Commercial and Economic Law in Ireland

Commercial and Economic Law in Ireland

Second Edition

Fidelma White

This book was originally published as a monograph in the International Encyclopaedia of Laws/Commercial and Economic Law.

Founding Editor: Roger Blanpain
General Editor: Frank Hendrickx
Volume Editors: Jules Stuyck & Evelyne Terryn

Wolters Kluwer

Published by:
Kluwer Law International B.V.
PO Box 316
2400 AH Alphen aan den Rijn
The Netherlands
E-mail: international-sales@wolterskluwer.com
Website: lrus.wolterskluwer.com

Sold and distributed in North, Central and South America by:
Wolters Kluwer Legal & Regulatory U.S.
7201 McKinney Circle
Frederick, MD 21704
United States of America
Email: customer.service@wolterskluwer.com

Sold and distributed in all other countries by:
Air Business Subscriptions
Rockwood House
Haywards Heath
West Sussex
RH16 3DH
United Kingdom
Email: international-customerservice@wolterskluwer.com

ISBN 978-94-035-2092-6

e-Book: ISBN 978-94-035-2130-5
web-PDF: ISBN 978-94-035-2164-0

This title is available on www.kluwerlawonline.com

The Author

Fidelma White is a graduate from the National University of Ireland and the London School of Economics. In 2009, she was awarded an LLD (Higher Doctorate based on Published Works) from the National University of Ireland. From 1991 to 1995, she taught Commercial Law and Public Law at the University of Sheffield in the United Kingdom. She has been a lecturer at University College Cork, Ireland, since 1995 and was appointed as Senior Lecturer in Law there in 2004. She teaches Introduction to Business Law, Commercial Law, E-Commerce Law and Consumer Law. Her research interests include commercial and consumer law. She acts as an External Examiner for a number of institutions and as a Consultant at national and European levels.

The Author

Table of Contents

Table of Contents

List of Abbreviations

BAI	Broadcasting Authority of Ireland
CAI	Consumer Association of Ireland
CCPC	Competition and Consumer Protection Commission
CIE	Córas Iompair Éireann
CJEU	Court of Justice of the European Union
ComReg	Commission for Communications Regulation
CRO	Companies Registration Office
CRU	Commission for Regulation of Utilities
DSA	Debt Settlement Arrangement
EC	European Community
ECB	European Central Bank
EEA	European Economic Area
EPC	European Patents Convention
EPO	European Patent Office
ESB	Electricity Supply Board
EU	European Union
EUIPO	European Union Intellectual Property Office
EUTM	European Union Trade Mark
IAA	Irish Aviation Authority
IBEC	Irish Business and Employers Confederation
ICTU	Irish Congress of Trade Unions
IDA	Industrial Development Agency
IFSC	International Financial Services Centre
IPCC	Irish Paper Clearing Company Ltd
ISE	Irish Stock Exchange
ISI	Insolvency Service of Ireland
LRC	Law Reform Commission
NCAs	National Competition Authorities
PCT	Patent Co-operation Treaty
PIA	Personal Insolvency Arrangement

List of Abbreviations

PRSA	Personal Retirement Savings Account
RSC	Rules of the Superior Courts
RTE	Radio Telefís Éireann
UCP	Uniform Customs and Practices relating to Documentary Credits
UK	United Kingdom
VHI	Voluntary Health Insurance Board

General Introduction

§1. General Background of the Country

I. Geography

1. Ireland is the third-largest island in Europe, behind Great Britain and Iceland. It lies to the northwest of Continental Europe, between 51.5° and 55.5° north latitude and between 5.5° and 10.5° west longitude. To the east of Ireland, separated by the Irish Sea, is the island of Great Britain; to the north, west and south is the Atlantic Ocean. Influenced by the Gulf Stream and prevailing winds from the south-west, Ireland has a mild but changeable climate, with few extremes. The average annual temperature ranges from 9°C to10°C: the coldest months are January and February with mean daily temperatures of between 4°C and 7°C; while July and August are the warmest with mean daily temperatures of between 14°C and 16°C. The total area of the island of Ireland is 84,412 square kilometres (32,595 square miles). The island comprises a ring of coastal mountains which surround a low central limestone plain.

2. The island of Ireland has two distinct jurisdictions: Ireland (also known as the Republic of Ireland) which covers five-sixths of the island (70,282 square kilometres or 27,136 square miles); and Northern Ireland which is part of the United Kingdom (UK) of Great Britain and Northern Ireland, and which covers the remaining one-sixth (14,139 square kilometres or 5,459 square miles) in the northeast. Traditionally, Ireland is subdivided into four provinces: Ulster, Munster, Leinster and Connacht; and thirty-two counties. Twenty-six of the counties are in Ireland, its capital being Dublin, while the remaining six (all in Ulster) are in Northern Ireland, its capital being Belfast. Ireland is the subject of this monograph.

II. Cultural Composition

3. Though once a very homogenous society, Irish society in recent years has become more diverse. In 2016, the total population was 4,761,865, an increase of 3.8% over the previous five years. Of this total, 4,082,513 of the population were described as Irish, with 535,475 being described as non-Irish. This latter figure included 122,515 from Poland; and 103,113 from the UK; with the next largest cohorts being Lithuanian (36,552); Romanian (29,186); Latvian (19,933); Brazilian (13,640); Spanish (12,112); Italian (11,732); French (11,661); German (11,531); Indian (11,465); from the USA (10,015); Slovakian (9,717); and Chinese (10,896).[1]

4. Article 44 of the Irish Constitution (1937) guarantees freedom of conscience and the free profession and practice of religion to all its citizens. Ireland remains predominately Catholic. Figures from 2016 identify 3,729,100 (78.3%) as Roman Catholic; 126,400 as Church of Ireland; 63,400 as Muslim; 62,200 as Orthodox; 37,400 as Christian; 24,200 as Presbyterian; and 14,300 as Hindu. Notably 468,400 claim no religion at all, an increase of 73.6% over the previous five years.[2]

III. Political System

5. Ireland is a Parliamentary democracy, founded upon a written Constitution (*Bunreacht na hÉireann*, 1937).[3] Article 6 of the Constitution implies a tripartite separation of powers between the legislative, executive and judicial branches of government.

6. The national Parliament, known as the *Oireachtas*, comprises the President (*an tUachtarán*) and two Houses, a House of Representative, known as *Dáil Éireann*, and a Senate, known as *Seanad Éireann*. Under Article 15.2.1° of the Constitution, the sole and exclusive power of making law for the State vests in the *Oireachtas*. Under the Constitution, general elections to *Dáil Éireann* must be held at least once every five years. All Irish citizens, and British Citizens, ordinarily resident and over 18 years of age and whose name appears on the electoral register are entitled to vote. Voting is by secret ballot on the principle of proportional representation in multi-seat constituencies, each voter having a single transferable vote. There are currently 158 members of *Dáil Éireann*. A general election to the *Seanad* must take place not later than ninety days after the dissolution of the *Dáil*. The *Seanad* comprises sixty members: eleven members are nominated by the *Taoiseach* (Prime Minister), six members are elected by university graduates and the remaining forty-three are elected from five panels of candidates representing specific vocational interests, including an Industrial and Commercial Panel.[4]

7. In accordance with Article 28 of the Constitution, the executive power of the State is exercised by the Government. The Constitution also provides that the Government shall consist of not fewer than seven and not more than fifteen members.[5] The Prime Minister (*an Taoiseach*), Deputy Prime Minister (*an Tánaiste*) and the

1. *See* Central Statistics Office, *Census 2016*.
2. *Ibid.*
3. Article 46 of the Constitution provides for its amendment by way of referendum. At the time of writing, there have been thirty-eight proposed amendments to the Constitution.
4. A proposal to amend the Constitution, the Thirty-Second Amendment, to abolish Seanad Éireann was rejected by the people in a referendum on 4 Oct. 2013.
5. Article 28.1.

Minister of Finance must be members of the *Dáil*. Other members can be members of the *Dáil* or the *Seanad*, but not more than two can be members of the *Seanad*.[6] The Government operates under a doctrine of collective responsibility[7] and is answerable to the *Dáil*.[8] The *Taoiseach* assigns Departments of State to individual members of the Government. Minister of State, who are not members of the Government, assist Government Ministers in their parliamentary and departmental duties. The *Taoiseach* is appointed by the President on the nomination of the *Dáil*[9] and must resign on ceasing to retain the support of the majority of the *Dáil*.[10]

8. As regards the judicial powers of State, Article 34 envisages a three-tiered court structure with, at its apex, a Court of Final Appeal (the Supreme Court), below that a Court of Appeal,[11] and below that again Courts of First Instance. The Courts of First Instance comprise the High Court and also courts of local and limited jurisdiction (i.e., the Circuit and District Courts). Article 35 of the Constitution guarantees the independence of the judiciary.

9. Other important offices established under the Constitution include that of the President, who is the directly elected Head of State but whose powers are largely ceremonial: the President normally acts on the advice of the Government.[12] There is also the Attorney General, the Government's legal advisor,[13] and the Comptroller and Auditor General who acts as an independent financial watchdog over public spending.[14]

10. With membership of the then European Economic Community from 1 January 1973, a further dimension was added to the Irish political system.[15] In particular, at the time of writing, there are eleven Irish members of the European Parliament (2019–2024), with two further MEPs due to take up their seats when the UK leaves the EU. Ireland contributes one member to the European Commission.

11. Despite the jurisdictional division of the island, under the Belfast Agreement[16] there are a number of all-island agencies and all-island policies pursued in a number of areas. For example, a North-South Ministerial Council was established

6. Article 28.7.
7. Article 28.4.2.
8. Article 28.4.1.
9. Article 13.
10. Article 28.10.
11. The Court of Appeal was established on 28 Oct. 2014, following the Thirty-third Amendment to the Constitution (1 Nov. 2013).
12. Articles 12–14.
13. Article 30.
14. Article 33.
15. European Communities Act, 1972.
16. The Belfast Agreement, also known as the Good Friday Agreement, was a major political development in the Northern Ireland peace process. It was signed on 10 Apr. 1998 (Good Friday) by the British and Irish Governments and endorsed by most Northern Ireland political parties, at the time. It was endorsed by the voters in Ireland (94% in favour) and Northern Ireland (71% in favour) in separate referenda on 23 May 1998.

as a forum in which ministers from the Irish Government and the Northern Ireland Assembly can discuss matters of mutual concern and formulate all-Ireland policies in six 'areas of co-operation', including agriculture, the environment, transport and tourist. Indeed, an increasing amount of commercial activity operates on an all-Ireland basis, particularly in the context of the EU. However, in June 2016, the UK voted to leave the EU ('Brexit'). The UK was originally scheduled to depart the EU on 29 March 2019, although, at the time of writing, this date has been extended to 31 January 2020. Therefore, the impact of Brexit on the Irish economy and its legal system remains to be seen.

IV. Population, Employment and Production Statistics

12. In 2016, the population of Ireland was recorded at just over 4.76 million, with just under 1.2 million in Dublin city and suburbs (the population of the whole island was approximately 6.6 million).[17] This is a significant increase from a modern historical low in the 1960s.

13. From the mid-1990s, Ireland experienced unprecedented levels of economic growth leading to a dramatic decrease in unemployment levels. This unprecedented economic growth saw the level of real Gross Domestic Product (GDP) almost double in size between 2000 and 2007. In 2005, the Organisation for Economic Co-operation and Development (OECD) estimated that in terms of GDP per capita, based on current Purchasing Power Parities, Ireland was ranked fourth in the world, with only the US, Norway and Luxembourg ranking higher.[18] Between 1993 and 2004, employment grew by 55%, with the employment rate exceeding the EU average by the end of this period. Correspondingly, unemployment rates decreased dramatically, with a marked decline in long-time unemployed figures. Between 2000 and 2007, the unemployment rate rested at around 4% of the population.

14. However, from 2008, there was a growth in unemployment figures, resulting from the economic crisis. This crisis was triggered by the global financial crisis but it was compounded by a domestic property bubble which when it burst bankrupted the main Irish banks and generated a fiscal crisis, with the fiscal deficit and debt-to-GDP ratio soaring. Ireland entered a recession in 2008 and was forced to seek financial support ('the bailout') from the European Central Bank (ECB), the European Commission and the International Monetary Fund ('the Troika') in 2010. A programme of austerity followed. The impact of this crisis on employment was felt immediately: unemployment rose from 4% in July 2007; to 14.8% in July 2012, despite a strong growth in emigration during this period. The unemployment rate peaked at 15.1% in early 2012. Ireland exited the Troika bailout in December 2013 and subsequent years saw the economy return to growth and hence the rate of unemployment has fallen steadily.[19] The European Commission has estimated that the

17. *See* Central Statistics Office, *Census 2016*.
18. OECD, *New GDP Comparisons Based on Purchasing Power Parity for the Year 2002* (2005).
19. *See* www.cso.ie.

Irish economy will grow by 4.1% in 2019; and it has forecast Irish GDP growth of 3.7% in 2020. As a result, in March 2019, the unemployment rate was 5.4%.[20]

V. Social and Cultural Values

15. Article 8 of the Constitution designates the Irish language as the first official language, while the English language is recognized as a second official language. English is however the language that is generally used, with Irish being spoken in *Gaeltacht* areas, mainly along the south and western seaboard. In the 2016 Census, the total number of persons who could speak Irish was 1.76 million.[21]

16. In terms of the world of arts, for an island of relatively small population, Ireland has made a disproportionately large contribution to world literature in all its branches, mainly in English. The Irish tradition of music and dance is also widely known.

17. With regard to sports, hurling and Gaelic football are the most popular sports in Ireland, with soccer, and rugby also being popular. Hurling and Gaelic football, along with Camogie, Ladies' Gaelic football, handball and rounders, make up the national sports of Ireland, collectively known as Gaelic Games. In general, Gaelic games are governed by the Gaelic Athletic Association (GAA), which is organized on an all-Ireland basis; traditionally, counties first compete within their province, and the winners then compete in the all-Ireland senior hurling and football championships. Many other sports are played and followed, including golf, horseracing, show jumping, greyhound racing, swimming, boxing, tennis, hockey and cricket.

§2. The Economic System

18. Ireland is a small, open, trade-dependent economy. This openness is reflected in the international mobility of its labour force and capital, in particular in the form of foreign direct investment. In recent decades, the Irish economy has been transformed from being agrarian and traditional manufacturing based to one increasingly based on the hi-tech and internationally traded services sectors.

19. Between the mid-1990s and 2007, unprecedented economic growth (in a phenomenon known as the 'Celtic Tiger') saw the level of Irish real GDP almost double in size. However, in line with the world economy, since 2007, Ireland has experienced a dramatic slow-down in economic growth. In September 2008, Ireland became the first Eurozone Member State to fall into recession with the onset of the world financial crisis and subsequent slow-down in the domestic property and construction markets. The first quarter of 2010 saw the economy return to growth

20. *See* www.cso.ie.
21. *See* www.cso.ie.

with an annual rate GDP of 2.3%.[22] In 2018, the Irish economy grew by 5.6%, the fastest growing economy in the EU. The export sector, dominated by foreign multinationals, remains a key component of Ireland's economy recovery.

§3. The Legal System

20. From the late twelfth century, Ireland was increasingly governed by English common law and in 1800 Ireland was fully integrated into the UK of Great Britain and Ireland by the Act of Union passed that year. The Anglo-Irish Treaty 1921, which marked the end of the War of Independence (1919–1921), led to the two-state solution: the Irish Free State, made up of twenty-six counties, established by the 1922 Constitution; and Northern Ireland comprising the remaining six counties. A new Constitution was passed by referendum in 1937, *Bunreacht na hÉireann*, which renamed the State 'Éire, or in the English Language, Ireland'.[23] In 1973, along with the UK and Denmark, Ireland joined the then European Economic Community. This necessitated an amendment to the Constitution to the effect that no provision of the Constitution could be invoked to invalidate any acts necessitated by membership of the European Community (now the EU) or to prevent EC (now EU) law having full effect in Irish law.[24]

21. Hence, with the exception of the written Constitution, the Irish legal system is quite similar to that in the UK. The system is based on the English common law and the procedural model is adversarial. Laws are not codified in the manner of the various Continental European codifications. Nor are there any comprehensive encyclopaedia of Irish law, as exists in Britain, such as *Halsbury's Laws*, and the United States, such as *American Jurisprudence*. Due to the absence of such comprehensive statements of the law in Ireland, it often can be very difficult for a person who is not a legal expert to find the appropriate rule on a particular matter. It is hoped that this monograph remedies that deficiency to some extent in the commercial and economic law field.

---

22. www.cso.ie.
23. Article 4. In 1949, Ireland declared itself a Republic and henceforth should be described additionally as the Republic of Ireland: *see further* the Republic of Ireland Act, 1948.
24. Article 29.4.3; *see further* European Communities Act, 1972 and *Doyle v. An Taoiseach* [1986] ILRM 693 where it was stated in the Supreme Court that Community law has the paramount force and effect of constitutional provisions.

Part I. Commercial Law

Chapter 1. Concepts and Sources of Commercial Law

22. Unlike the North American system, where there exists a Uniform Commercial Code, and many civil law jurisdictions, where there are commercial codes, there is no commercial code in Ireland. Therefore, Irish commercial law is neither integrated into one document nor is it peculiar to commercial transactions. Instead, commercial law is to be found in numerous pieces of legislation, and the common law, and to a large extent is based on contract law and personal property law, though these subjects are not exclusively relevant to commercial law.

23. The main sources of Irish commercial law are primarily legislation enacted by the *Oireachtas* (the National Parliament), most notably:

- the Cheques Act, 1959;
- the Sale of Goods and Supply of Services Act, 1980;
- the Bankruptcy Acts 1988–2015;
- the International Carriage of Goods by Road Act 1990;
- the Patents Acts, 1992–2017;
- the Trade Marks Act, 1996;
- the Merchant Shipping (Liability of Shipowners and Others) Act, 1996;
- the Central Bank Acts, 1942–2018;
- the Copyright and Related Rights Acts, 2000–2007;
- the Electronic Commerce Act, 2000;
- the Industrial Designs Act, 2001;
- the Competition Acts, 2002–2017;
- the Air Navigation and Transport (International Conventions) Act 2004;
- the Consumer Protection Act 2007;
- the Markets in Financial Instruments and Miscellaneous Provisions Act, 2007;
- the Arbitration Act 2010;
- the Central Bank Reform Act 2010;
- the Personal Insolvency Acts 2012–2015;
- the Competition and Consumer Protection Act 2014;
- the Companies Act 2014;
- the Knowledge Development Box (Certification of Inventions) Act 2017;
- the Mediation Act 2017;
- the Data Protection Act 2018.

24. Legislation enacted in the pre-1922 UK Parliament and which was carried over by the Constitution also plays a very significant role, most notably:

- the Bills of Lading Act, 1855;
- the Bills of Exchange Act, 1882;
- the Bills of Sale (Ireland) Acts, 1879–1883;
- the Factors Act, 1889;
- the Sale of Goods Act, 1893;
- the Marine Insurance Act, 1906.

25. Because Irish commercial law does not lend itself to definition and is diverse in its sources, it is useful to consider further the concept or characteristics of Irish commercial law. In doing so, it is worth noting that Irish commercial law shares many of the features of English commercial law.[25] Irish commercial law is largely based on transactions and not institutions. Hence, the focus of commercial law is on contracts and other arrangements. Areas such as partnership and company law are usually considered separately from commercial law.[26] Second, commercial law is concerned primarily with the dealing of merchants, or professional business persons, as opposed to consumers. Third, commercial law is centred on contract and the usages of the market. However, while much of commercial law is founded on contract law it is obvious that it extends into other areas including property,[27] tort, equity, restitution and insolvency law. The customs and usages of the market are also central to commercial law.[28] Much of the time commercial law reacts to and adopts new market practices. For instance, the common law recognized that a bill of lading was a document of title because merchants treated it as a document of title.[29] More recently, judges have had to consider the legal significance of new commercial practices including, for example, the use of retention of title clauses in sale of goods contracts.[30] Fourth, commercial law is concerned with a large mass of transactions in which each participant is a regular player, so that transactions are typical, repetitive and suitable for standardized treatment. Lastly, certain aspects of Irish commercial law, in more recent times, have undergone a harmonizing process, both at regional level, as a member of the EU,[31] and at an international level.

26. As noted above, as a matter of substantive law, commercial law coexists with many other aspects of Irish law, and cannot be easily identified as a separate body of rules. Equally, and until recently, at a procedural level, commercial law was

25. *See*, *generally*, Goode, Commercial Law (5th ed., Penguin 2017).
26. This contrasts with the approach of many civil jurisdictions where company law is considered part of commercial law. On the relationship between company and commercial law, *see* Sealy, *Company Law and Commercial Reality* Ch. 1 (Sweet & Maxwell 1984).
27. Commercial law relates principally to personal property law, e.g., goods, but land law cannot be excluded. Commercial finance is often secured on land by a mortgage or a charge, for instance.
28. Technically, a custom refers to a practice in a particular area, while a usage refers to a practice in a particular trade. Today, the terms are used interchangeably.
29. *Lickbarrow v. Mason* (1794) 5 Term Rep 683.
30. Retention of title clauses, now common in sale of goods contracts, were introduced into Irish and English law in the 1970s: *see further* paras 577–589.
31. European Union Act, 2009.

treated no differently from other aspects of civil procedure. In particular, disputes involving issues of commercial law are heard in the District Court, the Circuit Court or the High Court, depending on the amount which is at stake.[32] While in certain areas, such as bankruptcy,[33] company law[34] and arbitration,[35] the High Court is designated as the appropriate forum. However, as of 14 January 2004, the Commercial Court, a division of the High Court, was established, marking a significant change in commercial litigation in Ireland.[36] The Commercial Court is staffed by judges with a particular expertise in commercial matters, and it hears cases drawn from a dedicated 'commercial list'. To be admitted to the list, a case must come within one of the two categories: those specifically defined within the Rules (including almost any type of business dispute and various specific commercial disputes where the value of the claim or counterclaim exceeds EUR 1 million) and those where the Court can exercise its discretion having regard to the commercial and other aspects of the case. The intention is to offer a more coherent and speedy approach to the resolution of commercial law disputes, through techniques such as 'case management' whereby the judge actively manages the progress of the case to resolution. Reports to date suggest that these aims are being achieved.[37]

---

32. Currently, the District Court has civil jurisdiction in contract law and most other matters where the claim does not exceed EUR 15,000; the Circuit Court's civil jurisdiction relates mainly to actions where the claim does not exceed EUR 75,000, unless the parties consent otherwise; and there is no financial limit on the High Court's jurisdiction.
33. Rules of the Superior Courts (RSC), Ord. 76.
34. RSC, Ord. 74-5.
35. RSC, Ord. 56.
36. *See* RSC, Ord. 63A. This followed the recommendation, in 2002, of the Committee on Court Practice and Procedure, in its 27th Interim Report.
37. *See generally* Court Service, Annual Reports at www.courts.ie.

Chapter 2. The Economic Operators

27. Various categories of individuals and organizations participate in commercial activity and hence can be identified as 'economic operators'. The main economic operators are considered further below.

§1. The Sole Trader

28. A sole trader is an individual who pursues a commercial activity either in his/her own name or under a registered name.[38] Generally, any natural person is free to operate as a sole trader and to engage in any type of commercial activity which is lawful. There are no general prohibitions on who may take up any particular trade or business, nor are there any requirements of formal qualifications in order to engage in any business. However, a variety of authorization and licensing schemes exist in certain specific areas including certain professions, financial services, transport and the utilities sector, for instance.[39] Moreover, certain categories of individuals either have in the past or still are subject to specific legal restrictions.

I. Married Women

29. In the last century married women were not legally free to conduct business and to conclude contracts entirely on their own behalf. On being married, their property and any property they later would acquire vested in their husbands. Most of those impediments were removed in the nineteenth century,[40] and the remainder was swept away by the Married Women's Status Act, 1957. Moreover, the Employment Equality Acts, 1998 and 2004 and the Equal Status Acts, 2000–2012 seeks to promote equality, in particular by prohibiting discrimination in various areas, such as employment and the provision of goods and services to the public, on nine grounds, including gender and marital status.[41]

II. Minors

30. The age of majority was reduced to 18 years by the Age of Majority Act, 1985, although majority can be attained below that age where the person gets married. Those who are under the age of majority are called 'minors'. Although minors

---

38. Registration of Business Names Act 1963: *see further* paras 102–106, 242.
39. *See further* Part II, Ch. 2.
40. *See* Married Women's Property Acts, 1865, 1882, 1884, 1893, 1907.
41. The other grounds relate to: family status, sexual orientation, religion, age, disability, race and the Traveller community. This legislation seeks, *inter alia*, to transpose various EC measures, including, Council Directive 2000/43/EC (the Race Directive); Council Directive 2000/78/EC (the Framework Employment Directive) and Directive 2002/73/EC (the Gender Equal Treatment Directive).

are legally free to enter into contracts, the contracts they make will only be enforceable against them where the subject matter involves the minor acquiring 'necessaries'.[42] Accordingly, those who make commercial agreements with minors run the risk of not being able to enforce those contracts, should the minor wish to repudiate them.

III. Non-nationals

31. The position of non-nationals, that is persons who are not citizens of the State, is governed by the Aliens Act, 1935.[43] Unless they have been duly authorized by the Minister for Justice and Equality, in the form of a Business Permission, non-nationals, other than nationals of other European Economic Area (EEA) Member States[44] and Switzerland, are not permitted to engage in any business activity in the State. It has not been established whether or not a commercial agreement knowingly made with a non-national, who is unlawfully trading in the State, would be enforced by the courts.

§2. ORGANIZATIONS

32. The dominant form of business organization is the registered company although alternatives exist, namely partnerships and industrial and provident societies.[45]

I. Registered Companies

33. Registered companies[46] are regulated by the Companies Act 2014.[47] The 2014 Act consolidates and modernizes Irish company law and is designed to make it easier for companies to do business in Ireland. One of the main changes under the Act relates to the private company limited by shares (the 'private company'), which is the most common type of company in Ireland.[48] Pursuant to the 2014 Act, there are now two types of private company, which have replaced the former single form:

---

42. *See*, e.g., Sale of Goods Act, 1893, s. 2.
43. Non-nationals are referred to as 'aliens' under the 1935 Act.
44. The EEA comprises the Member States of the EU and Iceland, Liechtenstein and Norway.
45. In 2017, there were in excess of 215,000 registered companies in Ireland, although it is not possible to determine how many of these are involved in trading activity: CRO, Annual Report, 2017.
46. There are also a relatively small number of unregistered companies, established by royal charter or letters patent, which are subject to certain provisions of the Companies Act 2014.
47. The Companies Act 2014 commenced 1 Jun. 2015. The 2014 Act repealed the whole of thirteen former Companies Acts and a plethora of related legislation. *See further* Keane on Company Law (5th ed., Bloomsbury 2016).
48. The other main types of company include private unlimited companies (ULC); companies limited by guarantee (CLG) and public limited companies (PLC).

(i) a private company limited by shares ('LTD'); and (ii) a designated activity company ('DAC'). Within eighteen months of commencement of the 2014 Act, all existing private companies were required to convert to either an LTD or a DAC; any company which failed to take action was automatically converted to an LTD.

34. Companies can engage in practically every business and commercial activity, apart from certain professional occupations, like practising law, medicine, dentistry and veterinary medicine. Broadly speaking, anybody is free to register a company in Ireland or to acquire an already registered company 'off-the-shelf' and anybody, over the age of 18, is free to become a director of an Irish company, except for those disqualified for fraud, and the like, under the Companies Act. In addition, it is comparatively easy to form a private company. All that is required is that various documents are sent to Companies Registration Office (CRO),[49] with the requisite registration fee, namely:

- A constitution (setting out e.g., the company's name, that the members' liability is limited; the authorized share capital, and the identity of the 'subscribers' to the company).[50]
- A completed Form A1 containing various details such as the company name, its registered office, its e-mail address, details of its secretary and directors, their consent to acting as such, the subscribers and details of their shares (if any). This Form also incorporates a Declaration that the requirements of the Companies Act have been complied with, and as to which activity the company is being formed to engage in.

Registration can also be processed online. Where all documents are in order, a certification of incorporation will be issued, in due course. If the company is a public limited company (PLC) certain additional requirements regarding minimum capitalization must be satisfied.

35. How the company is to be governed and managed depends mainly on what the constitution states. The legislation requires certain matters to be done by the shareholders in general meeting and other matters to be done by the directors. But the members are legally free to allocate the great bulk of decision-making by the company in whatever manner suits them best. The norm is for the actual management of the company's business to be consigned to a board of directors, of which there must be at least one director. Companies must also have a secretary, who is mainly responsible for the administrative and legal side of things, and an auditor, who must be professionally qualified and is chosen each year at the annual general meeting.

---

49. www.cro.ie.
50. *See* Sch. 1 of Companies Act 2014.

36. The registered company has a number of features which make it an attractive vehicle for doing business. In particular, the registered company has a legal personality separate from that of its owners.[51] Thus, for example, company property is owned by the company and not the members or shareholders; the company can sue and be sued in its own name and a company has perpetual succession, that is, it does not expire when its members or shareholders die. Where liability is limited, the members' or shareholders' liability for the debts of the company, which it cannot pay, is limited (this limit is agreed on the establishment of the company or when shares are bought) and therefore the members or shareholders cannot be held personally liable beyond this limit. Lastly, a separate tax regime, with various rates, reliefs and incentives, exists for companies: for example, the standard corporation tax rate on trading income is currently 12.5%.

II. Foreign-Registered or External Companies

37. Companies which are registered abroad (known as 'external' companies under the Companies Act 2014) are legally free to do business in Ireland. If the association has a distinct legal personality in the State where it was incorporated, it will be treated in Ireland as a legal entity in its own right. Indeed, the growth in the Irish economy between 1997 and 2007 has been attributed, in part, to the large presence of foreign-registered or external companies (sometimes known as multinationals) attracted by various incentive schemes offered by government through the Industrial Development Agency (IDA).[52]

38. Any external company which establishes a branch in the State must be registered with CRO under Part 21 of the Companies Act 2014. The registration process requires the delivery of various forms (F12 for EEA companies or F13 for non-EEA companies) and documents, including a certified copy of the company's founding documents; a copy of the certification of incorporation; the latest accounts; and a filing fee. Certified translations may be needed. Moreover, the registration must take place within thirty days of the establishment of the branch in the State. Establishing a place of business connotes having a specified or identifiable place from which the company does business with some regularity. It is not sufficient that the foreign company acts through some local agent or through an Irish subsidiary or affiliate.

39. The provisions of the 2014 Act, regarding the prosecution of officers for non-compliance with companies legislation apply as much to external companies with a place of business here as they apply to Irish-registered companies. External companies are also subject to requirements regarding annual accounts.[53]

---

51. *Salomon v. Salomon & Co.* [1897] AC 22.
52. Industrial Development Acts 1986–2018: *see further* www.idaireland.com.
53. Companies Act 2014, ss 1303 and 1305.

III. Partnerships

40. Partnerships are not distinct legal bodies or entities in their own right; they are merely an association of the individual partners, without any separate legal personality.[54] Partners' rights and duties and the various incidents of their relationship are governed by the Partnerships Act, 1890. Partners carry joint and several unlimited liability for the unpaid debts of their firm. But it is possible to have limited partners, provided they take no active part in running the company's business. Partnerships can engage in practically every form of trade or commercial activity. For practical purposes, however, it is often preferable to have the association registered as a limited company – or indeed an unlimited company – rather than act as a partnership. Financial institutions and other bodies often find it more convenient to deal with registered companies.

IV. Industrial and Provident Societies

41. It is possible to carry on business as a registered industrial and provident society,[55] also known as a co-operative, which possesses a separate legal personality of its own and the members of which may enjoy limited liability. Some major businesses, especially in the food sector, take this form. In more recent years, however, the trend has been to move away from society status to becoming registered companies.

42. The governing legislation is the Industrial and Provident Societies Acts of 1893–2014. The legislation prohibits these bodies from being in the business of deposit taking. Apart from that, these societies can carry on any industry, business or trade authorized by their rules, whether wholesale or retail, including dealings of any description with land.[56] In order to establish an industrial and provident society, there must be at least seven persons who agree on a set of rules which deal with the several matters set out in the schedule to the 1893 Act. When those rules are registered with the Register of Friendly Societies and the Registrar is satisfied that all that Act's requirements have been satisfied, the society comes into being. The members have an extensive degree of freedom regarding how decision-making powers are to be allocated within their society. One attraction of doing business in this mode is that the Companies Act 2014 does not apply. Societies are subject to an annual requirement to submit audited accounts under the relevant legislation though.

§3. The State

43. Business activities are carried on by the State in two principal ways. First, a company can be established by special legislation, other than the Companies Act

54. *See* Twomey, *Partnership Law* (Butterworths 2000).
55. *See also* Building Societies Acts 1989–2006 and Credit Union Acts 1997–2012.
56. 1893 Act, s. 4.

2014, known as a statutory corporation. Most statutory corporations engaged in commercial activity are state-owned, such as the Electricity Supply Board (ESB), Radio Telefiś Éireann (RTE), Córas Iompair Éireann (CIE) and the Voluntary Health Insurance Board (VHI). Alternatively, the state many conduct commercial activity through companies registered under the Companies Act 2014, whereby the state is a shareholder.

Chapter 3. The Economic Institutions

44. The main economic institutions in the State can be segregated into governmental or state agencies and non-governmental or private bodies. On the governmental side of the line there are the Ministers, and the Department, of Business, Enterprise and Innovation, who have primary responsibility for overseeing and regulating commercial activities.[57] In the financial services sector, the Central Bank has extensive regulatory powers.[58] State agencies such as Enterprise Ireland,[59] which promotes exports and investment in research and development, among other things, and the Industrial Development Authority (IDA),[60] through the promotion of inward investment, play a vital role in encouraging the establishment and expansion of commercial enterprises. The main non-governmental institutions include the Irish Business and Employers Confederation (IBEC), the Irish Congress of Trade Unions (ICTU) and the various Chambers of Commerce.

§1. Professional Organizations, Chambers of Commerce

45. IBEC is the national representative body for Irish business and employers.[61] It represents over 7,500 member businesses and organizations, from all sectors to Government, the trade unions, other national interest groups and the general public. Numerous other business organizations exist, including: the Irish Small and Medium Enterprises Association (ISME);[62] the Construction Industry Federation (CIF);[63] the Retail, Grocery, Dairy and Allied Trades' Association (RGDATA);[64] while the agricultural sector is represented by the Irish Farmers Association (IFA)[65] and the Irish Creamery and Milk Suppliers Association (ICMSA),[66] amongst others. The professions are also well represented: solicitors and barristers by the Law Society and the Bar Association, respectively;[67] bankers by the Banking and Payments Federation of Ireland;[68] tax advisors by the Institution of Taxation;[69] and accountants by the Institute of Chartered Accountants of Ireland;[70] for example.

---

57. *See* www.dbei.gov.ie.
58. *See further* Part II, Ch. 2.
59. *See* www.enterprise-ireland.com.
60. Industrial Development Acts 1986–2003: *see further* www.idaireland.com.
61. *See* www.ibec.ie.
62. *See* www.isme.ie.
63. *See* www.cif.ie.
64. *See* www.rgdata.ie.
65. *See* www.ifa.ie.
66. *See* www.icmsa.ie.
67. *See* www.lawsociety.ie and www.lawlibrary.ie.
68. *See* www.bpfi.ie.
69. *See* www.taxireland.ie.
70. *See* www.icai.ie.

46. The central authority for the Irish trade union movement is the ICTU.[71] There are currently forty-four unions, representing all groups of workers – industrial, professional, managerial, clerical and unskilled – affiliated to Congress, north and south of the border, representing and campaigning on behalf of some 800,000 working people. Congress is the sole Irish affiliate of the European Trade Union Confederation (ETUC), the representative body for trade unions at the European level.

47. Chambers Ireland is a federal business organization comprising forty-two member chambers representing over 8,000 business members throughout the island of Ireland.[72] Each local chamber of commerce is made up of local business representatives who join together to promote the economic and social development of their community. Chambers vary in size, the largest being the Dublin Chamber of Commerce.[73]

§2. Advisory Bodies and Committees

48. There are no formal structures, comparable to those in several European states, whereby industrial, commercial and labour interests are consulted by the Government or provide advice to the Government. However, there are a number of opportunities available to the business community, and others, to have an input in relation to the development and implementation of public policy: namely, though lobbying,[74] and more particularly through pre-legislative consultation procedures and parliamentary scrutiny of policy by committees. The majority of business organizations engage in lobbying activities. First, while policy is being devised, it is quite common for a consultation process to be entered into whereby the relevant government department, or body, issues a consultation paper seeking responses from interested parties. Importantly, such consultation is not generally mandatory and it is left to the discretion of the relevant department or body how to react to the process. Nevertheless, consultation is a welcome opportunity for the business community to express its views and to seek to persuade government to take a particular approach. Equally, the parliamentary committee structure provides an opportunity to scrutinize and review public policy in a particular area. In this regard the Committee on Business, Enterprise and Innovation plays an important role.

49. At a broader level, between 1987 and 2009, Ireland utilized 'social partnership agreements', which many identified as being key to Ireland's former economic prosperity. What was notable about social partnership was the range of interested parties who negotiated and participated in the process, including the Government,

---

71. *See* www.ictu.ie.
72. *See* www.chambers.ie.
73. *See* www.dubchamber.ie.
74. *See* Regulation of Lobbying Act 2015.

trade unions, employers groups, farming organizations and the voluntary sector.[75] However, since the economic crash in 2008, such agreements no longer prevail in Ireland.

§3. THE COURTS

50. As noted above, on 14 January 2004, the Commercial Court, a division of the High Court, was established, marking a significant change in commercial litigation in Ireland. Where a dispute falls outside the jurisdiction of the Commercial Court, it may be heard before the District Court, the Circuit Court or the High Court, along with all types of cases, be they family law, administrative law, employment law, competition law or commercial law disputes. In a commercial context, the respective jurisdictions of these courts depend on the amount which is at stake or the rateable value of the land in question. In 2014, a new Court of Appeal was established, to hear appeals from the High Court thereby re-positioning the Supreme Court as more of a constitutional court.[76]

I. Commercial Court

51. The Commercial Court is staffed by judges with a particular expertise in commercial matters, and it hears cases drawn from a dedicated 'commercial list'. To be admitted to the list, a case must come within one of two categories: those specifically defined within the Rules and those where the Court can exercise its discretion having regard to the commercial and other aspects of the case.[77] The Rules refer to a wide range of business disputes where the value of the claim or counterclaim exceeds EUR 1 million, namely proceedings concerning:

– a business document, business contract or business dispute;
– the determination of any question of construction arising in respect of a business document or business contract;
– the purchase or sale of commodities;
– the export or import of goods;

75. This included the ICTU, Irish Business and Employers' Confederation (IBEC), Construction Industry Federation (CIF), Small Firms' Association (SFA), Irish Exporters' Association (IEA), Irish Tourist Industry Confederation (ITIC) and Chambers Ireland, Irish Farmers' Association (IFA), Irish Creamery Milk Suppliers' Association (ICMSA), Irish Co-Operative Organization Society Ltd (ICOS), Macra na Feirme, Irish National Organization of the Unemployed (INOU), Congress Centres Network, CORI Justice Commission, National Youth Council of Ireland (NYCI), National Association of Building Co-Operatives (NABCO), Irish Council for Social Housing (ICSH), Society of Saint Vincent de Paul, Age Action Ireland, The Carers Association, The Wheel, The Disability Federation of Ireland, Irish Rural Link, The Irish Senior Citizens' Parliament, The Children's Rights Alliance and Protestant Aid.
76. The Court of Appeal was established on 28 Oct. 2014, following the Thirty-third Amendment to the Constitution (1 Nov. 2013).
77. *See* RSC, Ord. 63A. This followed the recommendation, in 2002, of the Committee on Court Practice and Procedure, in its 27th Interim Report.

- the carriage of goods by land, sea, air or pipeline;
- the exploitation of oil or gas reserves or any other natural resource;
- insurance or reinsurance;
- the provision of services (not including medical, quasi-medical or dental services or any service provided under a contract of employment);
- the operation of markets or exchanges in stocks, shares or other financial or investment instruments, or in commodities;
- the construction of any vehicle, vessel or aircraft;
- business agency.

Also included are applications or proceedings relating to the Arbitration Act 2010 (except as regards the staying of legal proceedings) where the claim or counterclaim exceeds EUR 1 million; the Patents Acts 1992–2017, the Trade Marks Act 1996; the Copyright and Related Rights Acts 2000–2007, the Industrial Designs Act 2001 and the tort of passing-off.

52. The intention is to offer a more coherent and speedy approach to the resolution of commercial law disputes, through techniques such as 'case management' whereby the judge actively manages the progress of the case from commencement to resolution. One notable aspect of the new approach to litigation is the increasing extent to which judges, on the application of any of the parties or of their own motion, are willing to adjourn proceedings to allow the parties time to consider whether the proceedings should be referred to a process of mediation, conciliation or arbitration.[78]

II. High Court

53. In certain areas, such as bankruptcy,[79] company law[80] and arbitration,[81] the High Court is designated as the appropriate forum. Otherwise, there is no financial ceiling on the jurisdiction of the High Court. But if a case is brought before the High Court which would be more appropriate for one of the other two lower courts, the plaintiff stands to incur the costs penalty provided for in section 14 of the Courts Act, 1991.

III. Circuit Court

54. Currently, the Circuit Court has jurisdiction to hear claims up to EUR 75,000 for actions in contract, breach of contract, all torts and claims for damages unconnected with contracts. Where the parties agree on the matter, the Circuit Court has jurisdiction to hear disputes about sums in excess of this figure. If a case is brought

78. RSC, Ord. 63A, Rules 5 and 6.
79. RSC, Ord. 76.
80. RSC, Ord. 74-5.
81. RSC, Ord. 56.

in the Circuit Court which would be more appropriate for the District Court, on account of the amount recovered, the plaintiff stands to incur a costs penalty, the nature of which is set out in section 14 of the Courts Act, 1991.

IV. District Court

55. Currently, the District Court has jurisdiction to hear claims up to EUR 15,000 for actions in contract, breach of contract, most torts and claims for damages unconnected with contracts. Where the parties sign a consent, in the prescribed form, the District Court has jurisdiction over disputes for sums exceeding this amount.

V. Small Claims Court

56. Originally established as a consumer redress mechanism, the Small Claims Court extended its jurisdiction in 2010 to hear small B2B disputes in respect of any goods or services purchased in the ordinary course of a business, where the amount of the claim does not exceed EUR 2,000.[82]

§4. Commercial Arbitration

57. Arbitration is a process by which parties voluntarily refer their dispute to an impartial third person, an arbitrator, selected by them, for a decision, based on evidence and arguments to be presented before the arbitrator. The parties agree in advance that the arbitrator's determination, the award, will be final and binding upon them. Although there are no official statistics, arbitration is often the preferred form of commercial dispute resolution, in particular, in certain fields of business activity such as, commodity sales, construction, insurance and shipping. Many reasons are given as to why parties prefer arbitration over other forms of dispute resolution, including litigation. For example, arbitration gives the parties the freedom to select the arbitrator (who may have technical qualifications or trade experience), the parties can control the time and place of the proceedings, procedures can be more flexible than in a court of law and there is an absence of publicity as proceedings are held in private and awards are not published. Further, these features often lead to savings in time and costs.

58. Arbitration can be classified as either institutional or ad hoc, and domestic or international. Institutional arbitration is administered by one of the many specialized arbitration institutions under their own arbitration rules. In Ireland, there is the Chartered Institute of Arbitrators, for example.[83] This method has the advantage that

82. District Court (Small Claims) Rules 2009, SI 2009/519; *see further* Part 2, Ch. 5 VII.
83. *See* www.ciarb.org/branches/Ireland.; and www.arbitration.ie.

there is a pre-drafted set of procedural rules under which the arbitration will be conducted and each institution provides an experienced and trained staff to administer the arbitration. An ad hoc arbitration, on the other hand, is conducted under rules of procedure that are adopted for a specific dispute. These rules can be:

- drawn from an international organization, such as United Nations Commission on International Trade Law's (UNCITRAL'S) Arbitration Rules 1976, as revised;[84]
- drafted by the parties, the arbitration tribunal, or both, thus meeting the exact needs of the dispute.

In effect, with an ad hoc arbitration, an infrastructure for the arbitration process must be designed. Business persons, who are wary of institutional arbitration because of its formality, or apparent lack of neutrality, will often prefer ad hoc arbitration for these reasons.

59. Arbitration may also be classified as domestic or international. Prior to 2010, two statutory regimes regulated arbitration in Ireland. The Arbitration (International Commercial) Act, 1998, which applied the 1985 UNCITRAL Model Law in Ireland, provided a definition of international arbitration which combined factors relating to the nationality of the parties and the nature of the dispute.[85] Arbitrations which came within this definition were governed by the 1998 Act. Arbitrations which fell outside this definition were, by default, domestic arbitrations and were governed principally by the Arbitration Acts 1950 and 1980. This older legislation was more interventionist than the Model Law and was therefore identified as being in need of reform. In 2010, a new Arbitration Act was enacted which applies the Model Law to both domestic and international arbitration and thereby repeals the former legislation.[86]

I. Arbitration Act 2010

60. The Arbitration Act 2010 seeks to codify Irish arbitration law into a single statute and in doing so incorporates the 1985 UNCITRAL Model Law on International Commercial Arbitration in Ireland.[87] The Model Law is not an international convention; rather, it is a text which countries can adopt completely, or with amendment, thus going some way to achieving uniformity of national arbitration law. To date, legislation based on the Model Law has been enacted in eighty states (in a total of 111 jurisdictions) including Australia, Canada, New Zealand and the UK.[88]

84. *See* www.uncitral.org. These Rules are used in countries throughout the world with different legal, social and economic systems. The Rules do not have the force of law, rather they must be expressly adopted by the parties.
85. 1998 Act, s. 3.
86. 2010 Act, s. 4.
87. 2010 Act, s. 6. For text of 1985 Model Law, as amended, *see* Sch. I to 2010 Act.
88. *See*, e.g., the UK Arbitration Act 1996.

A. Application of the 2010 Act

61. Section 6 of the 2010 Act provides that the Model Law shall have force of law in Ireland and shall apply to both international commercial arbitrations and arbitrations which are not international commercial arbitration, i.e., domestic arbitrations. The Act came into effect on 8 June 2010, three months after its enactment,[89] and is stated to apply to arbitrations commenced on or after this operative date but not to arbitrations which have commenced before this date.[90]

B. The Arbitration Agreement

62. 'Arbitration agreement' is defined in the legislation with reference to Option 1 of Article 7 of the Model Law.[91] Accordingly, an 'arbitration agreement' is an agreement by the parties to submit to arbitration all or certain disputes which have arisen (a submission or *compromise)* or which may arise between them (an arbitration clause or *clause compromissoire)* in respect of a defined legal relationship, whether contractual or not.

63. A submission, in relation to existing disputes, is usually a very detailed document concerning, *inter alia,* the constitution of the arbitration tribunal, and the procedure to be followed, whereas, an arbitration clause, in relation to future disputes, often consists of a brief phrase:

> All disputes, arising in connection with this contract, shall be finally settled by reference to arbitration in Dublin: Irish law shall apply.

64. The 2010 Act makes clear that the arbitration agreement is not discharged, or frustrated, by the death of any party to the agreement and remains enforceable by or against the personal representative of the deceased.[92] Further, the 2010 Act contains rules in the event of bankruptcy of a party. In particular, if the assignee or the trustee in bankruptcy does not disclaim the contract containing the arbitration agreement, the agreement remains enforceable against the assignee or trustee.[93]

1. Form

65. While a valid oral arbitration agreement may exist at common law, the 2010 Act only applies where the arbitration agreement is 'in writing'.[94] 'In writing' is given a broad interpretation, in accordance with Option 1 of Article 7 of the Model

89. 2010 Act, s. 1(2).
90. 2010 Act, s. 4. *See also Osmond Ireland on Farm Business Ltd v. McFarland* [2010] IEHC 295.
91. 2010 Act, s. 2.
92. 2010 Act, s. 26.
93. 2010 Act, s. 27.
94. 2010 Act, s. 2.

Law, which makes clear that an arbitration agreement is in writing if its content is recorded in any form, whether or not the arbitration agreement or contract has been concluded orally, by conduct, or by other means. Further, this writing requirement is satisfied by an electronic communication provided the information contained therein is accessible so as to be useable for subsequent reference. An arbitration agreement can also be incorporated by reference, and, moreover, an arbitration agreement is in writing if it is contained in an exchange of statements of claim and defence in which the existence of an agreement is alleged by one party and not denied by the other. There is no requirement for the arbitration agreement to be signed.

2. Scope

66. The arbitration agreement determines the jurisdiction of the arbitrator and what disputes can be submitted to arbitration: the arbitrator must not exceed the power the parties have conferred upon him/her. Two questions need to be addressed in this regard:

- first, can the arbitrator decide the extent of his/her own jurisdiction?
- second, if the arbitration clause is contained in a contract, can the arbitrator decide whether that contract is void *ab initio* due to mistake or illegality, for example?

67. As to the first question, historically, the issue of substantive jurisdiction was seen as being one ultimately for the courts to resolve, not the arbitrator.[95] However, and in keeping with the more modern principle of the autonomy of the arbitral tribunal, Article 16 of the Model Law provides that an arbitration tribunal may rule on its own jurisdiction, including on objections in respect of the existence or validity of the arbitration agreement. This point is echoed in section 8 of the 2010 Act which addresses the construction of the Model Law and of arbitration clauses. It states:

> Where parties agree that disputes under a contract or agreement or disputes arising out of a contract or agreement shall be submitted to arbitration, this includes disputes as to the existence or validity of the contract or agreement. [96]

Other matters of jurisdiction would relate to whether the arbitral tribunal was properly constituted and what matters have been submitted to arbitration in accordance with the agreement.

68. As to the second issue, Article 16 states that an arbitration clause which forms part of a contract shall be treated as an independent agreement and a decision by the arbitral tribunal that the contract is null and void shall not entail *ipso jure* the

95. *Dalmia Dairy Industries v. National Bank of Pakistan* [1978] 2 Lloyd's Rep 223.
96. 2010 Act, s. 8(3).

invalidity of the arbitration agreement. Put simply, the arbitration agreement is severable from any underlying contract, again bolstering the autonomy of the arbitral tribunal.

69. As a matter of procedure, a plea that the arbitral tribunal lacks jurisdiction must be made in a timely fashion.[97] Where there is an objection as regards jurisdiction, at the outset of proceedings, such a plea must be raised not later than the submission of the statement of defence. Importantly, a party is not precluded from raising such a plea by merely appointing an arbitrator. Where there is an objection as regard jurisdiction, during the currency of proceedings, such a plea must be raised as soon as the matter alleged to be beyond jurisdiction is raised. Therefore, failure to object, in a timely fashion, may result in the party waiving his/her right to object. However, these strict requirements are tempered somewhat by the provision in the Model Law that the arbitral tribunal may, in either case, admit a later plea if it considers the delay justified.

70. The Model Law further provides that the arbitral tribunal may rule on the above pleas as either a preliminary question, or in an award on the merits.[98] If the arbitral tribunal rules as a preliminary question that it has jurisdiction, any party may request, within thirty days after receiving notice of the ruling, the High Court to decide the matter. There is no appeal from this decision of the High Court and while such request is pending the arbitral tribunal may continue proceedings and make an award.

3. Referral to Arbitration: Staying Litigation

71. Where, despite the existence of an arbitration agreement, both parties agree to pursue their claims through the courts, the arbitration agreement is overridden by this new agreement and rendered redundant. But, where one party, in opposition to the arbitration agreement, commences litigation, the court, at the request of the willing party, has the power to refer the parties to arbitration in order to give effect to the arbitration agreement and thereby stay the litigation. Under Article 8 of the Model Law this power is mandatory, unless the court finds that the agreement is null and void, inoperative or incapable of being performed.[99] The request for a stay must be made not later than when submitting the party's first statement on the substance of the dispute. Arbitral proceeding may nevertheless be commenced or continued and an award may be made, while the issue is pending before the court. Importantly, to provide finality, the 2010 Act provides that there is no appeal from any court determination, pursuant to Article 8 of the Model Law.[100]

---

97. Model Law, Art. 16(2).
98. Model Law, Art. 16(3) and 2010 Act, s. 9.
99. Similar mandatory powers existed under s. 5 of the Arbitration Act 1980: now repealed. *See further Feanmer v. L&M Keating* [2014] IEHC 295.
100. 2010 Act, s. 11(a).

C. Arbitrators and the Arbitration Tribunal

72. The 2010 Act provides, unless otherwise agreed by the parties, that the arbitral tribunal shall consist of one arbitrator.[101]

1. Appointment Procedure

73. The Model Law provides that parties are free to agree on the procedure of appointing an arbitrator. Failing such agreement, default procedures for a sole arbitrator and arbitrations with three arbitrators are outlined. For example, in an arbitration with a sole arbitrator, if the parties are unable to agree on the arbitrator, he/she shall be appointed, upon request of a party, by the High Court.[102]

74. The High Court is also empowered to assist in the constitution of the arbitral tribunal where:

(a) a party fails to act under an agreed appointment procedure;
(b) the parties, or two arbitrators, are unable to reach an agreement expected of them under an agreed procedure; or
(c) a third party, including an institution, fails to perform any function entrusted to it under an agreed appointment procedure.[103]

75. Importantly, the above decisions of the High Court are final and are not subject to an appeal. The Model Law does require the High Court to have due regard to a number of relevant factors in reaching the above decisions, including any qualifications of the arbitrators required by the agreement of the parties, any considerations likely to secure the independence and impartiality of the arbitrators and as regard sole and third arbitrators, the advisability of appointing an arbitrator of a nationality other than that of the parties.

2. Challenging an Arbitrator

76. Article 12 of the Model Law provides that an arbitrator must disclose 'any circumstances likely to give rise to justifiable doubts as to his impartiality or independence' without delay. This duty to disclose applies once a person is approached in connection with his/her possible appointment as an arbitrator and continues throughout the arbitral proceedings.

77. Moreover, an arbitrator may be challenged only if:

---

101. 2010 Act, s. 13.
102. Model Law, Art. 10(3) and 2010 Act, s. 9.
103. Model Law, Art. 10(4) and 2010 Act, s. 9.

(a) circumstances exist that give rise to justifiable doubts as to his/her impartiality or independence;
(b) he/she does not possess qualifications agreed by the parties.[104]

78. Procedures to challenge an arbitrator may be agreed by the parties and, in the absence of such an agreement, the Model Law contains default procedures.[105] Accordingly, a party who has become aware of grounds of challenge has fifteen days to submit, in writing, to the tribunal a statement of the reasons for the challenge. Unless the challenged arbitrator withdraws or the other party agrees, the arbitral tribunal shall decide on the challenge. If the challenge is unsuccessful, the challenging party may request, within thirty days' notice of the decision rejecting the challenge, the High Court to decide on the challenge: a decision from which there is no appeal. While the High Court decision is pending, the arbitral tribunal, including the challenged arbitrator, may continue with proceedings and make an award.

3. Termination of Arbitrator's Mandate

79. An arbitrator's mandate to act can be terminated in a number of ways. Article 14 of the Model Law states that where an arbitrator is unable to act or fails to act without undue delay, his/her mandate terminates if he/she withdraws voluntarily or if the parties agree on termination. Moreover, where there are concerns about an arbitrator's ability or willingness to act as outlined above, any party may request the High Court to decide on the termination of the arbitrator mandate: a decision from which there is no appeal.

4. Replacement of Arbitrator

80. Where an arbitrator's mandate is terminated, in whatever circumstances, a substitute arbitrator shall be appointed according to the rules which were applicable to the appointment of the arbitrator being replaced.[106]

5. Restrictions on Liability of Arbitrator and Others

81. The 2010 Act also provides for immunity to various actors, including institutions.[107] In particular, an arbitrator (including an employee, agent or advisor or

104. Model Law, Art. 12(2).
105. Model Law, Art. 13.
106. Model Law, Art. 15.
107. 2010 Act, s. 22.

expert) is given immunity for anything done or omitted in the discharge or purported discharge of his/her functions. Such immunity seeks to ensure the finality of arbitration awards.[108]

D. Proceedings

82. In practice, arbitral proceedings can vary from the very informal at one extreme (this can occur where the parties have an established trading relationship and a degree of trust exists between them) to court-like proceedings at the other (this might occur where large sums of money are involved or where the trading relationship has broken down and there is little likelihood of it being resurrected). Parties will need to be advised which type of proceedings best suit their needs. Where the parties have designated their own ad hoc arbitration or chosen institutional arbitration, the relevant rules of procedure will apply.

83. The Model Law, recognizing the autonomy of the parties, provides that the parties are free to agree on the procedure to be followed by the arbitral tribunal, subject to the provisions of the Model Law.[109] In particular, Article 18 states that the parties shall be treated with equality and each party shall be given a full opportunity of presenting his/her case (in line with the rules of natural justice). The Model Law provides a series of default rules, in the absence of agreement by the parties, in relation to, for example, the place of arbitration; the commencement of proceedings; statements of claim and defence; hearings and written proceedings; default of a party; experts and court assistance in taking evidence.

84. Moreover, the Model Law provides for the arbitral tribunal to order interim measures (akin to interlocutory injunctions):

(a) to maintain or restore the status quo;
(b) to take action to prevent (or to refrain from action likely to cause) harm or prejudice to the proceedings;
(c) to preserve assets out of which a subsequent award may be satisfied;
(d) to preserve evidence.

As regards (a) to (c) the party seeking the measure must satisfy the arbitral tribunal that harm not reparable by damages is likely to result if the measure is not ordered, and that there is a reasonable possibility that the requesting party will succeed on the merits of the claim.[110]

85. The Model Law further enables the arbitral tribunal to make preliminary orders, including ex parte orders, to support any interim measures and it contains a

108. *See generally*, *W v. Ireland* [1997] 2 IR 141.
109. Model Law, Art. 19.
110. Model Law, Art. 17.

specific regime for such orders.[111] The concurrent jurisdiction of the High Court to grant such interim measures is also recognized by the Model Law and the 2010 Act.[112]

86. Further to the Model Law, the 2010 Act provides that the arbitral tribunal may direct the examination of parties and witnesses under oath or affirmation, unless agreed otherwise by the parties.[113] Section 16 of the 2010 Act provides that the parties to an arbitral agreement can agree to consolidate proceedings with other arbitral proceedings, or that concurrent proceedings can be held. The arbitral tribunal does not have this power, unless conferred by the parties. This provision allows related claims to be heard together, saving time and costs. For example, disputes under a main contract and subcontracts occur frequently in the construction industry. Moreover, the arbitral tribunal may, subject to the agreement of the parties, order a party to provide security for the costs of the arbitration.[114]

E. The Award

87. The Model Law contains a series of default rules in relation to the award in Chapter VI, including provision for settlement in advance of an award,[115] and other grounds for termination of the arbitral proceedings (e.g., withdrawal of claimant or proceedings have become unnecessary or impossible).[116]

1. Applicable Law

88. The Model Law provides that the parties may choose the applicable law. Failing any such designation, the arbitral tribunal shall decide the applicable law as determined by the conflict of laws rules it considers appropriate.[117] Moreover, the arbitral tribunal may decide *ex aequo et bono* or as *amiable compositeur* but only if the parties have expressly authorized it to do so.

2. Form of Award

89. In relation to the award itself, the Model Law provides that the award must be made in writing and be signed by the arbitrator or arbitrators. Moreover, the

111. Model Law, Art. 17B & 17C.
112. Model Law, Art. 17J and 2010 Act, ss 9–10.
113. 2010 Act, s. 14.
114. 2010 Act, s. 19.
115. Model Law, Art. 30.
116. Model Law, Art. 32.
117. Model Law, Art. 28.

award must be reasoned unless the parties have agreed otherwise.[118] The final award has the effect of terminating the arbitral proceedings. There is also provision for correction of the award.[119]

3. Interest

90. The 2010 Act provides that the parties may agree on the arbitral tribunal's powers to award interest. In the absence of such an agreement, the arbitral tribunal may award simple or compound interest from the dates, at the rates, and with the rests, that it considers fair and reasonable.[120]

4. Costs

91. The 2010 Act states that 'costs', which include costs as between the parties and the fees and expenses of the arbitral tribunal (including fees and expenses of any experts), are to be decided by the parties, as they see fit.[121] In the absence of such agreement, the arbitral tribunal can determine by award the costs as it sees fit. And, as regards 'domestic' arbitrations (arbitrations which are not 'international commercial arbitrations'), there is provision for the taxation of costs.

5. Specific Performance

92. The 2010 Act also provides, unless agreed otherwise by the parties, that the arbitral tribunal may make an award requiring specific performance of a contract, other than a contract for the sale of land.[122]

F. Court Intervention

93. The Model Law is characterized by the principles of flexibility and arbitral freedom. Accordingly, the function of the court is to facilitate and support the arbitration process but not to interfere. We have seen above how the High Court may be called upon to assist the arbitral tribunal, for example, in staying litigation, in constituting the tribunal and in ruling on the tribunal's jurisdiction. Indeed, the 2010 Act provides that the High Court or Circuit Court may at any time during civil proceedings, if it thinks it appropriate, and, the parties consent, by order adjourn the

118. Model Law, Art. 31.
119. Model Law, Art. 33.
120. 2010 Act, s. 18.
121. 2010 Act, s. 21.
122. 2010 Act, s. 20.

civil proceedings to enable the parties to determine whether any or all of the matters in dispute might be resolved by arbitration.[123]

94. Judicial recourse against an award is also limited and may only be made by an application for setting-aside, in accordance with the Model Law.[124] Such an application must be made within three months of receiving the award, and, based on limited grounds including that:

- a party supplies evidence that a party to the agreement was incapacitated, or the agreement was not valid under the governing law;
- the court finds that the subject matter of the dispute is not capable of settlement by arbitration under the applicable law;
- the court finds that the award is in conflict with public policy.

G. Enforcement

95. A dual system of enforcement is envisaged in the Arbitration Act, 2010: one system applies to awards in arbitral proceedings which take place in the State and a second system of enforcement applies to 'foreign awards'.

1. Domestic Enforcement

96. Section 23 of the 2010 Act provides that an award is enforceable in the State either by action, or, by leave of the High Court, in the same matter as a judgment.[125] Therefore, an award may be relied on by the parties by way of defence, set-off, or otherwise in legal proceedings. The 2010 Act makes clear that Articles 35 and 36 of the Model Law, on recognition and enforcement, do not apply in respect of awards in arbitral proceedings which take place in the State.[126]

2. Enforcement of Foreign Awards

97. Historically, the main vehicle for enforcement of foreign awards was the New York Convention on the Recognition and Enforcement of Foreign Arbitral Awards (1958), adopted in Ireland originally in 1980 and now enacted in the Arbitration Act 2010.[127] The New York Convention was designed to provide a simple

123. 2010 Act, s. 32.
124. Model Law, Art. 34: *see*, e.g., *Snoddy v. Mavroudis* [2013] IEHC 285 on Court's reluctance to interfere with arbitrator's award. This contrasts sharply with the previous statutory regime in Ireland where an arbitral award was subject to judicial review on a number of grounds, namely, on grounds of the arbitrator's misconduct; error of law on the face of the award; by way of case stated; and by power to remit.
125. 2010 Act, s. 23.
126. 2010 Act, s. 23(3).
127. 2010 Act, s. 24: the Convention is re-produced in the Second Schedule to the 2010 Act.

and effective system for the recognition and enforcement of foreign awards. The New York Convention has been ratified by over 159 states.

98. The Convention applies to foreign awards, that is, awards made in the territory of a state other than the state where the recognition and enforcement of the award are sought.[128] In *Hiscox v. Outhwaite*,[129] where an arbitration was held in England but the award was signed in Paris, the House of Lords held, for the purposes of the New York Convention, that the award was made in Paris. This has the costly disadvantage of requiring the arbitrators to travel to the place of arbitration in order to sign the award. The 2010 Act and the Model Law avoid this problem by deeming the award to be made at the place of arbitration.[130]

99. Article III states that each Contracting State shall enforce arbitral awards in accordance with the rules set out in the Convention, thereby creating a general presumption for eligibility for enforcement. To obtain enforcement, the party must supply a duly authenticated original award or duly certified copy thereof, and the original agreement or duly certified copy thereof.[131] Enforcement can only be refused, at the request of the party against whom enforcement is sought, if that person can prove, for instance, that:

- a party to the arbitration agreement is under some incapacity;
- the arbitration agreement is not valid under the law to which the parties subjected it;
- a party was not given proper notice of the proceedings;
- the award deals with matters not within the arbitration agreement;
- the arbitral tribunal was improperly constituted;
- the award is not yet binding on the parties or has been set aside by a competent authority.[132]

100. Enforcement can also be refused if the competent authority where enforcement is being sought finds that: the subject matter is not capable of settlement by arbitration or contrary to public policy under the law of that country.[133]

101. In practice, the New York Convention has been overtaken by the Model Law as enacted in the Arbitration Act 2010. A party may now seek recognition and enforcement of an arbitration award under Articles 35 and 36 of the Model Law. Unlike the New York Convention, it allows enforcement of an arbitration award irrespective of where it was made. Moreover, the award does not need to be a foreign award, nor is there a requirement that it be given in a State which is a party to any particular Convention. The proofs required are set out in Article 35(2) of the

128. New York Convention, Art. 1(1).
129. [1991] 3 All ER 641.
130. Model Law, Art. 31(3).
131. New York Convention, Art. IV.
132. New York Convention, Art. V.
133. New York Convention, Art. V(2).

Model Law and are the same as those referred to in Article IV of the New York Convention: i.e., the original award and the original arbitration agreement or duly certified copies of each. If these are not in English or Irish then a translation will be required. The most common procedure used to enforce an award is an application for leave to enforce an award by way of a Special Summons. This is a summary court procedure which proceeds by way of Affidavit. Once leave to enforce the award has been obtained, all of the normal execution remedies under Irish law will be available against assets within the jurisdiction in order to satisfy the award.

Chapter 4. General Obligations of Economic Operators

102. The law imposes very few obligations of a general nature on the various economic operators, apart from the duties imposed on registered companies by the Companies Act 2014, most notably to file annual returns and other kinds of important information with the CRO.[134] The general obligations which exist relate to the registration on business names; taxation obligations; obligations in relation to employees' income tax, social welfare and pension entitlements; money laundering obligations; data protection obligations; and prompt payment obligations. These are outlined below.

§1. Registration of Business Names

103. Where the economic operator is doing business under a name or style which is not his/her or its real name, then that name must be separately registered under the Registration of Business Names Act, 1963. This requirement applies whether the operator is an individual, a partnership, a registered company or otherwise. The purpose is to make public the identities of those individuals, partnerships or corporate entities that are the legal entity behind the business name.

104. The Act identifies a variety of persons subject to business name registration.[135] In particular, any individual trading under a name which is not his/her true surname must register that name. Where a partnership carries on business other than under the true surname of all the partners, it must register the name it is using. This is also the case where there are corporate partners and the names of all of those partners are not included in the trading name. Where a registered company or other corporation carries on a business other than under the full corporate name, that business name must be registered. Regardless of what trading name is being used, every publisher of a newspaper must also register that fact under the 1963 Act. The above obligations apply where the economic operator has a place of business in the State and carries on business in the State.

105. The 1963 Act prescribes the manner and particulars of registration.[136] Accordingly, a signed statement in writing, in the prescribed form, containing the following particulars must be furnished to the registrar:

(a) the business name; in the case of a newspaper proprietor, the title of the paper;
(b) the general nature of the business;
(c) the principal place of the business;
(d) the date of adopting the business name;
(e) where the operator is:

134. *See* www.cro.ie. *See further Keane on Company Law* (5th ed., Bloomsbury 2016).
135. 1963 Act, s. 3.
136. 1963 Act, s. 4.

- a registered company or other body corporate, its true corporate name and also where either its registered office or principal office in the State is situated;
- a partnership, each partner's present Christian name and surname, any former names they had, their nationality if they are not Irish, their other business occupations and their usual residences. In the case of corporate partners, their registered office or their principal office in the State must be disclosed;
- an individual, his/her present Christian name and surname, any former names, nationality if not Irish, other business occupation, if any, and usual residence.

The registrar is identified in the Act as the registrar of companies.[137] Filing with CRO can be in paper or electronic form. A registration fee is payable and the above particulars must be registered within one month of adopting the business name.[138] Any changes must also be registered within one month of being made.[139]

106. Registration of a name may be refused on the grounds of undesirability; that refusal may be appealed to the High Court.[140] An index of all names registered under the Act is kept by the CRO and can be searched online.[141] Importantly, no new entity is created when a business name is registered and the fact that a particular name has been registered does not confer any special authority to use that name – use of that name may still constitute unlawful passing-off or breach of trademark, for instance.

107. A certificate that the business name used has been duly registered must be exhibited in a prominent position in the operator's principal office and in every branch office.[142] Furthermore, every business letter, circular and catalogue dispatched by a person who should have registered under the 1963 Act must set out certain information in legible characters.[143] An individual must disclose his/her present and any former names and nationality if not Irish. In the case of partnerships, there must be disclosed the present and former names of every partner, and their nationality, if not Irish. And, in the case of a body corporate, that information is its proper name, the names and any former names of its directors, and their nationality, if not Irish.

137. 1963 Act, s. 15.
138. 1963 Act, s. 6.
139. 1963 Act, s. 7.
140. 1963 Act, s. 14.
141. 1963 Act, s. 13 and s. 15; *see further* www.cro.ie.
142. 1963 Act, s. 8.
143. 1963 Act, s. 18.

§2. Taxation and Duty to Account

108. All persons subject to tax legislation are required to keep proper records and books of account. That duty is made express, for example, in section 84 of the Value-Added Tax Consolidation Act 2010 Act, which requires every person who is accountable for Value-Added Tax (VAT) to 'keep full and true records of all transactions which affect or may affect his liability to tax and entitlement to deductibility'. These records must be kept for at least a period of six years from the date of the latest transaction to which the records relate.[144] Since nearly all economic operators of any commercial significance are subject to VAT, they have an extensive statutory duty to keep proper records.[145] Furthermore, under section 281 of the Companies Act 2014 every company must keep adequate accounting records. Subsequent provisions specify various basic requirements in relation to accounting records; their location; access and period of retention.[146] In particular, these records must be kept by the company for at least six years after the end of the financial year containing the latest date to which the record relates. Failure to comply with these statutory requirements is a criminal offence.[147]

109. Moreover, every company which commences its trade, business or profession, must notify the Revenue Commissioners within thirty days from the date of commencement. The contents of that notice are set out in section 882 of the Taxes Consolidation Act 1997, and include:

a. the name of the company;
b. the address of its registered office;
c. the address of its principle place of business;
d. the name and address of its secretary;
e. the date it commenced its economic activity;
f. the nature of its trade, profession or business;
g. the date up to which its first accounts will be made up;
h. any other such relevant information.

110. Where it is requested to do so, a company must provide the Revenue Commissioners with a return of its profits for any period during which it was subject to corporation tax. That return must specify all sources of income taken into account, detail all disposals giving rise to chargeable gains and all allowable losses, and give

---

144. Value-Added Tax Consolidation Act 2010, s. 84(3).
145. A variety of persons are identified as not obliged to register for VAT, unless they elect otherwise, including a person, natural or legal, who supplies goods the total consideration for which does not exceed EUR 75,000 in any twelve-month period, or who supplies services the total consideration for which does not exceed EUR 37,500 in any twelve-month period: Value-Added Tax Consolidation Act 2010.
146. Companies Act 2014, ss 282–285.
147. Companies Act 2014, s. 286.

particulars on all charges deducted from income.[148] A similar obligation is imposed on individuals and partners subject to income tax.[149]

§3. Employees' Income Tax, Social Welfare and Pension

111. Where the economic operator has employees, he/she is then subject to obligations regarding the deduction and payment over of income tax and social welfare contributions. These requirements are set out principally in the Income Tax (Employments) (Consolidation) Regulations, 2001,[150] as amended, and in the Social Welfare (Collection of Employment Contributions by the Collector General) Regulations, 1979,[151] as amended. These lay down what records the employer must keep and the returns to be made; also, what sums should be deducted from remuneration and the amounts to be paid over to the revenue and social welfare authorities.

112. Moreover, since 15 September 2003, where employers do not operate an occupational pension scheme, they are required to ensure that their employees have access to a Personal Retirement Savings Account (PRSA), a form of flexible private pension savings account owned by the individual which can be transferred from job to job.[152] This involves the employer entering into a contract with a PRSA provider,[153] notifying employees of their right to contribute to a PRSA, allowing PRSA provider's access to employees at their workplace and making any relevant deduction from payroll, at the employee's request.

§4. Money Laundering Obligations

113. The Criminal Justice (Money Laundering and Terrorist Financing) Acts 2010–2018 seek to give effect to the Fourth European Directive on Anti-Money Laundering.[154] The Fourth Directive moves toward a more risk-focused framework than earlier directives and is notable for the requirement to create a central beneficial ownership register (the 'Central Register') operated by CRO. Following terrorist attacks in Europe in 2015 and 2016, a fifth Money Laundering Directive was adopted in 2018 and is due to be transposed in Member States in 2020.[155]

As well as creating a series of criminal offences in Part 2 of the 2010 Act, Part 4 designates various persons and bodies for money laundering purposes. Those designated include credit institutions, unless exempted; financial institutions, unless exempted; auditors, external accountants and tax advisors; solicitors, barristers;

148. Taxes Consolidation Act 1997, s. 884 and s. 951.
149. Taxes Consolidation Act 1997, ss 877–878, s. 880 and s. 951.
150. SI No. 559 of 2001.
151. SI No. 77 of 1979.
152. *See* Pensions (Amendment) Act 2002; *see further* www.pensionsboard.ie.
153. The Pensions Board and the Revenue Commissioners are jointly responsible for approving PRSA products.
154. Directive 2015/849 [2015] OJ L 141/73.
155. Directive 2018/843 [2018] OJ L 156/43.

estate agents and auctioneers, amongst others.[156] The effect of this designation is threefold. First, a designated person is under a statutory obligation to carry out a Business Risk Assessment to establish the money laundering/terrorist financing risk involved in its business. The Business Risk Assessment must be approved by senior management, must generally be documented and must be kept up-to-date. A record of the Assessment must be made available on request to the relevant competent authority.

114. Second, such bodies when providing services must exercise ‘customer due diligence’, which involves identifying customers (and beneficial owners) and verifying the customers’ identity, as well as assessing the risk posed by the customer/transaction with reference to various matters, including the Business Risk Assessment.[157] For instance, a private individual will generally be required to provide the following identifying information:

- a certified copy of a passport or driver’s license;
- proof of address such as a utility bill or a bank statement.

A limited private company will generally be required to provide the following:

- the original or certified copy of an electronic copy issued by the CRO of the Certificate of Incorporation or the Certificate to Trade of the company;
- the company’s Constitution/Memorandum and Articles of Association;
- the names of the company’s directors;
- proof of identity of at least two directors in line with those of a private individual as outlined above;
- a properly authorized mandate or Board Resolution to open the account and indicating the individuals in the entity who has authority to undertake transactions on the account.

115. The legislation also includes a category of ‘politically exposed’ persons and requires that designated bodies must take necessary steps to determine whether or not a customer is ‘politically exposed’ or is within certain degree of relationship with such a person.[158] Further, designed persons and institutions also have an ongoing monitor role in relation to customers.[159]

116. Third, such bodies must report to a Garda Síochána (the Irish police force) and the Revenue Commissioners (the Irish tax authority) any suspicion that a money laundering offence or a financing of terrorist offence has been or is being committed in relation to their business.[160]

156. 2010 Act, s. 25.
157. 2010 Act, s. 33.
158. 2010 Act, s. 37.
159. 2010 Act, s. 35.
160. 2010 Act, s. 44.

117. In support of the above, designated persons and institutions are required to put in place internal policies and procedures, including appropriate training.[161] They are also required to maintain records.[162] And, lastly, designed persons and bodies are subject to monitoring by various competent authorities, under the above legislation.[163]

§5. Data Protection Obligations

118. The EU's General Data Protection Regulation (GDPR)[164] came into force on 25 May 2018, replacing the previous data protection framework. As a Regulation, it does not generally require transposition into Irish law, as it is 'directly applicable'. Moreover, a new Data Protection Act 2018 was enacted establishing a Data Protection Commission (a multiperson Commission to replace the previously existing office of the Data Protection Commissioner), and giving further effect to the GDPR and related matters.[165] The GDPR seeks to emphasize transparency, security and accountability by data controllers and processors, while at the same time standardizing and strengthening the right of European citizens to data privacy.

119. The GDPR places responsibilities on persons who control and process personal data, as well as confer rights on individual data subjects, including rights to information; to access; to rectification and erasure (known as the right to be forgotten). In general term, if a natural or legal person controls or processes any data about a natural person, whether or not by automated means, then they are subject to six data protection principles. Accordingly, Article 5 of the GDPR provides that personal data must be:

(a) processed lawfully, fairly and in a transparent manner in relation to the data subject ('lawfulness, fairness and transparency');
(b) collected for specified, explicit and legitimate purposes and not further processed in a manner that is incompatible with those purposes; ('purpose limitation');
(c) adequate, relevant and limited to what is necessary in relation to the purposes for which they are processed ('data minimisation');
(d) accurate and, where necessary, kept up to date; ('accuracy');
(e) kept in a form which permits identification of data subjects for no longer than is necessary for the purposes for which the personal data are processed; ('storage limitation'); and

161. 2010 Act, s. 54.
162. 2010 Act, s. 55.
163. 2010 Act, Ch. 8.
164. Regulation 2016/679 on the protection of natural persons with regard to the processing of personal data and on the free movement of such data, and repealing Directive 95/46/EC, [2016] OJ L 119/1.
165. The Act also seeks to transpose EU Directive 2016/680 on the protection of natural persons with regard to the processing of personal data by competent authorities for the purposes of the prevention, investigation, detection or prosecution of criminal offences or the execution of criminal penalties, and on the free movement of such data, [2016] OJ L119/89; and to amend the Data Protection Acts 1988-2003.

(f) processed in a manner that ensures appropriate security of the personal data, including protection against unauthorised or unlawful processing and against accidental loss, destruction or damage, using appropriate technical or organisational measures ('integrity and confidentiality').

120. Many of the main concepts and principles of GDPR are much the same as those in the pre-existing legislative framework; however, there are some important developments in the GDPR. For example, before gathering any personal data, previous legislation required businesses and others to notify customers of their identity, the reasons for gathering the data, the use(s) it will be put to, who it will be disclosed to, and if it is going to be transferred outside the EU. Under Articles 13–14 of the GDPR, additional information must be communicated to individuals in advance of processing their data, such as the legal basis for processing the data, retention periods, the right of complaint where customers are unhappy with your implementation of any of these criteria, whether their data will be subject to automated decision-making and their individual rights under the GDPR. The GDPR also requires that the information be provided in concise, easy to understand and clear language. The rules for dealing with subject access requests also changed under the GDPR. In most cases, a data controller cannot charge for processing an access request, unless it can be demonstrated that the cost will be excessive. The timescale for processing an access request has also shortened, dropping from the previous forty-day period to the requirement that there should be no undue delay in processing an access request and, at the latest, they must be concluded within one month. Some organizations were previously required to notify the Data Protection Commissioner when they incurred a personal data breach. However, Article 33 of the GDPR brings in mandatory breach notifications. All breaches must be reported to the Data Protection Commission (DPC), typically within 72 hours, unless the data was anonymized or encrypted.

121. Article 35 of the GDPR also introduces mandatory Data Protection Impact Assessments (DPIAs) for those organizations involved in high-risk processing; for example, where a new technology is being deployed. Where the DPIA indicates that the risks identified in relation to the processing of personal data cannot be fully mitigated, data controllers are required to consult the DPC pursuant to Article 36 before engaging in the process. Moreover, Article 37 of the GDPR requires some organizations to designate a Data Protection Officer (DPO). Organizations requiring DPOs include public authorities, organizations whose activities involve the regular and systematic monitoring of data subjects on a large scale, and organizations who process what is currently known as sensitive personal data on a large scale. Lastly, Article 83 of the GDPR gives data protection authorities more robust powers to tackle non-compliance, including significant administrative fining capabilities of up to EUR 20,000,000 (or 4% of total annual global turnover, whichever is greater) for the most serious infringements. The GDPR also makes it considerably easier for individuals to bring private claims against data controllers when their data privacy has been infringed, and Article 82 allows data subjects who have suffered non-material damage as a result of an infringement to sue for compensation.

§6. Prompt Payment Obligations

122. The EC (Late Payment in Commercial Transactions) Regulations, 2012,[166] seek to encourage the prompt payment of commercial transactions. The Regulations apply to payments made as remuneration for commercial transactions.[167] 'Commercial transactions' means transactions between undertakings, or between an undertaking and a public authority, for the purposes of providing goods or services for remuneration.[168] However, there are a number of express exclusions from the application of the Regulations including:

– contracts made before 16 March 2013;[169]
– transactions with consumers;
– debts that are subject to insolvency proceedings instituted against the debtor.

123. Pursuant to the Regulations, there is an implied term of every commercial transaction that where the purchaser does not pay for the goods or services concerned by the relevant payment date, the supplier is entitled to interest ('statutory late payment interest') without the necessity of a reminder, on the amount outstanding under the contract concerned at the specified rate.[170] The relevant payment date is the date specified in the contract or where the contract is silent the relevant payment date is generally thirty calendar days after: receipt by the purchaser of the invoice; or the delivery of the goods or provision of the services; or acceptance or verification of the goods or services by the purchaser.[171] The sum payable under the Regulations is either the sum specified in the contract or the ECBs refinancing rate plus 8 percentage points.[172] Moreover, where late payment interest is payable, the supplier is also entitled to compensation towards the recovery cost, as specified in the Schedule.[173]

166. SI No. 580 of 2012, which transposes Directive 2011/7/EC on combating late payment in commercial transactions.
167. Regulation 3.
168. Regulation 2.
169. *See* former EC (Late Payment in Commercial Transactions) Regulations, 2002, SI 388 of 2002.
170. Regulation 4.
171. Regulation 2.
172. Regulation 5: this is the rate applied by the ECB to refinancing operations carried out before 1 January and 1 July in each year and published in the Official Journal of the European Communities.
173. Regulation 9.

Chapter 5. Business Assets and Commercial Property Rights

§1. Business Assets

124. The assets or property interests of any business fall into three distinctive legal categories: interests in land (real property); tangible moveables (a form of personal property traditionally known as chattels personal or *choses in possession*); and intangible moveables (a form of personal property also known as *choses in action*).

125. Interests in land, or real property, may comprise full or partial ownership of land, or anything permanently attached to the land, such as buildings. The rights, duties and incidents of land ownership are not ordinarily regarded as the subject of commercial law, even though land transactions may be an important feature of some businesses.[174] Ownership rights in land are almost always registered, the relevant information being registered in the Land Registry. In the case of so-called unregistered land, the registry is the Registry of Deeds.[175] The main purpose of these registrations is to protect priorities with respect to one's interest in the land; an interest which is not duly registered can be overridden comparatively easily by subsequent transactions in the property.

126. Tangible moveable comprises most notably goods and money. The rights, duties and incidents of proprietary rights in tangible moveables may be described as the Law of Personal Property – which in some quarters is used to denote commercial law. The ownership and transfer of goods is a core topic of commercial law and is considered further below in this monograph under the heading sale of goods.[176] Unlike land, there is no central national register for recording transactions in goods; an equivalent arrangement would be unnecessary and cumbersome. But where goods are pledged as security for obligations, it may be necessary to register the security agreement in the special register for bills of sale.[177] What are called floating charges given by companies over all or some of their goods or other property must be separately registered in the Registry of Companies.

127. Intangible moveables comprise legal rights which have no tangible form in themselves; the right can only be rendered fully effective by way of a court action. Intangible moveables may however be represented in the form of a document, and hence are known as *documentary intangibles*: examples include, bills of lading, insurance policies, negotiable instruments and shares in a company. Documentary intangibles are notable because the document represents the property rights which can be transferred by transfer of the document itself. Rights which are not documentary intangibles are called *pure intangibles*: examples include debts, goodwill

---

174. On the topic of land law, *see generally* Lyall, *Land Law in Ireland* (4th ed., Round Hall Sweet & Maxwell 2018); Wylie, *Irish Land Law* (5th ed., Bloomsbury 2013); and Pearse & Mee, *Land Law* (3rd ed., Thomson Reuters Round Hall 2011).
175. Since 4 Nov. 2006, both registry systems come under the control of the Property Registration Authority: *see* Registration of Titles and Deeds Act 2006; *see further* www.landregistry.ie.
176. *See* Ch. 9 §2 below.
177. *See* Ch. 10 §1 below.

and intellectual property rights. Within this category, trade names and a variety of forms of intellectual property are considered further in this chapter.

§2. Intellectual Property

128. As noted above, intellectual property comprises legal rights that are intangible; that is, they have no physical form.[178] They exist only because they are recognized by law, either statute or the common law; and generally they relate to the creative process. The main forms of intellectual property rights include: patents; trademarks; copyright and moral rights; database rights; performer's rights; design rights; and confidential information.[179] While intellectual property rights confer some positive rights on the right holder, the rights granted are predominately negative in nature. They include rights to stop others doing certain 'restricted acts': to stop pirates; counterfeiters; imitators; and, in some cases, third parties who have arrived at the same idea; without the license or permission of the right holder. Moreover, intellectual property rights are not prerequisites to exploitation: an invention can be exploited without registering a patent though registration provides temporary protection against imitators. Equally, intellectual property rights do not provide immunity against breach of other parties' rights (including intellectual property rights) and other public liabilities.

129. Intellectual property rights underpin much modern commercial activity. A business therefore needs to know:

- what intellectual property rights it has;
- what, if anything, it must do to protect those rights;
- how they may best be exploited;
- what action it may take against anyone who infringes those rights;
- how it may avoid infringing the rights of others.

I. Patents

130. Broadly speaking, patents protect inventions and thereby seek to encourage inventiveness. The governing legislation is the Patents Acts 1992–2017.[180] The 1992 Act is the principal Act, and as well as repealing pre-existing legislation, it

---

178. *See generally* Clark, Smyth, & Hall, *Intellectual Property Law in Ireland* (4th ed., Tottel 2016).
179. In addition, there are special systems of protection for plant varieties: *see* Plant Varieties (Proprietary Rights) Act 1980 and the Plant Varieties (Proprietary Rights) (Amendment) Act 1998; and semiconductor topographies: EC (Protection of Topographies of Semiconductor Products) Regulations 1988, SI No. 101 of 1998, which seeks to implement EC Directive on the legal protection of topographies of semiconductor products, Directive 87/54/EEC [1987] OJ L 24/36.
180. The 1992 Act was enacted on 27 Feb. 1992 and came into force on 1 Aug. 1992: SI No. 181 of 1992. It has been amended a number of times including by the Patents (Amendment) Act 2006; and the Patents (Amendment) Act 2012. *See* further the Knowledge Development Box (Certification of Inventions) Act 2017.

enabled ratification of the European Patents Convention (EPC) 1973,[181] and the Washington Patent Co-operation Treaty (PCT) 1970.[182] Section 128 of the 1992 Act empowers the Minister by order to give effect to any amendment of the EPC or the PCT, or any international treaty, convention or agreement relating to patents to which the state is or proposes to become a party. The wording of the 1992 Act closely follows that of the EPC and the PCT. Section 129 of the 1992 Act provides that judicial notice and notice by the Controller of Patents, Designs and Trade Marks shall be taken of, *inter alia*, the EPC, the PCT, any other international agreements, and, decisions or opinions of 'a competent authority' under the EPC.

131. The aim of the EPC is to enable a patent applicant to secure patent rights in a number of European jurisdictions by way of a single application to a centralized office, the European Patent Office (EPO), designating some or all of the thirty-eight Member States, including Ireland.[183] Where a 'European patent' is granted, it operates not as a unitary patent but as a bundle of national patents in the states designated by the applicant, subject to national patent law.[184] Work on developing a European unitary or single patent has been ongoing since 2000[185] and more recently has culminated in two EU Regulations, Regulation 1257/2012[186] and Regulation 1260/2012[187] on enhanced co-operation in the area of unitary patent protection. Under these Regulations unitary patent protection will be optional and coexist with national and European patents. A constitutional challenge by Spain to this unitary patent package was dismissed by the European Court of Justice[188] and pending ratification and implementation of the Unified Patent Court (UPC) Agreement,[189] it is predicted that unitary patent system will come into operation in 2019.

---

181. In 2017, the number of European applications designating Ireland was 165,629 and the number of granted patents designating Ireland was 101,196: Patents Office, *Annual Report 2017*. A revised EPC, known as EPC 2000, came into force on 13 Dec. 2007, and the EPC is now published in its 16th edition (2016).
182. In 2017, based on the international filing date and country of residence of the first named applicant, there were 477 filing from Ireland under the PCT system seeking 'international' patent protection: Patents Office, *Annual Report 2017*.
183. Unlike the failed Community Patent Convention (1989), an amendment to the Constitution was not deemed necessary to enable Ireland to ratify the EPC. The constitutionality of the 1992 Act can be questioned to the extent that the EPC provides for Boards of Appeal which hear appeals against decisions of Examining and Opposition Divisions of the EPO, and hence exercise a judicial function (*see Voest Alpine* [1987] OJ EPO 447; *Merrell Dow Pharmaceuticals v. Norton* [1996] RPC 76 at 82). However, support for the constitutionality of the 1992 Act is evidenced in the judgment of Keane J. in *ACW v. Ireland* [1994] 3 IR 232 at 243.
184. 1992 Act, s. 119.
185. COM(2000) 412 final.
186. [2012] OJ L 361/1.
187. [2012] OJ L361/89.
188. Cases C-146/13 and C-147/13.
189. In Ireland, ratification of the UPC Agreement will require a referendum to amend the Constitution: no date has currently been set for the referendum.

A. What Is Patentable?

132. The 1992 Act outlines the criteria for patentable inventions.[190] Section 9(1) of the 1992 Act, as amended, provides that:

> An invention, in all fields of technology, is patentable if it is susceptible to industrial application, is new and involves an inventive step.

'Invention' itself is not defined in the legislation. 'Industrial application' is defined in section 14 of the 1992 Act as follows:

> an invention is susceptible to industrial application if it can be made or used in any kind of industry, including agriculture.

EPO guidelines provide that the word 'industry' should be given a broad meaning and includes any physical activity of a 'technical character', that is, an activity which belongs to the useful or practical arts, as opposed to the aesthetic arts.[191] Importantly, 'industry' is not limited to the use of a machine or the manufacture of an item, but includes a process, and a substance or composition.

133. The term 'new' is explained in section 11(1) of the 1992 Act which states:

> An invention shall be considered to be new if it does not form part of the state of the art.
>
> The 'state of the art' comprises everything made available to the public, worldwide, including by means of written or oral description, by use, or otherwise.[192] The legislation does provide that certain disclosures will not be prejudicial to novelty, such as disclosures in breach of confidence, or, under certain conditions, the display of the invention at specified international exhibitions.[193]

134. 'Inventive step' is defined in section 13 of the 1992 Act which provides that:

> an invention qualifies if, having regard to the state of the art, it is not obvious to a person skilled in the art.

190. Chapter II of the 1992 Act conforms to the EPC, Arts 52–57; and the Strasbourg Convention 1963, Arts 1–5.
191. EPO Guidelines, C IV 5.1.
192. 1992 Act, s. 11(2).
193. 1992 Act, s. 12.

The courts have developed a number of tests for 'inventive step'.[194] For example, in *Rawls v. Irish Tyre & Rubber Services Ltd*,[195] based on similar wording to section 13, the High Court summarized the test for distinguishing invention from workshop improvement as follows:

> Has the improvement been a commercial success? Has it supplied a want? Has the problem awaited solution for many years and is the device novel and superior to that which has gone before? Is it used and is it widely used in preference to alternative devices? It is apparent that mere simplicity of the device is no objection, and a very slight advance, something approaching a scintilla, will suffice to support the invention. Moreover an ex post facto approach and analysis of the invention is to be guarded against, because it is easy to say after the event, that the whole thing was perfectly obvious in the popular sense of the word.

135. Further, in *Windsurfing International v. Tabur Marine*,[196] based on similar wording from the UK Patents Act, Oliver LJ stated that in assessing what is inventive and what is 'obvious', the court has to identify the inventive process and then it has to:

> assume the mantle of the normally skilled but unimaginative addressee in the art at the priority date and to impute to him what was, at that date, common knowledge in the art in question.[197]

The court must then identify the differences between the inventive step and the generally known matter and ask itself whether those differences constitute steps which would be obvious to the skilled but unimaginative addressee or whether the step involves some level of inventiveness.

136. More recently, Jacob L.J. restated the traditional four-step English test in *Pozzoli S.P.A. v. B.D.M.O. S.A.*[198] as follows:

(1) a. Identify the notional 'person skilled in the art'.
    b. Identify the relevant common general knowledge of that person.
(2) Identify the inventive concept of the claim in question or if that cannot readily be done, construe it).
(3) Identify what, if any, differences exist between the matter cited as forming part of the 'state of the art' and the inventive concept of the claim or the claim as construed.

---

194. *See also* EPO Guidelines C IV 11 for 'problem–solution' approach.
195. [1960] IR 11 at 30.
196. [1985] RPC 59.
197. [1985] RPC 59 at 73–74.
198. [2007] EWCA Civ 588, [2007] F.S.R. 37, 872 at 879.

(4) Viewed without any knowledge of alleged invention as claimed, do these differences constitute steps which would have been obvious to the person skilled in the art or do they require any degree of invention?

In contrast, the EPO adopts what is termed 'a problem and solution' approach, which involves three main stages:

(1) Determining the closest prior art.
(2) Establishing the technical problem to be solved.
(3) Starting from the closest prior art and the technical problem, then considering whether or not the claimed invention would have been obvious to the skilled person.

Importantly, this problem and solution approach is not a rule of law strictly speaking but, rather, a method of furnishing the court or tribunal with the correct mental reference to answer the fundamental question as to whether an alleged inventive step is obvious or not. In the Irish case *Glaxo Group Ltd v. Patents Act*[199] the more traditional four-stage English test was applied because it was agreed by the parties; however, Charleton J. expressed a preference for the European three-stage test in future cases (the judge also noted that either test would have led to the same result in this case).[200]

B. Exceptions to Patentability

137. There are a number of exceptions to patentability listed in sections 9 and 10 of the 1992 Act. Section 9(2) provides the following exceptions:

– a discovery, a scientific theory or a mathematical method;
– an aesthetic creation;
– a scheme, rule or method of performing a mental act, playing a game or doing business, or a program for a computer;
– the presentation of information.

These things are only excluded to the extent that a patent application or a patent relates to that thing *as such*:[201] anything more than 'that thing as such' may be patentable. So, for example, while a discovery is not patentable, a person who discovers a naturally occurring substance and a practical use for it may patent *the use of that thing*.

138. Section 10 contains three further exceptions to patentability. Section 10(1)(a) provides that inventions contrary to public order or morality shall not be

199. [2009] IEHC 277.
200. *See* further Re Boehringer Ingelheim Pharma GmbH & Co. KG & Patents Acts [2017] IEHC 495.
201. 1992 Act, s. 9(3).

patentable.[202] However, section 10(1)(a) further provides that inventions will not be regarded as contrary to public policy or morality only because they are prohibited by law. The words *public order or morality* are very general and hence open to wide interpretation. However, EPO Guidelines suggest that this exception will be invoked rarely.[203] The Guidelines provide that this exception is designed to prevent the patenting of inventions likely to induce riot or public disorder or to lead to criminal or generally offensive behaviour. Anti-personnel mines are identified in the Guidelines as an obvious example. In applying this exception, the EPO asks whether it is probable that the public in general would regard the invention as so abhorrent that the grant of patent rights would be inconceivable.[204]

139. Section 10(1)(b) excludes from patentability a plant or animal variety or an essentially biological process for the production of plants or animals other than a microbiological process or the products thereof.[205] Therefore, genetically modified organisms can be patented. This exception applies to varieties only and a plant or animal treated by a patentable process can be patented.[206] While not patentable, plant variety rights do arise under the Plant Varieties (Proprietary Rights) Act 1980, as amended.[207] The criteria for protection are that the variety must be distinct, uniform, stable and new.[208] The minimum period of protection is set at twenty-five years under this legislation.[209]

140. Lastly, section 10(1)(c) excludes a method for treatment of the human or animal body by surgery or therapy and a diagnostic method practised on the human or animal body.[210] However, section 10(2) clarifies that this exclusion does not apply to products, and in particular substances or compositions, for use in any such method.

141. Further exceptions to patentability are to be found in the EC (Legal Protection of Biotechnological Inventions) Regulations 2000[211] which transposes the

202. *See also* EPC, Art. 53(a).
203. C-IV, 4.1.
204. *See*, e.g., *Harvard/Onco -mouse* T19/90 (Harvard/Oncomouse) [1989] OJ EPO 451; [1990] OJ EPO 476; [1992] OJ EPO 589; (T315/03) [2005] EPOR 31 where a patent was granted for a genetically engineered mouse, Onco-mouse, which was more susceptible to carcinogens and therefore more useful in medical research.
205. *See also* EPC, Art. 53(b).
206. *See*, e.g., *Hybrid Plants/Lubrizol* [1990] EPOR 173.
207. *See* Plant Varieties (Proprietary Rights) (Amendment) Act 1998. The 1980 and 1998 Acts seek to implement the International Convention for the Protection of New Varieties of Plants (UPOV Convention) (1961, as revised in 1972, 1978 and 1991) and Regulation 2100/94 on Community Plant Variety Rights [1994] OJ L 227/1. The Regulation is closely modelled on the UPOV Convention. It introduces a parallel system of Community protection which coexists with national systems and which provides for the grant of plant variety rights which are valid throughout the EC.
208. 1980 Act, s. 5 and First Schedule, as amended; UPOV Convention, Art. 5.
209. 1998 Act, s. 15.
210. *See also* EPC, Art. 53(c).
211. SI No. 247 of 2000, which came into operation on 30 Jul. 2000.

EC Directive on the legal protection of biotechnological inventions.[212] The 2000 Regulations put beyond doubt the legal position that biotechnological inventions, including an element isolated from the human body, are patentable under national laws.[213] However, exceptions to patentability are listed in the Regulations. For example, Regulation 5(1) states that the human body and the simple discovery of an element from the human body are not patentable. Regulation 6(1) provides that inventions contrary to public order and morality are not patentable. In particular, excluded from patentability are:

- processes for cloning human beings;
- processes for modifying the germ line genetic identity of human beings;
- uses of human embryos for industrial or commercial use;[214]
- process for modifying the genetic identity of animals which are likely to cause them suffering without producing substantial medical benefits.[215]

C. Obtaining a Patent

142. As with trademarks, for example, the legal rights of a patent holder derive from registration.[216] A patent can be obtained for any patentable invention provided the proper statutory procedure is followed. Under the 1992 Act, the Patents Office[217] and the Controller of Patents, Designs and Trade Marks continue to administer the registration scheme.[218] Detailed rules govern the application, examination and grant process.[219] Each part of the process must be completed within prescribed time limits and fees are payable at various stages. In addition, an applicant will usually pay professional fees to a patent agent who assists the applicant through this technical and complex process, making the process even more expensive.[220] The process is outlined below.

---

212. Directive 98/44/EC, OJ L 213/13. A Dutch legal challenge to the Directive failed: *see* Case C-377/98.
213. Regulation 4.
214. *See Brüstle v. Greenpeace* (Case C-34/10), and *ISCC v. Comptroller General of Patents, Designs and Trade Marks* (Case C-364/13).
215. Regulation 6(2).
216. *See* 1992 Act, Part VII, ss 84–89 regarding the Register.
217. Based in Kilkenny: SI No. 293 of 1998. *See generally* www.patentsoffice.ie.
218. 1992 Act, s. 6, as amended by the Intellectual Property (Miscellaneous Provisions) Act 1998.
219. 1992 Act, ss 18–35; and the Patent Rules 1992–2012.
220. Re patent agents, *see* 1992 Act, ss 105–109. Importantly, professional privilege has been extended to communications with patent agents 'in relation to any matter concerning the protection of an invention, patent, design, or technical information or any matter involving passing-off': 1992 Act, s. 94. At the end of 2017, 86 individuals and 7 partnerships were registered as Patent Agents: Patents Office, *Annual Report 2017*.

1. Application[221]

143. An Irish patent application must be filed at the Irish Patents Office on a standard form, with the appropriate fee. The application must contain:[222]

- a request for the grant of the patent;
- a specification, that is a detailed technical description of the invention, including one or more claims for the patent, that is a detailed description of what the invention does;[223]
- any plans and drawings referred to in the specification and claims;[224]
- an abstract, or a concise summary of the specification.

144. The 'priority date' fixes the time at which the prior art is to be considered for the purpose of assessing the novelty of the invention.[225] The priority date is usually the date of filing the application. In order to claim early priority an inventor can pay the official filing fee and provide documentation containing:

- a request for grant of a patent
- information identifying the applicant
- a description of the invention
- reference to any previously filed application.[226]

Provided he/she files the claims and an abstract within twelve months from the date of filing, the application will proceed with priority given from the date of filing.[227]

2. Examination

145. Within about four weeks of filing, brief particulars of the application are published in the Patents Office Journal, which is published fortnightly, in hard and electronic form. This is the only information publicly available until the application is published. This occurs as soon as practicable after the expiry of eighteen months from the date of filing.[228]

221. In 2017, 268 applications for a national patent (137 for twenty-year full term; and 131 for ten-year short term) were received by the Irish Patents Office; a total of 1,166 applications were pending at 31 Dec. 2017; of these 180 were awaiting the submission of evidence of novelty: Patents Office, *Annual Report 2017*.
222. 1992 Act, s. 18. All these requirements need not be complied with on the date of filing.
223. The claims must define the matter for which protection is sought, be clear and concise and supported by the description: 1992 Act, s. 20.
224. The description must be sufficiently clear and complete for it to be carried out by a person skilled in the art: 1992 Act, s. 19(1). *See Rawls v. Irish Tyre and Rubber Services Ltd* [1960] IR 11.
225. 1992 Act, ss 25–27.
226. 1992 Act, s. 23.
227. Patent Rules 1992, Rule 19: SI No. 179 of 1992.
228. Earlier publication can be requested: 1992 Act, s. 28.

146. An applicant has two options at this stage. An applicant may submit to the Controller a statement that an application for the same invention has been made elsewhere, such as in the UK, or, in another state under the EPC. In addition, there must subsequently be filed evidence of novelty of the invention in the form of either an official search report issued on the relevant patent application or the grant of a patent.[229] Alternatively, an applicant can proceed by means of a search report requested from the Irish Patent Office,[230] subject to the payment of the appropriate fee.[231] The request and fee must be submitted within twenty-one months from filing. When completed, a search report is sent to the applicant who has two months to advise the Controller whether the application is to be withdrawn or maintained. If maintained, the search report is published and the applicant has four months within which to make amendments to the application or to advise the Controller that no amendments are being made. If this is not done, the Controller may refuse the application.[232] A limited examination is then carried out by the Patent Office under section 31 of the 1992 Act to determine whether the application complies with the legislation. The onus is placed on the applicant and his/her agent to ensure that the necessary requirements of patentability,[233] novelty,[234] inventive step,[235] industrial application,[236] clear and complete disclosure in the specification,[237] and clear and complete claims are complied with.[238] Failure to comply with these requirements could lead to revocation of the patent under section 58.[239]

3. Grant[240]

147. If all statutory formalities have been complied with, the Controller will request payment of a grant fee. Failure to pay within the time limit will mean that the application is deemed to be withdrawn.[241] Once the grant fee and any renewal fees have been paid, a certificate of grant of a patent will be issued.

229. 1992 Act, s. 30.
230. The search is actually carried out by the UK Patent Office.
231. 1992 Act, s. 29.
232. 1992 Act, s. 29(4).
233. 1992 Act, s. 9.
234. 1992 Act, s. 11.
235. 1992 Act, s. 13.
236. 1992 Act, s. 14.
237. 1992 Act, s. 19.
238. 1992 Act, s. 20.
239. *See further* para. 148 below.
240. In 2017, when 268 applications for patents were received by the Irish Patents Office, and a total of 1,166 applications were pending at 31 Dec. 2017, 87 patents were granted: Patents Office, *Annual Report 2017*. The number of patents in force on 31 Dec. 2017 was 169,453: Patents Office, *Annual Report 201*.
241. 1992 Act, s. 31(3).

D. Patent Owner's Rights

148. Once granted, a patent gives the owner a monopoly or exclusive right to exploit the invention.[242] Importantly, a patent does not authorize use, it is not a pre-requisite to exploitation and it does not provide immunity against breach of other parties' rights (including intellectual property rights) and other public liabilities.

149. Section 36 of the 1992 Act provides for a twenty-year patent from the date of filing of the patent application.[243] There is no provision for the extension of the period. Moreover, there is provision for a short-term patent, of ten years duration. Less strict rules as to patentability apply: the invention must be new, susceptible to industrial application and *not clearly lacking* an inventive step.[244]

150. Section 79 of the 1992 Act provides that the rules of law applicable to the ownership and devolution of personal property shall apply in relation to patent applications and patents, subject to the Act. A patent and a patent application is personal property and therefore, for example, can be assigned, licensed or charged by way of a mortgage.[245] Any changes in ownership or in an interest in a patent application once published or a patent must be recorded on the Register of Patents.[246] Failure to comply means that any document which has not been recorded will only be admitted as evidence of ownership or interest in court if the court so directs.[247]

151. Where a patent application or a patent is owned by two or more persons, there is a presumption that they hold the property as tenants in common in equal shares.[248] With a tenancy in common, the deceased's share forms part of his/her estate and passes under his/her will or on intestacy. One co-owner cannot assign any share in, or license, the patent, without the consent of all the other co-owners.[249]

152. Under the 1992 Act, there is provision in the legislation for the revocation of a patent, at any time during its life, by the High Court or the Controller, on stated grounds, which include: that the subject matter of the patent is not patentable;[250] or that the owner of the patent is not entitled to it.[251]

242. 1992 Act, Part II, Ch. VI, ss 40–46.
243. Subject to the payment of renewal fees payable in respect of the third and each subsequent year calculated from the date of filing of the patent application: Patent Rules 1992, Rules 33 and 34, SI No. 179 of 1992. Under the 1992 Act, s. 29 where a patent has lapsed following failure to pay a renewal fee, application can be made by the patentee, within three years of the patent lapsing, for restoration of the patent.
244. 1992 Act, ss 63–67. In 2017, 131 applications for short-term patents, out of a total of 268 applications, were received; and 27 short-term patents were granted: Patents Office, *Annual Report 2017*.
245. 1992 Act, s. 85.
246. 1992 Act, s. 85.
247. 1992 Act, s. 85(7).
248. 1992 Act, s. 80.
249. 1992 Act, s. 80(3).
250. 1992 Act, s. 58(a).
251. 1992 Act, s. 58(e). *See generally*, 1992 Act, ss 57–62.

E. Licenses

153. A patent owner may not wish, or be in a position, to exploit the patent fully. In such circumstances a patent owner may license the patent. Licenses are dealt with in Part IV of the 1992 Act. There are two types of license: voluntary or compulsory.

154. A voluntary license involves the patent owner applying to the Controller, at any time after the grant of the patent, to indicate that licenses as of right are available regarding the patent.[252] On application for a license of right, the patent owner must satisfy the Controller that he/she is not precluded by contract from granting licenses on the patent. The Controller must give notice to anyone listed on the Register as having an interest in the patent, such as another licensee, or a mortgagee. Once a license of right is entered on the Register, any person may obtain a license on terms to be agreed between the parties, or in default, on terms settled by the Controller.[253]

155. While there is no positive obligation placed on patent owners to exploit the patent, the compulsory license provisions seek to ensure such exploitation. A compulsory license cannot be applied for until after three years from the date of publication of the grant of the patent.[254] The grounds on which such an application can be made are set out in section 70 and include that:

- demand in the State for the subject matter of the patent is not being met or is not being met on reasonable terms;
- demand in the State for the product protect is being met by importation from outside the World Trade Organization (WTO);
- the establishment or development of commercial or industrial activities in the State is unfairly prejudiced.

F. Infringement and Remedies

156. Section 40 of the 1992 Act prohibits direct infringement, while section 41 prohibits indirect infringement. Infringement must occur in the State for the provisions of the 1992 Act to apply. A third party does not infringe where he/she has the consent, express or implied, of the owner of the patent. In *Betts v. Willmott*,[255] for instance, it was held that following the sale of a product, there is an implied license to use or resell. There is also an implied right to repair a patented product provided that such repair does not amount to the manufacture of a new product.[256]

252. The fees for renewal of a patent indicating that licenses, as of right, are available are halved: 1992 Act, s. 68(2)(d).
253. 1992 Act, s. 68(2)(a).
254. 1992 Act, s. 70.
255. (1871) LR 6 Ch. 239.
256. *See further Solar Thompson Engineering Co. Ltd v. Barton* [1977] RPC 537.

157. Section 40 classifies infringement according to whether the invention is a product, a process or the product of a process. For example, direct infringement in relation to a product arises by making, offering, putting on the market, using, importing or stocking the product for those purposes. In *Hoffman-Law Roche v. Harris Pharmaceutical Ltd,*[257] the concept of infringement, under equivalent wording,[258] was extended to include possession with the intention of using the product for trade purposes, and for securing of a profit. Whether this extended scope of infringement exists under the 1996 Act remains to be seen.

158. Indirect, or contributory, infringement, under section 41,[259] occurs where any person supplies or offers to supply any of the means, relating to an essential element of the invention, for putting the invention into effect. But indirect infringement does not occur where the 'means' are 'staple commercial products' except where the supply or offer is made for the purpose of inducing the person supplied to do an act which constitutes a direct infringement.[260] There is no definition of 'staple commercial product' though it may include generally available raw materials and goods suitable for uses, some of which would not amount to infringement.

159. Sections 42 and 43 limit the extent to which infringement proceedings can be taken by providing a number of exceptions to infringement. Acts which do not amount to infringement include:

- acts done privately for non-commercial purposes;
- acts done for experimental purposes;
- extemporaneous preparation of a medicine in a pharmacy for individual cases;
- acts which cannot be prevented under the Treaty of Rome.[261]

160. Under section 44, protection is provided from the date of first publication of the specification.[262] Hence, acts which occur prior to publication cannot constitute infringement. But, a patent must be granted before proceedings for infringement can commence.[263]

161. Infringement proceedings may be taken by a patent owner or by a licensee. However, before a licensee can take proceedings, the licensee must first request the patent owner to take proceedings and the patent owner must fail to do so within two

257. [1977] FSR 200.
258. That is, making, using, exercising or vending the invention, 1964 Act, s. 25.
259. *See* CPC, Art. 26.
260. 1992 Act, s. 41(2).
261. For example, where the owner of a patent has consented to goods made in accordance with his/her patent being placed on the market within the EU, the doctrine of exhaustion of rights may prevent him/her from complaining of the import of goods which would otherwise infringe his/her patent: *see*, e.g., *Merck & Co. Ltd v. Stephar BV* [1981] ECR 2063.
262. That is, eighteen months from the earliest priority date, or eighteen months after the date of application where no priority is claimed. *See further* 1992 Act, s. 56(3) under which damages can be reduced if it would not have been reasonable to expect from a consideration of the published application, that the patent would be infringed; *see also* EPC Art. 67.
263. 1992 Act, s. 56.

months of the request. The patent owner must then be joined as a defendant in the proceedings but is not liable for costs unless he/she enters an appearance and takes part in the proceedings.[264]

162. The scope of protection given by a patent is determined by the patent claim or claims and how a court interprets those claims. Prior to 1992, interpretation of claims was governed at common law. The English House of Lords adopted a 'purposive' interpretation, as opposed to a literal interpretation, of patent claims and this was approved by the Irish High Court in *Wavin Pipes Ltd v. The Hepworth Iron Co. Ltd.* [265] But the 1992 Act contains a Protocol on Interpretation in the Second Schedule, which derives from Article 69 of the EPC. Accordingly, the Protocol provides that in interpreting a patent, a court should adopt a middle ground between a strict literal interpretation and a more liberal interpretation, thereby providing fair protection of the patent owner and a reasonable degree of certainty for third parties.[266]

163. The burden of proving infringement, as is normal, rests on the patent owner or the licensee. However, this burden can shift. If the invention is a process for obtaining a new product, and if the same product is produced, there is a presumption that such a product is made using the patented process, unless the defendant can prove to the contrary.[267]

164. Section 47 provides for a series of remedies for infringement of a patent, including injunctive relief, an order for delivery up or destruction of the infringing product, damages or an account of profits and a declaration that the patent is valid and has been infringed. There is a restriction on recovery of damages for 'innocent' infringement[268] and in certain cases where the specification of the patent has been amended.[269] There is also provision in the legislation for a third party to seek a declaration of non-infringement.[270] These remedies are only available from the High Court, except regarding a short-term patent, where proceedings can be taken before the Circuit Court.[271] Lastly, a person aggrieved by groundless threats of infringement proceedings may seek an injunction to restrain such threats and damages.[272] A mere notification of the existence of a patent is not a threat.[273]

264. 1992 Act, s. 68(3).
265. [1982] FSR 32.
266. *See Actavis UK Ltd and others v Eli Lilly and Company [2017] UKSC 48* where the UK Supreme Court moved away from the former 'purposive approach' by effectively introducing a doctrine of equivalents and thereby demonstrating a convergence of UK law with the EPC and the law applied in other EU jurisdictions. This decision may be of persuasive value before an Irish Court.
267. 1992 Act, s. 46(1).
268. 1992 Act, s. 49(1).
269. 1992 Act, s. 49(3).
270. 1992 Act, s. 54.
271. 1992 Act, s. 66(4).
272. 1992 Act, s. 53.
273. 1992 Act, s. 53(4).

II. Trademarks

165. Trademarks are protected by statute in the form of the Trade Marks Act 1996,[274] as amended, and by the common law tort of passing-off.[275] The 1996 Act was introduced to meet our obligations under various EC measures,[276] and a number of international agreements.[277] In Ireland and the wider EU, trademarks can be registered at national level at the intellectual property (IP) offices of Member States, or in unitary form at EU level as a European Union Trade Mark (EUTM) at the European Union Intellectual Property Office (EUIPO) in Alicante. Under the overall system, national and European trademarks coexist and the same sign may be registered as a European and/or as a national trademark.

166. In 2009 the EU launched a review of the trademark system which culminated in the adoption of a new Trade Mark Directive, Directive 2015/2436,[278] and a new Trade Mark Regulation, Regulation 2015/2424, now codified as Regulation 2017/1001.[279] These reforms leave intact the main principles of trademark law and instead focus on making trademark registration systems in the EU more accessible and efficient for businesses in terms of lower costs and complexity, increased speed, greater predictability and legal security. These adjustments seek to ensure the complementary nature of the EUTM with national trademark systems. Notable changes include the removal of the requirement of 'graphic representation' for trademark registration; and new absolute and relative grounds for refusal/revocation. This EU reform package was implemented in Ireland by four Statutory Instruments[280] which introduced new provisions and amended certain existing provisions in the Trade Mark Act 1996, and related measures. These changes came into effect on 14 January 2019.

---

274. The 1996 Act was enacted on 16 Mar. 1996 and came into effect from 1 Jul. 1996: SI No. 199 of 1996.
275. *See* paras 243–254 below.
276. In particular, the EC Directive on trade marks: Directive 89/104/EEC, [1989] OJ L 40/1; and an EC Regulation on the Community trade mark: Regulation 40/94/EC, [1994] OJ L 11/1: both now repealed.
277. The Madrid Protocol relating to the International Registration of Marks (1989); and the Paris Convention for the Protection of Industrial Property (1883), as revised. The Protocol relating to the Madrid Agreement operates under the aegis of the WIPO. The Protocol permits trade mark owners to make, through their national trade mark offices, a single application to the WIPO in which they can seek protection for their marks in any or all countries party to the Protocol. The Madrid Protocol was ratified on 22 Jul. 2001 and came into force on 19 Oct. 2001: Trade Marks (Madrid Protocol) Regulations SI No. 346 of 2001. In 2017, 1,717 international registrations designating Ireland were received by the Patents Office: Patents Office, *Annual Report 2017*.
278. [2015] OJ L 336/1. Member States had until 14 January 2019 to transpose its provision into national law (bar Article 45 concerning the provision of an administrative procedure for revocation or a declaration of invalidity of a trade mark which comes into effect 14 January 2023.
279. [2017] OJ L 154/1, which entered into force on 23 March 2016. In EU law, Regulations are 'directly applicable' and thus do not have to be transposed into national law.
280. S.I. Nos 561–564 of 2017.

A. Registrability

167. A trademark can be registered if it complies with the statutory definitions and requirements. A trademark is defined as:

> any sign which is capable of distinguishing goods or services of one undertaking from those of other undertakings.[281]

The word 'sign' is not defined but is interpreted widely to include a three-dimensional sign, a hologram, and a sensory sign such as music or a sound,[282] smell, taste, feel or gesture. When seeking registration, it is no longer mandatory that the representation of a trademark must be 'graphic'. A sign can be represented in any appropriate form, although the representation must allow the examiner and the public to determine the clear and precise subject matter of the protection sought. The elimination of the 'graphic' representation requirement from the definition of trademark facilities the registration of non-traditional trademarks such as sound and motion marks.

168. The requirement that the mark must be 'capable of distinguishing goods or services of one undertaking from those of other undertakings' was an aspect of the previous 1963 Trade Marks Act. For example, in *Waterford Glass Ltd v. Controller of Patents Designs and Trade Marks,*[283] despite the geographical significance of the word 'Waterford', registration was allowed in relation to cut glass crystal because the mark had been used continually since 1952 and had achieved 100% factual distinctiveness. However, in *Masterfoods v. Controller of Patents, Designs and Trade Marks* [284] Kelly J identified a clear break between the policy underlying the 1963 Act and the new regime under the Trade Mark Directive and the 1996 Act. The case concerned an application to register two slogans as trademarks, including the slogan 'Top breeders recommend it' in relation to dog food. Registration had been refused by the Controller because the words were considered to be statements of fact and hence devoid of a distinctive character. The plaintiff appealed this decision to the High Court. Interestingly, a similar application by the plaintiff's predecessor, Mars GB Ltd, had been refused by the Controller under the 1963 Act and this refusal was upheld by Geoghegan J. in an *ex tempore* judgment delivered on 4 July 1996. With reference to the earlier decision, Kelly J noted that a major change to traditional trademark law has been brought about by the Trade Mark Directive, and the 1996 Act. Under the 1963 Act, there was a policy of not registering a mark which was incapable of distinguishing a trader's goods and was merely a commonplace description because to do so would give a monopoly over ordinary words which another trader might fairly wish to use. Kelly J noted that this policy was entirely

281. 1996 Act, s. 6(1), as amended.
282. In 2000, the Irish Patents Office registered its first 'sound mark': Patents Office, *Annual Report 2000*, 10.
283. [1984] FSR 390; [1984] ILRM 565.
284. [2003] IEHC 13.

set aside by the Directive and the subsequent decisions of the European Court.[285] In particular, Article 6 of the Directive (and section 15 of the 1996 Act) provided that registration of a trademark does not entitle the proprietor to prohibit a third party from using in the course of trade indications concerning '*the kind, quality, quantity, intended purpose, value, geographical origin, the time of production of goods or of rendering of service or other characteristics of goods or services*' provided that such use is in accordance with honest practices in industrial and commercial matters. Therefore, only where the proposed trademark amounts to no more than the usual way of designating the relevant goods or their characteristics can be said to be devoid of distinctive character. Accordingly, Kelly J found that the slogan was distinctive and the appeal was allowed.[286]

169. The 1996 Act, as amended, provides further that:

> a trade mark may, in particular, consist of words (including personal names), or designs, letters, numerals, colours, the shape of goods or of the packaging of goods, or sounds, provided that such signs are capable of being represented on the register in a manner which enables the Controller and the public to determine the clear and precise subject matter of the protection afforded to its proprietor.[287]

The reference to 'in particular' indicates that this list is not exhaustive.

170. The 1996 Act recognizes a number of *types* of trademark: some old; some new. The legislation retained the concept of 'certification mark'; that is, a mark indicating that the goods or services are certified by the proprietor as to origin, material, mode of manufacture of goods or performance of services, quality, accuracy or other characteristics.[288] The concept of 'collective mark' was introduced by the Act. A collective mark can be used to distinguish goods or services of members of an association which owns the mark from another association.[289] The 1996 Act also makes provision for the EUTM.[290] Since 1 January 1996, it has been possible to apply for a unitary or single EUTM, as an alternative to national registration. The main advantage of the EUTM is that it saves cost and time because one application to the EUIPO can lead to registration in all 28 Member States. The substantive law governing the EUTM is broadly similar to that of Member States national trademark law as harmonized by Directive 2015/2436.[291]

---

285. *See*, e.g., *Proctor & Gamble Company v. OHIM* [2001] ECR 1-625 – the *BABY-DRY* case.
286. In terms of the harmonizing objective of the Trade Marks Directive, it is also notable that this slogan was registered as a trade mark in the UK as of the 31 Oct. 1994.
287. 1996 Act, s. 6(2), as amended.
288. 1996 Act, s. 6(3) and s. 55; *see further* Second Schedule to Act.
289. 1996 Act, s. 6(3) and s. 54; *see further* First Schedule to Act.
290. *See* now Regulation 2017/1001, [2017] OJ L 154/1; and the 1996 Act, s.56.
291. [2015] OJ L 336/1. Member States had until 14 January 2019 to transpose its provision into national law (bar Article 45 concerning the provision of an administrative procedure for revocation or a declaration of invalidity of a trade mark which comes into effect 14 January 2023).

B. Grounds for Refusal

171. Grounds for refusal are either absolute or relative. The absolute grounds involve an inherent defect in the trademark applied for and are not related to any prior rights. In contrast, the relative grounds do not involve any inherent defects in the trademark applied for but relate to the existence of earlier rights.

172. The absolute grounds for refusal include that:

- the sign does not satisfy the section 6(1) definition;
- the trademark is devoid of distinctive character;
- the mark consists exclusively of signs or indications which may serve, in trade, to designate the kind, quality, quantity, intended purpose, value, geographical origin, the time of production of the goods or of rendering of services, or other characteristics of goods or services;
- the mark consists exclusively of signs or indications which have become customary in the current language or in the bona fide and established practice of the trade;
- the sign consists exclusively of the shape or another characteristic which results from the nature of the goods, or, is necessary to obtain a technical result, or, gives a substantial value to the goods;
- the mark is contrary to public policy or morality;
- the use of the mark is prohibited by law.[292]

173. Under the heading 'relative grounds for refusal', a trademark will not be registered if, for example:

- the mark is identical with an earlier trademark, and the goods or services for which the trademark is applied are identical with the goods or services for which the earlier trademark is protected;[293]
- because the trademark is identical with an earlier trademark and would be registered for goods or services similar to those for which the earlier trademark is protected, and there exists a likelihood of confusion on the part of the public, which includes the likelihood of association of the later mark with the earlier mark;[294]
- because the trademark is similar to an earlier trademark and would be registered for goods or services identical with or similar to those for which the earlier trademark is protected, and there exists a likelihood of confusion on the part of the public, which includes the likelihood of association of the later mark with the earlier mark;[295]
- the trademark is identical with or similar to an earlier trademark, where the earlier trademark has a reputation in the State and the use of the later trademark

292. 1996 Act, s. 8, s.9, ss 62 and 63, as amended.
293. 1996 Act, s. 10(1).
294. 1996 Act, s. 10(2)(a).
295. 1996 Act, s. 10(2)(b).

without due cause would take unfair advantage of or be detrimental to, the distinctive character or reputation of the earlier trademark.[296]

C. The Registration Process

174. As with patents, the legal rights of a trademark owner derive from registration.[297] Marks can be registered in one of forty-five classes: thirty-four in relation to goods; and eleven for service marks.[298] The classification is not entirely logical and a business may have to register in more than one class where the goods or services are thought to be similar. Detailed rules and procedures, beyond the scope of this monograph, regulate the registration process.[299] The following outlines the registration process.

1. Application

175. Applications for Irish trademarks are made to the Controller of the Patents Office.[300] Applications for an EUTM can no longer be filed through the Irish Patents Office and must be forwarded directly to the EUIPO, in Alicante, Spain.[301]

176. When filing an Irish trademark application, there are certain minimum formalities required to secure a 'filing date'.[302] This is usually the eventual date of registration under the 1996 Act,[303] and an infringement action can be taken from this date.[304] To secure a filing date, documents must be filed which:

- indicate that registration of a trademark is sought and the name and address of the person seeking registration;
- contain a representation of the mark for which registration is sought;
- indicate the goods or services which relate to the mark.[305]

Filing fees must be paid on application or within one month of the date of filing, otherwise the application is treated as abandoned.[306] Where priority is sought under

---

296. 1996 Act, s. 10(3), as amended.
297. *See* 1996 Act, s. 7(1) and Part IV concerning the Register and other administrative provisions.
298. 1996 Act, s. 39, as amended.
299. 1996 Act, ss 37–46; and the Trade Mark Rules, SI No. 199 of 1996.
300. 1996 Act, s. 37(1). The Patents Office is based in Kilkenny: SI No. 293 of 1998; *see further* www.patentsoffice.ie.
301. In 2017,there were 1,143 applications for an EUTM by Irish resident applicants.
302. 1996 Act, s. 38.
303. 1996 Act, s. 45(3).
304. 1996 Act, ss 13(3) and (4).
305. Trade Mark Rules, SI No. 199 of 1996, Rule 12.
306. Trade Mark Rules, SI No. 199 of 1996, Rule 12(5).

the Paris Convention,[307] then the application must be filed within six months from the date of filing of the first Convention application.[308]

2. Examination

177. Once an application is filed, there is no statutory time limit within which the application must be examined by the Patents Office. The purpose of the examination is twofold: (i) to ensure the necessary formalities of the 1996 Act and the Trade Mark Rules have been complied with; and (ii) to consider whether the substantive requirements of the 1996 Act and the Trade Mark Rules have been complied with, including whether the application should be refused on the absolute or relative grounds specified in the 1996 Act.[309] If following the examination it is found that any of these requirements have not been met, then an official action issues to the applicant allowing the applicant to make representations or to amend the application. Again, there are no statutory time limits and in practice there is a dialogue between the applicant and the relevant examiner. Where the applicant has failed to respond, or to satisfy the examiner that the requirements have been met, the application is refused.[310] Where the requirements are met, the application is accepted and proceeds to publication.

3. Publication

178. Once an application is accepted, following examination, it is published or advertised in the Patents Office Journal, a fortnightly publication, available in hard copy and online.[311] This allows third parties to oppose the application before registration. The 1996 Act includes a three-month opposition period which is not extendible.[312] There are no specified grounds for opposition. Hence, the grounds for opposition are the same as those which apply generally in relation to the refusal of registration: the absolute and relative grounds of refusal. Where an opposition is filed (with the relevant fee), the applicant must file, within three months, a counter-statement. If a counter-statement is not filed, the application is deemed withdrawn. If a counter-statement is filed, there follows a period in which both sides must file their evidence supporting their claims, with the Office, by way of statutory declaration. When the evidence is complete, both parties are invited to a hearing at which

307. The Paris Convention for the Protection of Industrial Property (1883), as revised; *see* 1996 Act, ss 60–65.
308. 1996 Act, s. 40(1).
309. 1996 Act, s. 42.
310. 1996 Act, s. 42(3).
311. 1996 Act, s. 43: *see* www.patentsoffice.ie.
312. Trade Mark Rules, SI No. 199 of 1996, Rule 18(1).

they are usually represented by their trademark agents or counsel.[313] Following the hearing, a decision is made and notified to the parties.[314]

4. Registration

179. If there is no opposition, or if any opposition is decided in favour of the applicant, then upon payment of the final registration fee, a certificate of registration will issue.[315] A mark is registered initially for ten years, renewable indefinitely for further periods of ten years, on payment of a renewal fee.[316] In legal proceedings, registration is prima facie evidence of the validity of the trademark.[317]

D. Owners' Rights and Dealing in Trademarks

180. Section 7(1) of the 1996 Act provides that a registered trademark is a property right obtained by registration under the 1996 Act and the owner shall have the rights and remedies provided for by the Act.[318] Further, section 26 describes a registered trademark as personal property and therefore, like other forms of personal property it can be traded by outright disposition such as an assignment, or by the owner permitting others to exploit his/her property by granting a license. Equally, it can be charged or gifted away. However, such dealings, to be fully effective, must comply with statutory formalities. Provision is made for the co-ownership of registered trademarks.[319]

181. Section 47 provides that the duration of a registered trademark is ten years from the date of registration (usually the filing date). Registration can be renewed indefinitely for further periods of ten years, provided the prescribed renewal fee is paid.[320] But, a trademark may be revoked on a number of stated grounds, including that, within five years of registration, the trademark has not been put to genuine use in the State and there are no proper reasons for non-use.[321]

182. Section 28 states that a registered trade mark, or an application,[322] is transferrable by assignment, testamentary disposition or otherwise, in the same way as other personal property, with or without the goodwill of a business. An assignment can be whole or partial. It may be partial, or limited, in that it applies to some but

313. On trade mark agents *see* 1996 Act, Part V. At the end of 2013, there were 205 individuals and four partnerships entered on the Register of Trade Mark Agents: Patents Office, *Annual Report 2013*.
314. This decision can be appealed to the High Court: 1996 Act, s. 79.
315. 1996 Act, s. 45.
316. 1996 Act, ss 47–48.
317. 1996 Act, s. 76.
318. A trade mark application is also treated as personal property: 1996 Act, s. 31(1).
319. 1996 Act, s. 27.
320. 1996 Act, s. 48.
321. 1996 Act, s. 51.
322. 1996 Act, s. 31(1).

not all of the goods or services for which it is registered; or it applies to use of the trademark in a particular manner or a particular locality.[323] But, to be effective, the legal assignment must be in writing and signed by or on behalf of the assignor.[324] Equitable assignment of a trademark may also be effected in which case there is no written requirement. A trademark may also be subject to an equitable charge, created in the same way as over other personal property.[325]

183. A trademark can also be licensed. This aspect of trademark law is of particular interest to those engaged in character merchandising, franchising and similar activities. Licensing was dealt with expressly for the first time in the 1996 Act.[326] To be effective, the license must be in writing and signed by or on behalf of the grantor.[327] In the absence of a written agreement, the purported licensee is in fact an infringer. A licensee may be entitled, under sections 34 and 35, to bring infringement proceedings in his/her own name.

184. There is provision under section 29 for the recording of certain transactions, such as assignments,[328] licenses and grants of security,[329] on the Register.[330] The Register is open for public inspection. Failure to record a registrable transaction brings with it a number of disadvantages. First, until an application to record a registrable transaction is made, it is ineffective against a person acquiring a competing interest in ignorance of the transaction.[331] Second, a licensee may be unable to bring infringement proceedings in his/her own name. And, third, a person may be unable to recover damages or an account of profits.[332]

E. Infringement

185. Both the civil and criminal law is used to protect the position of trademark owners and licensees. It is not possible to commence infringement proceedings before the date of publication of the registration of the trademark,[333] though the effective date of registration is the filing date. Damages can therefore be claimed from this date. Equally, no offence can be committed prior to the date of publication.[334]

---

323. 1996 Act, s. 28(2).
324. 1996 Act, s. 28(3).
325. 1996 Act, s. 28(5).
326. *See generally*, 1996 Act, ss 32–36.
327. 1996 Act, s. 32(3).
328. An equitable assignment will not be registered: 1996 Act, s. 30.
329. 1996 Act, s. 29(2).
330. *See further* Rule 45 of the Trade Mark Rules 1996, SI 199 of 1996. In 2013, out of a total of 84,725 trade marks on the Register, 1,458 were the subject of an assignment; while 6 were the subject of a licence: Patents Office, *Annual Report 2013*.
331. 1996 Act, s. 29(3)(a).
332. 1996 Act, s. 29(4).
333. 1996 Act, ss 13(3) and 13(4)(a).
334. 1996 Act, ss 13(3) and 13(4)(b).

186. The legislation provides that infringement proceedings can be brought by the owner of a registered trademark and/or a licensee.[335] Under section 35, an exclusive licensee can take infringement proceedings in his/her own name. However, under section 34, subject to the provisions of the licence, any other type of licensee is generally entitled to call on the proprietor of the registered trademark to take infringement proceedings in respect of any matter which affects the licensee's interests. Otherwise, the licensee may only bring proceedings for infringement of a trademark with its proprietor's consents. Where infringement proceedings are brought by a licensee in these circumstances, the licensee may not, without the leave of the Court, proceed with the action unless the proprietor is either joined as a plaintiff or added as a defendant.

187. Section 13 states that the owner of a registered trademark has exclusive rights in the trademark and such rights are infringed by the use of the trademark in the State without the owner's consent. Importantly, there is no need to prove a reputation or to show actual or likely damage as is the case with the tort of passing-off. Section 14 specifies various infringing acts, which mirror the relative grounds for refusal set out in section 10. Accordingly, a person infringes a registered trademark if that person uses in the course of trade[336] a sign which:

– is identical with the trademark, in relation to goods or services which are identical with those for which it is registered;[337]
– because the sign is identical with the trademark and is used in relation to goods or services similar to those for which the trademark is registered, and there exists a likelihood of confusion on the part of the public, which includes the likelihood of association of the sign with the trademark;[338]
– because the sign is similar to the trademark and is used in relation to goods or services identical with or similar to those for which the trademark is registered, and there exists a likelihood of confusion on the part of the public, which includes the likelihood of association of the sign with the trademark;[339]
– is identical with or similar to the trademark irrespective of whether it is used in relation to goods or services which are identical with, similar to, or not similar to, those for which the trademark is registered where the trademark has a reputation in the State and the use of the sign, being without due cause, takes unfair advantage of, or is detrimental to, the distinctive character or the reputation of the trademark.[340]

188. 'Use' of a sign includes:

– affixing it to goods or their packaging;

---

335. 1996 Act, s. 13, s. 18, s. 34 and s. 35.
336. *See Arsenal Football Club v Matthew Reed*Case 206/01, [2002] E.C.R. I-10273.
337. 1996 Act, s. 14(1).
338. 1996 Act, s. 14(2)(a).
339. 1996 Act, s. 14(2)(b).
340. 1996 Act, s. 14(3), as amended.

- offering or exposing goods for sale, putting them on the market or stocking them for those purposes under the sign, or offering or supplying services under the sign;
- importing or exporting goods under the sign;
- using the sign on business paper or in advertising;
- using the sign as a trade or company name or part of a trade or company name;
- using the sign in comparative advertising in a manner that is contrary to the European Communities (Misleading and Comparative Marketing Communications) Regulations 2007 (S.I. No. 774 of 2007).[341]

189. When taking infringement proceedings it may be necessary to establish that a sign and a mark are *identical* or *similar*, or that the goods or services to which the sign and mark relate to are *identical* or *similar*. *Société LTJ Diffusion v. Sadas Vertbaudet SA* was the first opportunity for the European Court of Justice to comment on the issue of the identical nature of signs and marks.[342] In *Diffusion* the claimant was a French company that produced clothing under the trademark *Arthur*. The defendant operated a mail order business selling, among other things, children's clothing including a range named 'Arthur et Félicie'. The defendant registered its mark as a French national trademark and also applied to register the mark as a Community trademark (the precursor to the EUTM). The application was opposed by the claimant on the basis of Article 5(1)(a) of the Directive, on which section 14(1) of the 1996 Act was based. The French court referred the following question to the Court of Justice:

> Does the prohibition in Art 5(1)(a) … cover only identical reproduction, without addition or omission, of the sign or signs constituting a mark or can it extend to:
>
> 1. reproduction of the distinctive element of a mark composed of a number of signs;
> 2. full reproduction of the signs making up the mark where news signs are added?

190. In reaching its decision, the Court emphasized that Article 5(1)(a) should be interpreted strictly so as to avoid the application of the section to situations which were more specifically protected under Article 5(1)(b) of the Directive (transposed in section 14(2) of the 1996 Act). The Court therefore held that a mark and a sign were identical where 'the former reproduces, without any modification or addition, all the elements constituting the latter'. This relatively straight-forward test was complicated by a supplementary finding whereby the Court held that the perception of the identical nature had to be made globally from the perspective of the average consumer, bearing in mind that the consumer (who is deemed to be reasonably

341. 1996 Act, s. 14(4), as amended.
342. Case C-291/00, [2003] FSR 34.

observant and circumspect), rarely has an opportunity to make a side-by-side comparison of the mark and the sign, but rather must rely on his own imperfect recollection of the mark. In those circumstances the Court accepted that the mark and the sign might still be considered to be identical for the purposes of Article 5(1) even though objectively they were not identical.

191. This test was applied by the English Court of Appeal in *Reed Executive plc v. Reed Business Information Ltd.*[343] The case concerned the use by the defendants of the mark *Reed* in the form of a logo incorporating the words 'Reed Business Information', in connection with an online recruitment service. The claimant had registered the trademark *Reed* in Class 35 for employment agency services. One of the questions for consideration by the Court was whether the use of the words 'Reed Business Information' in the form of a logo amounted to use of an identical mark. The leading judgment was given by Jacob L.J. who noted the ambiguous nature of the decision in the *Diffusion* case; however, he went on to apply the 'strict' approach. Applying this to the facts, Jacob L.J. held that 'Reed Business Information' was not identical to the mark *Reed* on the basis that the words 'business information' would not go unnoticed by the average consumer. In reaching this conclusion, Jacob L.J. did not rule out the fact that consumers could confuse Reed Business Information with Reed Employment but if so that would be a matter of similarity of the marks, not identity.

192. As well as addressing the identical or similar nature of signs and marks and goods or services, the courts have also had to consider the sometimes additional requirement that, *there exists a likelihood of confusion on the part of the public, which includes the likelihood of association of the sign with the trade mark.* This phrase has been the subject of a number of cases before the English courts and the ECJ.[344] Broadly speaking, at issue was the point whether *likelihood of association* is an alternative to *likelihood of confusion* and hence proof of either one would lead to infringement, or whether *likelihood of association* is an element of *likelihood of confusion*, requiring proof of *likelihood of confusion* to establish infringement. In *Wagamama v. City Centre Restaurants plc,*[345] an attempt was made to interpret the identical UK provisions, to include what is known as 'non-origin association'. The plaintiff ran a popular Japanese restaurant, registering its name as a trademark in relation to restaurant services. The defendant opened an Indian restaurant calling it 'Raja Mama's', the first of a chain. The plaintiff argued that the relevant UK provision should be widely interpreted, following Benelux law, to include non-origin association, that is, if the sign called to mind the registered trademark, there is infringement. Laddie J rejected the broad view, finding that the concept of *likelihood of association* is not an alternative to that of *likelihood of confusion*, but an element of it. On the facts, and applying the narrow view, the court found that there was an infringement because the public would confuse the two and assume that they

343. [2004] EWCA Civ 159; [2004] ETMR 56.
344. *See also Smithkline Beecham v. Antigen* [1999] ILRM 190.
345. [1995] FSR 713.

were connected. The reasoning of the English court in *Wagamama* has since been followed broadly by the ECJ in *Sabel v. Puma*,[346] and *Canon v. MGM*.[347]

193. In assessing the *likelihood of confusion* more generally, it has been held that account must be taken of all the circumstances of the case including the degree of similarity of the two marks, including visual, aural and conceptual similarity; the likelihood that the public will make an association between the two marks; and the distinctiveness of the earlier mark, such distinctiveness being either inherent or enhanced by a reputation enjoyed on the market.[348] These factors were applied in Ireland in *Cofresco Frischhal v. The Controller of Patents, Design and Trade Marks*.[349] In that case, the plaintiff was the registered proprietor of a community trademark '*TOPPITS*' in respect of low-cost plastic re-sealable containers for kitchen and general household use. The second named defendant applied to register the mark '*TUB-ITS*' in respect of a similar class of goods. The Controller disallowed the plaintiff's objections and the plaintiff appealed to the High Court. There Finlay Geoghegan J. held that that there was not a likelihood of confusion between the registered mark and the mark sought to be registered, taking into account the above factors, and this was so despite the fact that the goods in question were low-cost and primarily purchased in a self-service context, where a consumer would have an imperfect recollection of the earlier trademark and where as a matter of probability there would be no detailed examination of the mark when purchasing. Moreover, it was held that where goods are sold to the general public for consumption or domestic use, as opposed to goods sold in a specialized market, decision-makers, whether a hearing officer or judge, were entitled to give their own opinion as to the likelihood of deception and confusion and in doing so were not confined to the evidence of witnesses at the trial or hearing.

F. Defences to Infringement

194. There are limits on the effect of a registered trademark and these operate as defences to infringement. Section 15, as amended, provides for a number of such defences. For example, a registered trademark is not infringed:

(a) by the use of another registered trademark;[350]
(b) provided that such use is in the course of trade in accordance with honest practices in industrial and commercial matters by a person who:
   - uses the name or address of a third party, where that third party is a natural person;

346. C-251/95, [1997] ECR I-6191, [1998] 1 CMLR 445.
347. C-39/97 [1999] 1 CMLR 77.
348. *Sabel BV v. Puma AG* [1997] 1 ECR I-6191; *Canon Kabushiki Kaisha v. Metro-Goldwyn-Meyer Inc.* [1998] ECR I-5507.
349. [2007] IEHC 187, [2007] 1 IR 582, [2007] 2 ILRM 430.
350. 1996 Act, s. 15(1).

- uses signs or indications which are not distinctive or which concern the kind, quality, quantity, intended purpose, value, geographical origin, the time of production of goods or of rendering of the service or other characteristics of goods or services;
- uses the trademark where it for the purpose of identifying or referring to goods or services as those of the proprietor of that trademark, in particular where that use is necessary to indicate the intended purpose of a product or service, in particular, as accessories or spare parts.[351]

The phrase *honest practices in industrial or commercial matters* is clearly open to wide interpretation but, as noted above, case law suggests that an objective 'reasonable man' test will be applied to determine what is *honest*.[352]

195. In addition, and in keeping with the doctrine of exhaustion under EU law, the owner of a registered trademark cannot complain that his/her rights are infringed when the mark is used on goods which have been put on the market in the EEA by the owner or with his/her consent.[353] However, the owner may complain of infringement where he/she has 'legitimate reasons ... to oppose further dealings in the goods' for instance where the goods have been altered after being first marketed.[354]

196. A defendant in infringement proceedings may challenge the validity of the registration of the plaintiff's mark, on the grounds that it should not have been registered.[355] Where such a challenge succeeds, the mark will be declared invalid and removed from the Register.

G. *Remedies*

197. Both the civil and criminal law is used to protect the position of trademark owners and licensees. As regards civil remedies, the legislation provides that where a registered trademark is infringed, the owner and/or a licensee can sue for damages or an account of profits, an injunction or otherwise.[356] Usually, a plaintiff will seek an injunction to prevent the defendant from continuing to use the mark, and damages for any losses caused by the defendant's use of the mark, or an account of profits. Additionally, a successful party will normally be awarded costs against the other party.

351. 1996 Act, s. 15(2).
352. *European Ltd v. Economist Newspapers Ltd* [1996] FSR 431; *Cable & Wireless plc v. British Telecommunications plc* [1998] FSR 383.
353. 1996 Act, s. 16(1). *See further Davidoff, A&G Imports & Levi-Strauss v. Tesco*, Joined Cases C414/99, C415/99 and 416/99 approving *Silhouette International v. Hartlauer* C-355-96 [1998] 2 CMLR 593.
354. 1996 Act, s. 16(2).
355. 1996 Act, s. 52.
356. 1996 Act, s. 18 and s. 34.

198. Damages are awarded on the basis of compensation for loss suffered as a result of infringement. A plaintiff seeking damages must prove that the infringement *caused* the loss suffered (such as loss of profit on sales, loss of license income and losses resulting from damage to product reputation). Importantly, innocent infringement is no defence to a claim for damages.[357]

199. Rather than seeking damages based on the plaintiff's loss, the plaintiff can elect to require the infringer to account for the profits made on the infringing activities. This remedy is useful where it is difficult to measure the plaintiff's loss, or where an account of profits yields a larger sum to the plaintiff than a damages claim, as where the infringer makes sales to customers who are not customers of the trademark owner, or where sales are made at a higher price than that offered by the trademark owner.

200. As well as granting interlocutory and perpetual injunctions to prevent further infringement, the legislation also provides for orders for erasure of an infringing sign,[358] for delivery up of infringing goods,[359] for the disposal of infringing goods,[360] and grants various search and seizure powers to facilitate the taking of infringement proceedings.[361]

201. Criminal remedies are provided for in sections 92–95 which cover matters such as fraudulent use of a trademark, including counterfeiting,[362] falsification of the Register[363] and falsely representing a trademark as being registered.[364]

202. Lastly, there is provision to deal with groundless threats of infringement proceedings. A person so threatened can apply for:

- a declaration that the threats are unjustified;
- an injunction against the continuance of the threats;
- damages in respect of any loss sustained as a result of the threats.[365]

Mere notification that a trademark is registered or that an application for registration has been made does not constitute a threat. The jurisdiction conferred by section 24 relates to the *threat* of proceedings. Once an action is commenced, section

357. *Gillette UK Ltd v. Edenwest Ltd* [1994] RPC 279.
358. 1996 Act, s. 19.
359. 1996 Act, ss 20–22.
360. 1996 Act, s. 23.
361. 1996 Act, s. 25.
362. 1996 Act, s. 92.
363. 1996 Act, s. 93.
364. 1996 Act, s. 94.
365. 1996 Act, s. 24.

24 jurisdiction is spent and the court is seized of the matter. Hence, it has been held that a party threatening proceedings may pre-empt a section 24 application by issuing proceedings.[366]

III. Copyright and Related Rights

203. Copyright is a property right which is defined principally within the terms of the Copyright and Related Rights Acts 2000–2007.[367] Copyright is different from other intellectual property rights, such as patents and trademarks, in that it arises automatically and is not dependent upon registration. In *Phonographic Performance (Ireland) Ltd v. William Cody and Princes Investments Ltd*,[368] Keane J was of the opinion that the author's right to copyright derives from Articles 40.3.2° and 43 on private property, in the Constitution. Hence, the right cannot be abolished but is regulated by legislation. Section 17 of the 2000 Act further identifies copyright as a property right. The 2000 Act repealed the vast majority of the earlier legislation in this area,[369] and sought to meet our obligations under various EC Directives and international treaties and to consolidate the law into one piece of legislation. The 2000 Act remains the principal statute, although it has been amended a number of times. The EU has recently adopted a new Directive on Copyright in the Digital Single Market, Directive 2019/790.[370] The Directive seeks to respond to new business models and new actors in the digital market and to enhance cross-border access to content online and to provide wider opportunities to use copyright materials in education, research and cultural heritage. It is most notable perhaps for offering greater protection to press publications concerning online uses (Article 15) and placing greater obligations on online content-sharing service providers to ensure copyright protection (Article 17). This Directive must be transposed by 7 June 2021 by Member States.

A. The Subject Matter of Copyright

204. Section 17(2) of the 2000 Act provides that copyright subsists in:

– original literary, dramatic, musical or artistic works;

---

366. *Symonds Cider v. Showerings (Ireland) Ltd* [1997] 1 ILRM 481. Cf. *Trebor Bassett Ltd v. The Football Association* [1927] FSR 211.
367. The 2000 Act, the principal statute, was enacted on 10 Jul. 2000, and, barring four minor provisions, came into effect from 1 Jan. 2001: *see* SI Nos 404–411 of 2000; SI No. 427 of 2000 and SI No. 157 of 2007. *See also* the Copyright and Related Rights (Amendment) Act 2004 and the Copyright and Related Rights (Amendment) Act 2007.
368. [1994] 2 ILRM 241 at 247, reversed on other grounds in the Supreme Court, [1998] 2 ILRM 21.
369. 2000 Act, s. 10 and the Second Schedule. The 2000 Act repealed, *inter alia*, all of the Copyright Act 1963 other than s. 59; the Performers' Protection Act 1968; the Copyright (Amendment) Act 1987; ss 2–3 of the Intellectual Property (Miscellaneous Provisions) Act 1998; the EC (Legal Protection of Computer Programs) Regulations, 1993; and the EC (Term of Protection of Copyright) Regulations, 1995.
370. [2019] OJ L 13/92.

- sound recordings, films, broadcasts or cable programmes;
- the typographical arrangement of published editions;
- original databases.

205. An important general distinction is drawn between ideas and the expression of ideas. Copyright law protects the *expression* of ideas only.[371] Accordingly, section 17(3) provides that copyright protection shall not extend to ideas and principles which underlie any element of a work. Moreover, copyright cannot subsist in a literary, dramatic or musical work, or an original database, unless it is recorded in writing or otherwise.[372] And, copyright cannot subsist in a sound recording until the first fixation of the sound recording is made.[373]

206. A work which is literary, dramatic, musical, artistic or a database must be original to attract copyright protection. For a work to be 'original' it has been held that it must be a product of the author's labour, skill and capital and not a copy of someone else's work.[374] In the Supreme Court in *Gormey v. EMI Records (Ire) Ltd* [375] Barron J stated:

> originality does not require the work to be unique, merely that there should have been original thought. Where there is treatment of materials already in existence it is necessary to show some new approach. It cannot be copied directly. The work must truly belong to the person claiming to be author.[376]

207. The concept of 'originality' has more recently been considered by the Court of Justice in the context of Directive 2001/29, the Information Society Directive.[377] In *Infopaq International A/S v. Danske Dagblades Forening*,[378] Infopaq produced summaries of articles in Dutch newspapers and other periodicals which is then sent to clients via e-mail. Using a 'data capture process' the articles were scanned and ultimately reduced to eleven words abstracts which were printed on paper. Dankse Dagblades Forening, a professional association of Danish daily newspaper publishers, became aware of Infopaq's activities and considered its acts were reproductions for which it needed the authorization of the relevant copyright owners. Litigation was commended in the Danish courts and a preliminary reference was made to the Court of Justice. A preliminary issue before the Court concerned the meaning of 'reproduction'. Article 2 of the Directive provides that authors have the exclusive right to authorize or prohibit the reproduction, in whole or in part, of their works,

371. *University Press Ltd v. University Tutorial Press Ltd* (1916) 2 Ch. 601 at 608–609; *see also Baigent v. Random House* [2007] EWCA Civ 247.
372. 2000 Act, s. 18(1).
373. 2000 Act, s. 19.
374. *University Press Ltd v. University Tutorial Press Ltd* (1916) 2 Ch. 601.
375. [2000] 1 IR 74; [1999] ILRM 178.
376. [2000] 1 IR 74 at 93.
377. [2001] OJ L L167/10.
378. Case C-5/08, [2009] ECR I-6569.

and therefore the Court found it necessary to identify when a 'work' attracts copyright protection. With reference to the Berne Convention, the Court found that literary and artistic works are intellectual creations. Further, the Court concluded that copyright only subsists in original works if they represent the author's own intellectual creation. Accordingly:

> It is only through the choice, sequence and combination of [those] words that the author may express his creativity in an original manner and achieve a result which is an intellectual creation.[379]

The Court thus ruled that printing eleven words may be a reproduction if these words are the expression of the intellectual creation of their author. The extent to which this European definition differs from the tradition common law test of labour, skill and capital remains to be seen. Following *Infopaq,* it has been held in England that newspaper headlines are capable of being original literary works, both independently and as part of the articles to which they relate.[380]

208. 'Literary work' is defined in section 2 of the 2000 Act as meaning: a work, including a computer program,[381] but does not include a dramatic or musical work, or an original database, which is written, spoken or sung. 'Written' is defined as including any form of notation or code, whether by hand or otherwise and regardless of the method or medium in or on which it is recorded.[382] Case law provides many examples of what constitutes and what does not constitute a literary work. For example, books,[383] newspaper reports[384] and law reports[385] have been protected by copyright as literary works. The work does not need to have literary merit: exam papers,[386] and business letters,[387] have also been protected as literary works. In contrast, it has been held that names,[388] titles[389] and words[390] are not generally protected by copyright.[391]

209. Also protected by copyright are neighbouring or 'related rights' such as sound recordings, films, broadcasts, cable programmes and typographical arrangement of published works. Neighbouring rights can be distinguished from the right

379. Case C-5/08, para. 45.
380. *Newspaper Licensing Agency Ltd v. Meltwater Holdings BV* [2011] EWCA Civ 890.
381. *See further* the Software Directive, Directive 91/250/EEC, [1991] OJ L 122/42.
382. 2000 Act, s. 2(1).
383. *Folens v. O ' Dubhghaill and Joyce* [1973] IR 255.
384. *Hall v. Crosbie & Co.* (1931) 66 ILTR 22.
385. *Hodges v. Walsh* (1840) 2 IR EQ R 266.
386. *University Press Ltd v. University Tutorial Press Ltd* (1916) 2 Ch. 601.
387. *British Oxygen Co. Ltd v. Liquid Air Ltd* [1925] Ch. 383.
388. *Exxon Corporation v. Exxon Insurance Consultants International Ltd* [1982] RPC 69, no copyright in the name 'Exxon'.
389. *Dicks v. Yates* (1881) 18 Ch. D 76, no copyright in the novel title 'Splendid Misery'.
390. *Wombles Ltd v. Wombles Skips Ltd* [1975] FSR 488, no copyright in the word 'Wombles'.
391. Such a name, title or word may the subject of a registered trade mark (*see further* paras 166–199 above) and may be protected at common law by the tort of passing-off (*see* paras 248–259 below).

described above, that is, literary, dramatic, musical and artistic works, and databases, in that they do not arise by virtue of authorship. Rather neighbouring rights tend to be entrepreneurial in nature, and exploitative of a literary or musical work, for example.

210. Under the 2000 Act, databases may be protected by copyright under Part II, or, by a new property right,[392] known as the database right, under Part V, depending on the originality of the work.[393] These rights are independent of each other (though a database protected by copyright can also benefit from the protection offered by the database right) and of any copyright or other intellectual property rights which might exist in the individual contents of the database.[394]

211. A database means:

> a collection of independent works, data or other materials, arranged in a systematic or methodical way and accessible by whatever means but excludes computer programs used in the making or operation of a database.[395]

Where the database is 'original' it will receive copyright protection.[396] 'Original database' is defined as:

> a database in any form which by reason of the selection or arrangement of its content constitutes the original intellectual creation of its author.[397]

The owner of copyright in a database is the author, and the author of a database is identified as the natural person or group of persons who created the base.[398] Prior to the 2000 Act, databases of very low originality received copyright protection in Irish law.[399] It would appear that this position has changed with the 2000 Act. Where the database is lacking originality, it will not receive copyright protection but may receive a lower level of protection, known as the database right, under Part V of the 2000 Act.[400]

---

392. 2000 Act, s. 321(1).
393. These provisions seek to implement EC Database Directive: Directive 96/9/EC, [1996] OJ L 77/20.
394. 2000 Act, s. 17(3) and s. 321(3).
395. 2000 Act, s. 2(1).
396. 2000 Act, s. 17(2)(d).
397. 2000 Act, s. 2(1).
398. 2000 Act, s. 21(g).
399. *See*, e.g., *RTE and ors v. Magill TV Guide* [1990] ILRM 534.
400. For the 'database right' *see* paras 236–239 below.

B. The Period of Protection

212. The periods vary depending on the subject matter being protected.[401] For example, the copyright in:

(a) literary, dramatic, musical or artistic works or original databases expires seventy years after the death of the author, irrespective of when the work was first lawfully made available to the public;[402]
(b) a film expires seventy years after the last of the following persons dies:
   - the principle director;
   - the author of the screenplay;
   - the author of the dialogue;
   - the author of the music specifically used in film.[403]
(c) a sound recording expires:
   - fifty years after the sound recording is made;
   - where it is first lawfully made available to the public during the period specified above, fifty years after the date of such making available;
   - in certain circumstances, including where the sound recording is first created on or after 1 November 2013, seventy years after the date of such making available.[404]

C. Identifying the Owner of Copyright

213. Generally, the creator of the work, such as the author of a literary work, owns the copyright in that work. Sometimes, however, the creator is not easily identified and there are exceptions to this general rule. In three provisions, Chapter 2, in Part II of the 2000 Act, deals with the issue of authorship and ownership of copyright.

214. Section 21 states that the author means the person who creates a work and includes, in the case of:

- a sound recording, the producer;
- a film, the producer and the principal director;
- a broadcast, the person making the broadcast;
- a cable programme, the person providing the cable programme service in which the programme is included;
- a typographical arrangement of a published edition, the publisher;

401. 2000 Act, Part II, Ch. 3, which implements the EC Term of Protection Directive 93/98/EEC, [1993] OJ L 290/9.
402. 2000 Act, s. 24; *see* further s.24(1)(A) in relation to duration of copyright in musical composition with words.
403. 2000 Act, s. 25.
404. 2000 Act, s. 26, as amended by SI No. 411/2013.

- a computer-generated work, the person by whom the arrangements necessary for the creation of the work are undertaken;
- an original database, the individual or group of individuals who made the database;
- a photograph, the photographer.

215. Section 22 addresses the issue of 'joint-authorship', that is where the contribution of each author is not distinct from that of the other author(s). For example, a film is treated as a work of joint-authorship, unless the producer and the principal director are the same person.[405]

216. Section 23 contains exceptions to the general rule that the owner of copyright is the creator. In particular, where a copyright work is produced by an employee in the course of employment, copyright vests in the employer, unless specified to the contrary in the employment contract. Where a work is commissioned, copyright vests in the author of the work in the usual way. Thus, if an independent contractor is commissioned to produce a work, such as a report or a computer program, he/she will own the copyright in that work. In order to avoid this, the person commissioning the work may require the contractor to agree to assign to him/her the copyright in the work.

D. Formalities and Qualification for Protection

217. There is no registration requirement for copyright protection in Ireland, under the 2000 Act. Copyright is acquired automatically provided that the statutory requirements are met. Chapter 18 of Part II of the 2000 Act deals with the issue of qualification for copyright protection. For instance, for a work to qualify for copyright protection, the author must be a qualifying person, defined as including:

- an Irish citizen;
- a citizen, or subject of, or an individual domiciled or ordinarily resident in the State, or in any country, territory, state or area to which the relevant provisions of this part extends;
- a body incorporated under Irish law;
- a partnership or body unincorporated under Irish law.

  Additionally, section 184 provides that a work shall qualify for copyright protection where it is first lawfully made available to the public:
  - in the State;
  - in any country, territory, state or area to which the relevant provisions of this Part extends.[406]

405. 2000 Act, s. 22(2).
406. 2000 Act, ss 188–189.

E. The Rights of a Copyright Owner

218. The rights of a copyright owner are outlined in section 17 and Chapter 4 of Part II of the 2000 Act. Section 17(1) provides:

> Copyright is a property right whereby … the owner of the copyright in any work may undertake … certain acts in the State, being acts which are designated by the Act as acts restricted by copyright in a work of that description.

Section 37 expands on this provision by listing three broad categories of 'restricted acts'. It provides that:

> the owner of the copyright in a work has the exclusive right to undertake or authorise others to undertake all or any of the following acts, namely:
>
> – to copy the work;
> – to make available to the public the work;
> – to make an adaptation of the work.

219. The right to copy, or the 'reproduction right',[407] is developed further in section 39 of the 2000 Act which provides that copying, in relation to any work, includes:

– storing the work in any medium;
– making of copies which are transient or incidental to some other use of the work.[408]

Moreover, copying in relation to an artistic work includes making a copy in three dimensions of a two-dimensional work and vice versa. Copying in relation to a film, TV broadcast or cable programme includes making a photograph of the whole or a substantial part of any image forming part of the film, broadcast or programme.[409] And, copying in relation to a typographical arrangement of a published edition includes making a reprographic copy of the arrangement.[410]

220. Section 40 spells out the nature of the making available right as including:

– making available copies of a work over the Internet;
– performing, showing or playing a copy of the work in public;

407. 2000 Act, s. 39(2).
408. 2000 Act, s. 39(1)(a); but *see* 2000 Act, ss 80–82 which permit, *inter alia*, making back-up copies of computer programs, and making copies of computer programs to achieve interoperability between computer programs.
409. 2000 Act, s. 39(1)(c).
410. 2000 Act, s. 39(1)(d).

- broadcasting a copy of the work;
- including a copy of the work in a cable programme service;
- issuing copies to the public;[411]
- renting copies of the work;[412]
- lending copies of the work.[413]

221. The right to make an adaptation of a work is considered further in section 43 and, for example, in relation to a literary or dramatic work, film, sound recording, broadcast, cable programme or typographical arrangement of a published edition includes:

- a translation, arrangement or other alternation of the work;
- a version of a dramatic work which is converted into a non-dramatic work, and vice versa;
- a version of a work in which the story or action is conveyed wholly or mainly by means of pictures in a form suitable for reproduction.[414]

However, where a person proposes to play a sound recording in public, or, include a sound recording in a broadcast or a cable programme service, he/she may do so without the prior consent of the copyright owner provided, he/she agrees to pay royalties to the relevant licensing body, and he/she complies with the relevant statutory provision.[415]

F. Dealing in Copyright

222. Sections 17(1) and 120(1) of the 2000 Act specify that copyright is personal or moveable property and therefore it can be traded, by outright disposition such as an assignment for payment, or by the owner permitting others to exploit his/her property by granting a license. Equally, like other forms of property, it can be charged or gifted away. However, such dealings to be fully effective must comply with statutory formalities. Chapter 8 of Part II of the 2000 Act covers dealings in copyright works. Section 120(1) provides:

> The copyright in a work is transmissible by assignment, by testamentary disposition or by operation of the law, as personal or moveable property.

---

411. Known as the distribution right. While a copyright holder can control distribution, this is limited by the European 'doctrine of exhaustion', recognized by the 2000 Act, s. 41, whereby once a work has been put into circulation in the EEA by or with the consent of the copyright owner, the subsequent distribution within the EEA cannot be prohibited or controlled.
412. Known as the rental right, *see further* 2000 Act, s. 42, as amended.
413. Known as the lending right, *see further* 2000 Act, s. 42, as amended.
414. 2000 Act, s. 43(2).
415. 2000 Act, s. 38.

An assignment may be whole, or partial. In the latter case, the assignment may relate to one or more but not all of the acts which a copyright owner can undertake, the 'restricted acts', or it may relate to a part but not whole of the period of copyright protection.[416] An assignment may also be described as partial where it is limited geographically. Future copyright can also be assigned by the prospective owner of a work not yet created.[417] An assignment, whether whole or partial, must be in writing and signed by the assignor.[418] There is also authority to support the notion of an equitable assignment of copyright where, for example, the strict legal formalities have not been complied with,[419] or where there is an agreement to assign copyright in an existing work, at some time in the future.[420] Because there is no public registration system with regard to copyright, an assignee is taking a risk that there is no prior assignment which would take priority over his. If there is, then the assignee has a personal cause of action against the assignor, but has no proprietary claims over the copyright.

223. Assignment of copyright must be distinguished from a license agreement in relation to a copyright work. With an assignment, the copyright owner transfers all or part of his/her property rights in the copyright work. With a license agreement, no property in the copyright work is transferred, but the licensee is given permission to undertake some or all the 'restricted acts' in relation to the work. Section 37(2) states:

> The copyright in a work is infringed by a person who without the licence of the copyright owner undertakes ... any of the acts restricted by copyright.

This permission may be personal to the licensee and, if so, cannot be transferred.

224. Under the 2000 Act, an exclusive license is defined as a license in writing and signed by a copyright owner which authorizes the licensee, to the exclusion of all other persons, including the copyright owner, to undertake 'restricted acts' in relation to the work. Otherwise, there are no statutory formalities, though it is advisable that any license be in writing. A license granted by the owner of copyright is binding on every successor in title except a purchaser in good faith for valuable consideration without notice, actual or constructive.[421]

---

416. 2000 Act, s. 120(2).
417. 2000 Act, s. 121.
418. 2000 Act, s. 120(3).
419. *Brooker v. John Friend Ltd* [1936] NZLR 743; *Wah Sang Industrial Co. v. Takmay Industrial Co.* [1980] FSR 303; *Batjak Production Inc v. Simitar Entertainment (UK)* [1996] FSR 139.
420. *Western Front Ltd v. Vestron* [1987] FSR 66; *Wah Sang Industrial Co. v. Takmay Industrial Co.* [1980] FSR 303; *Batjak Production Inc v. Simitar Entertainment (UK)* [1996] FSR 139.
421. 2000 Act, ss 120(4) and (5).

G. Infringement[422]

225. As noted above, section 37(2) provides:

> The copyright in a work is infringed by a person who without the licence of the copyright owner undertakes … any of the acts restricted by copyright.

Further, section 37(3) states that:

> References to the undertaking of an act restricted by copyright in a work shall relate to the work as a whole or to any substantial part of the work and to whether the act is taken directly or indirectly.

Hence, infringement is broadly defined and can relate to the work as a whole or to a substantial part of the work, and it can be direct or indirect. Infringement may also be secondary in nature. The concept of 'secondary infringement' is dealt with in Chapter 5 of Part II of the 2000 Act. Accordingly, secondary infringement includes:

– dealing with infringing copy;[423]
– providing the means for making an infringing copy;[424]
– permitting use of premises for infringing performances;[425]
– permitting use of apparatus for infringing performances.[426]

226. Section 38 provides an exception to infringement by allowing the playing of a sound recording in public, or the inclusion of a sound recording in a broadcast or cable programme service, without the prior permission of the copyright owner, provided a payment is made to the relevant licensing body and the statutory provision is complied with.

H. Permitted Acts

227. The 2000 Act contains a number of permitted acts in relation to copyright works; in other words, defences to infringement. Their purpose is to balance the rights of copyright owners and other users. The main 'permitted act' is referred to as 'fair dealing' and this applies to all works, under the 2000 Act. 'Fair dealing' is defined, for the first time in the 2000 Act, as:

---

422. *See* Chs 4 & 5 of Part II of the 2000 Act.
423. Dealing includes: selling; renting; lending; or offering to sell, rent or lend; importing; having possession of; 2000 Act, s. 45.
424. Providing the means include: making; selling, renting or lending; or offering to sell, rent or lend; importing or having possession of an article specifically designed for making copies; 2000 Act, s. 46.
425. 2000 Act, s. 47.
426. 2000 Act, s. 48.

> making use of a work … for the purpose and to an extent which will not unreasonably prejudice the interests of the owner of the copyright.[427]

For example, 'fair dealing' with a work for the purposes of research or private study shall not infringe copyright.[428] Fair dealing with a work for the purposes of criticism or review shall not infringe copyright where accompanied by an acknowledgment.[429] Further permitted acts or defences exist in relation to education;[430] prescribed libraries and archives;[431] public administration;[432] designs;[433] computer programs;[434] original databases;[435] and type-faces, amongst others.[436]

I. Remedies on Infringement

228. Where a person's copyright has been infringed, the legislation offers a variety of civil remedies and criminal sanctions, both supported by strong presumptions of ownership in copyright works.[437] Section 127 of the 2000 Act provides that infringement of copyright in a work is actionable by the copyright owner. Furthermore, section 135(1) provides that an exclusive licensee has the same rights and remedies in respect of matters occurring after the grant of the license as if the license had been an assignment. Where infringement proceedings are brought by a copyright owner, or an exclusive licensee, in respect of which they have concurrent rights, the owner or the licensee cannot, without the leave of the court, bring proceedings unless the other party is joined as a plaintiff or added as a defendant.[438]

229. The remedies available for breach of copyright include damages, or an account of profits, and injunctions.[439] Additionally, a successful party will normally be awarded costs against the other party.

230. Under section 128(1), a court may award such damages as, having regard to all the circumstances, it considers just. Damages are awarded on the basis of compensation for loss suffered as a result of infringement. A plaintiff seeking damages must prove that the infringement *caused* the loss suffered (such as loss of profit on sales, loss of license income and losses resulting from damage to product reputation). However, the 2000 Act provides that where the infringement is innocent, no

427. 2000 Act, s. 50(4).
428. 2000 Act, s. 50.
429. 2000 Act, s. 51.
430. 2000 Act, ss 53–58.
431. 2000 Act, ss 59–70.
432. 2000 Act, ss 71–77.
433. 2000 Act, ss 78–79.
434. 2000 Act, ss 80–82.
435. 2000 Act, s. 83.
436. 2000 Act, ss 84–85.
437. Chapters 9–15 of Part II of the 2000 Act.
438. 2000 Act, s. 136.
439. 2000 Act, s. 127(2).

damages can be awarded.[440] In addition to or as an alternative to compensatory damages, a court may award aggravated and/or exemplary damages where, for example, the breach of copyright is flagrant.[441] Alternatively, a plaintiff can seek an account of profits. The rationale behind this remedy is to ensure that the infringer does not profit from his/her wrongful conduct.[442] As well as granting interlocutory and perpetual injunctions, to prevent further infringement, a court can grant orders of delivery up,[443] and powers of seizure, following a court order,[444] or otherwise,[445] may be conferred. Such powers are very important when piracy of copyright works is alleged.

231. The 2000 Act contains strong presumptions of ownership in favour of copyright holders to facilitate the taking of civil and criminal legal proceedings.[446] For instance, copyright is presumed to exist in a work until the contrary is proved.[447] And, the plaintiff is presumed to be the owner, or exclusive licensee, until the contrary is proved.[448]

232. Beyond the civil remedies available to a copyright owner or exclusive licensee, the 2000 Act prescribes specific criminal offences.[449] Moreover, the 2000 Act provides for substantial financial sanctions for copyright offences: up to EUR 1,875 and/or twelve months imprisonment on summary conviction; and up to EUR 125,000 and/or five years imprisonment on indictment.[450]

J. Moral Rights

233. The above rights and legal protections are largely based on providing and protecting the financial or economic interests of 'authors'. The 2000 Act, in Chapters 7 and 11 of Part II, recognizes for the first time in Irish law the moral rights of authors. Accordingly, even after the transfer of an author's economic rights, the author's moral rights remain. This aspect of the legislation seeks to implement our international obligations under Article 6*bis*(1) of the Berne Convention for the Protection of Literary and Artistic Works (Paris Act, 1971).[451]

---

440. 2000 Act, s. 128(2).
441. 2000 Act, s. 128(3).
442. *House of Spring Gardens Ltd v. Point Blank Ltd* [1984] IR 611.
443. 2000 Act, s. 131; *see further* 2000 Act, s. 138 for six-year time limit on this remedy.
444. 2000 Act, s. 132.
445. 2000 Act, s. 133.
446. 2000 Act, Ch. 12 of Part II of the 2000 Act, s. 139. These presumptions were first introduced in the Intellectual Property (Miscellaneous Provisions) Act 1998, ss 2–3, which sought to comply with international obligations, in particular under the TRIPs Agreement 1994.
447. 2000 Act, s. 139(2).
448. 2000 Act, s. 139(3).
449. 2000 Act, Ch. 13 of Part II.
450. 2000 Act, ss 140(7) and (8).
451. These rights may also be protected by the Constitution, the common law of contract, passing-off and defamation.

234. The author of a work[452] has the following moral rights recognized by the 2000 Act:

- the paternity right, that is, the right to be identified as the author of a work;[453]
- the integrity right, that is, the right to object to derogatory treatment of a work;[454]
- the right not to have work falsely attributed to him/her, as author;[455]
- a right to privacy in photographs and film when commissioned for private or domestic purposes.[456]

There is, as yet, no reported Irish case law on the moral rights of authors, though case law from other jurisdictions is informative. For example, in *Snow v. Eaton Centre,* [457] the plaintiff sculptor was granted an order for the removal of Christmas decorations from a snow geese sculpture by him that had been commissioned by the defendant shopping centre because the decorations distorted the sculpture in a prejudicial manner contrary to his integrity right. In *Clark v. Associated Newspapers Ltd,*[458] a mock diary column in the defendant newspaper which purported to be written by the well-known politician Alan Clark, and which carried his photograph, was held to amount to false attribution of the work to the plaintiff politician.

235. The paternity right, the integrity right and the right to privacy in photographs and films exist for the same period of time as the relevant economic rights.[459] In contrast, the right not to have the work falsely attributed subsists twenty years after the death of the person on whom it is conferred.[460] While the economic rights which comprise copyright are *personal property* which can be sold or licensed, moral rights are *personal rights* and hence cannot be assigned or transferred,[461] except by devolution on death.[462] Significantly, though, they can be waived.[463] Any waiver must be in writing and signed by the person waiving the rights.[464] The waiver may relate to a specific work or works, or to works generally; it can relate to existing or future works.[465] The waiver may be conditional or unconditional, revocable or irrevocable.[466] Sections 137 and 138 provide that a breach of

452. 'Work', for the purpose of the moral rights provisions, is defined as meaning: a literary, dramatic, musical, or artistic work, or film: 2000 Act, s. 2(1).
453. 2000 Act, s. 107 and exceptions listed in s. 108. *See further Rowe v. Walt Disney Productions* [1987] FSR 38.
454. 2000 Act, s. 109 and exceptions and qualifications provided for in ss 110–111.
455. 2000 Act, s. 113.
456. 2000 Act, s. 114.
457. [1982] 70 CPR 105; *see also Morrison Leahy Music Ltd v. Lightbound* [1993] EMLR 144; *Pasterfieldv. Denham* [1999] FSR 168.
458. [1998] 1 All ER 959.
459. 2000 Act, s. 115(1).
460. 2000 Act, s. 115(2).
461. 2000 Act, s. 118.
462. 2000 Act, s. 119.
463. 2000 Act, s. 116.
464. 2000 Act, s. 116(2).
465. 2000 Act, s. 116(3)(a).
466. 2000 Act, s. 116(3)(b).

moral rights is actionable as a breach of statutory duty owed to the author, and damages, injunctive relief and other remedies are available.

K. Performers' Rights

236. Since copyright protects *expressions* which are fixed in some medium, performances, such as a singer's rendition of a song or an actor's performance in a role are not protected by copyright. Parts III and IV of the 2000 Act provide for a regime of rights, exceptions and sanctions in respect of performers' rights and rights in performances which is broadly parallel to those provided in Part II in relation to copyright.

237. 'Performance' means a performance of any actors, singers, musicians, dancers or other persons who act, sing, deliver, play in, interpret, or otherwise perform literary, dramatic, musical or artistic works or expressions of works of folklore, which is a live performance given by one or more individuals, and shall include a performance of a variety act or any similar presentation.[467] The key requirement relates to the live nature of the activity.

238. Performers' rights include:

- the exclusive right to authorize or to prohibit the making of a copy of a recording of a performance: the reproduction right;[468]
- the exclusive right to authorize or to prohibit the making available to the public of copies of a recording of a performance;[469]
- the exclusive right to authorize or to prohibit the issuing of copies of a performance to the public: the distribution right;[470]
- the exclusive right to authorize or to prohibit the renting or lending of copies of a recording of a performance;[471]
- a right to equitable remuneration from the owner of the copyright in a sound recording of a performance for its exploitation.[472]

239. These rights generally expire fifty years after the date of the performance.[473] The moral rights of performers are recognized in Part IV of the 2000 Act.

467. 2000 Act, s. 202(1).
468. 2000 Act, s. 204.
469. 2000 Act, s. 205.
470. 2000 Act, s. 206.
471. 2000 Act, s. 207.
472. 2000 Act, s. 208.
473. 2000 Act, s. 291, as amended.

L. Database Right

240. As noted above, under the 2000 Act, original databases may be protected by copyright under Part II, and non-original databases by a new property right, known as the database right,[474] under Part V.[475] The database right is described as sui generis[476] and affords lesser protection than copyright.

241. A database means:

> a collection of independent works, data or other materials, arranged in a systematic or methodical way and accessible by whatever means but excludes computer programs used in the making or operation of a database.[477]

Under Part V, where a database lacks 'originality' but has involved 'a substantial investment' in obtaining, verifying or presenting the contents of a database, the maker has rights to do certain acts, known as 'restricted acts', and to restrict others from doing those acts.[478] 'Substantial investment' is defined broadly: 'investment' includes any investment, whether of financial, human or technical resources;[479] while 'substantial' means substantial in terms of quantity or quality or a combination of both.[480]

242. Restricted acts comprise mainly extraction[481] or re-utilization[482] of the contents of the database.[483] Lawful users[484] cannot be prevented from extracting or re-utilizing insubstantial parts of the contents of the database,[485] but repeated and systematic extraction or re-utilization of insubstantial parts of the contents of the database which conflicts with the normal exploitation of the database is prohibited as unreasonably prejudicing the legitimate interests of the maker.[486] Certain acts are permitted in relation to the database right including:

- in relation to non-electronic databases, fair dealing by a lawful user for research and private study;[487]

---

474. 2000 Act, s. 321(1).
475. These provisions seek to implement EC Database Directive: Directive 96/9/EC, [1996] OJ L 77/20.
476. *See* Chapter III of Database Directive 96/9/EC, [1996] OJ L 77/20.
477. 2000 Act, s. 2(1).
478. 2000 Act, s. 321.
479. 2000 Act, s. 320(1).
480. 2000 Act, s. 320(1).
481. 'the permanent or temporary transfer of all or a substantial part of the contents to another medium by any means in any form': 2000 Act, s. 320.
482. 'making available to the public all or a substantial part of the contents of a database by the distribution of copies, by renting, by on-line or by other forms of transmission'; 2000 Act, s. 320.
483. 2000 Act, s. 324.
484. Defined as 'any person who, whether under a licence to undertake any of the acts restricted by any database right in the database, or otherwise, has a right to use the database': 2000 Act, s. 320(1).
485. 2000 Act, s. 327.
486. 2000 Act, s. 324(3).
487. 2000 Act, s. 329.

– fair dealing by lawful users for educational purposes;[488]
– anything done in relation to public administration.[489]

243. It is the *maker* of the database, and not the author (these may be the same person though not necessarily) who enjoys the database right, because it is the maker who has made the necessary investment in the database.[490] But such makers, if natural persons, must be nationals of a Member State or habitually resident in the EU or, if legal persons, must have their registered office or principal place of business in the EU. The database right lasts for fifteen years from the end of the year in which the database was created.[491] Any substantial alternations to the database will recommence this period flowing afresh.[492]

IV. Registered Designs[493]

244. The governing legislation is the Industrial Designs Act 2001,[494] which seeks, *inter alia*, to implement an EC Directive on the legal protection of designs.[495] Broadly speaking, this legislation is expansionist in nature: for instance, it widens the definition of industrial design and extends the period of protection.

245. Under the 2001 Act, 'design' is defined as meaning:

> the appearance of the whole or a part of a product resulting from the features of, in particular, the lines, contours, colour, shape, texture or materials of the product itself or its ornamentation.[496]

488. 2000 Act, s. 330.
489. 2000 Act, ss 331–336.
490. 2000 Act, ss 322–323.
491. 2000 Act, s. 325.
492. 2000 Act, s. 325(3).
493. Also, the Community Design Regulation, 6/2002/EC, entered into force on 6 Mar. 2002 and introduced into Irish law for the first time the concept of unregistered design rights: *see further Karen Millen Ltd v. Dunnes Stores & Anor* [2007] IEHC 449.
494. The Industrial Designs Act 2001 was enacted on 27 Nov. 2001, and was commenced on 1 Jul. 2002: *see* SI No. 275 of 2002. *See also* the Industrial Design Regulations 2002, SI No. 280 of 2002.
495. Directive 98/71/EC, [1998] OJ 1 289/28. The 2001 Act also enables the state to ratify the Hague Agreement concerning the International Registration of Industrial Designs (1999) which provides an international register of design, maintained by the WIPO in Geneva. An international application for registration of a design may be filed, designating the countries where design registration is sought and this takes effect in each designated country as is the application was filed nationally. *See also* the Community Design Regulation, adopted 12 Dec. 2001, Regulation 6/2002 [2002] OJ L 3/1 which provides for a Community-wide registration system for designs, similar to the trade mark regime. This Regulation entered into force on 6 Mar. 2002: *see further* SI No. 27 of 2003.
496. 2001 Act, s. 2(1).

'Product' means:

> any industrial or handicraft item, including parts intended to be assembled into a complex product,[497] packaging, get-up, graphic symbols and typographic type-faces, but excluding computer programs.[498]

These definitions substantially expand the meaning of design. For example, there is no longer a requirement for 'eye appeal' or aesthetic character or industrial applicability, as under the previous legislation.[499] The inclusion of colour, texture and 'materials of the product itself' clearly goes beyond earlier law also. The definition of product is broader than the definition of 'article' under the previous legislation, and permits the registration of designs for products which have no other function than to carry the design. So, designs for packaging, get-up and graphic symbols are registrable.

246. A design to be registered, and hence protected, must be *new* and have *individual character.*[500] A design is 'new' where:

> no design identical to it has been made previously available to the public before the filing date.[501]

Designs are deemed to be identical if their features differ only in immaterial details.[502] A design will have 'individual character' if:

> the overall impression it produces on the informed user differs from the overall impression produced on such a user by a design which has been made available to the public before the filing date.[503]

A design will be deemed to have been 'made available to the public' if it has been:

> published following registration or otherwise, or exhibited, used in trade or otherwise disclosed, except where these events could not reasonably have become known in the normal course of business to the circles specialising in the sector concerned, operating within the EEA.[504]

497. 2001 Act, s. 2(1).
498. 2001 Act, s. 2(1).
499. Industrial and Commercial (Property) Act 1927, s. 3 and *Allibert SA v. O ' Connor* (1981) FSR 613.
500. 2001 Act, s. 11.
501. 2001 Act, s. 12(1).
502. 2001 Act, s. 12(2).
503. 2001 Act, s. 13.
504. 2001 Act, s. 2(1).

Significantly, 'universal novelty' is now required; previously local novelty only was required.[505] But disclosure in confidence to a third party will not destroy novelty.[506]

247. A design right does not subsist in features of appearance of a product which are solely dictated by technical function,[507] and a design right does not subsist in a design which is contrary to public policy and morality.[508]

248. The author or owner of a design is the person who created it, unless the design is created in the course of employment, in which case, the owner is the employer, unless there is an agreement to the contrary.[509] On registration,[510] the term of protection is initially five years, renewable for further five-year periods, up to a maximum of twenty-five years.[511] The rights of the design owner are stated to be the exclusive right to use the design and to prevent any unauthorized use.[512] In particular, 'use' includes the making, offering, putting on the market, importing, exporting or the using of a product in which the design is incorporated or to which it is applied, or stocking such a product for those purposes. There is no requirement that the design be applied to a product for infringement to occur. There is also a litany of 'permitted acts', in relation to a design right including:

- acts done privately and for non-commercial purposes
- acts done for experimental purposes
- acts of reproduction for the purpose of making citations or of teaching.[513]

249. A design, if registered, may be declared invalid on a number of stated grounds including if:

- it does not fall within the definition of design;
- it is not new or has individual character;
- it has been made available to the public prior to filing;
- it is functional;
- the holder of the design is not entitled to it under the law of the Member State concerned;
- the design is on conflict with a prior design.[514]

---

505. 1927 Act, s. 64.
506. 2001 Act, s. 2(7).
507. 2001 Act, s. 16.
508. 2001 Act, s. 21(1)(a).
509. 2001 Act, ss 17–19.
510. On registration *see* Chs 3 and 4 of Part 2 the 2001 Act.
511. 2001 Act, s. 43.
512. 2001 Act, s. 42(4). *See further* Chs 7 and 8 of Part II the 2001 Act on infringement of design rights and remedies, respectively.
513. 2001 Act, s. 48.
514. 2001 Act, s. 47.

Article 17 of the Design Directive provides that a design registered in a Member State shall also be eligible for protection under the law of copyright.[515] However, section 79 of the Copyright and Related Rights Act 2000 contains an important exception from copyright protection.[516] Section 79(1) provides that copyright infringement will not arise by the making of an object in three dimensions of a two-dimensional work (namely, to make a product from a drawing) if the object would not appear to a non-expert to be a reproduction of the work. Moreover, the 2001 Act amends the Copyright and Related Rights Act 2000 to the effect that copyright in a design registered under the 2001 Act expires twenty-five years after filing, or the date of expiry of copyright under the 2000 Act, whichever is the sooner.[517]

§3. Trade Names

I. Business Names

250. Persons or bodies may trade either under their own name or under a different name, what may be called a business name. As has been explained in Chapter 4,[518] where they trade under a business name, prescribed details must be separately registered under the Registration of Business Names Act, 1963, and must be disclosed in various business letters and other documents. However, registration of a name under this Act of itself confers no right to use that name. But if a person trades under a name, be it his/her own or a business name, for a significant duration, he/she may thereby acquire certain exclusive rights to use that name which can be defended in an action for the tort of passing-off.

II. Passing-Off[519]

251. While section 7(1) of the Trade Marks Act 1996 makes it clear that a registered trademark is a property right which derives from registration, section 7(2) provides that the common law of passing-off remains unaffected by the 1996 Act. Broadly speaking, passing-off involves one trader representing his/her goods or services to be those of another so as to mislead the public and thereby cause an appreciable risk of detriment to the other trader. For example, in *Jameson v. Dublin Distillers Co Ltd*,[520] the plaintiff, John Jameson & Son, produced whiskey of a high reputation. The defendant acquired a business known as William Jameson & Co which also produced whiskey but whose sales had been falling for some years. In

515. Cf. 1927 Act, s. 172 which provided that copyright did not subsist in designs capable of being registered and which were intended to be industrially multiplied.
516. Repeating the provisions of the Copyright Act, 1963, s. 14(7), as amended.
517. 2001 Act, s. 89 and 2000 Act, s.31A.
518. *See* paras 102–106 above.
519. *See generally*, McMahon & Binchy, *Law of Torts* (4th ed., Bloomsbury Professional 2012) Ch. 31; Clark, Smith & Hall, *Intellectual Property Law in Ireland* (4th ed., Bloomsbury 2016).
520. [1900] 1 IR 43.

1898, the defendant decided to sell their whiskey under the name 'Jameson's Whiskey', omitting the prefix 'William'. It was held that the defendant had unlawfully passed-off their product as that of the plaintiff because the evidence showed that the name of 'Jameson's Whiskey' had become so identified with the plaintiff that its use without qualifying words by the defendant to show that it was their whiskey was likely to mislead purchasers into believing that the whiskey was made by the plaintiff.

252. In *Reckitt & Colman Products v. Borden Inc,*[521] Lord Oliver outlined three essential features of passing-off which the plaintiff must establish:

(1) a goodwill or reputation attaching to the goods or services which in the minds of the public is associated with an identifying 'get-up' (e.g., brand name, trade description, individual features, labelling or packaging) and which is distinctive specifically of the plaintiff's goods or services;
(2) that the defendant made a misrepresentation (intentional or otherwise) which leads or is likely to lead the public to believe that the goods or services offered by the defendant are in fact offered by the plaintiff;
(3) proof that the plaintiff has suffered or is likely to suffer as a result of the erroneous belief engendered by the defendant's misrepresentation.

Each feature is examined in turn.

A. *Goodwill*

253. Goodwill has been defined as:

> the benefit and advantage of the good name, reputation connection of a business. It is the attractive force which brings in custom. It is the one thing which distinguishes an old established business from a new business at its start.[522]

It is clear, from case law, that the necessary goodwill can be established quite quickly. In *Stannard v. Reay,*[523] for example, the plaintiff and defendant both established chip-shops under the name 'Mr Chippy', but the plaintiff did so three weeks earlier than the defendant. The court, in granting an injunction against the defendant, held that the plaintiff had built up trade very quickly and therefore could be said to have established the necessary goodwill. Moreover, the geographical scope of a business reputation or goodwill can be extensive. For example, in *C&A Modes*

521. [1990] 1 WLR 491 at 499, approved by Laffoy J in *DSG Retail Ltd v. World Ltd* (unreported, High Court, 13 Jan. 1998); *see also Erven Warnick Besloten Vennootschap v. J Townend & Sons (Hull) Ltd* (the 'Advocaat' case) [1979] AC 731 at 741, applied in numerous Irish cases including *Falcon Travel Ltd v. Owners Abroad Group plc* [1991] 1 IR 175; *An Post v. Irish Permanent plc* [1995] 1 IR 140; *Smithkline Beecham plc v. Antigen Pharmaceuticals Ltd* [1999] 2 ILRM 190.
522. *Inland Revenue v. Muller ' s & Co ' s Margarine Ltd* [1901] AC 217.
523. [1967] RPC 589.

Ltd v. C&A Waterford Ltd,[524] the plaintiff was a well-known British chain-shore which operated in England and Northern Ireland. The defendant, an Irish company, used the letters 'C&A' with the intention of leading customers to connect their business with that of the plaintiff. Although the plaintiff did not have a store in the Republic of Ireland there was evidence that a large number of people travelled from the Republic to Northern Ireland to shop at the plaintiff's store there. Therefore, goodwill was established and the action for passing-off succeeded.

B. Misrepresentation Causing Confusion

254. It is clear that imitation of a product alone without confusion is insufficient to base a passing-off action. In *Adidas Sportsschuhfabricken Adi Dassler KG v. Charles O'Neill,*[525] the plaintiff was a well-known German sports gear company which used a distinctive three strips on its goods. The plaintiff sought an injunction to prevent the defendant's use of three strips on its sports gear. It was held that the defendant's conduct did not constitute passing-off because the defendant was a well-established sports gear manufacturer and its goods were boxed with its name marked clearly thereon and hence no confusion was created.

255. These tests for determining confusion are the likely impression on the passing or unwary customer.[526] It is no defence to claim that an observant person making a careful examination of the goods or services would not have been confused. For example, in cases involved packaged goods, the court will consider the 'get-up' of the goods and, in many cases, Irish courts have focused on the packaging rather than the names and content. For instance, in *Polycell Products v. O'Carroll,*[527] an injunction was granted in relation to an adhesive product in packaging similar in colour and design to the plaintiff's product even though the names of the products were reasonably different: 'Polycell' and 'Clingcell'. Again, in *United Biscuits v. Irish Biscuits,*[528] the two products in question were 'Cottage Creams' and 'College Creams'. Despite a similarity in names and type, the plaintiff's action for passing-off failed because the packaging was very different and therefore there was no risk of confusion.

256. Whether there is confusion is a matter of evidence. Likelihood of confusion was established in *Guinness Ireland Group v. Kilkenny Brewing Company Ltd,*[529] where the defendant was engaged in a different type of business from the plaintiff. An injunction was granted against the use of the name 'Kilkenny Brewing Company' by the defendant, a company whose purpose was to hold land, on which was situated a microbrewery, rather than to be a trading company for the business

524. [1976] IR 198.
525. [1983] ILRM 112; cf. *Gabicci v. Dunnes Stores Ltd* (unreported, High Court, 31 Jul. 1991).
526. *Singer Manufacturing Co. v. Loog* (1882) 8 AC 15 at 18; *An Bord Trachtála v. Waterford Foods plc* [1994] FSR 316.
527. [1959] Ir Jur Rep 34.
528. [1971] IR 16.
529. [1999] 1 ILRM 531.

carried on at the microbrewery. There was evidence, from three persons 'very experienced in the licensed trade' that consumers would be likely to get the impression that the defendant brewed 'Kilkenny Irish Beer', the plaintiff's product.

C. Damage

257. The requirement of damage is an area of uncertainty. Earlier cases suggest that there is no need to prove actual damage: the assumption is that confusion in the minds of the public of itself causes damage.[530] However, *Stringfellow v. McCain Foods GB Ltd*[531] suggests a move away from this traditional position. There, the plaintiff was the owner of a night-club 'Stringfellows'. The defendant manufactured a brand of potato-chips called 'Stringfellows' and advertised it using a family disco dancing in their kitchen. The Court of Appeal held that although the advertising campaign may have led some members of the public to confuse the two, there was no damage to the plaintiff's goodwill established. Also, the plaintiff was not merchandising his name on other products: the fact that he/she might merchandise in the future was rejected as a basis for damage and was mere speculation.

258. In the Irish case of *Falcon Travel Ltd v. Owners Abroad Group plc,*[532] the former approach seems to have prevailed. There, the plaintiff traded in package holidays to the public since the 1970s and had established a good reputation. The defendant was a UK company also trading in holidays since the 1980s, but originally it restricted itself to the UK market. In 1988, the defendant moved into the Irish market, issuing brochures and opening an office. The defendant was aware of the plaintiff but believed there would be no confusion because both businesses were very different: the plaintiff was relatively small in comparison with the defendant which was a large wholesaler. However, in fact, a lot of confusion was caused. The plaintiff received telephone calls, correspondence and threats of legal action which should have been directed at the defendant. Furthermore, a newspaper article confused two businesses when the defendant's customers were stranded in Turkey. The defendant argued that the plaintiff had suffered no loss, in fact, it had an increased turnover. Murphy J. stated that it had to be proved that the plaintiff suffered damage; however, he appears to have decided that appropriating the plaintiff's name is sufficient damage without the need to show further actual damage.

D. Remedies

259. Damages, to compensate for the resulting loss, such as the diversion of sales or injurious association, and an injunction to prevent any further confusion, may be available in an action for passing-off. Actual deception is not needed[533] and

530. *See*, e.g., *Drapier v. Trist* [1939] 3 All ER 513.
531. [1984] RPC 501.
532. [1991] 1 IR 175.
533. *Jameson v. Dublin Distillers Co. Ltd* [1900] 1 IR 43 at 55.

there is no need to prove intention to deceive,[534] but if either are proved the case will be stronger. Nominal damages may be awarded where there is no intention to deceive. In *Michelstown Co-op Agricultural Society v. Goldenvale Food Products Ltd,*[535] the court considered that, in general, damages would be an inadequate remedy in passing-off cases, the appropriate remedy being an injunction.

260. The circumstances in which a court will grant an injunction to restrain passing-off were considered by the Court of Appeal in *British Telecommunications plc v. One in a Million Ltd.*[536] The Court concluded that an injunction could be granted in three types of cases:

(1) where actual passing-off is established or threatened;
(2) where the defendant is a joint-tortfeasor with another in passing-off, either actual or threatened;
(3) where the defendant has equipped himself/herself or intends to equip another with an instrument of fraud in which case the court will intervene on a *quia timet* basis.

In *British Telecommunications plc v. One in a Million Ltd,* the defendant had registered Internet domain names identical or similar to several well-known business organizations, including, 'bt.org' and 'marksandspencer.com'. The Court found that the registration of such names amounted to a representation to the public that the person registering was connected with the name and thus constituted passing-off. Additionally, it held that the registration amounted to 'an instrument of fraud' which could be restrained by injunction either if the name, by reason of its similarity to that of an existing business, would inherently lead to passing-off, or even if the name would not inherently lead to passing-off, if it was produced to enable passing-off to be committed, was adapted to be used for passing-off or was likely to be used fraudulently.

261. In *B&S Ltd v. Irish Auto Trading Ltd,*[537] the principles of *America Cynamid,*[538] in relation to interlocutory injunctions, were adopted. Hence, the applicant must show that there is a fair question to be tried and the injunction will be granted or refused on the balance of convenience.[539] It has been argued that these principles

534. *Guinness Ireland Group v. Kilkenny Brewing Company* [1999] 1 ILRM 531; *Smithkline Beecham plc v. Antigen Pharmaceuticals Ltd* [1999] 2 ILRM 190.
535. Unreported, High Court, 12 Dec. 1985, approved in *Symonds Cider & English Wine Co. Ltd v. Showerings (Ireland) Ltd* [1997] 1 ILRM 481.
536. [1998] 4 All ER 476, [1998] FSR 265.
537. [1995] 2 ILRM 152.
538. [1975] AC 396.
539. *See further Contech Building Products Ltd v. Walsh & Ors* [2006] IEHC 45.

should not be strictly applied in passing-off cases. In such circumstances, the outcome of interlocutory proceedings often determines the final outcome of any dispute, hence, it was argued, that a court should consider the substance of the case at an interlocutory stage. This argument was rejected in *Symonds Cider v. Showerings (Ireland) Ltd.*[540]

262. It is important to remember that the tort of passing-off seeks to protect the trader and not the public. Hence, it is no defence to show that the defendant's goods or services are better or cheaper than those of the plaintiff, or that the resulting competition is good for the general public.[541]

540. [1997] 1 ILRM 481. *See also Miss World Ltd & Ors v. Miss Ireland Beauty Pageant Ltd & Ors* [2004] IEHC 14; and *Contech Building Products Ltd v. Walsh & Ors* [2006] IEHC 45.
541. *Incorporated Law Society of Ireland v. Carroll* (unreported, High Court, 24 Jan. 1995).

Chapter 6. Bankruptcy and Related Institutions

263. Bankruptcy connotes the rules governing the division of the estate of an individual who has become insolvent. Company liquidation connotes the dividing up of the assets of a company which is being wound up, often because it is insolvent. Where the company being wound up is insolvent, many rules from the bankruptcy code are transposed to the liquidation. Both the bankruptcy and the companies legislation contain machinery for facilitating compromises between the debtor and his/her creditors, thereby avoiding an actual bankruptcy or liquidation. One very important personality in this whole area is the receiver, a device not strictly confined to bankruptcy and insolvency situations.

§1. Receivers

264. A receiver is someone who is duly appointed to take possession of certain assets, usually with a view to selling them and paying off a creditor out of the proceeds of their sale. Money judgments are often enforced in this manner – by the court appointing what is called a receiver by way of equitable execution to seize and realize the judgment debtor's assets.[542] Another ground on which a court will appoint a receiver is where a secured creditor's security is in jeopardy; the receiver's primary function there is to protect and preserve that security. Where land has been charged as security for obligations, one common mode of enforcing that security is by appointing a receiver whose task is to sell the land.

265. Perhaps the commonest receiver in the commercial world is the receiver appointed by a secured creditor under express authority contained in the security instrument. Most company debentures and comparable security documents authorize the creditor to appoint a receiver and manager in the event of default or in several other itemized circumstances. A typical clause to this end will read as follows:

- whenever the principal sum falling due under the agreement becomes payable;
- whenever the company fails to pay any instalment, or the principal sum or the interest, due under the agreement;
- whenever the company contravenes any of several covenants contained in the security instrument;
- whenever the company ceases or threatens to cease carrying on its business;
- whenever a resolution is passed, a petition is presented or an order is made to wind-up the company;
- whenever the company acts in such a way as endangers or jeopardizes the security created by the debenture;
- whenever any prior debenture becomes enforceable against the company.

542. RSC Ord. 45.

266. Traditionally, the principles and rules governing receivers were predominantly based on case law – on the law of contract and on the principles of equity. The extent of the receiver's authority depends largely on the clause which enables his/her appointment and the actual instrument of appointment. Usually he/she will be given express authority to manage the business in question for a period, in the hope that a better price can be obtained by selling all or part of the business as a going concern. He/she is an agent of whoever appointed him/her but frequently he/she will also be designated as an agent of the debtor too.[543] Within a corporate context, Part 8 of the Companies Act 2014 deals with the appointment of receivers; powers and responsibilities of receivers and regulation and enforcement of their duties. In particular, section 437 provides that a receiver of the property of a company has power to do, in the State and elsewhere, all things necessary or convenient to be done for or in connection with, or as incidental to, the attainment of the objectives for which the receiver was appointed. The provision then provides a litany of powers in addition to any powers conferred by an order or instrument.[544] This provision is new and was designed address the problem of poorly drafted debentures.

§2. Compromises and Schemes with Creditors

267. There are numerous statutory mechanisms which facilitate debtors entering into some compromise or scheme with their creditors. The first three schemes outlined here concern compromises with individuals; the remainder concern compromises with companies.

I. Deed of Arrangement

268. Where the creditors have agreed to some compromise, the terms can be recorded in what is called a deed of arrangement and registered in the High Court Central Office under the Deeds of Arrangement Act, 1887. A duly registered deed binds all the parties to it but cannot adversely affect non-parties. Instruments of this nature are rarely used these days. Indeed, companies cannot enter into deeds of arrangement qua debtors.[545]

II. Court-Supervised Arrangements with Insolvent Individual

269. Part IV of the Bankruptcy Act, 1988, enabled insolvent individuals to obtain a moratorium from their creditors, during which time they could propose and agree terms of settlement with their creditors, in certain circumstances. This aspect of 1988 is now repealed[546] and instead, from 31 July 2013, the Personal Insolvency

543. *See Bula Ltd v. Crowley (No. 3)* [2003] 1 IR 396.
544. Companies Act 2014, s. 437(3).
545. *Re Rileys Ltd* [1903] 2 Ch. 590.
546. Personal Insolvency Act 2012, s. 6 and Schedule.

Act 2012 offers two main options for arrangements with creditors, utilizing the services of a Personal Insolvency Practitioner (PIP) and under the supervision of the Insolvency Service of Ireland (ISI) and the court.[547]

270. First, there is the Debt Settlement Arrangement (DSA).[548] This arrangement is limited in that it only applies to unsecured debt. A DSA must be agreed by the debtor and approved at a creditor's meeting by 65% (in value) of creditors. In addition it must be processed by the ISI and approved by the appropriate Court.[549] Under a DSA, a debtor's unsecured debts subject to the DSA, will be settled over a period of up to five years (extendable to six years in certain circumstances). If successfully complied with, the debtor will be discharged from debts specified in the DSA at the end of the period.

271. Second, there is the Personal Insolvency Arrangement (PIA). Unlike the DSA, the PIA can include secured and unsecured debt, although a limit of EUR 3 million applies to the amount of secured debt that can be included in a PIA, unless all secured creditors consent to the inclusion of a higher amount. A PIA must be agreed by the debtor and approved at a creditors' meeting by a qualified majority of creditors. In addition it must be processed by the ISI and approved by the court.[550] Under a PIA, a debtor's unsecured debts will be settled over a period of up to six years (extendable to seven years in certain circumstances) and the debtor will be released from those unsecured debts at the end of that period. Secured debts can be restructured under a PIA. Depending on the terms of the PIA, the debtor may be released from a secured debt at the end of PIA period or the secured debt can continue to be payable by the debtor (although perhaps on restructured terms).

III. Composition Within Bankruptcy

272. Even where the individual debtor has been adjudicated bankrupt, sections 38–41 of the Bankruptcy Act, 1988, as amended, enables him/her to still propose a compromise with his/her creditors. If that has the support of three-fifths in number and value of the creditors and is acceptable to the court, the bankruptcy will terminate and the settlement will become binding on all the creditors.

547. Personal Insolvency Act 2012 (Commencement) (No. 3) Order 2013, SI No. 285/2013. The 2012 Act also makes provision for a third option, which is not court supervised, knows as a Debt Relief Notice (DRN). This option only applies where the qualifying debts do not exceed EUR 20,000 and the debtor's income is very low. The DRN process enables eligible insolvent debtors to write off their debts where they can prove they are not in a position to repay them and it is unlikely their financial situation will improve in the next three years: 2012 Act, ss 25–47.

548. Personal Insolvency Act 2012, ss 55–88.

549. Where the total liabilities of a debtor are in excess of EUR 2,500,000, the appropriate court is the High Court; otherwise the appropriate court is the Circuit Court: Personal Insolvency Act 2013, s. 5.

550. Where the total liabilities of a debtor are in excess of EUR 2,500,000, the appropriate court is the High Court; otherwise the appropriate court is the Circuit Court: Personal Insolvency Act 2013, s. 5.

IV. Company Schemes of Arrangement

273. Part 9, Chapter 1 of the Companies Act 2014, enables companies to reach a settlement with their creditors, via a scheme of arrangement.[551] Accordingly, where a scheme of arrangement with creditors is proposed, the directors of the company may convene a meeting of creditors, or, on application, the High Court may convene the meeting.[552] Meetings must be held of each class of creditors who may be affected in order to consider what is being proposed.[553] Under the 2014 Act, the High Court has an explicit power where it is exercising its discretion to convene a scheme meeting to give directions on the appropriate meetings to be held.[554] Where any class agrees to a proposal by a special majority,[555] all members of the class are bound to provide certain further conditions are met.[556] But classes which do not approve of the proposals in this manner are not bound by them. In a new provision, section 453(4), state creditors, such as the Revenue Commissioners, are given express power to vote in favour of a scheme even though it might result in less than 100% in the euro being paid to the Commissioners. In the past, the Revenue Commissioners, as a preferred creditor, were often an objecting creditor in these schemes, on the grounds that the Commissioners have no authority to compromise taxes which are due and payable. Advertisement of the passing of the scheme resolution(s) and the application to the court to approve the scheme in 'at least two daily newspapers circulating in the district where the registered office or principal place of business of the company is situated' is now a condition of the scheme becoming effective. Moreover, where a scheme is approved by the court, the company must deliver a copy of the scheme order to the Registrar of Companies within twenty-one days after the date of making of the order and the scheme order takes effect immediately on such delivery.[557] Importantly, it is not necessary for a company to be insolvent for it to make use of this procedure, and for some companies this procedure may present a preferable alternative to examinership as a method of business rescue.

V. Court Protection and Supervised Examination of Companies

274. An examinership process was first introduced in Ireland in 1990,[558] modelled on Part IV of the Bankruptcy Act 1988 and resembling somewhat the 'Chapter 11' bankruptcy procedure in the United States. Today, Part 10 of the Companies Act 2014 regulates examinership, dealing with appointment of an examiner, powers

551. *See* previously ss 201–203 of the Companies Act 1963, as amended.
552. Companies Act 2014, s. 450.
553. *See* Companies Act 2014, s. 452 for requirement of 'scheme circular'.
554. Companies Act 2014, s. 450(3).
555. 'Special majority' means a majority in number representing at least 75% in value of the creditors or class of creditors or members or class of members, as the case may be, present and voting either in person or by proxy at the scheme meeting: Companies Act 2014, s. 449.
556. Companies Act 2014, s. 453.
557. Companies Act 2014, s. 454.
558. Companies (Amendment) Act, 1990.

of an examiner, liability for third parties for debts of a company in examination and conclusion of examinership. Importantly, the legislation states that a person cannot be appointed as an examiner unless he or she would be qualified to act as a liquidator, and, hence the new professional qualification requirements for liquidators also apply to examiners.[559]

275. If a company is insolvent, an outside examiner can be appointed by the court to investigate its affairs, principally to ascertain if all or part of its business is viable.[560] Where a favourable conclusion is reached in that regard, the examiner will then seek to negotiate a compromise with the various classes of creditors. If at least one class of creditors and of the shareholders accept his/her proposals, they can then be put before the court, which has an extensive discretion. If the court approves the proposed settlement, or approves it as altered, then all classes of creditors are bound by it – and not just the classes which voted for the settlement.

276. From the time the petition for protection is lodged in court and up to the ending of the examination, the company is protected from adverse action by its creditors in numerous ways; for instance, they cannot repossess property let to the company, they cannot levy execution against its assets, a receiver cannot be appointed over all or part of its assets and a winding up petition cannot be presented.[561] If the court consents, the examiner can become involved in the actual management of the company in a number of ways.[562]

VI. Administration of Insurance Companies

277. A somewhat similar system exists for non-life insurance companies under the Insurance (No. 2) Act, 1983, as amended, whereby an administrator can be appointed over the affairs of an insolvent insurer. But the initiative for any such appointment lies with the Central Bank.[563] Also, the administrator's primary function is not to draw up proposals for settlement, against a short deadline. His/her job is to manage the business with a view to eventually rehabilitating it or else disposing of the business in some way.

559. Companies Act 2014, 519.
560. Both the High Court and the Circuit Court have jurisdiction in this regard: Companies Act 2014, s. 509.
561. Companies Act 2014, s. 520.
562. Companies Act 2014, s. 524; and Ch. 3 Part 10 more generally.
563. Central Bank Acts 1942–2010.

§3. Personal Bankruptcy

278. Irish bankruptcy law was substantially reformed and consolidated in the Bankruptcy[564] Act, 1988 (hereinafter the 1988 Act).[565] More recently, the Personal Insolvency Act 2012 has made a number of important changes to this legislation, including by reducing the bankruptcy period from twelve to three years.[566] The bankruptcy period has since been reduced to one year.[567]

279. Where a person is adjudicated bankrupt, his/her assets will vest in the Official Assignee (or exceptionally in a special trustee), who will sell those assets and divide the proceeds among his/her unsecured creditors. When all of that is done, the debtor may be able to obtain a discharge from bankruptcy on fulfilling certain conditions. All bankruptcy matters are dealt with in the High Court, usually by a judge specially assigned for that purpose.

I. Initiating the Bankruptcy

280. The procedure for initiating bankruptcy is presenting a petition to the court on the grounds that the debtor has committed what is termed an act of bankruptcy.[568] A debt of more than EUR 20,000 must be due to the creditor/petitioner, except of course where the debtor petitions for his/her own bankruptcy.[569] Details of the procedure for presenting the petition and subsequent matters are set out in the Bankruptcy Rules.[570]

281. What constitutes an act of bankruptcy for these purposes is defined in section 7(1) of the 1988 Act, as amended, being any of the following:

a. if in the State or elsewhere, the debtor makes a conveyance or assignment of all or substantially all of his/her property to a trustee or trustees for the benefit of his/her creditors generally;
b. if in the State or elsewhere he/she makes a fraudulent conveyance, gift, delivery or transfer of his/her property or any part thereof;
c. if in the State or elsewhere he/she makes any conveyance or transfer of his/her property or any part thereof, or creates any charge thereon, which would under this or any other Act be void as a fraudulent preference if he/she were adjudicated bankrupt:

564. *See* Sanfey, M. & Holohan, B. *Bankruptcy Law and Practice in Ireland* (2nd ed., Round Hall Press 2010); Forde, M. & Simms, *Bankruptcy Law* (2nd ed., Round Hall 2009).
565. Based in part on the Budd Committee *Report on Bankruptcy* (Prl. 2714, 1972).
566. Based on the LRC *Report on Personal Debt Management and Debt Enforcement* (LRC 100, 2010).
567. 1988 Act, s. 85, as amended by the Bankruptcy (Amendment) Act 2015, s.10.
568. 1988 Act, s. 7, as amended.
569. 1988 Act, ss 8, 11 and 15, as amended.
570. RSC, Ord. 76 on Bankruptcy: SI No. 120 of 2012. Traditionally, these procedural rules are strictly enforced: *see O ' Maoileoin v. Official Assignee* [1989] IR 647; *In the matter of Gerard Sherlock, A Bankrupt* [1995] 2 ILRM 493.

a. if the individual has been the subject as a debtor to a Debt Settlement Arrangement which has been terminated under section 83 of the Personal Insolvency Act 2012;
b. if the individual has been subject as a debtor to a Debt Settlement Arrangement which under section 84 of the Personal Insolvency Act 2012;
c. if the individual has been subject as a debtor to a Personal Insolvency Arrangement which has been terminated under section 122 of the Personal Insolvency Act 2012;
d. if the individual has been subject as a debtor to a Personal Insolvency Arrangement which under section 123 of the Personal Insolvency Act 2012 is deemed to have failed.

d. if with intent to defeat or delay his/her creditors he/she leaves the States or, being out of the State, remains out of the State or departs from his/her dwelling house or otherwise absents himself/herself or evades his/her creditors;
e. if he/she files in the Court a declaration of insolvency;
f. if execution against him/her has been levied by the seizure of his/her goods under an order of any court or if a return of no goods has been made by the sheriff or county registrar, whether by endorsement on the order or otherwise;
g. if the creditor presenting a petition has served upon the debtor in the prescribed manner a bankruptcy summons, and he/she does not within fourteen days after service of the summons pay the sum referred to in the summons or secured or compound for it to the satisfaction of the creditor.

282. Most bankruptcy petitions are presented under the last of these headings. This involves first applying to the court for a bankruptcy summons, which will be issued if the debtor was notified of the application and at least EUR 20,000 is owing to the applicant. That summons will then be served and if, within the next fourteen days, the debt is not paid, the debtor is deemed to have committed an act of bankruptcy.

II. Effects of Adjudication

283. To be adjudicated a bankrupt has drastic personal effects on the debtor as well as on his/her property. He/she cannot be elected to or sit as a member of the Oireachtas or of any local authority. He/she cannot be a director of a company, except where the court permits him/her to act on such terms as the court lays down. He/she is debarred from engaging in several professions and occupations, for instance practising as a solicitor, acting as a company auditor or as a stockbroker.

Bankrupts are not permitted to obtain credit in excess of EUR 650 without disclosing that they are undischarged bankrupts.[571] Moreover, while they are not prohibited entirely from trading, if they engage in business under any other name they must disclose their bankruptcy to the persons they deal with.[572]

284. Subject to some exceptions, the bankrupt's property immediately vests in the Official Assignee, who is an official attached to the High Court and is responsible for the administration of bankrupts' estates.[573] Exceptionally, the property can be vested in a specially selected trustee in bankruptcy. Any vesting in the Assignee or a trustee is 'subject to equities', meaning without prejudice to all rights of third parties in the property.[574]

285. The property or interests of which the bankrupt is not divested in this manner include the following:

- Property not actually acquired or property already disposed of. Many of the reported cases focusing on incomplete sales transactions are concerned with whether or not the bankrupt buyer or seller of goods remained their owner on the day he/she was adjudicated bankrupt.
- Necessities for living: section 45(1) of the 1988 Act, as amended, allows the bankrupt to retain personal effects and equipment for his/her trade up to a value of EUR 6,000. He/she can also apply to the court for an order that necessities exceeding that value should not be taken from him/her.
- Property held in trust: under section 44(4) of the 1988 Act this property belongs to someone else, beneficially.
- Pension assets under section 44A of the 1988 Act; although income from such a pension does vest in the Official Assignee.
- Third-party insurance: section 62 of the Civil Liability Act, 1961, prevents the proceeds of an insurance policy, covering damage caused by the bankrupt to another personally or to his/her property, from vesting in the insolvent estate. Instead, those funds are held in a form of trust for the benefit of the party claiming compensation from the bankrupt.
- Social welfare benefits: section 283 of the Social Welfare Consolidation Act, 2005, does not permit benefits payable under that Act to vest in the Assignee or trustee in bankruptcy.

286. Bankruptcy does not have any uniform impact on contracts to which the bankrupt was a party. It all depends on the nature and the terms of each contract. Sometimes the bankruptcy will be treated as either repudiating the contract or bringing it to an end by way of frustration. On other occasions, the contract will vest in

571. 1988 Act, s. 129(a), as amended by the Euro Changeover (Amounts) Act 2001.
572. 1988 Act, s. 129(b).
573. 1988 Act, s. 44.
574. *Re Nolan and Stanley* [1949] IR 197; *see*, e.g., 1988 Act, s. 136(2).

the Official Assignee or in the trustee in bankruptcy, if there is one. Where a contract survives bankruptcy but is having a particularly onerous effect on the insolvent estate, the Assignee as trustee can apply to the court to rescind that contract.[575]

III. Asset-Swelling Measures

287. There are a number of rules which for convenience may be subsumed under the broad umbrella of 'asset-swelling' measures. These are aimed at protecting the insolvent estate against further depletion and recovering property which was improperly transferred out of that estate, often with a view to defeating the creditors. The main provisions of this effect are as follows.

A. Disclaiming Onerous Property and Contracts

288. Where the insolvent estate contains property or contracts[576] which are a substantial drain on its resources, an application can be made that they should be disclaimed. A not infrequent subject of applications of this kind is leases; the debtor would have leased property at a rent which presently is far above its economic value to the estate. Where disclaimer is allowed, the other contracting party is entitled to be compensated for the loss he/she thereby suffered.

B. Examination[577]

289. The Official Assignee has extensive authority to examine the bankrupt and others about transactions in his/her property. Where a bankrupt fails to co-operate he/she can be examined under oath in Court. This power can be very useful when seeking to track assets which seem to have disappeared.

C. Fraudulent Conveyance

290. Section 10 of the Fraudulent Conveyances Act, 1634, empowers the court to set aside conveyances and other transfers of assets by an insolvent debtor, done in order to defeat or delay his/her creditors. No strict time limit is set for the operation of this section. Where the transfer in question was gratuitous, there would be relatively little difficulty in proving the improper intent. But the fact that the transfer was made for valuable consideration does not always put it outside the legislation; if it possesses the indicia or 'badges of fraud', it will be struck down.

575. 1988 Act, s. 56.
576. 1988 Act, s. 56.
577. 1988 Act, s. 21.

D. Fraudulent Preference

291. By fraudulent preference is meant paying off one creditor before other creditors get paid where there is no plausible commercial justification for paying that person first. The term fraud here is something of a misnomer; a more appropriate word might be an unfair or an improper preference. Where a bankrupt pays one or a handful of creditors with the intention of preferring them over the other creditors, his/her payment is a fraudulent preference. And if it was made during the three years preceding his/her adjudication as a bankrupt, section 57 of the 1988 Act, as amended, provides that the payment can be recovered by the Official Assignee for the benefit of the estate. This principle also applies to certain other transactions by the bankrupt which are comparable to him/her paying a creditor in those circumstances. The main concern in the cases decided under this provision is ascertaining whether the insolvent carried out the impugned transaction with the requisite 'fraudulent' intent. There are several stock situations where that intent is readily inferred by the courts.

E. Voluntary Settlement

292. A voluntary settlement is a gift. Section 59 of the 1988 Act, as amended, provides that every such settlement made within three years of the debtor being adjudicated a bankrupt can be set aside on the application of the Official Assignee. Furthermore, where it can be shown that the debtor was insolvent when he/she made a gift, the settlement can be set aside when made during the five years prior to the adjudication. In either of these cases, no question of ascertaining the settlor's true intent arises; once the transaction can fairly be characterized as a gift, it can be struck down if made within the relevant three or five-year period. Many of the modern cases concern transfers of the family home between spouses, where the marriage has broken down, and subsequently that arrangement would be challenged as a voluntary settlement. Whether it indeed fits that description depends on all the circumstances of the case. There are special rules for marriage settlements made within the three years prior to the adjudication.

F. Transfer at Substantial Under-Value

293. At times a transaction by an insolvent debtor on the virtual eve of his/her bankruptcy may be highly suspect but it cannot be fitted under any of the above headings. In particular, he/she has sold property at a very advantageous price to one of his/her friends or relations. Section 58 of the 1988 Act, as amended, now strikes at that kind of transaction, where it occurred within three years of the adjudication. If the property was sold at substantially below its market value or the transaction otherwise caused the debtor's estate to be significantly diminished, the court can set aside the entire transaction.

IV. Proving Debts and Distribution to Creditors

294. Having got in and then disposed of so much of the bankrupt's estate as is reasonably possible, the Official Assignee will then proceed to pay the creditors at least a proportion of the amounts they are owed. The secured creditors can look to their security; they are unsecured creditors for the difference between the value of their security and the amount of their debt.

295. The costs of administering the estate must be paid before any of the bankrupt's debts.[578] Moreover, there is a category of 'preferential' creditor who must get paid before the ordinary unsecured creditors can receive any payment.[579] They are, principally, the Revenue Commissioners, in respect of a variety of revenue debts; local authorities in respect of one year's unpaid rates; employees of the bankrupt in respect of certain unpaid wages and other forms of remuneration.

296. All unsecured creditors will be paid the same percentage in the Euro. Several of the rules regarding the kinds of debts and liabilities which can be 'proved' in the bankruptcy are highly technical, for instance, those regarding contingent claims, interest, costs, set-off and what is called 'double proof'. Only creditors who have duly proved their debts will be paid.

V. Discharge

297. Where all his/her creditors are paid off in full, the bankrupt will obtain a discharge and can resume ordinary commercial activities.[580] A discharge can also be obtained where all the creditors so agree. Otherwise, a bankrupt is entitled to automatic discharge one year from the date of being adjudicated bankrupt.

§4. Company Liquidation

298. Company liquidation, or winding up, is largely regulated by statute, namely Part 11 of the Companies Act 2014.[581] Many of the rules and procedures for company liquidation resemble those for bankruptcy.

I. Initiating the Liquidation

299. The Companies Act 2014 continues to recognize that there are three ways of commencing the liquidation or winding up of an insolvent company: a members'

578. 1988 Act, s. 80.
579. 1988 Act, s. 81.
580. 1988 Act, s. 85, as substituted by s. 157 of the Personal Insolvency Act 2012.
581. *See also* RSC, Ord. 74, SI No. 121 of 2012.

voluntary winding up; a creditors' voluntary winding up; and a compulsory winding up by the court (sometimes known as an 'official winding up').[582] The Companies Act 2014 has sought to streamline the provisions dealing with these three forms. With a members' voluntary winding up, following a 'summary approval procedure' or a special resolution to wind-up the company, a liquidator is appointed by the members.[583] A related method is the creditors' voluntary winding up whereby the members resolve to wind-up the company on the grounds of insolvency, but in this case the liquidator is chosen by the creditors and he/she is answerable to them.[584] The compulsory winding up resembles the bankruptcy procedure; a petition is presented to the High Court to have the company wound up on a compulsory basis, and the court appoints a liquidator.[585] A company may be wound up by the court on a number of grounds, most commonly if the company is insolvent, that is, unable to pay its debts.[586] A company is deemed to be unable to pay its debts in a number of circumstances, such as where a creditor to whom the company is indebted in a sum exceeding EUR 10,000 serves a demand in writing and the company fails to pay within twenty-one days, or if execution issued on a judgment in favour of a creditor of the company is returned unsatisfied in whole or in part, or if it is proved to the satisfaction of the court that the company is unable to pay its debts, and in determining whether a company is unable to pay its debts, the court shall take into account the contingent and prospective liabilities of the company.[587] If the petition succeeds, the Court appoints a liquidator, who becomes an officer of the Court and is principally accountable to the court. Pursuant to the Companies Act 2014, for the first time, there is a statutory obligation for a person to have certain qualifications prior to being appointed as a liquidator.[588]

II. Effects of a Winding Up

300. Commencement of a winding up freezes various transactions that concern the company, as outlined below. A voluntary winding up commences once the appropriate resolution is passed.[589] A compulsory winding up is deemed to have commenced not when the winding up order is made but when the petition for a winding up is presented in the Central Office of the High Court.[590]

582. Companies Act 2014, ss 561–562.
583. Companies Act 2014, ss 578–584.
584. Companies Act 2014, ss 585–588.
585. Companies Act 2014, ss 568–577.
586. Companies Act 2014, s. 569.
587. Companies Act 2014, s. 570.
588. Companies Act 2014, ss 633–635.
589. Companies Act 2014, s. 590.
590. Companies Act 2014, s. 589.

A. *Shareholders*

301. From the time a winding up commences, any transfer of shares in the company done without the sanction of the liquidator is void, unless the court orders otherwise.[591]

B. *Directors*

302. From the date of commencement of the winding up, a company must cease to carry on its business, except so far as may be required for the beneficial winding up of the company.[592] Moreover, at the same time, all the powers of the directors of the company shall cease, unless in the case of a winding up by the court or a creditors' voluntary winding up, the continuance of those powers is sanctioned by a committee of inspection or the creditors, or in the case of a members' voluntary winding up, the members in general meeting sanction the continuance of those powers.[593]

C. *Contracts*

303. In general, the advent of liquidation has no immediate effect on contracts with the company. However, there are contracts with express and even implied terms that liquidation either lawfully terminates them or constitutes a repudiatory breach of them. Express provisions to that effect are often contained in leases. As with bankruptcy, there is a procedure whereby the liquidator may apply to disclaim onerous contracts.[594]

D. *Litigation*

304. Once a winding up order has been made, a provisional liquidator appointed, or a resolution for voluntary winding up passed, all proceedings against the company are stayed and no action can be commenced unless by leave of the court and subject to such terms as the court may impose.[595] The powers of the liquidator, which are enumerated in Table A of section 627, include the power to commence any legal proceedings in the name of the company and to defend any legal proceedings in the name of the company.

591. Companies Act 2014, s. 602.
592. Companies Act 2014, s. 677(1).
593. Companies Act 2014, s. 677.
594. Companies Act 2014, ss 615–616.
595. Companies Act 2014, s. 678.

E. Company Property

305. Once appointed, the liquidator must take into his or her custody, or under his or her control, all the property to which the company is or appears to be entitled.[596] However, unlike the position in bankruptcies, the company's property does not automatically vest in the liquidator. The liquidator may apply to the court to have title to all or part of that property vested in him/her.[597] Moreover, any disposition of the company's property made without the sanction of the liquidator, and after the commencement of the winding up, is void, unless the court orders otherwise.[598] The principle governing decisions by the court to uphold any such disposition is that:

> since the policy of the law is to procure so far as practicable rateable payments of the unsecured creditors' claims, … the court should not validate any transaction or series of transactions which might result in one or more pre-liquidation creditors being paid in full at the expense of other creditors, who will receive only a dividend, in the absence of special circumstances making such a course desirable in the interests of the unsecured creditors as a body.[599]

F. Creditors' Remedies

306. Section 603 deals with the voidance of executions against company property. Accordingly, and unless a court orders otherwise, any attachment, sequestration, distress or execution put in force by a creditor against the property of the company, after the commencement of winding up, is void.

307. Moreover, where a creditor has issued execution against the goods or lands of a company, or attached any debt due to the company, and the company is subsequently wound up, the creditor shall not be entitled to retain the benefit of the execution or attachment against the liquidator in the winding up of the company unless the creditor has completed the execution or attachment before the commencement of the winding up.[600] Furthermore, before the goods taken in execution are sold or the execution is completed, the liquidator may demand that the sheriff return those goods.[601] However, rights arising under these two latter provisions may be set aside by the court[602] and a purchaser in good faith, under a sale by the sheriff, acquires a good title against the liquidator.[603]

596. Companies Act, s. 596.
597. Companies Act 2014, s. 614.
598. Companies Act 2014, s. 602.
599. *Re Gray ' s Inn Construction Co.* [1980] 1 WLR 711 at 717.
600. Companies Act 2014, s.606.
601. Companies Act 2014, s. 607.
602. Companies Act 2014, s. 606(4) and s. 607(5).
603. Companies Act 2014, s. 606(3).

308. Commencement of a winding up is a crystallizing event which converts any floating charge on all or part of the company's property into a fixed charge. A winding up does not prevent the appointment of a receiver under a debenture, nor does it affect the receiver's entitlement to dispose of the charged assets. But it puts an end to the receiver's express authority to manage the business and to enter into contracts binding on the company for that purpose.

III. Asset-Swelling Measures

309. The whole purpose of winding up a company is to pay off its creditors, according to their priorities, and to distribute anything that might remain among the members or shareholders, according to their rights to repayment of capital and to participation in any surplus. Not alone is the machinery of liquidation organized to this end but the Companies Act 2014 Act contains some major rules that protect creditors and investors against unfair advantage being taken of the company. Several of these are designed to prevent unfair discrimination between creditors. Although section 619 of the 2014 Act applies the general law of bankruptcy to some aspects of winding up insolvent companies, it has been held that this provision, which was replicated in the former Companies Act 1963, did not import those bankruptcy rules that have the effect of increasing the insolvent's assets which are available for the creditors.[604] Nevertheless, various other provisions of the 2014 Act either apply or adapt some of those 'asset-swelling' rules to company liquidations.

A. Examination

310. Chapter 11 of Part 11 of the Companies Act 2014 deals with the court's powers in winding up a company. In particular, section 671 covers the court power to summon persons for examination. Accordingly, the court may summon any officer of the company, any person known or suspected to have in his or her possession any property of the company or supposed to be indebted to the company, or any person whom the court deems capable of giving information relating to the promotion or formation of the company, its trade or dealings, or its affairs or property. These persons may be required to produce any documents related to the company that they possess.[605] They may be required to set out in a written statement an account of transactions between themselves and the company.[606] They moreover may be examined on oath.[607] They may not refuse to answer any question on the grounds that they might incriminate themselves, and any answer by the person to

---

604. *Re Irish Attested Sales Ltd* [1962] IR 70.
605. Companies Act 2014, s. 671(4).
606. Companies Act 2014, s. 671(5).
607. Companies Act 2014, s. 671(3).

such a question may be used against that person in any proceedings except proceedings for the prosecution of that person for an offence (other than perjury).[608] Information gained from these examinations frequently provides the foundation for misfeasance suits and for proceedings for fraudulent or reckless trading. If in the course of an examination of this nature it appears that any person being questioned owes the company money or holds property belonging to it, the court may direct that the money be paid or the property be delivered up to the liquidator.[609]

B. Restitution of Assets Improperly Transferred

311. Section 608 of the 2014 Act facilitates recovery of company assets which have been disposed of in any way that defrauded the company, its creditors or its members. Any liquidator, creditor or contributory of a company which is being wound up, can apply and, if they satisfy the court that the assets were disposed of in that manner, the court is empowered to order its repayment or recovery. That order can be made against any person who appears to have the use, control or possession of such property or of the proceeds from its sale or any development of the property. In deciding to make any order of this nature, account must be taken of the interest of any bona fide purchaser for value of the property.

C. Fraudulent Conveyance

312. Section 10 of the Fraudulent Conveyances Act, 1634, declares void a very wide category of transfers of property by a debtor done with the intention to defraud his/her creditors. The power to set aside transfers of property on these grounds is not an exclusive bankruptcy jurisdiction. This power applies just as much to property transfers made by companies as to transfers by individuals.

D. Unfair Preference

313. What has been said above about fraudulent preferences in bankruptcy applies also to company liquidations but the new Companies Act 2014 has changed the wording from 'fraudulent preference' to 'unfair preference' to clarify that 'fraud' is not a feature of the relevant provisions.[610] Accordingly, a payment or comparable transaction done within six months of the liquidation commencing, with a view to preferring the other party over the remaining creditors is invalid. Moreover, if the person preferred is closely connected with any of the company's directors, the relevant period is extended to two years and the burden of proof is reversed, that is, it is for the preferred connected person to demonstrate that the transaction was done without the proscribed preferential intent. If the company gave a floating charge

---

608. Companies Act 2014, s. 671(7).
609. Companies Act 2014, s. 672.
610. Companies Act 2014, ss 604–605.

over all or part of its assets at any time during the twelve months prior to the liquidation commencing, the charge is invalid if it is shown that the company was indeed insolvent when it was given.[611] Whereas in the above situation the main focus is on the company's intentions at the time in question, here the principal concern is whether the company was not solvent at the time.

E. Fraudulent Trading

314. Where it can be proved that the company was engaged in what is called 'fraudulent trading', those responsible for managing its business at the time can be held liable both in civil law and criminal law. Section 610 imposes civil liability for fraudulent trading, where any person was knowingly a party to the carrying on of any business of the company with intent to defraud creditors of the company. In such circumstances the court may order that the person shall be personally responsible, without any limitation of liability, for all or any part of the debts or other liabilities of the company as the court may direct. Criminal liability is based on section 722.

F. Reckless Trading

315. On account of the obvious difficulties in establishing a case of fraudulent trading, a new head of liability was introduced in 1990, known as 'reckless trading'.[612] The sanction is unlimited liability for all or part of the unpaid debts; there is no equivalent criminal offence and only officers of the company can be held accountable for reckless trading.

316. What constitutes reckless trading is defined in section 610(3) of the Companies Act, 2014 as follows:

> an officer of a company shall be deemed to have been knowingly a party to the carrying on of any business of the company in a reckless manner if
>
> a. the person was a party to the carrying on of such business and, having regard to the general knowledge, skill and experience that may reasonably be expected of a person in his or her position, the person ought to have known that his or her actions or those of the company would cause loss to the creditors of the company, or any of them, or
> b. the person was a party to the contracting of a debt by the company and did not honestly believe on reasonable grounds that the company would be able to pay the debt when it fell due for payment as well as all its other debts (taking into account the contingent and prospective liabilities).

611. Companies Act 2014, s. 597.
612. Companies Act 2014, s. 610.

IV. Proving Debts and Distributions to Creditors

317. Section 619 of the Companies Act 2014 provides that the rules of bankruptcy law apply the respective rights of secured and unsecured creditors and to proving debts of an insolvent company. Accordingly, what has been said above about proof and priority in bankruptcy also applies in this context. The liquidator's job is to distribute whatever sum he/she can fetch for the company's assets among its creditors. Where all secured and preferential creditors (the Revenue, the rates and employees) are paid off, the remainder is distributed among the unsecured creditors ranking pari passu.[613]

613. *See generally* Companies Act 2014, Ch. 7.

Chapter 7. Negotiable Instruments

318. Commercial law has developed a number of payment methods to suit the needs of the commercial community. Amongst the most important, from a legal perspective, are bills of exchange. Although their use today is limited mainly to the commercial sphere, and in particular, international trade, the law on bills of exchange forms the basis of our understanding of a range of other payment mechanisms. Therefore, this chapter concentrates on bills of exchange while considering briefly a number of other mechanisms, such as cheques, promissory notes, bank drafts, automated payments and electronic fund transfers (EFT). Documentary credits and performance bonds are especially important in international transactions and also are considered briefly below.

§1. Negotiable Instruments

319. Bills of exchange, promissory notes and cheques are contractual documents but are distinct and valuable in that they are all negotiable instruments. An instrument is a document which evidences title to a legal right, such as a right to enforce a debt. A negotiable instrument has three features which distinguish it from other contractual rights. First, merely being in possession of a contractual document does not normally allow the holder to enforce the contract; only the parties (or their assignees) to the contract can enforce it by action, under the doctrine of privity of contract. However, the lawful holder of a negotiable instrument can enforce it by action. Second, as an instrument which evidences title to a legal right, a property right, it can therefore be transferred. Generally rights under a contract can only be transferred by formal assignment.[614] However, a negotiable instrument can be transferred without formal assignment, either simply by delivery to the transferee or by delivery and endorsement with the name of the transferee. The transferee is then able to enforce the legal obligation evidenced by the instrument. Third, the transferee of a *negotiable* instrument, unlike other contractual assignments where the transferee takes subject to equities, may take it free of any defects in the transferor's title and defences which could have been set-up against the transferor.[615]

§2. Bills of Exchange

320. A bill of exchange is an order by one person (the *drawer*) to another person (the *drawee*) to pay a sum of money to a person (the *payee*). The payee may enforce the bill himself/herself by presenting it for payment in accordance with its terms, or may sell (or 'discount') it to a third party, transferring it to the third party in return for an immediate cash payment. The transferee will then enforce the bill in due course, or may in turn himself/herself transfer it. Importantly, a bill contains

614. *See*, e.g., Supreme Court of Judicature (Ireland) Act 1877, s. 28(6).
615. *See Belfast Banking Co. v. Doherty* (1879) 4 LR (Ir) 124 at 134.

an *unconditional* contractual undertaking to pay a sum of money to the payee.[616] Hence, the undertaking to pay contained in the bill is largely independent of any underlying transaction, so that the bill can be enforced regardless of any alleged breaches in the underlying contract.[617] The drawer and drawee are parties to the bill and are liable to honour the payment undertaking. The drawee is the person primarily liable to honour the bill; however, liability depends on signature. The drawer is therefore immediately liable on the bill but the drawee is only liable on it if it is presented to him/her for acceptance and he/she accepts the obligation it contains by signing it.

321. Today, bills of exchange are used mainly in a commercial context. In relation to international sales, where goods are sold and are being transported abroad, frequently the seller draws a bill on the buyer for the price, under which the buyer is to make payment at the stated time. The seller can then 'discount' that bill at his/her bank or through the bills market, thereby obtaining cash before the goods are actually delivered to the buyer. Bills are particularly appropriate where goods are being sold on credit. For instance, if the price is to be paid six months after the goods are shipped, a bill can be drawn at the time of shipment and immediately discounted, the seller thereby getting the funds which the buyer does not have to pay for another six months. Bills are also used as a means of raising credit for business operations, when drawn under acceptance credits. In order to raise finance, by agreement, an enterprise may draw a bill on a bank, whereby the bank agrees to pay money on a specified date to the drawer or to someone designated by him/her. The drawer will then discount the bill. When the payment date arrives, the person who acquired the bill from the drawer or his/her successor in title will present it for payment to the accepting bank. A related type of transaction is where one enterprise allows another to draw a bill on it, so that the drawer can raise finance. This is called an 'accommodation bill', whereby the drawee simply accommodates the drawer in his/her quest for funds, on the understanding that the drawer will put the acceptor in funds by the time payment is due.

322. Therefore, the great attraction of bills of exchange is their negotiable nature, including their transferability and their autonomy from the underlying transaction. The law relating to bills of exchange is contained in the Bills of Exchange Act 1882,[618] a consolidating statute which sought to codify the pre-existing case law on bills of exchange, cheques and promissory notes.

I. Definition

323. The 1882 Act defines a bill of exchange as:

616. *Walek v. Seafield* [1978] IR 167; *Nova (Jersey) Knit Ltd v. Kammgarn Spinnerei GmbH* [1977] 2 All ER 463.
617. The only exception to this general rule is where the breach gives rise to a total failure of consideration for which the bill was given or a partial failure in a quantified amount: *Nova (Jersey) Knit Ltdv. Kammgarn Spinnerei GmbH* [1977] 2 All ER 463 at 480.
618. *See also* the Cheques Act 1959; and the Consumer Credit Act 1995, s. 41.

> an unconditional order in writing addressed by one person to another, signed by the person giving it, requiring the person to whom it is addressed to pay on demand or at a fixed or determinable future time a sum certain in money to or to the order of a specified person, or to bearer.[619]

An instrument which does not comply with these conditions is not a valid bill of exchange:[620] it can be described as 'incomplete' or 'inchoate'. However, any person in possession of an incomplete bill has prima facie authority to complete it.[621]

II. Transfer

324. A significant number of bills of exchange are not presented for payment by the original payee but are transferred to a third party (usually in return for payment) who may present the bill themselves or transfer it again to another party. Prima facie, all bills of exchange are transferable unless their transferability is restricted by the parties. A bill payable 'to X only', or crossed 'not transferable' or 'not negotiable' is not transferable.[622] The method by which a bill is transferred depends on whether it is a bearer bill or an order bill.[623] A bearer bill can be transferred by simple delivery.[624] Delivery means the transfer of possession, actual or constructive, from one person to another.[625] In contrast, an order bill is transferred by endorsement and delivery.[626] In order to endorse a bill the payee must sign his/her name, either on the reverse of the bill or on a slip of paper attached to the bill and known as an 'allonge'.[627] The endorsement may be general, special or restrictive.

325. A 'general' endorsement consists merely of the payee's signature. Its effect is to convert an order bill into a bearer bill, so that after a general endorsement the bill can be transferred by simple delivery.[628] However, any holder can convert a generally endorsed bill back into an order bill by writing the name of a person as transferee/payee above the endorser's signature. A 'special' endorsement consists of the payee's signature together with the name of a person to whom the bill is to be transferred, for example, 'pay F White' printed above the endorser's signature.[629] This converts a bill into an order bill. A 'restrictive' endorsement limits the further transfer of the bill, either by prohibiting further transfer or by indicating that it is transferred in order to be dealt with in a particular way.[630] For instance, the bill in the example above might be endorsed by the payee 'pay F White only' in which case

619. 1882 Act, s. 3(1).
620. 1882 Act, s. 3(2).
621. 1882 Act, s. 20.
622. 1882 Act, s. 8(1).
623. 1882 Act, s. 8(2).
624. 1882 Act, s. 31(2).
625. 1882 Act, s. 2.
626. 1882 Act, s. 31(3).
627. 1882 Act, s. 32(1).
628. 1882 Act, s. 34(1).
629. 1882 Act, s. 34(2).
630. 1882 Act, s. 35.

F White cannot further transfer the bill. In the absence of a restrictive endorsement there is (in theory) no limit to the number of times a bill may be transferred.

A. Forged and Unauthorized Signatures

326. An order bill can only be transferred by endorsement with the signature of the payee or last endorsee. This makes an order bill more secure against theft than a bearer bill. The legislation provides that a forged or unauthorized signature has no effect, and the transferee acquires no title to the bill through a forged or unauthorized endorsement.[631] The distinction between a forged endorsement and one which is merely unauthorized is unclear and may be difficult to draw but it is clear that an unauthorized endorsement can, while a forged endorsement cannot, be ratified.[632] However, a forged endorsement is not wholly ineffective. A person who takes a bill as a result of a forged endorsement can enforce the bill against the person who transferred the bill to him/her (the forger) but not against persons who became parties to the bill before the forgery. Further, a person who takes a bill as a result of forged endorsement may be able to retain it as against the true holder if the holder is estopped from setting up the forgery or unauthorized signature. In addition, where a bill is drawn payable to a non-existent or fictitious payee, it is treated as a bearer bill so that it can be transferred without endorsement.[633] A person to whom such a bill is endorsed can therefore acquire title to it and enforce it notwithstanding the fact that the signature on the bill is a 'forgery' since his/her title to the bill does not depend on the signature.

III. Holders

327. The person entitled to enforce a bill of exchange, by presenting it for payment or by taking enforcement proceedings if it is dishonoured, is called 'the holder' of the bill. Only payment to the holder of a bill can discharge the payer's liability on the bill. The holder of a bearer bill is the bearer; the holder of an order bill is the payee or endorsee in possession of it.[634] The 1882 Act recognizes three classes of holder, each with different rights:

- holders;
- holders for value;
- holders in due course.

631. 1882 Act, s. 24.
632. 1882 Act, s. 24.
633. 1882 Act, s. 7(3).
634. 1882 Act, s. 2.

Since 'holder' status depends, at least in part, on possession of the bill,[635] only one person can be a holder of a bill at any time. Having decided who is the holder, it will then be necessary to classify the holder into one of these three classes above in order to decide what rights he/she enjoys and what, if any, defences can be raised against him/her if he/she seeks to enforce the bill. The basic distinction between the three classes relates to the giving of consideration for the bill.

A. Mere Holder

328. A mere holder is a person in possession of the bill where no value has ever been given for the bill. The mere holder has fewest rights. He/she is entitled:

- to transfer the bill
- to insert the date in the bill if it has been omitted and
- to present the bill for payment.

However, he/she cannot benefit from the negotiable aspect of the bill, and so his/her rights are subject to prior equities and defects.

B. Holder for Value

329. A holder will be a holder for value[636] if he/she, or any previous holder,[637] provided consideration for the bill. For this purpose consideration is defined widely to include any consideration which would be sufficient to support a simple contract, or an antecedent debt or liability of the person against whom the bill is to be enforced.[638] This appears to be an exception to the rule that past consideration is not sufficient consideration.

C. Holder in Due Course

330. A holder for value can enforce the bill even though the person against whom he/she enforces it received no consideration for his/her promise to pay; however, other defences may be raised against a holder for value; for instance, that the bill was obtained by fraud or duress. A holder in due course,[639] however, can enforce the bill free from all defences and defects in title or his/her predecessors in

635. 1882 Act, s. 2.
636. 1882 Act, s. 27.
637. 1882 Act, s. 27(2).
638. 1882 Act, s. 27(1).
639. 1882 Act, s. 29.

title: in these circumstances the bill is truly negotiable. Every holder is rebuttably presumed to be a holder in due course.[640] A holder in due course is defined in section 29(1) of the 1882 Act as:

> a holder who has taken a bill complete and regular on the face of it, under the following conditions, namely,
>
> a. that he became the holder of it before it was overdue and without notice that it had previously been dishonoured, if such was the fact;
> b. that he took the bill in good faith [641] and for value, and that at the time the bill was negotiated to him he had no notice of any defect in the title of the person who negotiated it.

331. The meaning of 'holder in due course' was one of the issues which arose in *Shield Life Insurance Co Ltd & O'Callaghan v. Ulster Bank.*[642] In this case the defendant bank argued that it was a holder in due course and hence that it held the bill free from any previous defects in title. Two separate frauds had been perpetrated by an insurance broker, O'Callaghan. With regard to the first fraud, Mrs Murphy drew a cheque on her bank in favour of the plaintiff, Shield Life, which she gave to O'Callaghan for transmission to the plaintiff. O'Callaghan endorsed the cheque with the name of his own company and took the cheque to his own bank, the defendant bank, where he lodged some of the proceeds to his office account and the remainder to his client account. He later withdrew the amount from his client account. In an action for conversion by the plaintiff, Shield Life, the defendant bank argued that it was a holder in due course because it took the cheque in good faith for value. While assuming that the defendant bank had given value for the cheque when it credited the amount of the cheque to its customer's account before receiving payment through the clearing system, the court found that the bank was not a holder in due course for three reasons. First, to be a holder in due course, a person must first be a holder, as defined in section 2 of the 1882 Act, which: 'means a payee or indorsee of a bill ... or the bearer thereof'. Bearer, in turn, 'means the person in possession of the bill ... which is payable to bearer'. The court found that the defendant did not come within any of these definitions. The payee was the plaintiff, Shield Life, and therefore there could be no bearer, and the cheque had not been properly endorsed to the bank and so the bank was not an endorsee. Second, there was an irregularity on the face of the cheque because it had not been endorsed by the payee before being transferred. And third, the absence of an endorsement meant that the bank had notice of the defect in title of the person negotiating the cheque.

---

640. 1882 Act, s. 32(2).
641. 1882 Act, s. 90 defines good faith as an action done honestly, whether it is done negligently or not. It has been held that a holder will not have acted in good faith if he/she has been willfully blind and deliberately avoided having notice of possible defects: *Jones v. Gordon* (1877) 2 All Cas. 616; *Bank of Ireland v. EBS* [1998] 2 ILRM 451.
642. [1995] 3 IR 225.

332. Once a bill has come into the hands of a holder in due course, all prior defects in title are cured. Subsequent holders can therefore enforce the bill against all persons who became party to it before it came into the hands of the holder in due course, free of all defects in title, even if they are aware of them. The only exception is that a person who acquires a bill through a holder in due course cannot take free of defects if he/she was party to the conduct which gave rise to the defect.[643]

IV. Liability on a Bill of Exchange

333. The general rule is that every person who puts his/her name to a bill, as drawer, acceptor or endorser, becomes liable on it and the bill can be enforced against him/her by persons to whom it is subsequently transferred. In addition, a person who transfers a bearer bill may be liable in certain circumstances if it is dishonoured. The person primarily liable is the acceptor or, if the drawee fails to accept, the drawer; other parties are only liable if the person primarily liable fails to honour the bill.

A. *Capacity*

334. No one can be held liable on a bill unless he/she has the capacity to incur contractual liability.[644] So, for example, an infant or minor will not be liable on a bill. Where a party lacks capacity he/she cannot be held liable on the bill but the bill remains valid and fully enforceable against other parties.

B. *Signature*

335. A person's liability on a bill prima facie depends on him/her having signed it.[645] Difficulties arise if a person whose signature appears on a bill claims that it was placed there without his/her authority. The signature may be forged or unauthorized.[646] A person whose signature on a bill is forged incurs no liability unless he/she is estopped from asserting the forgery, as, for instance, if, having become aware that his/her signature on the bill had been forged, he/she stood by while the person seeking to enforce the bill gave value for it. If the drawer's signature on the bill is forged there is no bill of exchange at all. In the case of unauthorized signatures, a person incurs no liability on a bill through an unauthorized signature unless

643. 1882 Act, s. 29(3).
644. 1882 Act, s. 22.
645. 1882 Act, s. 23.
646. 1882 Act, s. 24.

(i) he/she is estopped from denying the signor's authority or (ii) he/she subsequently ratifies the signature. An agent who signs a bill on behalf of his/her principal may incur personal liability on it if he/she signs his/her own name, unless his/her signature clearly indicates that he/she signs as agent and does not undertake personal liability.[647]

C. Delivery

336. Every contract on a bill is incomplete and revocable until the bill is delivered.[648] The only exceptional case, where liability is complete without delivery, is if the drawee of a bill notifies the person entitled to payment that he/she accepts the bill. 'Delivery' means the transfer of possession, actual or constructive, from one person to another.[649] Delivery may be conditional: for instance, if a person orders goods and gives the seller a bill of exchange for the price, he/she may deliver the bill conditionally on delivery of the goods. Since delivery is necessary to complete liability on a bill, a person who signs a bill and then loses it, or has it stolen, is prima facie not liable on it. However, it is rebuttably presumed that a bill has been delivered by every signatory to it and if the bill comes into the hands of a holder in due course it is irrebuttably presumed that it has been delivered by all prior parties to it.[650] Hence, the transferability of bills is promoted.

D. The Undertakings

337. Each person who becomes a party to a bill by signing and delivering it gives certain contractual undertakings relating to its payment. In addition, each party is bound by certain estoppels relating to existing facts and events prior to his/her becoming a party to the bill.

1. Acceptor

338. The acceptor is the party primarily liable on the bill. By accepting the bill he/she undertakes that at maturity he/she will honour the bill in accordance with the terms of his/her acceptance. In addition, as against a holder in due course, he/she is estopped from denying (a) the drawer's existence, capacity and authority to draw the bill; (b) the genuineness of the drawer's signature; and (c) the payee's existence and capacity to endorse the bill.[651]

647. 1882 Act, s. 26(1).
648. 1882 Act, s. 21.
649. 1882 Act, s. 2.
650. 1882 Act, s. 22(2).
651. 1882 Act, s. 54.

2. Accommodation Party

339. A person may accept a bill in order to promote its image by lending the value of his/her name to the bill to increase its marketability. Such a person is referred to as 'an accommodation party'.[652] Where a person accepts a bill as an accommodation party the drawer, and not the acceptor, is primarily liable on the bill.

3. Drawer

340. The drawer's liability can be described as secondary in that the drawer does not undertake to pay the bill. Instead, the drawer undertakes that on presentation the bill will be accepted and paid and that if not he/she will compensate the holder or any endorsee who pays the bill, provided that the necessary dishonour proceedings are taken. The drawer's undertaking to pay compensation following dishonour will normally include the value of the bill, plus interest and the cost of enforcement.[653] As against a holder in due course, he/she is estopped from denying the existence of the payee and his/her capacity to endorse the bill.[654]

4. Endorser

341. Each person who endorses the bill becomes party to it and gives the same undertakings as the drawer.[655] He/she is estopped, as against a holder in due course, from denying the genuineness and regularity of the drawer's signature or of any endorsements prior to his/her own.[656] In addition, as against subsequent endorsees he/she is estopped from denying that the bill was valid and that he/she had a good title to it at the time of his/her endorsement.[657]

342. The drawer and endorsers of the bill can avoid liability on it by drawing/endorsing it 'without recourse', in which case he/she will add the words 'without recourse' or 'sans recourse' after his/her signature to indicate to future parties that he/she accepts no liability for the bill's being honoured.

---

652. 1882 Act, s. 28.
653. 1882 Act, s. 57.
654. 1882 Act, s. 55(1).
655. 1882 Act, s. 55(2)(a).
656. 1882 Act, s. 55(2)(b).
657. 1882 Act, s. 55(2)(c).

5. Transferor of a Bearer Bill

343. A bearer bill can be transferred by delivery, without signature, and hence the transferor of a bearer bill does not become a party to the bill. However, a person who transfers a bearer bill by simple delivery gives the following warranties to the transferee:

(a) that the bill is genuine as it purports to be
(b) that he/she has the right to transfer it
(c) that he/she is not aware of any facts which make the bill worthless.[658]

If the holder of a bearer bill signs it, he/she becomes a party to the bill and is liable as an endorser.

V. Procedures for Enforcement

344. Unless a bill is an accommodation bill, the person primarily liable to honour it is the drawee. However, if he/she fails to honour it, either by refusing to accept or pay it, the holder may take steps against any prior party to the bill to enforce their undertakings with regard to the bill, as described above. The 1882 Act prescribes certain steps which the holder must take on dishonour if he/she is to enforce the bill against anyone other than the drawee; generally failure to take the prescribed steps will release some or all previous parties from liability on the bill.

A. *Presentation of the Bill*

345. Generally, the holder must present the bill (unless it is a demand bill):[659]

- for acceptance
- for payment.

A bill payable 'X days after sight' must be presented for acceptance to fix the date of payment,[660] and it must be presented within a reasonable time.[661] If the bill is not presented within a reasonable time, the drawer and any prior endorsers are released from liability.[662] Where a bill expressly stipulates that it must be presented for acceptance, or where a bill is drawn payable elsewhere than at the residence or place

658. 1882 Act, s. 58.
659. 1882 Act, s. 39.
660. 1882 Act, s. 39(1).
661. 1882 Act, s. 40(1). On what constitutes 'reasonable time' *see* s. 40(3).
662. 1882 Act, s. 40(2).

of business of the drawee, it must be presented for acceptance.[663] Otherwise, presentation for acceptance is not required.[664] The statutory rules on acceptance are set out in sections 39–44 and are very detailed. For example, where required, presentation must be to the drawee or his/her authorized representative (often a bank).[665] Presentation may be excused in certain circumstances, as where presentation is impossible despite the exercise of reasonable diligence.[666] But, presentation is not excused because the holder believes that the bill will not be accepted on presentation.[667]

346. All bills of exchange must be presented for payment in accordance with the statutory rules.[668] If not properly presented, the drawer and any prior endorsers are released from liability.[669] Generally, presentation for payment must take place at the correct time and place. For instance, where the bill is a 'time bill' it must be presented for payment on the day the bill falls due.[670] Where the bill is a demand bill, it must be presented for payment within a reasonable time of its issue to make the drawer liable and a reasonable time after its endorsement to make the endorser liable.[671] Presentation for payment may be excused in limited circumstances, as where presentation is impossible despite the exercise of reasonable diligence,[672] but otherwise, failure to present for payment at the proper time and place operates to release prior parties.

B. *Notice of Dishonour*

347. Once presented, the drawee must deal with the bill of exchange either by discharge or by dishonour. If the drawee fails to accept the bill as drawn,[673] or, having accepted it, fails to pay it,[674] the bill is dishonoured by non-acceptance or non-payment, as appropriate. In that case the holder can enforce the undertakings given by the drawer or endorsers but in order to do so must within a reasonable time give

663. 1882 Act, s. 39(2).
664. 1882 Act, s. 39(3).
665. 1882 Act, s. 41(1).
666. 1882 Act, s. 41(2).
667. 1882 Act, s. 41(3).
668. 1882 Act, ss 45–46.
669. 1882 Act, s. 45.
670. 1882 Act, s. 45(1).
671. 1882 Act, s. 45(2). On what constitutes 'reasonable time' *see* s. 45(2). There is a difference, for example, in what is reasonable for an ordinary holder presenting a cheque for payment and for a banker presenting a customer's cheque for payment, with the ordinary holder being given more time: *Royal Bank of Ireland v. O ' Rourke* [1962] IR 159 where it was held that a bank presenting a cheque for payment was not bound to present the cheque for payment on the day it received it, but had until post time the following day to transmit it to the paying bank. *See also Brennan v. Bank of Ireland* (unreported, High Court, 23 May 1985); cf. *Barclays Bank plcv. Bank of England* [1985] 1 All ER 385.
672. 1882 Act, s. 46(2).
673. 1882 Act, s. 43.
674. 1882 Act, s. 47.

notice of dishonour to every previous party to be held liable.[675] The legislation contains detailed rules on the timing and content of the notice.[676] Notice of dishonour is excused in certain circumstances,[677] but generally failure to notify any party of dishonour in accordance with the legislative rules will release that party from liability on the bill,[678] unless the bill is subsequently negotiated to a holder in due course. A notice of dishonour given by one party to another protects not only the person giving the notice but also all intermediate parties in the liability chain.[679]

VI. Defences to Liability

348. A person against whom it is sought to enforce a bill of exchange may raise a number of defences in order to seek to avoid liability. The validity of some of these defences depends on whether the relationship between the person seeking to enforce the bill and the person against whom the bill is to be enforced is immediate or remote. The relationships between drawer and drawee, drawer and payee, and endorser and endorsee are all immediate: all other relationships are remote. Thus, the relationship between a person to whom a bill is endorsed and the original acceptor of the bill is remote.

349. First, as against an immediate party, a person may avoid liability on a bill by showing that his/her undertaking on the bill is voidable on the grounds of duress, misrepresentation or undue influence. These are personal defences and cannot be raised against a remote party who is a holder in due course. Further, as against an immediate party, a person may avoid liability by showing that there is a total failure of the consideration for which that undertaking was given; there may be such a failure as a result of a breach of the underlying contract. This is also a personal defence. Second, a person may deny liability to the person seeking to enforce the bill by showing that that person has no title to it, because it was stolen, for example, or, by showing that he/she is not a party to the bill on the grounds that /her signature on the bill was forged or placed there without his/her authority. Third, a person may deny liability by showing that there is no valid bill, because the statutory requirements for a valid bill are not fulfilled. Fourth, a person other than the acceptor may avoid liability by showing that the required proceedings were not taken on dishonour. And lastly, a person may avoid liability by showing that the bill has been materially altered without his/her consent.[680] If a bill is materially altered and the alteration is apparent, the bill is wholly avoided as against all persons who became party to the bill before the alteration, unless they consent to it. Where the alteration is not apparent, a holder in due course may enforce the bill against persons who

---

675. 1882 Act, s. 48, esp. s. 49(12) on reasonable time. *See further Royal Bank of Ireland v. O ' Rourke* [1962] IR 159.
676. 1882 Act, s. 49.
677. 1882 Act, s. 50.
678. 1882 Act, s. 48.
679. 1882 Act, ss 49(3) and (4).
680. 1882 Act, s. 64(2).

became party to it prior to the alteration in accordance with its original terms. An altered bill may be enforced *as altered* against any person who becomes party to it after the alteration.

VII. Discharge of the Bill

350. The person primarily liable on a bill of exchange is the drawee/acceptor. However, if he/she fails to honour the bill, the holder may either:

- seek to enforce his/her undertaking on the bill by legal action; or
- enforce the bill against one of the other parties liable on it, provided the appropriate proceedings have been taken on dishonour.

If anyone other than the drawee/acceptor pays the bill, all subsequent parties are discharged from liability but the bill generally remains enforceable against prior parties. An endorser who pays a bill may either:

- cancel all endorsements subsequent to his/her own and reissue it for value; or
- enforce the bill against a previous party.

If the drawer pays the bill he/she may enforce it against the drawee/acceptor, unless it was an accommodation bill. The undertakings contained in the bill therefore remain enforceable until the bill is discharged.

351. A bill may be discharged in the following ways. First, by payment in due course by or on behalf of the drawee/acceptor. A payment is only 'in due course' if made:

- on or after maturity
- to the holder
- in good faith without notice of any defect in the holder's title.[681]

Second, a bill can be discharged by the acceptor becoming the holder of the bill because any legal action by the holder against himself/herself would be impossible.[682] Third, a bill may be discharged by the holder renouncing his/her rights either on the bill as a whole or against one or more individual parties.[683] Fourth, a bill may be discharged by cancellation of the bill or of the liability of one or more parties.[684] And lastly, a bill may be partially discharged where it is materially altered without the assent of all parties liable on the bill.[685]

---

681. 1882 Act, s. 59(1).
682. 1882 Act, s. 61.
683. 1882 Act, s. 62.
684. 1882 Act, s. 63.
685. 1882 Act, s. 64.

§3. CHEQUES

352. The use of cheques is now in decline with the rise in the use of other payment mechanisms including automated payments, such as direct debits and standing orders. Nevertheless, cheques remain an important payment method in business-to-business payments.[686]

I. Definition

353. A cheque is defined by section 73 of the Bills of Exchange Act 1882 as:

> a bill of exchange drawn on a banker payable on demand.

It follows therefore that a valid cheque must satisfy the requirements for a valid bill of exchange.[687] In general, the law applicable to bills of exchange applies equally to cheques although there are rules which apply specifically to cheques and not bills of exchange.[688] However, cheques are used very differently from other types of bills of exchange. Commonly cheques are used to withdraw cash or to pay a third party: they are rarely negotiated.

354. A cheque is an order from a customer to his/her bank to pay money in accordance with the terms of the cheque. The bank makes the payment out of its own funds and recoups the amount by debiting the customer's account, hence reducing its indebtedness to the customer.[689] Unlike other bills of exchange, a cheque is not accepted by the drawee, so that the bank on which it is drawn is under no obligation to the payee to honour the cheque. Instead, primary liability on a cheque falls on the drawer.[690] However, the drawee bank is, in all cases, under an obligation to its customer to honour cheques drawn by him/her so long as there are sufficient funds in his/her account to meet the cheque. Where a bank wrongfully dishonours a cheque when there are funds available,[691] the bank is liable to the customer for breach of contract and the customer can sue the bank for damages for any loss

686. *See* ECBs *Statistical Data Warehouse (*formerly *Blue Book)* which describes payment system instruments, payment systems and securities settlement systems in all Member States of the EU: *see further* https://www.ecb.europa.eu/stats/payment_statistics/payment_services/html/index.en.html.
687. *See* para. 311 above.
688. *See* Part III of the 1882 Act and the Cheques Act 1959.
689. *Foley v. Hill* (1848) 2 HLC 28.
690. This rule was modified where a cheque was supported by a cheque guarantee card, in which case the bank was under an obligation to the payee, but that obligation was based on the undertaking contained in the guarantee card rather than any undertaking in the cheque itself: *First Sport Ltd v. Barclays Bank plc* [1993] 3 All ER 789. However, from 31 Dec. 2011, the cheque guarantee card scheme in Ireland ceased to operate due to limited usage of the scheme and the decline in cheque numbers more generally.
691. *Marzetti v. Williams* 1 B & Ad 415.

caused. Moreover, where a cheque is returned unpaid, the wording on the cheque, such as 'refer to drawer', may be defamatory thereby allowing the customer to sue for damages for defamation.[692]

II. Obtaining Payment

355. A payee can obtain payment of the sum ordered in the cheque in three different ways. First, as a bill of exchange, a cheque can be presented to the drawee for cash payment. Hence, a payee can personally present the cheque for payment at the bank branch where it is drawn, that is, the branch where the drawer holds his/her account. This may be impractical for the payee and so second, as an alternative, a payee can use his/her own bank to act as agent to present the cheque for payment on his/her behalf. In such circumstances, the cheque is presented through the clearing system, and the cheque is credited to the payee's account by his/her own bank. Third, a cheque may be transferred to a third party for an immediate cash payment. In effect the third party buys the cheque and presents it for payment on its own behalf. However, the choice of payment may be limited by a crossing on the cheque, affecting its transferability.

III. Crossing Cheques

356. As a bill of exchange, a cheque is a negotiable instrument and hence is transferable. However, such transferability exposes the holder or payee to the risk of theft or fraud. Crossings or other markings on a cheque can restrict its transferability and hence make it more secure. Different forms of crossing have different legal effects. Three forms of crossing are covered in the 1882 Act: a general crossing; a special crossing; and a not-negotiable crossing. A further type of crossing, 'account payee', has no legislative basis in Ireland.

357. The simplest form of crossing is a general crossing. This is effected by drawing two parallel lines across the face of the cheque; the words 'and company' or '& Co' can be inserted between the lines.[693] As a result, the cheque must be presented for payment through a bank account; it cannot be cashed. Alternatively, a cheque can be specially crossed. This involves inserting the name of a particular bank between the parallel lines,[694] and the effect is that the cheque can only be presented for payment at the bank named. In addition, generally or specially crossed cheques can be marked or crossed with the words 'not negotiable'. This type of

692. *Pike v. Hibernian Bank* [1950] IR 195; *Kinlan v. Ulster Bank* [1928] IR 171 at 183; *Jayson v. Midland Bank Ltd* [1968] I Lloyd's Rep 409.
693. 1882 Act, s. 76(1).
694. 1882 Act, s. 76(2).

crossing negatives the negotiability of the cheque, that is, if the cheque is transferred, the transferee can obtain no better title than the transferor. Importantly, such a crossing does not prevent the cheque from being transferred.[695]

358. In order to make cheques more secure, the practice has developed of generally crossing a cheque and putting the words 'account payee' or 'account of F White' between the two parallel lines. The intention is to ensure that the cheque can be lodged into the payee's or F White's account only. The legal effect of this type of crossing is unclear,[696] and has been addressed by legislation in the UK. There, under the Cheques Act 1992, such a crossing has the effect of rendering the cheque non-transferable and valid only as between the parties thereto.[697] No similar legislation exists in Ireland.

IV. The Clearing System

359. The cheque clearing system is operated by the Irish Paper Clearing Company CLG (Irish Paper Clearing Company Ltd (IPCC)).[698] But, not all cheques are cleared through the IPCC: some cheques can be collected locally. As noted above, a cheque can be presented for payment at the bank branch where it was drawn, that is, at the drawer's branch. In these circumstances the cheque can be cleared internally at the branch, and payment can be received in one business day, without the need for the services of the IPCC. Similarly, if a cheque is presented for payment at a different branch of the same bank on which it is drawn, payment can be made through the bank's internal collection system without the need to utilize the clearing system operated by the IPCC. However, where a payee lodges a cheque with his/her own bank, a bank different from the bank on which the cheque is drawn, the payee's bank acts as his/her agent in presenting the cheque for payment.[699] This presentation is operated through the clearing system. Today, presentation of a cheque for payment involves a bilateral exchange of cheques between members of the IPCC. Settlement of the cheques exchanged each day is made on a multilateral net basis, and takes place through members' accounts held at the Central Bank. The whole process is slow taking from three days, if the cheque is honoured, to five days, where the cheque is dishonoured, to complete. Because most cheque payments involve two banks, the collecting and the paying bank, cheques are particularly susceptible to theft and fraud. As a result, legislation offers collecting and

695. 1882 Act, s. 81; *see also Shield Life Insurance Co. Ltd & O ' Callaghan v. Ulster Bank* [1995] 3 IR 225.
696. *National Bank v. Silk* [1891] 1 QB 435.
697. The 1992 Act inserted a new s. 81(a)(1) into the 1882 Act.
698. The members of this Company include the main banks, and the Central Bank. Where a non-member bank wishes to use the system they must engage a member bank to act as agent on their behalf.
699. On presentation of bills of exchange for payment *see* 1882 Act, s. 45. *See further Royal Bank of Ireland v. O ' Rourke* [1962] IR 159.

paying banks protection where cheques are forged provided generally that the paying bank acts in good faith and in the ordinary course of business,[700] or that the collecting bank acted in good faith and without negligence.[701]

§4. Promissory Notes

360. A promissory note is a promise to pay a sum of money. Banknotes are promissory notes; notes other than banknotes are no longer widely used other than in international transactions. They may be used as a form of security for a loan, the lender requiring the borrower to provide a promissory note for the amount of the loan.[702] A promissory note is defined as:

> an unconditional promise made in writing by one person to another signed by the maker, engaging to pay on demand or at a fixed or determinable future time, a sum certain in money to, or to the order of, a specified person or to bearer.[703]

A valid note must comply with all aspects of this definition. A note must be distinguished from an IOU which is a mere acknowledgement of a debt rather than a promise to pay. The definition of a promissory note is similar to that of a bill of exchange and the law relating to bills and notes is largely similar. It follows that a note can be transferred and negotiated in the same way as a bill. The law relating to notes is contained in Part III of the Bills of Exchange Act 1882. The main difference between bills and notes is that a note is never accepted: it is a promise, rather than an order, to pay. And since, unlike a bill, a note is not accepted, liability to honour a note falls on the maker and any endorser.

§5. Bank Drafts

361. A bank draft is a draft drawn by a bank on itself requiring it to pay a specified amount to a named payee. A bank draft does not qualify as a bill of exchange because the drawer and the drawee/acceptor are not separate persons.[704] However, although bank drafts are not bills of exchange or cheques, they are made subject to the Cheques Act 1959.[705] Bank drafts are commonly used where the payee wishes to be as certain of payment as may be possible. Because the draft is drawn on a bank there is little doubt as to payment, unless the bank becomes insolvent. Bank drafts can also be used by persons who do not hold a current account or have chequebook facilities.

700. 1882 Act, ss 60 and 80, and the Cheques Act 1959, s. 1.
701. Cheques Act 1959, s. 4; *see further Shield Life Insurance Co. Ltd & O ' Callaghan v. Ulster Bank* [1995] 3 IR 225.
702. Their use is restricted by the Consumer Credit Act 1995, s. 41.
703. 1882 Act, s. 83.
704. 1882 Act, s. 3.
705. 1959 Act, s. 1(2).

§6. Automated Payments and EFT

362. Developments in technology have led to huge changes in modern banking practices and the development of a variety of different payment service providers. Traditional payment methods, such as cheques, are in decline, while automated payments and electronic funds transfers (EFTs) are on the increase.[706] Moreover, banking and other payment services are being provided directly to the office or the home via the Internet or mobile phone rather than in person at the bank's branch office.

363. Automated payments comprise standing orders, direct credits and direct debits. Payments may be initiated either by the payer or by the payee. Credit transfers are initiated by the payer and are used for regular repeat payments. In contrast, direct debits are initiated by the payee, who obtains authority from the payer to order the payer's bank, for example, to make such payments as the payee may demand from time to time. Direct debits are used for regular payments where the amount may differ, such as with utility bills and mortgage repayments at a variable rate. Automated payments offer convenience all around. Payments are made directly from the payer's bank or other payment service provider to the payee's bank/payment service provider. Where repeat payments have to be made, such as with standing orders or direct debit mandates, one written authority is all that is needed. Automated payments also reduce the potential for fraud.

364. EFTs describe a number of different systems in which the instruction to a credit institution or payment service provider to make a payment to the credit of a particular payee, or to debit a particular account, is given by electronic means, normally using a computer system.[707] Examples include the use of automated teller machines (ATMs) used for cash withdrawals, and EFT at point of sale (EFTPOS) used for the payment of goods or services. These latter two mechanisms offer convenience and security to consumers, though they are of limited use to business customers as payment mechanisms.

365. Payment services, including automated payments and EFTs, are now regulated in the EU by Directive 2015/2366 on payment services in the internal market (PSD2)[708] which replaces the first Payment Services Directive[709] and makes important changes to the regulatory framework, including by expanding the range of services that come within its scope; clarifying the extent of user/consumer rights and provider obligations; and introducing more stringent security and authentication requirements. Its underlying rationale is to facilitate market entry of new providers, technical innovations, and efficiency of the provision of payment services thereby enhancing the EU's Digital Market and growth in e-commerce.

---

706. *See* above. *See also* Directive 2009/110/EC on the supervision of the business of electronic money institutions [2009] OJ L267/7.
707. *See further* UNCITRAL's Legal Guide on Electronic Funds Transfers (1987): *see* www.uncitral.o rg.
708. Directive (EU) 2015/2366 on payment services in the internal market, [2015] OJ L 337/35.
709. Directive 2007/64/EC [2015] OJ L 337/35 transposed in Ireland by the European Communities (Payment Services) Regulations 2009 (S.I. No. 383 of 2009): both now repealed/revoked.

366. The PSD2 is transposed in Irish law by the European Union (EU) (Payment Services) Regulations 2018[710] (the '2018 Regulations'). In summary, the 2018 Regulations set out the authorization framework for payment service providers in Part 2; Part 3 outlines information and transparency requirements; while Part 4 sets out parties' rights and obligations in relation to the provision and use of payment services. Most of the 2018 Regulations came into force on 13 January 2018. However, due to delays in the development of the required Regulatory Technical Standards (RTS) in respect of authentication and security, some provisions will not come into force until 18 months from the date that the RTS enters into force.[711] Commencement of these measures is now expected in late 2019/early 2020.

367. The information requirements and the substantive requirements, rights and obligations in Parts 3 and 4 apply in respect of payment service providers established in the State or providing a payment service to a user in the State, including through an agent.[712] Most of the requirements can be contracted out of, except in contracts involving consumers and microenterprises.[713]

368. Regulation 93 addresses the limited obligations of a payment service user. These include using a payment services instrument in accordance with the terms governing its issue and use, although these terms must be 'objective, non-discriminatory and proportionate'. Further, the users must notify the payment service provider, without undue delay on becoming aware of the loss, theft, misappropriation or unauthorized use of the payment instrument. Importantly, the user's failure to comply with these and other obligations will result in the reduction/ removal of provider liability in respect of unauthorized payments.

369. Regulation 94 deals with the obligations of the service provider in relation to payment instruments. These include:

- making sure that the personalized security features of the payment instrument are not accessible to anyone other than the user;
- not sending any unsolicited payment instruments, other than as a replacement for an existing instrument;
- ensuring that appropriate means are available to enable the user to contact in respect of fulfilling notification requirements;
- to provide, on request, a means for the user to prove for eighteen months after giving a notification that he/she did notify;
- preventing the use of the instrument once notification is given.

370. Regulation 95 provides that a payment service user is entitled to rectification from the payment service provider of any unauthorized or incorrectly executed payment transaction. However, this only arises where the user notifies the provider

710. SI No 6 of 2018.
711. 2018 Regulations, Reg.1(3).
712. 2018 Regulations, Reg.3(1)(a).
713. 2018 Regulations, Reg.62(2) and (3) (re Part 3); Reg.85(1) and (2) (re Part 4).

without undue delay on becoming aware of any such transaction giving rise to a claim and no later than thirteen months after the debit date.

371. Regulations 97 and 98 deal with unauthorized payment transactions. Accordingly, the payment service provider is liable for unauthorized payments, under Regulation 97, provided the payer concerned has given notice. The provider must refund to the payer immediately the value of the transaction, and, if necessary, restore the debited payment account to the state it would have been in had the transaction not taken place. However, Regulation 98 limits the scope of Regulation 97 in a number of ways. For instance, the payer must bear the loss of unauthorized payments up to a total of EUR 50, if the transaction resulted from the use of a lost or stolen payment instrument or from the misappropriation of the instrument. Moreover, the payer bears all losses arising from the use of an unauthorized payment if he/she incurred these by acting fraudulently or with gross negligence or if he/she failed to fulfil his/her obligations under Regulation 93.

§7. Documentary Credits

372. Where, under the contract of sale, payment is to be by documentary credit, the buyer is required to enter an arrangement with a bank whereby the bank gives an undertaking that, provided certain conditions are met, the bank will pay the seller. The conditions that are normally to be fulfilled relate to the presentation by the seller of shipping documents for the goods being sold. Once the credit is opened, the seller can ship the goods and present the documents required under the sales contract to the bank. Provided the documents correspond with the instructions given to the bank by the buyer, the bank will pay the seller. The bank's undertaking to pay can take several forms. For example, the bank may agree to pay the seller cash, immediately on presentation of the shipping documents, or at some fixed date, such as, ninety days, thereafter. Alternatively, the bank may agree to accept bills of exchange drawn on it by the seller (an acceptance credit). Or, the bank may agree to discount bills drawn by the seller on the buyer (a negotiated credit). Here, the seller will normally endorse such bills 'without recourse'.

373. Significantly, the bank's undertaking to pay is recognized as creating an obligation independent or autonomous of the underlying sales contract. Therefore, a seller looks first to the bank for payment and cannot look to the buyer for payment unless the bank defaults. As a result, a bank must honour its undertaking to pay, provided the relevant conditions are met, regardless of any problems which might arise under the sales contract, for example, where the seller is in breach of the sales contract. A court will not grant the buyer an injunction to prevent the seller from drawing on the credit in such a situation;[714] nor will it grant a buyer an injunction against the bank making payment.[715] For example, in *GPA Group plc v. Bank*

714. *Hamzeh Malas Inc v. British Imex Industries* [1958] 1 QB 542.
715. *Discount Records Ltd v. Barclays Bank Ltd* [1975] 1 WLR 315.

of Ireland and EUROCONTROL,[716] the plaintiff leased aircraft worldwide while the second defendant, EUROCONTROL, was responsible for the collection of route charges. EUROCONTROL detained five GPA aircraft because of failure by the leasee to pay route charges. EUROCONTROL agreed to release the aircraft to GPA in return for a letter of credit from GPA in the sum of USD 3,000,000 for the benefit of EUROCONTROL. A letter of credit was drawn on the first defendant bank which provided for payment on presentation of a demand certificate either (i) signed by the officers of both GPA and EUROCONTROL; or (ii) signed by the officers of EUROCONTROL and attaching a final and binding court order of a competent jurisdiction for the amount claimed (in respect of which the time for appeal shall have passed). Subsequently, GPA argued that the leasee, and not GPA, was responsible for route charges and therefore GPA sought assurance that EUROCONTROL would not seek payment under the letter of credit. EUROCONTROL refused to make such an assurance. The bank received a demand certificate, duly signed by EUROCONTROL officers and attaching a consent order of the English High Court against the leasee purportedly in compliance with the letter of credit. GPA argued that the demand certificate did not comply with the letter of credit and was granted an interim injunction restraining the bank from making payment. However, a permanent injunction to restrain payment was refused. The High Court stated that when a letter of credit is issued and confirmed by a bank, the bank is obliged, save in the case of fraud, to pay if the documents are, on their face, in order. The court found that the documents were prima facie in order and the terms of the letter of credit were satisfied. The High Court also stated that the honouring of a letter of credit should not be lightly prohibited by the courts. And, the policy of the courts was to require immediate compliance with a demand for payment. Furthermore, the bank's obligation cannot be affected by disputes between its customer and third-party beneficiaries under the letter of credit. As a result, a documentary credit gives a seller an almost certain promise of payment.[717]

374. Documentary credits are not regulated by statute. The relevant law is found in the common law which is largely based on commercial practice. The majority of documentary credits are made expressly subject to the Uniform Customs and Practices relating to Documentary Credits (UCP), promoted by the International Chamber of Commerce (ICC).[718] The UCP is revised periodically in keeping with commercial practice: the current version is UCP 600 (2007).

---

716. [1992] 2 IR 408; *see also GPA Group plc v. Bank of Ireland* and EUROCONTROL (unreported Supreme Court, 9 Nov. 1995) where the Supreme Court observed that while letter of credit was irrevocable and must be paid when documents are in order and the terms of the credit satisfied, that does not mean that a dispute cannot arise between the parties other than the bank.

717. In *Mitsui & Co. Ltd v. Flota Mercante Grancolombiana SA* [1989] 1 All ER 951, [1988] 1 WLR 1145 it was stated that 'even the most copper-bottomed letter of credit sometimes fails to produce payment', per Staughton LJ at 957, 1153. In that case, it was held that a seller who had retained title on shipment, still retained title even though he had received 80% of the price with the balance secured by a documentary credit.

718. *See generally*, www.iccwbo.org.

§8. Performance Bonds

375. Performance bonds are used to secure the performance of a wide range of contractual and other obligations. For instance, with an international sale of goods, financed by documentary credit, the buyer may require some assurance that the goods will be shipped and can therefore require the seller to arrange a performance bond, so that, in default of shipment, the sum fixed in the bond will become payable. The person who arranged the bond is called the 'account party' while the recipient of the bond is called the 'payment party'. The essential feature of a performance bond is that it is provided by a creditworthy institution, such as a bank, offering the payment party/beneficiary a guarantee of performance and in default, monetary compensation from the reliable paymaster. While performance bonds perform the function of guarantees, they have been treated by the courts as broadly analogous to documentary credits.

376. The autonomous nature of performance bonds and the danger for account parties of demand bonds is illustrated by the Supreme Court case *Celtic International Insurance v. Banque Nationale de Paris.*[719] The case involved a construction contract between Mahon & Phillips Ltd, a customer of the defendant bank, and the South Eastern Health Board, whereby the defendant undertook to pay to the plaintiff a sum of money, if demanded, provided that such a claim was accompanied by a certificate from the South Eastern Health Board indicating that the sum of money was owing to them. Subsequently, a receiver was appointed to Mahon & Phillips and the benefit of the construction contracts assigned to another construction company. The Health Board issued the necessary certificate and made a call on the performance bond, but the defendant refused to pay. The Supreme Court held that a bank which gives a performance guarantee must honour it according to its terms. The bank should neither be concerned with the relations between the parties to whom the guarantee is given and the party whose performance is guaranteed nor as to whether the party to whom the guarantee is given has performed his/her contractual obligations or is in default. The bank must make payment pursuant to the guarantee on demand if this has been stipulated. The only exception to this rule being where it is clear that there has been fraud on behalf of the person to whom the guarantee is given. Where a bank makes payment under a bond, the bank is entitled to reimbursement from the account party.

719. [1995] 2 ILRM 518; *see also Edward Owen Engineering Ltd v. Barclays Bank International* [1978] 1 QB 179.

Chapter 8. Stock and Commodity Exchanges

377. Currently, there is only one exchange operating within the State, namely, the Irish Stock Exchange (ISE) plc. There are no commodity exchanges, as such.

§1. The Stock Exchange

378. In 2018, the ISE plc was acquired by Euronext, a pan European exchange covering Belgium, France, Ireland, the Netherlands, Portugal and the UK, and now trades as Euronext Dublin. Previously, a stock exchange has operated in Dublin since 1793 and was given statutory recognition in 1799.[720] In 1971, the Dublin Exchange amalgamated with the Cork Exchange. Then, in 1973, along with a number of other regional exchanges in the UK, they merged with the London Stock Exchange to form the International Stock Exchange of the UK and the Republic of Ireland Limited. In 1995, the UK and Irish exchanges separated, and under the Stock Exchange Act 1995, the ISE became an autonomous entity, a company limited by guarantee under the Companies Acts. In 2014, the ISE altered its corporate structure to a plc, facilitating the 100% acquisition by Euronext in 2018.

379. The ISE plc is regulated by the Central Bank with regard to the Markets in Financial Instruments Directive,[721] along with its accompanying Regulations,[722] collectively known as 'MiFID 2'. This legislation established requirements in respect of the provision of investment services and activities in the EU. In particular, requirements are established in respect of authorization and operation of investment firms, stock exchanges and other types of trading venues. MiFID 2 which replaced MiFID 1 (Directive 2004/39/EC), is transposed in Irish law by the EU (Markets in Financial Instruments) Regulations, 2017.[723]

380. The EU (Markets in Financial Instruments) Regulations 2017 define a 'regulated market' as:

> a multilateral system operated or managed (or both managed and operated) by a market operator which, brings together or facilitates the bringing together, of multiple third-party buying and selling interests in financial instruments – in the system and in accordance with its non-discretionary rules – in a way that results in a contract, in respect of the financial instruments admitted to trading under its rules or systems (or both) and in accordance with Part 7.[724]

And, the 2017 Regulations define a 'market operator' as:

---

720. Stock Exchange (Dublin) Act 1799.
721. Directive 2014/65/EU, [2014] OJ L 173/349.
722. Regulation 600/2014/EU, [2014] OJ L173/84.
723. SI No. 375 of 2017.
724. Reg. 3.

one of more persons who manage or operate (or both manage and operate) the business of a regulated market and may be the regulated market itself.[725]

381. Thus, under the 2017 Regulations, the Main Securities Market of the ISE is ‘a regulated market’; the ISE plc is the ‘market operator’ of the Main Securities Market and other markets which are Multilateral Trading Facilities (MTFs). The ISE currently operates three other securities markets: Euronext Growth, the Global Exchange Market (GEM) and the Atlantic Securities Market (ASM). The ISE also complies with the requirements of various European Directives, including the Prospectus Directive, the Transparency Directive, and the Market Abuse Directive in relation to securities listed and admitted to trading on the main securities market.

382. In brief, the ISE provides a market for a wide range of securities, including equities, corporate bonds, government bonds, investment funds, exchange traded funds and specialist securities – with many of the fund services providers based in the International Financial Services Centre (IFSC). The primary list of equities is the Main Market, Euronext Dublin and, at the time of writing, there were twenty-nine companies whose shares were listed on this Market. The index of listed shares is known as the ISEQ index.

725. Reg. 3.

Chapter 9. Commercial Contracts

383. Contracts for the sale of goods and the supply of services together represent the mainstay of commerce and trade. Traditionally, sale of goods contracts has been considered the most important commercial transaction; however, contracts for the supply of services have, more recently, increased in importance, in particular in the financial services sector. Both sale of goods and supply of services contracts are considered in more detail in this chapter. But as a preliminary, an outline of the general principles of contract law will set the context.

§1. General Principles of Contract Law

384. Contract law is the medium through which the majority of commercial transactions and relationships are structured. Specific rules exist in relation to many commercial contracts, including sale of goods, agency and insurance. However, where specific rules do not exist, the general rules of contract law apply. The aim of this section is to outline these general rules of contract law under three headings: contract formation; terms of contract; and discharge of contractual obligations.[726]

I. Contract Formation

385. A contract can be defined as a legally enforceable agreement or promise. In general, there are three requirements for the formation of a contract:

- agreement
- consideration
- intention to create legal relations.

A. Agreement

386. An agreement is a reasonably definite understanding between the parties. An agreement is made up of two parts, in law: (i) an offer on certain terms; and (ii) an acceptance of the offer.

726. For a more detailed analysis the leading texts on Irish contract law are McDermott, Contract Law (2nd ed., Bloomsbury Professional 2017); Clark, Contract Law in Ireland (8th ed., Thomson Round Hall 2016); Enright, Principles of Irish Contract Law (Clarus Press 2007) and Friel, Contract Law (2nd ed., Round Hall 2000).

1. Offer

387. An offer is any statement or conduct, indicating a clear intention to contract on terms that are reasonably definite. A distinction is made in law between offers and invitations to treat, that is, invitations seeking offers. Examples of invitations to treat include:[727]

- statements reserving the right to negotiate further;
- displays of goods in shop windows[728] or on shelves;[729]
- price lists, circulars and other advertisements;[730]
- requests for bids by an auctioneer;[731]
- requests for tenders.[732]

388. Offers are generally regarded as revocable until acceptance, hence offers can be withdrawn at any time up to acceptance.[733] However, to be effective, the withdrawal must be communicated to the offeree.

2. Acceptance

389. An acceptance is an expression by which the offeree indicates consent to be bound by the terms of the offer. An acceptance must be manifested in words or conduct, and this manifestation must be communicated to the offeror. Different rules apply depending on the means of communication:

- Oral acceptance must be received by the offeror.[734]
- Acceptance by post is effective from posting.[735] Further, once an acceptance is posted, the offer cannot be withdrawn.
- It has yet to be determined by an Irish court whether a dispatch or receipt rule applies to acceptance by electronic communications, such as by e-mail or via the

---

727. The following are general rules. Where, for example, a display or advertisement indicates an intention to be bound to reasonably definite terms, it may constitute an offer: *see*, e.g., *Carlill v. Carbolic Smoke Ball Company* [1893] 1 QB 256; *Kennedy v. London Express Newspapers* [1931] IR 532.
728. *Minister for Industry & Commerce v. Pim* [1966] IR 154.
729. *PSGB v. Boots Cash Chemists* [1953] 1 All ER 482.
730. *Grainger & Son v. Gough* (1896) AC 325.
731. A bid is an offer which the auctioneer accepts at the fall of the hammer: Sale of Goods Act 1893, s. 58.
732. Tenders are offers, leaving the person who made the request for tender to choose whether to accept or not. But *see Harvela v. Royal Trust Bank of Canada* [1986] AC 207, [1985] 2 All ER 966.
733. A promise to keep an offer open can only be enforced where the promise is supported by consideration: *see further* paras 376–386 below.
734. *Entores v. Miles Far East Crpn* [1955] 2 QB 327; *Brinkibon v. SSS mbH* [1983] 2 AC 34.
735. *Kelly v. Cruise Catering Ltd* [1994] 2 ILRM 394, 397–398.

WWW, although English authority suggests that the dispatch rule applies to communications by e-mail.[736] However, once this issue is decided, the Electronic Commerce Act 2000 contains rules to determine when and where an electronic communication is dispatched or received.[737]

It is sometimes said that silence cannot amount to acceptance;[738] but it seems that this is not an absolute rule. Normally silence will not provide an unequivocal indication of acceptance but in certain circumstances it may amount to acceptance.[739]

390. A distinction is drawn between acceptances and counter-offers. Where a person purports to accept an offer but, in doing so, alters the terms, this is viewed as a counter-offer. A counter-offer is treated as a new offer, terminating the original offer, which the offeror can choose to accept or reject.[740] Where the parties use standard form documentation as part of the negotiating process, this can lead to a *battle of forms.* For instance, in *Butler Machine Tool v. Ex-Cell-O Corp*[741] the plaintiff seller quoted for the supply of goods to a potential buyer subject to its standard terms of sale which included a statement that '[t]hese terms and conditions shall prevail over any terms and conditions in the buyer's order'. One of the clauses in the seller's terms of trading was a price variation clause. The buyer placed an order on its own trading terms which did not include a price variation clause. The buyer's order form had a tear-off slip at the bottom which was an acknowledgment of receipt of order which stated '[w]e accept your order on the terms and conditions stated thereon'. The seller filled-in the acknowledgment receipt and returned it to the buyer. A dispute arose and the question was whether there was a contract, and if so, on whose terms. The English Court of Appeal found that the quotation was an offer, including a price variation clause. However, the buyer's order altered the terms under which it was willing to contract and so this was a counter-offer on new terms, with no price variation clause. The acknowledgement of receipt returned by the seller constituted an acceptance because by filling-in the acknowledgement the seller was taken to have assented to the buyer's terms. This finding was despite the fact that the seller's terms of trading included the phrase that 'these terms and conditions shall prevail over any terms and conditions in the buyer's order'.

B. Consideration

391. Barring agreements in deeds, an agreement alone will not be enforced by the courts: it must be supported by 'consideration'. Essentially, consideration is that which is given in return for an agreement or a promise; sometimes referred to as

736. *See Thomas and Gander v. BPE Solicitors* [2010] EWHC 306 (Ch); The Pamela [1995] 2 Lloyd's Rep. 249.
737. Electronic Commerce Act 2000, s. 21; *see also* EC (Directive 2000/13/EC) Regulations, 2003, Regulation 14, SI No. 68 of 2003.
738. *Felthouse v. Bindley* (1863) 1 New Rep 401.
739. The Leonidas D [1985] 2 All ER 796, [1985] 1 WLR 925.
740. *Brinkibon v. SSS mbH* [1983] 2 AC 34.
741. [1979] 1 All ER 965.

'mutuality of obligation'. Consideration may be the price paid under a contract but not necessarily. Indeed, one promise may be consideration for another promise. For example, in *Ryanair v. O'Keeffe*[742] the plaintiff was the 1 millionth passenger on Ryanair and, when asked, she agreed to participate in promotional activities on behalf of Ryanair in return for free flights on Ryanair. Subsequently, the extent of her free flights was limited by Ryanair and she argued that Ryanair was in breach of contract. The court first has to decide whether there was a contract between the parties and, in particular, whether the plaintiff had supplied consideration for Ryanair's promise of free flights or whether the promise of free flights was a mere gift, not supported by consideration, and hence not contractually binding. The High Court found that the surrender by the plaintiff of her anonymity and privacy and her active participation in the generation of publicity amounted to real consideration and hence a contract existed which had been breached and damages were awarded.

The doctrine of consideration is unique to the common law system and is complex, being based on a number of rules. These rules are outlined below.

1. Consideration Must Move from the Promisee

392. Where two people, A and B, have an agreement, in order for A to enforce B's part of the agreement, A must show that he provided consideration for B's promise. In other words, consideration must move from the promisee.[743] Likewise, in order for B to enforce A's part of the agreement, B must show that he provided consideration for A's promise.

2. Adequacy of Consideration Irrelevant

393. In enforcing agreements, the courts are not concerned with the *adequacy*, or value, of consideration.[744] For example, it is not unusual to have a contract where the consideration is nominal, one cent or one Euro, even though the actual value of the transaction is much higher.

3. Consideration Must Be Sufficient

394. In the majority of commercial contracts, finding consideration to support an agreement or a promise does not cause a problem. However, problems can arise concerning the 'sufficiency' of consideration and the variation of contracts.

---

742. [2003] 1 IRLM 14.
743. *Thomas v. Thomas* (1842) 2 QB 851.
744. *Westlake v. Adams* (1858) 5 CBNS 248.

a. Past Consideration Is Not Sufficient

395. Consideration must be 'sufficient' and past consideration is not sufficient consideration.[745] This means that consideration being provided for a promise must be given when the promise is made or after the promise is made, but not *before* the promise is made. Consideration is past, for example, when goods are sold and, at some time subsequently, the seller gives a guarantee as to their quality.[746]

b. Performance of Existing Duty Is Not Sufficient

396. Another aspect of this rule is that the performance of an existing duty is not sufficient consideration. The general rule is that where A is under a legal or contractual duty to B, performance of that duty (or a promise to perform that duty) is not consideration for a new promise from B. It follows, where A provides fresh consideration, by doing anything beyond his original promise, the new promise can be enforced.[747]

c. Part Payment of an Existing Debt Is Not Sufficient Consideration

397. Moreover, if a liquidated sum is owed by A to B, a promise by B to accept a lesser sum in full satisfaction of the whole debt will not bind B, because the debtor has only part performed his duty to pay his creditor. Hence, the creditor can sue the debtor for the balance of the debt.[748]

d. Consideration to a Third Party

398. Another aspect of the rule, that consideration must be sufficient, concerns the question whether consideration to a third party T, can be valid consideration for a contract between A and B. For instance, can performance of a duty owed to T be sufficient consideration for a promise between A and B. It seems, following the English case *New Zealand Shipping v. Satterthwaite,*[749] that this is possible. In that case, A (stevedores) had contracted with T (shipowners) to unload goods from T's ship. Some of the goods being unloaded belonged to B who promised that he would not sue A for any damages caused during the unloading. It was held that B's promise not to sue was enforceable because it was supported by consideration (B received a benefit) from the promisee, and that consideration was the unloading of the goods, despite the fact that A was already obliged to unload the goods under his contract with T.

745. *Eastwood v. Kenyon* (1840) 11 Ad & El 438.
746. *Roscorla v. Thomas* (1842) 3 QB 234.
747. *Stilk v. Myrick* (1809) 2 Camp. 317, 170 ER 1168; cf. *Williams v. Roffey Bros* [1991] 1 QB 1 but *see* more recently in *Ireland Truck & Machinery Sales v. Marubeni Komatsu* [1996] 1 IR 12.
748. Pinnel's Case (1602) 5 Co. Rep. 117a; *Foakes v. Beer* (1884) 9 App. Cas. 605.
749. [1975] AC 154, [1974] 1 All ER 1015.

e. Variation of Contract Terms

399. A significant problem, caused by the doctrine of consideration, relates to the variation of contract terms. As noted above, consideration must be sufficient and past consideration is not sufficient. This means that consideration being provided for a promise must be given when the promise is made or after the promise is made but not before the promise is made. Therefore, new contractual terms, or variations, cannot be incorporated into the contract after the contract is made, unless the promisee provides new consideration for the new term or variation. Hence, for every variation there must be fresh consideration. This difficulty can be avoided where the initial contract includes a term allowing one or both parties to vary the contract in specified circumstances: a 'variation clause'.

f. Waiver and Estoppel

400. Even where a promise, such as a variation, is not supported by sufficient consideration, the promise may still bind the promisor under the doctrines of waiver and 'promissory estoppel'. At common law, where a party agrees not to insist on his/her strict legal rights, or represents that he/she will not insist on strict performance, he/she may be held to have waived his/her right to strict performance. In *Charles Rickards Ltd v. Oppenhaim,*[750] under a sales contract, a car chassis was to be built and delivered by 20 March. It was not delivered in time but the buyer continued to press for delivery until 29 June at which point he gave notice to the seller that he would not accept delivery if it was not made within four weeks. Delivery was not made until October at which time the buyer refused to accept it. The English Court of Appeal found the buyer had waived the original delivery date but by giving reasonable notice of his intention to insist on delivery, he was entitled to reject the goods when his four-week deadline was not satisfied.

401. A similar doctrine exists in equity whereby if one party promises that he/she will not insist on his/her strict contractual rights, he/she will not be allowed to retract that promise, if the promise has been acted upon by the other party. The doctrine is referred to as equitable or 'promissory' estoppel.[751] The exact scope of the doctrine is unclear but it would appear that the following requirements exist:

- The promisor must make an unambiguous statement, express or implied, that he/she will not insist on his/her strict legal rights.
- The promisee must have relied on that promise, perhaps acting to his/her detriment, but this is not clear.
- It must be inequitable to allow the promisor to retract his/her promise.

Where the doctrine applies, its effect is to suspend, not extinguish, contractual rights. Hence, the promisor can return to the original terms of the contract by giving

750. [1950] 1 KB 616, [1950] 1 All ER 520: *see also* para. 465.

751. *Hughes v. Metropolitan Railway Co.* (1877) 2 App. Cas. 439, *Central London Property Trust Ltd v. High Tress House Ltd* [1947] KB 130, *Kenny v. Kelly* [1988] IR 457.

reasonable notice. Significantly, promissory estoppel is said to operate as 'a shield, not a sword', in that it creates no new rights of action for the promisee; it merely acts as a defence for the promisee.

C. Intention to Create Legal Relations

402. The third requirement for the formation of a valid and enforceable contract is that there must be an intention to create legal relations between the parties to the contract. This requirement causes little difficulty in a commercial context because, in relation to commercial transactions, there is a presumption that there is an intention to create legal relations. However, this intention is only presumed and parties in commercial transactions may lack the necessary intention to create legal relations.[752] For example, in *Kleinwort Benson Ltd v. Malaysia Mining Corporation Ltd,*[753] a creditor agreed a loan with a subsidiary company based on two letters of comfort provided by the parent company along the following lines:

> It is our policy to ensure that the business of the subsidiary is at all times in a position to meet its liabilities to you under the loan agreement.

The subsidiary company went into liquidation and the creditors sought repayment from the parent company. The English Court of Appeal held that the letters of comfort were not intended to create a contractual promise as to future conduct. The court took the view that letters of comfort are generally regarded as intended to create a moral but not a legal binding obligation.

D. Formalities

403. In general, where there is an agreement, supported by consideration and an intention to create legal relations, there are no further requirements as to form, for a valid and enforceable contract. The contract can be concluded orally, or in writing, or it may be implied from the conduct of the parties. A written contract may be useful for evidential purposes but writing is not essential.

404. There are several important statutory exceptions to this general rule. For example, under section 2 of the Statute of Frauds (Ireland) 1695, contracts of guarantee must be evidenced in writing and signed by the party to be charged, that is, sued. Under section 51 of the Land and Conveyancing Law Reform Act 2009, contracts for the sale or other disposition of land must also be evidenced in writing and signed by the person against whom the action is brought. Similarly, under section 4 of the Sale of Goods Act 1893, a contract for the sale of goods of the value of IEP 10 (EUR 12.70) or more is not enforceable by action unless:

---

752. *Rose and Frank Co. v. J R Crompton Bros* [1925] AC 445, [1924] All ER Rep 245.
753. [1989] 1 WLR 379. *See also British Steel Corpn v. Cleveland Bridge and Engineering Co. Ltd* [1984] 1 All ER 504 on letters of intent.

- the buyer accepts, and actually receives, part of the goods sold;
- the buyer gives something in earnest to bind the contract;
- the buyer has made part payment;
- there is a note or memorandum in writing of the contract and signed by the party to be charged, that is, sued.[754]

405. Under the EC (Commercial Agents) Regulations 1994 and 1997,[755] which implement the EC Directive on self-employed commercial agents,[756] a 'commercial agency' contract is not valid unless evidenced in writing.[757] Lastly, a variety of formal requirements apply to certain specific contracts entered into with consumers, in order to protect the consumer.[758] For example, credit sales, contracts of hire purchase and other hire contracts with consumers are all regulated by the Consumer Credit Act 1995 which includes various formal requirements.[759] Moreover, consumer buyers of goods, services and digital content are also protected by a series of formal requirements in relation to on-premises contracts and off-premises contracts and distance contracts pursuant to the EU (Consumer Information, Cancellation and other Rights) Regulations 2013.[760] Under these Regulations, for instance, certain specified information must be provided by the trader to the consumer, on paper or on another durable medium, within a specified time. Failure to provide this information may mean that aspects of the contract are unenforceable by the trader and a trader who fails to comply with these formal information requirements commits an offence.[761]

E. Defects in Formation

406. When contracts are being formed an event may occur, or, one party may do something which he/she should not do, which results in a defect in the formation of the contract. There are different types of defect, each having different consequences.

1. The Effect of a Defect

407. A distinction is made between defects which render a contract void or voidable. A void contract is one that never existed, and hence never had any legal effect such that the parties do not owe, and never have owed, any legal obligations to each

754. *See further* para. 460.
755. SI No. 33 of 1994 and SI No. 31 of 1997.
756. Directive 86/653/EEC, [1986] OJ L 382/17.
757. Article 13(2) and Regulation 5, 1994: *see further* para. 670.
758. *See further* Part II, Ch. 5, §2 on consumer law.
759. Re credit sales *see* Part III; re hire purchase *see* Part VI; and re other hire contracts *see* Part VII.
760. S.I. No. 484 of 2013. These Regulations transposed Directive 2011/83 on consumer rights, [2011] OJ L304/64, into Irish law.
761. *See*, e.g., Regs 7(8), 9(4), 10(10) and 12(5) of S.I. No. 484 of 2013.

other. Any money paid under a void contract, or any property transferred, is returnable. In contrast, where a contract is found to be voidable this means that the innocent party, that is, the party not responsible for the defect, has a choice or an option: he/she can allow the contract to continue or he/she can rescind or set aside the contract. Where the contract is rescinded, it is set aside from the beginning and each party is required to return benefits received, as far as is possible. But until the contract is rescinded, it remains valid.

2. The Defects

408. The main defects which render a contract void or voidable are: mistake; misrepresentation; and duress or undue influence.[762] Each has a very particular meaning, in law, leading to different consequences.

a. Mistake

409. Mistake is a relatively narrow ground. For instance, if a purchaser of oats buys grain thinking it is old oats, where in truth it is new oats, this is not what would be categorized as a mistake, in law. When the law recognizes a mistake, the contract is rendered void at common law.[763] For example, where two parties agreed to the sale of an item that does not exist, though both parties believed it to exist, it is said that they share a common mistake and the contract is void. The contract may also be void where the parties are at cross-purposes. In *Raffles v. Wichelhaus,*[764] there was a contract to buy cotton, shipped from Bombay on a ship called 'Peerless'. There was in fact two ships called 'Peerless', both sailing from Bombay with cotton, one in October and the other in December. The buyer thought that he/she was buying the October shipment, the seller thought that he/she was selling the December shipment. As a result, the parties were at cross-purposes and the contract was found to be void.

410. Problems can arise where A contracts with B, mistakenly believing him to be C. The issue is whether A intended to contract with B or C. Where the parties do not deal face to face, it is possible to establish that A intended to contract only with C, and hence there is no contract with B.[765] Where the parties deal face to face, the

762. Contracts may also be rendered void for illegality.
763. Equity may recognize a wider variety of mistakes making a contract voidable instead of void: *see*, e.g., *Solle v. Butcher* [1950] 1 KB 671.
764. (1864) 2 H&C 906.
765. *Cundy v. Lindsey* (1878) 3 App. Cas. 459; *Shogun Finance Ltd v. Hudson* [2003] UKHL 62, [2004] 1 AC 1101, [2004] 1 All ER 641.

objective interpretation of the circumstances is that A intends to deal with the person before him.[766] In these circumstances, B will normally be responsible for A's 'mistake' because he fraudulently misled him, and the contract will be voidable for misrepresentation.[767]

b. Misrepresentation

411. Where one party to a contract makes an untrue statement in relation to a material fact – a misrepresentation – before the contract is concluded, and this induces the other party to enter the contract, then the contract may be voidable for misrepresentation. The misrepresentation may be made fraudulently, negligently, or innocently. As well as being able to rescind the contract, the innocent party may be entitled to damages from the person making the misrepresentation.[768] For example, in *Fenton v. Schofield,* [769] a vendor of land made a statement that over the previous four years a river running through the land had yielded 300–350 salmon a year and that he had spent IEP 15,000 renovating the property. Both statements of fact were untrue and the vendor knew of this. A purchaser paid IEP 17,000 for the property on the strength of these statements. The plaintiff sued for fraudulent misrepresentation and was awarded damages based on the difference between what the land was worth and what it was represented to be worth. Similarly, in *Connor v. Potts,*[770] a seller of two farms described them as comprising 443 acres, which he believed to be true. The purchase price was calculated at GBP 12 10s an acre; however, there was in fact only 376 acres. Following a finding of innocent misrepresentation, it was held that the plaintiff was entitled to specific performance of the contract at a reduced price.

c. Duress or Undue Influence

412. The essence of contract law is that two parties freely consent to being bound to each other. Where consent is given only because pressure is put on a party, in the form of duress or undue influence, then this may lead to a defect in formation and the innocent party may be able to set aside the contract. Threats to a person's life, person or property have been recognized as constituting duress.[771] More recently, the courts have recognized the concept of 'economic duress' which is particularly important in a commercial context. The equitable doctrine of undue influence is wider than the common law concept of duress and includes the situation where pressure is exerted without any threats. Equity gives further relief where a

766. *Phillips v. Brooks* [1919] 2 KB 243; *Lewis v. Avery* [1972] 1 QB 198, [1971] 3 All ER 907; cf. *Ingram v. Little* [1961] 1 QB 31, [1960] 3 All ER 332.
767. *See* para. 396 below.
768. Damages may be available at common law for fraudulent and negligent misrepresentation. Under the Sale of Goods and Supply of Services Act 1980, Part V which applies to sale of goods contracts, hire purchase agreements, agreements for the letting of goods, and contracts for the supply of services, damages are also available for non-fraudulent misrepresentation: s. 45.
769. (1966) 100 ILTR 69.
770. [1897] IR 534.
771. *See*, e.g., *Williams v. Baley* (1866) LR 1 HL 200.

relationship between the parties is such that it gives rise to a presumption that one party exercised undue influence over the other. Such relationships include that of: parent and child; and trustee and beneficiary. Other relationships, such as husband and wife, may be included where the party challenging the transaction can show that they reposed trust and confidence in the other party.[772]

F. A Duty to Trade Fairly?

413. While there is no general duty to act in good faith in Irish contract law, the accumulation of the above doctrines of mistake, misrepresentation, duress and undue influence, amongst others, go some way to producing a similar effect. More directly, but within a consumer context only, Part 3 of the Consumer Protection Act 2007 transposes into Irish law Directive 2005/28/EC on unfair commercial practices and in doing so, arguably, imposes a general duty to trade fairly.[773] 'Commercial practice' is broadly defined and means any conduct (whether an act or omission), course of conduct or representation by a trader in relation to a consumer transaction, including any such conduct or representation made or engaged in before, during or after the consumer transaction.[774] 'Consumer transaction' means a promotion or supply of a product to a consumer; while 'product' covers both goods and services, again broadly defined.[775] Pursuant to Part 3, a range of unfair,[776] misleading[777] and aggressive[778] commercial practices are prohibited. Moreover, the legislation lists thirty-two activities that are always prohibited, including false claims:

- that the trader or product has an approval, authorization or endorsement that it does not have;
- that the trader is about to cease trading;
- about cures for illnesses;
- indicating that the product is free when it costs the consumer more than the reasonable costs responding to the representation or collecting the product or having it delivered;

---

772. *See*, *Barclays Bank v. O ' Brien* [1994] 1 AC 180; and *Royal Bank of Scotland v. Etridge (No. 2)* [2001] 3 WLR 1021. In an Irish context *see Bank of Nova Scotia v. Hogan* [1997] 1 ILRM 407; *Ulster Bank v. Fitzgerald,* Unreported, High Court, O'Donovan, J., 9 Nov. 2001; *Danske Bank v. Madden* [2009] IEHC 319; *Tynan v. County Registrar for Kilkenny* [2011] IEHC 250; and *Ulster Bank v. Roche* [2012] IEHC 166.
773. [2005] OJ L 149/22.
774. 2007 Act, s. 2.
775. For example, goods is defined as meaning real and personal property, including minerals, trees or crops, whether on, under or attached to land or not; gas, electricity or water; computer software; tickets or like evidence of a right to be in attendance at a particular place at a particular time or times or a right of transportation; any voucher, coupon or other document or thing intended to be used as a substitute for money in the payment, in whole or in part, for a product or otherwise exchanged for a product: 2007 Act, s. 2. *Cf.* definition of goods for the purpose of the Sale of Goods Acts 1893 and 1980: *see* 9.2.5.
776. 2007 Act, s. 41.
777. 2007 Act, ss 42–51.
778. 2007 Act, ss 52–54.

– that there is limited available to encourage quick sales.[779]

414. Many of the practices prohibited by Part 3 of the Consumer Protection Act 2007 would make any subsequent contract void or voidable on the grounds of mispresentation, duress or undue influence. However, the legislation goes much further. First, it prohibits certain behaviour which would not affect the validity of the contract at common law and second, the sanction for breach of the legislation is both civil (including a claim for exemplary damages for the consumer[780]) and criminal.[781]

G. Rights of Cancellation

415. There may exist a right to lawfully cancel a contract after its formation. Such a right is normally given as a form of consumer protection. For instance, under Part 4 of the EU (Consumer Information, Cancellation and other Rights) Regulations 2013[782] a consumer has a right to cancel off-premises contracts and distance contracts, for the sale of goods, supply of services and digital content, within a fourteen day period. Further, rights of cancellation exist under the Consumer Credit Act 1995.[783]

H. Privity of Contract

416. Privity of contract describes the relationship between the parties to a contract. The doctrine of privity of contract provides that only the parties to the contract may sue to enforce the terms of the contract:

> it has been decided that, where the foundation of the right of action is rested upon contract, no one can maintain an action who is not a party to the contract.[784]

There are exceptions to the doctrine. The most important exception, in a commercial context, relates to the law of agency. Accordingly, where a person A enters a contract with another person T, on behalf of and with the authority of another person P, the contract which arises exists between P and T – A having no contractual rights or obligations under the contract.[785] Another exception exists where a contractual right between X and Y is transferred or assigned to a third party Z. Despite

779. 2007 Act, s. 55.
780. 2007 Act, s. 74.
781. 2007 Act, s. 79 on fines and imprisonment.
782. S.I. No. 484 of 2013. These Regulations transposed Directive 2011/83 on consumer rights, [2011] OJ L304/64, into Irish law.
783. *See*, e.g., s. 58(5) with regard to hire purchase arrangements.
784. *Murphy v. Bowen* (1866) IR 2 CL 506 *per* Monahan CJ at 512.
785. *See further* paras 644–699.

the existence of various exceptions, the doctrine of privity has been strongly criticized, and Ireland is part of a growing minority of jurisdictions which remain loyal to the doctrine. The Law Reform Commission published a Report on Privity of Contract and Third Party Rights which proposes legislative reform of the doctrine of privity to allow third-party beneficiaries to enforce rights under a contract.[786] However, at the time of writing, this Report had not been implemented.

II. Terms of the Contract

417. Once a contract is properly formed, the contractual obligations of the parties are to be found in the terms of the contract. It is therefore, important to be able to identify the terms of a contract and to classify them according to their status. Where contracts are in writing, this task may be less difficult than with oral contracts. In particular areas of commercial law, such as international trade, standard form contracts play an important role. However, as noted above, there is no general legal requirement that contracts be recorded in writing and many commercial contracts are made informally, either face to face, over the telephone, or e-mail.

A. Mere Representations, Representations and Terms

418. In the negotiations which lead to the formation of a contract, parties may make numerous statements, either orally or in writing. A buyer may describe a particular type of product to perform a particular function; a seller may go to great lengths to highlight the features and advantages of his/her product over competitors' products. Not every word spoken between the parties forms part of any subsequent contract. In the event of a dispute arising later it may be necessary to determine the legal status of these various statements.

419. Generally, there are three categories of statement. The law distinguishes between mere representations, representations and terms of the contract. The classification of statements is based on the intention of the parties, objectively assessed by a court. Mere representations, sometimes referred to as 'mere puffs', are statements which are intended to have no legal effect. Mere representations probably include advertising claims and sales talk, which are usually exaggerated to entice a customer to purchase: they are not actionable.

420. Other statements are either representations or terms of the contract, or both.[787] A representation is a pre-contractual statement of fact which encourages the other party to enter the contract but it is not a term of the contract. In contrast, a term of the contract is any statement which is intended to have contractual effect and hence, is contractually binding on the parties. Determining whether a statement is a representation or a term of the contract depends on the intention of the parties.

786. LRC 88 – 2008.
787. Sale of Goods and Supply of Services Act 1980, s. 44.

This in turn will depend on the court's view, based on the facts of the case. As a result, it is difficult to predict the status of any statement with certainty. Case law can be difficult to reconcile in this regard but it does suggest that certain statements are more likely to be terms than representations, such as: statements made close in time to the conclusion of the contract;[788] statements which are particularly important to the hearer;[789] and statements made by an expert to a non-expert.[790]

421. Representations and terms of the contract give rise to legal liability, if false.[791] Where a representation is factually false this may amount to a misrepresentation which renders the contract voidable and damages may be payable.[792] Where a term of the contract is broken or breached, the innocent party can sue the person responsible for the breach, claiming damages and may be able to terminate, or end, the contract.[793] The classification between representations and terms is no longer as important as it once was. Liability for breach of contract is strict, so that an innocent party can claim damages for breach of a term of the contract even though the statement was made innocently, believing it to be true. Prior to 1980, damages were only available for misrepresentation where the false statement was made fraudulently,[794] or negligently.[795] However, the Sale of Goods and Supply of Services Act 1980,[796] provides that damages are payable for non-fraudulent misrepresentation.[797] However, the maker of the statement can avoid liability if he/she can show that he/she had reasonable grounds to believe and did believe that the statement was true. This reduces the incentive that used to exist for an innocent party to argue that a statement was a term of the contract. But other distinctions remain. Where a term of the contract is breached, the innocent party may be able to terminate the contract. Termination is *prospective* in nature, releasing the parties from their future obligations to each other. In contrast, where there is a misrepresentation, the innocent party may be able to rescind the contract. Rescission is *retrospective* in nature, seeking to restore the parties to their pre-contractual positions.

---

788. *See Routledge v. McKay* [1954] 1 All ER 885, [1954] 1 WLR 615, cf. *Schawel v. Reade* [1913] 2 IR 81.
789. *See Bannerman v. White* (1861) 10 CBNS 844.
790. *See Dick Bentley Productions Ltd v. Harold Smith (Motor) Ltd* [1965] 2 All ER 65, [1965] 1 WLR 623; cf. *Oscar Chess v. Williams* [1957] 1 All ER 325, [1957] 1 WLR 370. *See generally Bank of Ireland v. Smith* [1966] IR 646, *per* Kenny J.
791. A person may be liable for the false statements of his/her agent, and, where goods are supplied on credit to a person dealing as a consumer, the credit supplier will be liable for false statements made during negotiations by the supplier of goods: Sale of Goods and Supply of Services Act, s. 14.
792. *See* para. 396 above.
793. *See* paras 438–448 below.
794. Using the tort of deceit: *see* McMahon & Binchy, *Law of Torts* Ch. 35 (4th ed., Butterworths 2013).
795. Under the authority of *Hedley Byrne & Co. Ltd v. Heller & Partners Ltd* [1964] AC 465, [1963] 2 All ER 575.
796. This legislation is limited in its application to contracts for the sale of goods, hire purchase agreements, other arrangements for the letting of goods, as defined, and contracts for the supply of services: 1980 Act, s. 43.
797. 1980 Act, s. 45(1).

Furthermore, damages for breach of contract and misrepresentation are assessed differently, and the right to terminate may be lost more quickly than the right to rescind.

B. Individually Negotiated or Standard Terms

422. The terms of a contract can be individually negotiated, whereby the parties negotiate each individual term, or standard in format. Many commercial contracts are made on standard terms promoted by trade or professional organizations. Standard terms of sale and purchase are quite common, as are standard terms in insurance, carriage, construction and banking contracts.

1. Incorporation of Terms by Reference

423. The terms of a contract can derive from various sources: advertising, oral statements, letters and standard terms printed in a master document or, on the back of standard form documentation, such as order forms, and invoices, or more commonly today online. Such terms may be incorporated into any contract 'by reference', provided that the terms are introduced no later than the time when the contract is concluded. Any statement made after the conclusion of the contract will be unenforceable unless supported by further consideration.[798] Incorporation by reference can occur in three ways, by:

(a) signature
(b) notice
(c) course of dealings.[799]

a. Signature

424. When a party signs a document containing a set of terms, he/she is prima facie bound by the terms even if the party has not read the terms. In *L'Estrange v. Graucob Ltd*,[800] the plaintiff bought a machine on terms contained in a document described as a 'Sales Agreement'. Some of the clauses were in 'legible but regrettably small print'. The plaintiff signed the 'Sales Agreement' but did not read the terms. The court held that she was bound by the terms:

> When a document containing contractual terms is signed then, the party signing is bound, and it is wholly immaterial whether he has read the document or not.[801]

---

798. *See* paras 376–386 above.
799. *Noreside Construction Ltd v. Irish Asphalt Ltd* [2014] IESC 68.
800. [1934] 2 KB 394.
801. *Ibid.* at 403, *per* Scrutton LJ; *see further Slattery v. CIE* (1968) 106 ILTR 71.

This rule can operate harshly, especially in a consumer context, but it is justified by the objective approach to contract: a person who signs a document containing contractual terms appears to be assenting to those terms.

b. Notice

425. Standard terms can be incorporated by reference where the terms are made available or reasonable notice of the terms is given to the other party at the time the contract is made.[802] Again, it usually does not matter whether the other party has read the terms. Whether reasonable notice of the terms has been given will depend on the facts of the case, but the test is objective, so that, provided sufficient has been done to bring the terms to the notice of persons generally, no account is taken of subjective factors. Where the term to be incorporated is unusual, then even more care must be taken to give reasonable notice, for example, by printing it in bold or larger print.[803]

c. Course of Dealings

426. Lastly, where parties have contracted in the past and incorporated a standard set of terms, such past 'course of dealings' may be enough to ensure that the standard terms are part of any future contract. However, there seems to be a requirement of *consistent* dealing before this argument will work.[804]

2. Statutory Regulation of Standard Terms

427. The EC (Unfair Terms in Consumer Contracts) Regulations 1995, as amended,[805] represent a major departure in Irish contract law which traditionally has been non-interventionist in its general approach to contracts. Under these Regulations, any standard term in a contract between a business and a consumer which is 'unfair' is void. Importantly, individual consumers, the Competition and Consumer Protection Commission (CCPC), and others, can seek to enforce these Regulations. The Regulations are considered further in Part II.[806]

---

802. *Parker v. South Eastern Railways Ltd* (1877) 2 CPD 416, [1874–1880] All ER 116; *see also Carroll v. An Post National Lottery* [1996] 1 IR 443.
803. *Interfoto Picture Library v. Stilletto Visual Programmes* [1988] 1 ER 348; *see further Western Meats Ltd v. National Ice and Cold Storage* [1982] ILRM 99.
804. *McCutcheon v. David MacBrayne Ltd* [1964] 1 All 430.
805. SI No. 27 of 1995 and SI No. 307 of 2000.
806. *See* paras 973–976.

C. Conditions, Warranties and Innominate Terms

428. Once the terms of the contract have been distinguished from mere representations and representations, they can be classified into three different categories: conditions, warranties or innominate terms. Different consequences follow the breach of these different terms.

429. Traditionally, there were two classifications: conditions and warranties. A condition is a more important term of the contract when compared with a warranty. The difference between the two becomes apparent when you compare the effect of the breach of a condition with a breach of warranty. Where a term which is classified as a warranty is broken, the innocent party is entitled to damages only. However, where the term which is broken is classified as a condition, then the innocent party is entitled to damages and to terminate the contract.

430. The strict division between conditions and warranties can be criticized for being inflexible. For instance, where a term is classified as a condition, the innocent party can terminate the contract even though the effect of the breach might not be very serious.[807] Innominate or 'intermediary' terms represent the middle ground between conditions and warranties.[808] Where an innominate term is breached, the effect depends on the seriousness of the breach. If the breach is not serious, the innocent party is limited to a claim in damages. In contrast, if the effect of the breach is serious, the innocent party can claim damages and terminate the contract. This flexibility gives a court more discretion to decide what is the fairest remedy in a given situation although it also brings a degree of uncertainty.

431. Parties to a contract may seek to define their obligations by classifying the terms of a contract as conditions and warranties, for example. While courts seek to give effect to the intentions of the parties, they are not bound by such classifications. Where a term is identified as a 'condition', a court might nevertheless find that the parties did not intend that the breach of the term would entitle the innocent party to terminate the contract.

D. Express and Implied Terms

432. All terms of a contract are either express or implied. An express term is one expressed or stated, and agreed by the parties either by word of mouth or in writing. Express terms arise from the express wishes of the parties: one of the principles of contract law being to give effect to the intentions of the parties.

433. Into every contract, a court can imply further terms. In *Tradax (Ireland) v. Irish Grain Board Ltd*, it was stated that:

---

807. *See*, e.g., *Cehave v. Bremer* [1975] 3 All ER 739.
808. *See Hong Kong Fir v. Kawasaki* [1962] 2 QB 26; *Irish Telephone Rentals v. ICS Building Society* [1991] ILRM 880.

> this power must be exercised with care. The Courts have no role in acting as contract makers, or as counsellors, to advise or direct which agreement ought to have been made by two people, whether businessmen or not, who choose to enter into contractual relations with each other.[809]

These sentiments hold true in relation to commercial contracts, although where a party to the contract is a consumer there is now a substantial body of law which seeks to regulate the content of consumer contracts.[810] Generally, a court can imply a term on three different grounds: on the facts; in law, or, based on trade custom and usage.

1. Implied by Fact

434. Based on the express terms of a contract, a court may imply further terms into the contract to flesh out the express terms of the contract or to give business effect to the contract.[811] This is an important function of the courts especially where the parties have failed to address all the necessary terms of the contract. The law in this area was restated in *Carna Foods v. Eagle Star*[812] where Lynch J quoting MacKinnon LJ in *Shirlaw v. Southern Foundries*[813] stated:

> Prima facie that which in any contract is left to be implied and need not be expressed is something so obvious that it goes without saying: so that if while the parties were making their bargain an officious bystander were to suggest some express provisions for it in their agreement, they would testily suppress him with a common 'oh of course'.[814]

Lynch J also quoted Lord Pearson in *Trollope v. NWMRHB*:[815]

> An unexpressed term can be implied if and only if the court finds that the parties must have intended that term to form part of their contract: it is not enough for the court to find that such a term would have been adopted by the parties as reasonable men if it had been suggested to them: it must have been a term that went without saying, a term necessary to give business efficacy to the contract, a term which although not tacit, formed part of the contract which the parties made for themselves.[816]

809. [1984] IR 1 at 14, *per* O'Higgins CJ.
810. *See further* Part II Ch. 5.
811. *Luxor v. Cooper* [1941] AC 108.
812. [1997] 2 ILRM 449.
813. [1939] 2 KB 206 at 227.
814. [1997] 2 ILRM 449 at 504.
815. [1973] 2 All ER 260 at 268.
816. [1997] 2 ILRM 449 at 504–505.

2. Implied in Law

435. Terms are implied in law where they are required by the Constitution, legislation or the common law. For example, into every contract of employment the common law implies a term that the employee will not disclose confidential information;[817] and the Constitution implies a right to disassociate.[818] Probably the most important terms implied by law, in a commercial context, arise from the Sale of Goods Act 1893 and Sale and Supply of Goods and Services Act 1980. Pursuant to this legislation, terms are implied into contracts for the sale of goods and the supply of services concerning the title of goods supplied,[819] and the quality of goods and services supplied, amongst others.[820]

3. Implied by Usage

436. Lastly, a court can imply a term into a contract based on custom and usage.[821] Not every trade custom will receive judicial recognition. The trade custom must be reasonable, consistent with the express terms of the contract and universally recognized in the trade as a legally binding custom.[822]

E. Terms Excluding or Limiting Liability

437. Generally, at common law, the court will enforce an exclusion clause as long as it forms part of the contract and it is clearly drafted to cover the situation. Between parties of equal bargaining strength, exclusion clauses allow the parties to allocate risk and plan their relationship. However, the use of exclusion clauses can be abused by a party in a stronger bargaining position, particularly where the other party is a consumer. As a result, the common law developed rules to deal with widely drafted clauses. In addition, the Sale of Goods and Supply of Services Act 1980 contains special rules on the exclusion of liability for breach of the statutory implied terms, based on a distinction between commercial and consumer sales.[823] Moreover, the EC (Unfair Terms in Consumer Contracts) Regulations 1995, as amended, offer further protection for consumers from unfair terms, including exclusion clauses.[824]

817. *Robb v. Green* [1895] 2 QB 315.
818. *Educational Co. Ltd v. Fitzpatrick (No. 2)* [1961] IR 345.
819. *See* paras 469–484 below.
820. *See* paras 485–541 and paras 638–639 below.
821. Technically, a custom refers to a practice in a particular area, while a usage refers to a practice in a particular trade. Today, the terms are used interchangeably.
822. *Paxton v. Courtnay* (1860) 2 F&F 131; *O ' Reilly v. Irish Press* (1937) ILTR 194; *O ' Connaill v. The Irish Echo* [1958] 92 ILTR 156.
823. *See* paras 963–967. Similar rules apply under the Consumer Credit Act 1995 to hire purchase and other hire contract.
824. *See* paras 426, 973–976.

1. Common Law

438. Generally, at common law, a court will enforce an exclusion clause provided: (i) it is properly incorporated; and (ii) it is clearly drafted to cover the situation.

a. Incorporation

439. To be effective, the exclusion clause must form part of the contract, that is, it must be properly incorporated before the contract is concluded. The rules on incorporation of contract terms are examined above.[825] Indeed, many of these rules were developed with exclusion clauses in mind.

b. Drafting

440. Obviously, the exclusion clause must be clearly drafted to cover the situation which gives rise to liability in the first place. Where an exclusion clause is ambiguous, a court will interpret the exclusion clause against the party seeking to rely on it and hence in favour of the person against whom it is being enforced. This rule of interpretation is known as the *contra proferentem* rule. As a result, exclusion clauses must be drafted clearly and unambiguously.

c. The Doctrine of Fundamental Breach

441. Partly because of the fear that, in some contracts, parties were trying to exclude their liability for failure to perform even the most basic, or fundamental, terms of the contract, the courts developed the doctrine of fundamental breach. The issue is whether an exclusion clause can exclude liability for fundamental breach of contract. The courts have reacted to such clauses in two different ways by saying that:

- an exclusion clause can never excuse a fundamental breach;
- an exclusion clause may excuse a fundamental breach depending on the construction of the clause.

In one line of English cases the first position was preferred, but, in *Photo Production v. Securior,*[826] the House of Lords adopted the second approach. There, the plaintiff had engaged the defendant security firm to make periodic visits during the night to their factory. An employee of the security firm on one of these visits lit a small fire which got out of hand and burnt down the factory and contents causing a loss of GBP 615,000. The plaintiff sued and the defendant sought to exclude its liability on the basis of a clause which provided:

825. *See* paras 406–409 above.
826. [1980] AC 827; *see also Suisse Atlantique* [1967] AC 361. *See further Western Meats Ltd v. National Ice and Cold Storage Co. Ltd* [1982] ILRM 99.

> 'Under no circumstances' was the defendant to be 'responsible for any injurious act or default by any employee ... unless such act or default could have been foreseen and avoided by the exercise of due diligence' of the defendant.

The English Court of Appeal found that the defendant was in fundamental breach of contract by failing to do what in essence it had promised to do and that an exclusion clause can never excuse such a fundamental breach. On appeal, the House of Lords disagreed and found that the clause was completely clear, it covered the defendant's position and hence was effective. Therefore, under English law, there is no common law prohibition on the use of such clauses. Unfortunately, the position in Ireland is not so clear. The leading authority here is *Clayton Love v. B & I Transport*,[827] a case decided before the later English authorities setting out the above rule, which favours a stricter approach to the use of such clauses. However, though not over-ruled, its future application has been rendered uncertain by its age and the later English and Irish authority.[828]

2. Sale of Goods and Supply of Services Act 1980

442. The above rules apply to contracts in general; however, additional rules apply in particular areas. In a commercial context, the Sale of Goods and Supply of Services Act 1980 provides the most important source of such additional rules. The Sale of Goods Act 1893 and Sale of Goods and Supply of Services Act 1980 imply various terms as to the title and the quality of goods and services supplied in contracts for the sale of goods and supply of services.[829] Liability for breach of some of these terms can never be excluded.[830] In other cases, liability for breach of the terms can never be excluded where the buyer deals as a consumer,[831] but otherwise 'fair and reasonable' exclusion is permissible.[832]

3. The EC (Unfair Terms in Consumer Contracts) Regulations

443. The Sale of Goods and Supply of Services Act 1980 regulates the exclusion of seller's liability for breach of the statutory implied terms only. All other terms in a sale of goods and a supply of services contract, whether exclusionary or not, are regulated by the common law,[833] and, in certain circumstances, by the EC

827. (1970) 104 ILTR 157.
828. *See*, e.g., *ESL Consulting Ltd v. Verizon (Ireland) Ltd & Anor* [2008] IEHC 369, [2010] 2 IR 426. *See further* Clark, *Contract Law in Ireland* paras 7-48–7-51 (7th ed., Thomson Round Hall 2013) and Friel, *The Law of Contract* 205–207 (2nd ed., Round Hall Sweet & Maxwell 2000).
829. *See further* paras 469–484; 485–541; and 638–639.
830. Liability for breach of 1893 Act, s. 12, can never be excluded: 1893 Act, s. 55(3), as substituted by the 1980 Act, s. 22: *see further* para. 484.
831. Defined in 1980 Act, s. 3: *see further* para. 535.
832. For example, this rule applies to ss 13–15 of the 1893 Act: 1893 Act s. 55(4), as substituted by the 1980 Act, s. 22: *see further* para. 535.
833. *See* paras 421–424 above.

(Unfair Terms in Consumer Contracts) Regulations 1995[834] and 2000.[835] The Regulations seek to implement the EC Directive on Unfair Terms in Consumer Contracts.[836] In essence, they seek to protect consumers from unfair contract terms. The Regulations are considered in more detail in Part II, Chapter 5.

F. The Parol Evidence Rule

444. Generally, under the parol evidence rule, where a contract is reduced to writing neither party can rely on evidence extrinsic to the written contract, whether oral or written, to add to or vary the terms of the written contract. The rationale for the rule is to promote certainty. It is assumed that where the parties have gone to the trouble of reducing their agreement to writing that the written document represents fully their agreement and that the parties intend their relations to be governed by that written document and by it alone. The rule is however subject to many refinements and exceptions. For example, the rule only relates to evidence as to the *content* of a contract: it does not apply where evidence is introduced to show that the contract is not properly formed. Further, the rule only prevents a party relying on extrinsic evidence as to the *express* terms of a contract: intrinsic evidence can be introduced to show that the term ought to be implied.

III. Discharge of Contractual Obligations

445. The obligations of the parties under a contract can be discharged, or brought to an end, in a number of ways:

- by consent of the parties
- by performance
- under the doctrine of frustration and
- sometimes, following a breach of contract.

Each in outlined further below.

A. Consent

446. Because the formation of a contract is based on the consent of the parties, parties are free to agree to terminate a contract, before or during performance, by mutual consent. However, as with formation of a contract, consideration is required. This is usually not a problem where both sides agree to terminate the contract when

834. SI No. 27 of 1995.
835. SI No. 307 of 2000.
836. 93/13/EEC, [1993] OJ L 95/29.

both still have obligations to perform: mutual promises represent sufficient consideration for each other. But where only one party is discharged, that party must supply some further consideration.[837]

B. Performance

447. Where parties perform their duties, in accordance with the terms of the contract, their contractual duties are said to be discharged, or ended. However, performance must meet exactly with the terms of the contract and where performance is less than is required by the contract, this can amount to a breach of contract. An illustration of this rule can be found in *Re Moore v. Landauer*,[838] where a sales contract required that tins were to be packed and delivered in cases of thirty tins. The correct total of tins was delivered; however, some cases contained only twenty-four tins. This was held to be a repudiatory breach of contract and the buyer did not have to pay or accept the goods.

448. Insignificant deviations from the terms of the contract may be allowed under the *de minimis* exception. What amounts to 'insignificant' depends on each particular case. In *Wilensko v. Fenwick*,[839] sellers sold timber of specified measurements to the buyers. Just under 1% of the timber failed to meet the exact specification and this was held to be a breach of contract. In contrast, in *Shipton Anderson & Co v. Weil Bros*,[840] where there was a contract for the sale of not more than 4,950 tons of wheat, an extra 55 pounds were delivered, an excess of 0.0005%. The court found that this excess was so slight that the buyer could not argue that the seller had failed to perform his obligation under the contract. In commercial contracts it seems likely that the *de minimis* exception will be narrowly construed. To avoid this problem, an express term should be included in a commercial contract to allow for minor variations in performance. In practice, most business persons would not seek to terminate a contract for slight variations, they would rather deal with a lesser, or excess, delivery by adjusting the contract price.

C. The Doctrine of Frustration

449. Under this doctrine the parties' obligations under a contract may be discharged by operation of the law. A contract is said to be frustrated where:

– it becomes impossible to perform the contract
– the purpose of the contract is not achievable
– performance becomes illegal.

---

837. *See* variation of contract at para. 384 above.
838. [1921] 2 KB 519.
839. [1938] 3 All ER 429.
840. [1912] 1 KB 574.

1. Impossibility of Performance

450. The occurrence of certain events between the time of the making of the contract and the performance of the contract can lead to the contract being frustrated. For instance, where the subject matter of the contract is destroyed, the contract may be frustrated. In *Asfar v. Blundel,*[841] there was a contract for the sale of dates. The dates were on a barge which sank and the dates were impregnated with river water and sewage. Physically the dates still existed, they were recovered from the river and could be used to distil alcohol. However, in a commercial sense, the dates were destroyed or perished, and hence the contract was frustrated. Equally, where a contract places a personal duty on a party, the death of that party may frustrate the contract.

451. The doctrine of frustration only relieves the parties from their respective obligations under the contract where the performance of the contract is impossible, not merely impracticable. *Neville & Sons v. Guardian Builders Ltd*[842] illustrates this point. The defendant entered into a contract with the plaintiff whereby the plaintiff was to build houses on the defendant's land. A term of this agreement required the defendant to give the plaintiff permission (a license) to enter the land. However, the defendant's land was landlocked and it had no access to a nearby road. The defendant sought to gain the necessary access by purchasing adjoining land owned by the County Council. There were delays in buying the adjoining land, because the County Council wanted to impose conditions on the sale to which the defendant would not agree. The plaintiff grew impatient and sought an order for specific performance. The plaintiff argued, in its defence, that the contract was frustrated. The Supreme Court stated that frustration of a contract takes place when a supervening event occurs without the default of either party and for which the contract makes no sufficient provision. Further, the frustrating event must so significantly change the nature of the outstanding contractual rights and obligations from what the parties could reasonably have contemplated at the time of the contract's execution that it would be unjust to hold them to its stipulations in the new circumstances. In such a case, the parties are discharged from further performance of the contract and the court has the power to declare the contract at an end. On the facts, the court found that if the defendant had purchased the County Council land, the building could start. However, the County Council had insisted on certain conditions to the sale and the defendant was not happy to contract on those terms. This, according to the Supreme Court, should not be classified as a supervening event which significantly changes the nature of the outstanding contractual rights and obligations. The performance of the contract had become more onerous but was not frustrated. It is essential that the frustrating events are outside the control of the parties; you cannot have self-induced frustration.[843] In the *Neville* case, getting ownership of the County Council land to give effect to the license with the plaintiff was not outside the control of the defendant, and hence the contract was not frustrated.

841. [1896] 1 QB 123.
842. [1995] ILRM 1.
843. *Herman v. Owners of SS Vicia* [1942] IR 304.

2. Purpose Frustrated

452. This is a narrow ground which is based on a series of cases involving the hiring of rooms to view the coronation of King Edward VII. Due to illness, the coronation was postponed. The rooms were still available but there was nothing to view and so the contracts were frustrated. Other cases illustrate the limits of this ground. For instance, where a property has been bought for redevelopment and it turns out that redevelopment cannot happen, or becomes more difficult, because the property is 'listed', this has been held not to amount to frustration.[844] Also, a sales contract to export or import goods is not frustrated where there are export or import restrictions.[845]

3. Illegality

453. Where the performance of a contract becomes illegal, such as where a trade embargo is imposed after the contract is made, it is frustrated.

4. Effect of Frustration

454. The effect of frustration is that the contract ends automatically, and the parties are discharged from all future obligations. In *Kearney v. Saorstat & Continental Shipping*,[846] the plaintiff's contract of employment ended when his ship sank and so when he later died his wife was unable to benefit from workman's compensation insurance which was dependent on the continued existence of an employment contract. Any obligations arising before the frustrating event are still effective in law.

D. Breach of Contract

455. A breach of contract does not discharge the contract, or either party. But, a breach may entitle the innocent party to terminate the contract and thus treat himself/herself as discharged from his/her outstanding contractual obligations. Generally, where a party does not do what he/she is required to do under the terms of the contract, his/her failure to properly perform is sufficient to establish liability: liability is strict; it is not dependent on fault. However, in some areas, contractual liability is based on fault, such as with contracts for the supply of services under section 39(b) of the Sale of Goods and Supply of Services Act 1980.[847] Where a party fails to perform his/her contractual obligations, without lawful excuse, there is a breach of contract. There are a number of remedies available for a breach of contract including: termination, damages and specific performance.

---

844. *AIP v. Walker* [1976] 3 All ER 509.
845. *CCGCIE v. Tradax* [1983] 1 Lloyd's Rep 250.
846. (1943) Ir Jur Rep 8.
847. *See* para. 638 below.

1. Termination

456. Breach of a term of the contract does not necessarily terminate the contract, only where there has been a breach of a condition or an innominate term, where the consequences of the breach are serious, is the innocent party entitled to treat the breach as a repudiation of the contract and terminate the contract.[848] The innocent party can accept or reject that repudiation. Where he/she accepts the repudiation the contract is terminated and the parties' outstanding obligations under the contract are discharged. Or, the innocent party can choose to affirm the contract and pursue a claim in damages only. Where a warranty has been breached, the remedy is damages only. The parties are not discharged from their obligations under the contract: the contract continues.

2. Damages

457. Despite the principle *pacta sunt servante*, where one party fails to perform his/her obligations under a contract, the courts will rarely force performance. The usual contract law remedy is damages, not an order for specific performance. Damages are available for every breach of contract whether the term breached is a condition, an innominate term or a warranty. This contrasts with the discretionary nature of an order for specific performance.

a. The Compensation Principle

458. An award of damages seeks to compensate the innocent party.[849] It is said the purpose of damages, in contract law, is to put the innocent party in the position he/she would have been in had the contract been performed. Following on from this compensation principle a number of observations can be made. First, because damages are supposed to compensate, they are only payable where a party has suffered a loss. If no loss is suffered, the court may recognize that a legal right has been breached but because there is no loss, there is no need for compensation and so nominal damages may be awarded. Second, the purpose of damages in contract law is to compensate the innocent party and not to punish the person in breach of contract and so punitive damages are not available in contract law.

b. Types of Loss

459. Following a breach of contract, an innocent party can be compensated for physical injury, property damage and more commonly in a commercial context, financial loss.

848. *See*, e.g., *Athlone RDC v. Campbell (No. 2)* (1912) ILTR 142, *Dundalk Shopping Centre v. Roof Spray Ltd* [1990] ILRM 377.

849. *Doran v. Delaney* [1999] 1 IR 303 per Geoghegan J at 308.

c. Causation

460. A plaintiff can only recover damages if there is a causal link between the breach of contract and his/her loss. Where the loss is not caused by the breach of contract, no damages are available.

d. Remoteness

461. When a contract is breached, a series of events can occur which cause the plaintiff loss. However, a defendant is not liable for every event which follows from a breach of contract: it is said that where the loss is too remote, or too far away from the breach, the defendant will not be liable. The leading authority on contractual remoteness is *Hadley v. Baxendale.*[850] In that case, the plaintiff ran a mill. The shaft in the mill broke and had to be sent to the makers in Greenwich as a model for a new shaft. The defendant agreed to carry the shaft to Greenwich but in breach of contract, delayed its delivery for a few days, leaving the mill idle. The legal issue was whether the defendant should be liable for lost profits which resulted from the mill being idle which resulted from the delay in delivery. The court held that this loss was too remote and it laid down the following test:

- the loss must arise naturally from the breach;
- the loss must be such that it might reasonably be in the minds of the parties at the time they made the contract as the probable result of the breach.

In *Hadley v. Baxendale,* it appears that the defendant did not know that the mill would be kept idle until the new shaft arrived.

e. Mitigation

462. Where there has been a breach of contract, there is a duty placed on the innocent party to mitigate or minimize his/her loss. Where an innocent party pursues a claim for damages and the court finds that he/she has failed to take all reasonable steps to mitigate his/her loss, his/her damages will be reduced by an amount to arrive at an amount of damages as if he/she had mitigated his/her loss.[851]

f. Measure of Damages

463. The measure of damages, or the *quantum,* is the actual amount of money payable. Specific rules exist in relation to the type of loss caused. For example, where the claim is for *expectation loss*, the measure is the difference in value between the performance rendered and the performance actually contracted for, or the cost of remedying the defective performance and bringing it up to the contractual standard. Where the claim is for *reliance loss,* the measure of damages is the cost of the action (inaction) on reliance on the contract.

850. (1854) 9 Ex 341.
851. *See*, e.g., *Cullen v. Horgan* [1925] 2 IR 1.

g. Time of Assessment

464. The general rule is that the time of assessment of the amount of damages is the date of the breach. However, an innocent party is usually given some time after the breach to assess the position and decide what is best to do (in order to mitigate, for instance), and so damages are then assessed at the end of that time, rather than the day of the breach. Other times the innocent party will not learn of the breach until days, or weeks, after it has occurred. In such circumstances, damages are assessed when the innocent party knew or should have known of the breach.

h. Penalty Clauses and Liquidated Damages Clauses

465. The above rules, especially on remoteness and the measure of damages, can make it very difficult to predict what damages may be payable following a breach of contract. To avoid such uncertainty, commercial contracts often contain a clause providing that a fixed sum is payable on breach of contract: a 'liquidated damages clause'. Where the clause represents a reasonable pre-estimate of the loss it will be enforced, but where the clause is excessive and acts as a sort of deterrent against breach, then it is called a 'penalty clause' and the courts will not give effect to it. The leading authority for distinguishing the two is *Dunlop v. New Garage & Motor*,[852] where a four-stage test was established, the most important element being that:

> a sum is a penalty where it is extravagant when compared with the greatest loss that could conceivable follow the breach.

3. Specific Performance

466. An order for specific performance is only available where damages would not be sufficient to compensate the party. In most commercial contracts damages will be sufficient compensation and hence specific performance has limited application in commercial dealings. Damages might not be sufficient compensation where there was a contract to sell unique goods, for example. As noted above, there is no right to specific performance; the court has a discretion whether to grant it or not.

852. [1915] AC 79; *see also*; *O ' Donnell & Co. Ltd v. Truck and Machinery Sales Ltd* [1998] 4 I.R. 1; *Sheehan v Breccia* [2018] IECA 286; and *Flynn & Anor v Breccia* [2018] IECA 273.

§2. SALE OF GOODS

467. Commercial contracts for the sale of goods are governed by the Sale of Goods Act 1893, as amended by Part II of the Sale of Goods and Supply of Services Act 1980.[853] Together this legislation is referred to as the Sale of Goods Acts 1893 and 1980.[854] These Acts set out the rights and duties of the parties; however, neither are codes in the sense that they do not contain all the applicable rules. Much of the law can be found outside the Acts in the common law. Section 61(2) of the 1893 Act, provides that 'The rules of the common law, including the law merchant' shall apply to contracts for the sale of goods, except insofar as they are modified by the Act. For instance, the common law rules on mistake,[855] frustration[856] and damages[857] are modified in the legislation. Other relevant areas of the common law, including contractual formation, and the doctrine of privity remain untouched by the legislation.

468. An important feature of the Sale of Goods Acts 1893 and 1980 is that many of the rules contained therein operate by default, that is, they apply unless the parties have agreed otherwise. This approach reflects the laissez-faire policy which dominated the late nineteenth century whereby the purpose of commercial law generally, and sales law in particular, was to provide a framework within which merchants could transact. Merchants were free to decide what suited them best, and only where they omitted to address a particular issue, such as the place of delivery, would the legislation step-in to provide that the place of delivery is the seller's place of business.[858]

469. Accordingly, today, in the commercial context, many sales of goods are governed by standard form contracts which contain detailed rules specific to the contract in question, the default rules in the legislation being inappropriate. These standard terms can either be drafted by one of the parties to the contract (usually the dominant party with the terms being offered on a 'take-it-or-leave-it' basis) and hence are 'private' between the parties or adopted from a set of standard terms promoted by a trade organization. In certain sectors of the economy, such as the grain trade or the oil trade, this latter type of standard form contract is prevalent.[859] Where a dispute arises in these circumstances, any resolution will usually revolve around the particular wording of the standard form contract in question, the legislation forming a backdrop to the dispute.

853. Where the buyer is a consumer, this legislation is supplemented by the European Communities (Certain Aspects of the Sale of Consumer Goods and Associated Guarantees) Regulations 2003, SI No. 11 of 2003; *see further* Part II, Ch. 5, §2 on consumer law.
854. 1980 Act, s. 9.
855. 1893 Act, s. 6.
856. 1893 Act, s. 7.
857. 1893 Act, ss 51–54.
858. 1893 Act, s. 29(1).
859. For example, in international trade, GAFTA (the Grain and Feed Trade Association) and FOSFA (the Federation of Oil Seeds and Fats Association) promote standard form sales contracts.

470. In 2008 an expert group, the Sales Law Review Group, was established to advise the Government on reform of the law on sale of goods and related matters and to make recommendations for a scheme of legislation capable of providing a statutory sales law framework appropriate to modern-day conditions and needs. In 2011, the Group published its final report containing 124 recommendations for reform.[860] The Report recommends the repeal of the existing Sale of Goods Act 1893 and the Sale of Goods and Supply of Services Act 1980 and the introduction of a new Sale of Goods Act dealing primarily with commercial sales and separate primary legislation dealing with consumer transactions. Key specific recommendations for reform are identified throughout below. The Report has been accepted in principle by the Government,[861] and at the time of writing, draft legislation was being prepared.

I. Application of Legislation

471. The Sale of Goods Acts 1893 and 1980 only apply to contracts for the sale of goods as defined in the legislation. Section 1(1) of the 1893 Act defines a contract for the sale of goods as:

> a contract whereby the seller transfers or agrees to transfer the property in goods to the buyer for a money consideration, called the price.

Further, a contract of sale can be in one of two forms: a sale, or, an agreement to sell. This point is made in section 1(3):

> Where under a contract of sale the property in the goods is transferred from the seller to the buyer the contract is called a sale; but where the transfer of the property in the goods is to take place at a future time or subject to some condition thereafter to be fulfilled the contract is called an agreement to sell.

Hence, a *sale* operates as an executed contract and a conveyance, in one. An *agreement to sell* is merely a contract. Some further act or event is necessary before the property in the goods can vest in the buyer under the contract. But both are contracts of sale and come within the legislative definition. The various elements of this definition: the parties; the property; the price; and the goods are examined further below.

860. *Report on the Legislation Governing the Sale of Goods and Supply of Services* (Dublin, Prn. A11/1576, 2011).
861. *See* Press Release: Bruton Announces Major Overhaul of Consumer Law, 18 Oct. 2011, available at http://www.djei.ie/press/2011/20111018.htm.

A. The Parties

472. It is well established that the requirement, in the statutory definition of a contract for the sale of goods, that the property be transferred from one party to another means that there must be two distinct parties: a seller and a buyer. The seller and the buyer can be part-owners of the same goods,[862] but the same person cannot be both the seller and the buyer.

B. Transfer of the Property

473. The essence of a contract for the sale of goods is the transfer of property in the goods from the seller to the buyer. 'Property' is defined in section 62 of the 1893 Act as meaning the general property in the goods, and not merely a special property. In this sense, 'property' means the absolute legal interest in the goods, or 'ownership'. Where the intention of the parties is not to pass property or ownership, the contract is not a contract of sale within the meaning of the legislation. Therefore, contracts of hire and hire purchase are excluded. Moreover, section 61(4) of the 1893 Act provides that the legislation does not apply to any transaction in the form of a sale that is intended to operate by way of mortgage, pledge, charge or other security.[863] Specific rules on the passing of property are set out in sections 16–19 of the 1893 Act and are outlined in section VII.[864]

C. The Price

474. The goods must be sold for 'a money consideration, called the price'. If the consideration for the goods under the contract is in any form other than money consideration, the contract will not be a contract of sale within the terms of the legislation. Where, for example, the consideration for the goods is other goods, as is the case with a contract of barter, the transaction falls outside the Sale of Goods Acts. Or, where for example, money is traded for money (except money in curia), as is the case with a foreign exchange transaction, again the Sale of Goods Acts have no application. Section 8 of the 1893 Act provides for the setting of the price. Accordingly, the price can be fixed by the contract, or by an agreed manner, or it may be determined by the course of dealings between the parties. Otherwise, a reasonable price is payable, and what is a reasonable price is a question of fact dependent on the circumstances of each case.

---

862. 1893 Act, s. 1(1).
863. *See further* Part I, Ch. 10.
864. *See* paras 590–603 below.

D. The Goods

475. The subject matter of the contract must be goods. Goods are defined in section 62 of the 1893 Act as including 'all chattels personal other than things in action and money'. In Irish law, all property can be classified as real or personal. Real property includes land and anything permanently attached to the land, such as buildings. Personal property is all property except real property. Personal property divides into chattels real (mainly leasehold interests in land) and chattels personal. Chattels personal are those items which are not chattels real. Chattels personal subdivide broadly into two classes: tangibles moveables (or *choses in possession)* such as goods and money; and intangible moveables (or *choses in action*). Therefore, goods are a type of personal property. But excluded from the definition of goods under the Sale of Goods Acts are certain types of personal property: things in action, and money. Things in action (or *choses in action*) are legal rights that are intangible in form, such as debts, shares in a partnership or a company, and intellectual property rights – copyright, patents and trademarks. Goods in comparison are tangible, movable and visible in nature. Also, excluded from the definition of goods is money, meaning legally recognized tender. Money in curia, such as antique coins, is goods for the purpose of the legislation.

476. Certain items clearly come within the above definition and are well recognized as goods, for the purpose of the Sale of Goods Acts. For example, ships, aircraft, motor vehicles and domestic animals are all goods. The matter is not so straight-forward in relation to other items though. Electricity and other forms of energy, while clearly capable of being sold, have never been defined as goods, for the purposes of the Sale of Goods Acts. Also, there is no Irish authority on whether human remains and body parts, products and genetic material (such as organs, blood and sperm) are goods. Perhaps of more commercial significance is the legal status of computer software. Again, there is no Irish authority on this point. In *St Albans City and District Council v. International Computers Ltd*,[865] Sir Ian Gildewell stated *obiter*, in the Court of Appeal, that while a disk was clearly goods, a program or software, 'being instructions or commands telling the computer hardware what to do', of itself was not. The implication of the above case law is clearly unsatisfactory in that the law applicable to a particular transaction will depend on whether software has been delivered on a physical medium such as a disk or a CD (in which case it could be classified as a sale of goods) or whether it has been downloaded online (in which case it could be categorized as a supply of services, or as a contract sui generis to which the statutory rules do not apply). Despite recognizing the unsatisfactory state of the law, the Sales Law Review Group did not recommend amending the definition of goods to include digital content, nor did it recommend

865. [1996] 4 All ER 481. In *Saphena Computing Ltd v. Allied Collection Agencies Ltd* [1995] FSR 616 the court avoided classifying a supply of software which was adapted to the customer's needs because it was common ground that the law was the same whether it was a supply of services or a sale of goods. A contract to write a new programme for a customer is clearly capable of being a contract for the supply of services: *see Salvage Association v. CAP Financial Services Ltd* [1995] FSR 654.

that digital content should be treated, *as goods*. Instead, it recommended that a comprehensive consultative process on the issues of whether strict liability standards are suitable for software contracts and on whether there is a need for a specialized instrument dealing with software transactions should be undertaken in advance of any further consideration of legislative regulation in this area.[866]

477. The statutory definition of goods in section 62 of the 1893 Act expressly includes 'emblements, industrial growing crops and things attached to or forming part of the land which are agreed to be severed before sale or under the contract of sale'. Emblements are annual crops grown by agricultural labour; industrial growing crops are similarly cultivated but are not expected to mature within one year. Both emblements and industrial growing crops can be contrasted with naturally occurring crops or plants. Naturally occurring crops come under the heading 'things attached to or forming part of the land'. Provided there is an intention to sever any growing thing from the land before the sale or under the contract of sale, the transactions will probably be a sale of goods.

E. Formalities

478. At common law, a contract for the sale of goods required no formalities. This position is reflected in the opening lines of section 3 of the 1893 Act, which provides that subject to the provisions of this Act, or any other Act, a contract of sale may be made in writing, by word of mouth, partly in writing and partly by word of mouth, or may be implied from the conduct of the parties. But section 4(1) of the 1893 Act (which derives from the Statute of Frauds (Ireland) 1695) provides that a contract for the sale of goods of the value of IEP 10 (EUR 12.70) or more is not enforceable by action unless:

- the buyer accepts, and actually receives, part of the goods sold;
- the buyer gives something in earnest to bind the contract;
- the buyer has made part payment;
- there is a note or memorandum in writing of the contract and signed by the party to be charged, that is, to be sued.

Section 4 of the 1893 Act was repealed in the UK in 1954, following a recommendation of the Law Revision Committee.[867] Similarly, the Sales Law Review Group has recommended the repeal of section 4 of the 1893 Act on the basis that it is archaic.[868]

866. Sales Law Review Group, *Report on the Legislation Governing the Sale of Goods and Supply of Services* (Dublin, Prn. A11/1576, 2011) para. 2.29.
867. UK Law Reform (Enforcement of Contracts) Act 1954, s. 1.
868. Sales Law Review Group, *Report on the Legislation Governing the Sale of Goods and Supply of Services* (Dublin, Prn. A11/1576, 2011) para. 3.23.

II. The Duties to Deliver, Accept and Pay

479. Part III of the Sale of Goods Act 1893, sections 27–37, is entitled 'Performance of the Contract'. The first provision of this Part, section 27, sets out the core duties of the parties, under a contract for the sale of goods. Section 27 provides that it is the seller's duty to deliver the goods, and the buyer's duty is to accept and pay for the goods, in accordance with the terms of the contract. If either party fails in these core duties, they will be in breach of the contract.

480. Delivery is defined simply as the 'voluntary transfer of possession from one person to another'.[869] Delivery can be affected in two ways: by actual delivery (i.e., the physical transfer of possession of the goods[870]) or constructive delivery (i.e., the transfer of *control* over the goods, without the physical transfer of possession).

481. Unless the parties have agreed otherwise, the place of delivery is the seller's place of business, if he/she has one, or if not, his/her residence.[871] Under section 32(1) of the 1893 Act, where under the contract of sale the seller is required to send the goods to the buyer, delivery to a carrier, whether named by the buyer or not, for the purpose of transmission to the buyer, is prima facie deemed to be delivery of the goods to the buyer. If, on the other hand, the carrier is the seller's agent, delivery to the carrier does not constitute delivery to the buyer. Further, under section 32(2) of the 1893 Act, unless otherwise authorized by the buyer, the seller is required to make a reasonable contract with the carrier, on behalf of the buyer. If the seller fails to do so and the goods are damaged in transit, the buyer may decline to treat delivery to the carrier as delivery to himself/herself and he/she can hold the seller responsible in damages.

482. All expenses of and incidental to putting the goods in a deliverable state[872] are borne by the seller, unless otherwise agreed.[873] But the legislation does not contain rules as to the expense of delivery itself. At common law, however, the expenses of and incidental to making delivery fall on the seller, and any expenses in relation to preparing for or receiving delivery fall on the buyer. This rule can be varied by the parties, such as in contracts on *cif*, *fob*, or *ex works* terms.

483. If the seller is obliged under the contract to send the goods to the buyer and no time is fixed, the seller is required to send them within a reasonable time.[874] Otherwise, if no time is fixed, a court would usually imply that the goods should be

869. 1893 Act, s. 62.
870. 1893 Act, s. 29(1) provides that it is a question depending on the terms of the contract whether the seller should send, or the buyer take possession of, the goods.
871. 1893 Act, s. 29(1).
872. Goods are in a 'deliverable state' when they are in such a state that the buyer would under the contract be bound to take delivery of them: 1893 Act, s. 62(4).
873. 1983 Act, s. 29(5).
874. 1893 Act, s. 29(2).

delivered within a reasonable time.[875] What is reasonable will depend on the circumstances of the case. If goods are delivered late, the seller is in breach of contract and the buyer can sue for damages. However, if the duty to deliver at or within a specific time is classified as a condition, time is said to be 'of the essence', and late delivery entitles the buyer to reject the goods, terminate the contract and sue the seller for damages, even if the delay is slight. Under section 10(1) of the 1893 Act, whether the time for delivery is 'of the essence', or merely a warranty depends on the terms of the contract. However, it has been held that in ordinary commercial contracts for the sale of goods the time for delivery is prima facie of the essence.[876] This is a presumptive rule that can be rebutted.

484. In relation to the time of delivery, and as of 14 June 2014, separate rules for consumer sales have been introduced into the Sale of Goods Act 1893, pursuant to the EU (Consumer Information, Cancellation and other Rights) Regulations 2013.[877] Accordingly, unless the parties have agreed otherwise, the seller must deliver the goods by transferring the physical possession or control of the goods to the consumer buyer without undue delay and not later than thirty days from the conclusion of the contract.[878] Where a seller fails to deliver the goods at the time agreed with the consumer buyer, the buyer may require the seller to make the delivery within an additional period of time appropriate to the circumstances. However, this option to extend the delivery time does not apply where:

(a) the seller has refused to deliver the goods;
(b) delivery of the goods within the time agreed with the consumer buyer is essential, taking into account all the relevant circumstances at the time of the conclusion of the contract;
(c) the consumer buyer has informed the seller prior to the conclusion of the contract that delivery on or by a specified date is essential.[879]

Where the seller fails to deliver the goods as originally agreed, or within any additional period of time, the consumer buyer may treat the failure as a breach of a condition of the contract, which entitles the buyer to repudiate the contract.[880] In these circumstances, the seller must, without undue delay, reimburse all sums paid under the contract,[881] and a claim for damages may also be available.

485. Section 30 of the 1893 Act sets out details of the amount to be delivered and what happens if the wrong quantity is delivered. Essentially, unless the seller

875. *Hick v. Raymond and Reid* [1893] AC 22.
876. *Hartley v. Hymans* [1920] KB 475, *per* McCardie, J, 483–484; *see also Charles Rickards v. Oppenhaim* [1950] 1 KB 616.
877. SI No. 484/2013, Regulation 30.
878. Sale of Goods Act 1893 s. 29(2B).
879. Sale of Goods Act 1893 s. 29(2C).
880. Sale of Goods Act 1893 s. 29(2E).
881. Sale of Goods Act 1893 s. 29(2F).

delivers the exact amount, barring minute differences under the *de minimis* doctrine,[882] the buyer can reject the goods and terminate the contract. Further, section 31 provides that, unless otherwise agreed, the buyer is not obliged to accept delivery of the goods by instalments.

486. The remedies under section 30 are default remedies and are stated to apply subject to any usage of trade, special agreement or course of dealing between the parties.[883] Section 30 applies in three sets of circumstances. First, where the seller delivers a lesser quantity than that contracted for, the buyer is given two options. He/she may: (i) reject the quantity of goods delivered; or (ii) accept the quantity of goods delivered and pay for them at the contract rate, that is, the price payable is reduced proportionately to the quantity delivered.[884] In either case, the buyer also has the right to sue for damages for the seller's breach, for non-delivery. Where the price is prepaid he/she is entitled to a refund of the full price under option (i), or to a refund of part of the price equal to the undelivered amount under option (ii). Second, where the seller delivers a greater quantity than that contracted for, the buyer is given three options. He/she may: (i) accept the contract quantity and reject the rest; (ii) reject the whole quantity; or (iii) accept the whole quantity delivered and pay for them at the contract rate, that is, the price will be increased in proportion to the amount delivered.[885] Again, the buyer may be able to claim damages for the seller's failure to deliver the correct quantity, but option (iii) is effectively an offer for a new contract, and where the buyer accepts the greater quantity, it appears that he/she is precluded from claiming damages for delivery of the wrong quantity. Finally, where the seller delivers goods he/she contracted to sell mixed with goods of a different description, the buyer is given two options. He/she may: (i) accept the goods which match the contract description and reject the rest; or (ii) reject the whole quantity delivered.[886] The Sales Law Review Group has recommended the repeal of this last provision – section 31(3) – because of its limited nature and instead has recommended that future legislation should give buyers a right of partial rejection of goods not in conformity with the contract and which do not form part of a commercial unit.[887]

487. The combination of the default remedies, and a narrow *de minimis* rule, can operate harshly on sellers where deliveries are made and they are not of the correct quantity contracted for. To mitigate such harshness, the default rules are frequently modified by express terms which describe the quantity to be delivered in approximate terms (e.g., '100,000 litres, plus or minus 5%') or including a price variation clause whereby the price can vary in line with the quantity delivered, although outer limits on the maximum and minimum amount to be delivered would need to be agreed. Moreover, the Sales Law Review Group has recommended that the right of

882. *Shipton Anderson & Co. v. Weil Bros* [1912] 1 KB 574.
883. 1893 Act, s. 30(4).
884. 1893 Act, s. 30(1).
885. 1893 Act, s. 30(2).
886. 1893 Act, s. 30(3).
887. Sales Law Review Group, *Report on the Legislation Governing the Sale of Goods and Supply of Services* (Dublin, Prn. A11/1576, 2011) para. 8.39.

buyers to reject for delivery of a wrong quantity should not apply in commercial contracts of sale where the excess or shortfall is so slight that it would be unreasonable to reject the whole of the goods.[888]

III. Implied Terms as to Title

488. The passing of property in the goods, from the seller to the buyer, is identified in the statutory definition of a sale of goods contract as an essential ingredient. But at common law, a seller's act of selling did not necessarily warrant that he/she had the right to sell. Today, section 12 of the Sale of Goods Act 1893, as substituted by section 10 of the 1980 Act, implies various undertakings, on the part of the seller, as to title in contracts for the sale of goods.

489. Section 12(1) implies one condition and two warranties. First, section 12(1)(a) implies a condition that, in relation to a sale, the seller has the right to sell the goods, and in relation to an agreement to sell, that he/she will have the right to sell the goods at the time property is to pass. Further, section 12(1)(b) implies a warranty that the goods are free and will remain free from any charge or encumbrance not disclosed to the buyer before the contract is made; and a second warranty that the buyer will enjoy quite possession of the goods.

490. Section 12(1) implies these undertakings 'in every contract of sale, other than one to which subsection (2) applies'. This provision is unique, among the statutory implied terms, with regard to its width of application. In contrast, section 13 of the 1893 Act applies only to sales by description; while section 14 of the 1893 Act, applies only to sales in the course of a business.[889] Again, unlike the majority of the other statutory implied terms, liability for breach of the section 12 undertakings can never be excluded. Furthermore, the remedies for breach of these undertakings are more extensive than for the other implied terms.

491. Section 12(2) allows the seller to limit the title he/she passes to the buyer under the contract of sale but requires disclosure to the buyer. Accordingly, where the sale is for a limited interest in goods, there is an implied warranty, under section 12(2)(a), that all charges or encumbrances known by the seller have been disclosed to the buyer before the contract is made, and there is an implied warranty, under section 12(2)(b), that neither the seller, nor any third party, nor anyone claiming under them will disturb the quiet possession of the buyer. This provision would apply where a seller expressly or impliedly contracts to sell a limited title to goods.

888. Sales Law Review Group, *Report on the Legislation Governing the Sale of Goods and Supply of Services* (Dublin, Prn. A11/1576, 2011) para. 8.35.

889. *See further* paras 489–492 and para. 501 below.

A. The Right to Sell

492. Section 12(1)(a) does not refer to the seller's title to the goods, nor does it require the seller to be 'the owner' of the goods.[890] Section 12(1)(a) simply requires that the seller has 'the right to sell'. Clearly, a thief does not have the right to sell goods that he/she has stolen and so he/she can be sued by a buyer for breach of section 12(1)(a), if he/she can be found. Where an owner authorizes an agent to sell his/her goods, the agent has the right to sell, and the owner's title will be passed to the buyer. But, it is arguable that, based on case law, where an owner of goods can be stopped by process of the law from selling the goods, he/she does not have the right to sell and is in breach of section 12(1)(a). In *Niblett v. Confectioner' Materials Ltd,*[891] the defendant seller agreed to sell 3,000 cases of tinned condensed milk, to be shipped from New York to London, to the plaintiff buyer. When the goods arrived, one instalment of 1,000 cases was labelled 'Nissly'. The well-known Nestlé company obtained an undertaking from the seller not to deal further with any similar tins because, it was admitted that, any such dealing would infringe Nestlé's trademark. The plaintiff buyer in order to deal with his tins, and avoid any potential problems with the Nestlé company, had to remove the labels from the tins, at considerable expense, and sell the goods for the best price obtainable. It was held by the Court of Appeal that the buyer was entitled to damages because the seller did not have the right to sell the goods and so was in breach of section 12(1).[892]

493. Section 12(1)(a) states that there is an implied condition on the part of the seller that, in the case of a sale, the seller has the right to sell the goods, and in the case of an agreement to sell, he/she will have such right at the time when property is to pass. Therefore, where there is a *sale*, the seller must have the right to sell immediately, otherwise he/she will be in breach of section 12(1)(a). But, where there is an *agreement to sell*, a seller who does not have the right to sell the goods when he/she concludes the sale agreement is not in breach of section 12(1)(a). Between the time of the agreement and the time for the passing of property under the contract, the seller must acquire the right to sell the goods. So, for example, a seller can contract to sell goods which he/she does not own, and provided that he/she acquires the right to sell them, by buying the goods himself/herself, before property is due to pass under the first contract, he/she will not be in breach of section 12(1)(a).

890. There may be an express term in the contract requiring that the seller be 'the owner' of the goods being sold at the time the agreement is entered into, or some future time, such as delivery: *see*, e.g., *Barber v. NSW Bank* [1996] 1 All ER 906, [1996] 1 WLR 641, where such an express term was identified as a condition.

891. [1921] 3 KB 387; *see also O ' Reilly v. Fineman, Ir Jur Rep* 36 and *The Irish Digest 1939 – 1948* Col 107.

892. It was further held, by Atkin LJ, that the seller was in breach of the warranty as to quiet possession under s. 12(2).

494. The requirement to have the right to sell is identified in the legislation as a condition. Generally, where a condition is breached, the buyer may treat the contract as repudiated, reject the goods and sue for damages for any loss caused. However, a buyer may loose the right to reject the goods where he/she is deemed to have accepted them under sections 34 and 35 of the 1893 Act. Under section 35 a buyer will be deemed to have accepted goods where he/she: (i) intimates acceptance; (ii) does an act inconsistent with the ownership of the seller; or (iii) keeps the goods, without good and sufficient reason, without rejecting them. These standard rules on rejection and acceptance would appear not to apply to a breach of section 12. More particularly, where the breach consists of the seller's failure to pass good title to the goods sold, the buyer is prima facie entitled to recover the whole of the purchase price paid because of a total failure of consideration on the part of the seller.

495. The leading case in this area is the English case of *Rowland v. Divall.*[893] There the defendant, S, bought a car, in good faith, from a thief, T, and resold it to the plaintiff, B1, a car-dealer, for GBP 334. Two months later, the car-dealer, in turn, sold it on to a third party, B2, for GBP 400. Another two months later, the police repossessed the car on behalf of the original owner, O. B1 returned the price of the car, GBP 400, to B2, and then claimed GBP 334 from S on the basis that there was a total failure of consideration because of the breach of section 12. S admitted liability for the breach but defended the claim by arguing that B1, and any subsequent buyers, obtained a benefit from the contract of four months use of the car, and further, that B1 could not reject the car, because it had been repossessed by its owner. Despite these arguments, the Court of Appeal upheld B's claim allowing a total refund of the price. The reasoning is not clear but it appears, in part, to be based on the notion that the whole object of a sale is to pass property and B1 did not get such property.[894] Further, the Court of Appeal held that because the breach had been so fundamental, there could be no acceptance in these circumstances. The rule in the legislation preventing rejection once the goods have been accepted[895] did not apply here because, according to Atkin LJ, the rule only applies to sales, and where no title is passed, as was the case here, the transaction is not a sale.[896]

496. As well as claiming a total refund of the purchase price, a buyer who has incurred further expenses, may make a claim in damages. Where, for example, it transpires after several months, that the seller of a car did not have the right to sell

893. [1923] 2 KB 500. Despite much criticism of the case, *Rowland v. Divall* was applied by the Irish Supreme Court in *United Dominion Trust (Ireland) Ltd v. Shannon Caravans Ltd* [1976] IR 225 and more recently approved, by the English Court of Appeal in *Barber v. NSW* [1996] 1 All ER 906.

894. Atkin LJ stated: 'the buyer has not received any part of that which he contracted to receive – namely the property and right to possession – and, that being so, there has been a total failure of consideration'; [1923] 2 KB 500 at 507.

895. To be found in s. 11(1)(c) of the original 1893 Act; *see* now s. 11(3) of the 1893 Act, as substituted by s. 10 of the 1980 Act.

896. Scrutton LJ noted that B's inability to reject the car was a result of it being repossessed by the true owner and was therefore a direct consequence of the seller's breach.

it, the buyer, as well as reclaiming the price, may make a claim in damages for the cost of insurance, tax, maintenance and even defending the action against the true owner.[897]

B. Free from Encumbrances and Quite Possession

497. Section 12(1)(b) implies two further undertakings on the part of the seller. First, there is implied a warranty that the goods are free and will remain free until the time when property is to pass, from any charge or encumbrance not disclosed to the buyer before the contract is made. This provision is of little practical relevance. The rights of any person entitled to a charge or encumbrance over goods, such as a security interest in the goods, depends on them having possession of the goods. Without possession, the charge or encumbrance is equitable in nature, and would be overridden by a bona fide purchaser for value without notice of the charge or encumbrance.

498. Second, there is an implied warranty that the buyer will enjoy quite possession of the goods except insofar as it may be disturbed by the owner or other person entitled to the benefit of any charge or encumbrance so disclosed.[898] For example, in *Rubicon Computer Systems Ltd v. United Paints Ltd,*[899] there was a contract to supply a computer system. Following installation and part payment a dispute arose. The supplier had installed a 'time-lock', which when activated rendered the system unusable. It was held, *inter alia,* that the supplier's installation of the 'time-lock' constituted wrongful interference with the goods and accordingly there was a breach of the buyer's right to quite possession. Breach of this undertaking is not limited to physical interference with the goods. This part of the provision may overlap with section 12(1)(a). In *Niblett v. Confectioner' Materials Co. Ltd,* Atkin LJ considered that the warranty as to quiet possession had been broken because the buyer had to strip off the labels before he could deal with the goods.

499. There will be a breach if the buyer is disturbed in possession by the wrongful acts of the seller, or any person claiming under him/her; or by the lawful acts of any other person, including the true owner.[900] But, there is authority that there will be no breach where the buyer's possession is disturbed by the wrongful acts of third parties,[901] although this is not expressed in the wording of the provision.

---

897. *See*, e.g., *Warman v. Southern Counties Car Finace Corpn Ltd* [1949] 2 KB 576, [1949] 1 All ER 711.

898. Atkin LJ in *Niblett v. Confectioners ' Materials* [1921] 3 KB 387 at 403 states that: 'Probably this warranty resembles the covenant for quiet enjoyment of real property by a vendor who conveys as beneficial owner in being subject to certain limitations, and only purports to protect the purchaser against lawful acts of third persons and against breaches of the contract of sale and tortious acts of the vendor himself.

899. (2000) 2 TCLR 453.

900. *Mason v. Burningham* [1949] 2 KB 545.

901. *The Playa Larga* [1975] 1 WLR 218.

500. Unlike section 12(1)(a), the implied warranty as to quiet possession is a continuing warranty. This is illustrated by the English case, *Microbeads AC v. Vinhurst Road Markings Ltd,*[902] where a buyer was disturbed by a person who acquired a patent in relation to the goods, a road-marking machine, after they were sold to the buyer. There was no breach of the seller's right to sell because, at the relevant time, no such patent had been acquired and hence the seller did have the right to sell; but there was a breach of the warranty of quiet possession. Further, the buyer's right of action does not begin to run until he is disturbed, and, under the Statute of Limitations 1957, he has six years from that time to pursue a section 12 action.[903]

501. Unlike section 12(1)(a) where the requirement that the seller has a right to sell applies at different times, depending on whether the contract is a sale or an agreement to sell, the implied warranties in section 12(1)(b) apply from the time of the contract, even with regard to an agreement to sell.

502. The undertakings in section 12(1)(b) are warranties, breach of which gives rise to a right to claim damages,[904] but not to reject the goods and treat the contract as repudiated.

C. Exclusion of Liability

503. Section 55(3) of the 1893 Act, as substituted by section 22 of the 1980 Act, provides that any term exempting from all or any part of the provisions of section 12 shall be void. Therefore, no one can exclude or restrict the implied terms as to title regardless of whether the buyer is dealing as a consumer or not. In contrast with the rules on exclusion of liability in relation to the implied terms as to quality, under sections 13–15 of the 1893 Act, where a reasonable exclusion may be made where the buyer is not dealing as a consumer, this rule in relation to section 12 illustrates the primacy, or fundamental nature, of section 12 amongst the implied terms. Of course, as noted above, section 12(1) does not apply where the sale is for a limited interest in the goods under section 12(2). Accordingly, the implied terms in section 12(1) can be effectively avoided where the seller sells a limited interest in goods and discloses this fact. The rules on the exclusion of liability for breach of the statutory implied terms, do not apply to international sale of goods contracts, as defined in section 61(6)(b) of the 1893 Act.

IV. Implied Terms as to Quality

504. As noted above, the core duties of the parties to a contract for the sale of goods are set down in section 27 of the Sale of Goods Act 1893. Section 27 provides that it is the seller's duty to deliver the goods, and the buyer's duty to accept

902. [1975] 1 All ER 529, [1975] 1 WLR 218.
903. Statute of Limitations, 1957, s. 11(1)(a) and (2)(a).
904. Under the Sale of Goods Act 1893, ss 53–54; *see* paras 561–568 below.

and pay for the goods, 'in accordance with the terms of the contract of sale'. Under this heading, we are concerned with the seller's duty to deliver the goods in accordance with the statutory implied terms concerning the nature and quality of the goods supplied under a contract of sale. Where a seller fails to deliver goods in accordance with these terms, he/she will be in breach of contract. Moreover, because all the statutory implied terms in this area, bar three,[905] are classified as conditions of the contract, the buyer will be entitled to reject the goods, treat the contract as repudiated, and sue for damages for any resulting loss. These remedies place the buyer in a strong bargaining position. A buyer may waive his/her right to reject the goods and terminate the contract, and simply claim damages, or, a buyer may loose his/her right to reject the goods if the buyer is deemed to have accepted them under sections 34 and 35 of the 1893 Act.[906] Of course, to be entitled to any of these remedies the buyer must prove that the loss sustained was *caused* by the seller's breach of contract,[907] and the loss must not be too remote from the breach.

505. The Sale of Goods Act 1893, in its original form, governed Irish sales law for the majority of the last century. However, in the 1960s and 1970s, concerns were raised about the suitability of the 1893 Act to a modern society and economy. In particular, it was argued that the interests of consumers in sale transactions were not being protected.[908] In response to these concerns, the Sale of Goods and Supply of Services Act 1980 was enacted. These changes were more consumer than commercially orientated and were similar to the provisions of the then new UK Sale of Goods Act 1979.[909] It has been opined in the UK, with reference to their equivalent implied terms, that 'it is now unrealistic to treat the basic principle of the law as *caveat emptor* rather than *caveat venditor*'.[910] The same can be said of the Irish position.

506. Today, sections 13 and 14 of the Sale of Goods Act 1893, as substituted by section 10 of the Sale of Goods and Supply of Services Act 1980, imply three conditions relating broadly to the quality of goods supplied under a sale of goods contract. Section 15 of the 1893 Act, as substituted by section 10 of the 1980 Act, implies similar terms in contracts of sale by sample. Basically, section 13 requires that the goods supplied correspond with description; section 14(2) requires that the

905. 1893 Act, s. 12; 1980 Act, s. 12.
906. On buyer's remedies, *see* paras 542–571 below.
907. *See*, e.g., *O ' Regan v. Micro-Bio (Ireland) & Intervet* (unreported, High Court, 26 Feb. 1980), at 9–11 where a major issue was whether birds died because of the effect of being vaccinated with a defective vaccine or whether the birds were already infected with a disease before they were vaccinated. Expert evidence resolved the matter in favour of the plaintiff.
908. *See* Whincup, *Consumer Protection Law in America, Canada and Europe* (Dublin: National Prices Commission, Occasional Paper No. 9); National Consumer Advisory Council Report to Minister for Industry and Commerce (10 Dec. 1974), Chs 1 and 2; and 309, *Dáil Debates*, Cols 1100–1106 (23 Nov. 1978).
909. The initial identical nature of English and Irish sales law (effectively from 1893–1973, though some minor changes started to appear from the 1950s), and the later similar nature of English and Irish sales law (1973 to date) has meant that English case law has always been a vital source of analysis and guidance for Irish courts.
910. Adams & MacQueen, ed., *Atiyah ' s Sale of Goods* (12th ed,, Harlow, Pearson 2010), 140.

goods supplied are of merchantable quality; and section 14(4) requires that the goods supplied are fit for the buyer's particular purpose.

A. Correspondence with Description

507. Section 13(1) of the 1893 Act provides that where there is a contract of sale by description, there is an implied condition that the goods shall comply with the description. There are three elements to any section 13 claim. First, section 13 only applies where there is a sale by description; second, the contractual words of description must be identified; and lastly, the goods supplied must be compared with the contractual words of description to determine whether there is a breach of contract or not. These elements are examined further below.

1. When Is a Sale a Sale by Description?

508. Clearly, where the goods being sold are not seen by the buyer, as is the case with sales of future or unascertained goods, there must be a description relied on by the buyer by which the goods can be identified and sold. So, a sale of future or unascertained goods will always be a sale by description.[911] But even where goods are seen by the buyer, there may be a sale by description.[912] The legislation provides that a sale shall not be prevented from being a sale by description because the goods are exposed for sale and selected by the customer.[913] Thus, sales from retail outlets where goods are packaged or labelled in some way and set out for display, such as in supermarkets, may be sales by description.[914]

509. In order for goods to be sold by description, the descriptive words must be influential in the sale. The circumstances must be such that the parties might reasonably expect the description to influence the buyer in his/her decision to buy the goods: an objective test. For instance, in *Egan v. McSweeney*,[915] the plaintiff purchased coal from the defendant for domestic use. When lit, some of the coal

911. 'The term 'sale of goods by description' must apply to all cases where the purchaser has not seen the goods, but is relying on the description alone … . The most usual application of that section no doubt is the case of unascertained goods, … ' *Varley v. Whipp* [1900] 1 QB 513 at 516 *per* Channel J.

912. Lord Wright in *Grant v. Australian Knitting Mills Ltd* [1936] AC 85 at 108 stated: 'There is a sale by description even though the buyer is buying something displayed before him on the counter; a thing is sold by description, though it is specific, so long as it is sold not merely as a specific thing, but as a thing corresponding to a description, e.g: woollen undergarments, a hot-water bottle, a second hand reaping machine.' *See also O ' Connor v. Donnelly* [1944] Ir Jur Rep 1 at 8, *per* Gavin Duffy J.

913. 1893 Act, s. 13(2).

914. The National Consumer Advisory Council had recommended that 'sales by description should include self service sales': *see* Briefing Document in relation to the Sale of Goods and Supply of Services Act 1980.

915. (1956) 90 ILTR 40; *see also O ' Connor v. Donnelly* [1944] IR Jur Rep 1 at 6; and *McDowell v. Sholedice* (unreported, Supreme Court, 31 Jul. 1969).

exploded causing injury. The plaintiff argued, *inter alia*, that there was a breach of the then section 14(2) of the 1893 Act, on merchantable quality, which only applied where goods were bought by description. Davitt P found that this was a sale by description. He stated:

> *Whether it was made by word of mouth, or by means of a postcard, the plaintiff must have made known her requirements by describing them and by ordering two bags of coal. I think it is reasonably clear that what she wanted was coal and not coke, or turf,; and that she relied on her description to ensure that she got what she wanted.*[916] *(emphasis added)*

510. In the more recent English case of *Harlingdon and Leinster Enterprises Ltd v. Christopher Hull Fine Art Ltd,*[917] the importance of reliance was again highlighted.[918] There an oil painting, sold for GBP 6,000 by the defendant art dealer, was described as being by Gabriele Münter, a German expressionist. This attribution was based on the painting's description in an art catalogue some years earlier. However, the seller emphasized that he had no expertise in this area of fine art and the seller appears to have made it clear that he considered that the buyer, who was also an art dealer, knew more about these matters than he did himself. The buyer had inspected the catalogue and the painting before the purchase. It was later discovered that the painting was a fake, worth about GBP 50 to GBP 100. The buyer sought to reject the goods on the basis that, *inter alia*, there was a breach of the implied condition as to description, under section 13(1) of the UK Sale of Goods Act 1979.[919] The majority of the Court of Appeal held, on the facts, that the parties could not reasonably have contemplated that the buyer was relying on the seller's attribution, in view of the disclaimer by the seller, and the relative expertise of the parties. Hence, the sale was not a sale by description.

511. It can therefore be stated, as a general rule, that where descriptive words are used to refer to the goods being sold, and it is reasonable that the buyer would rely on those words, the sale will be a sale by description. In practice, the vast majority of sales will be sales by description. *Benjamin's Sale of Goods* gives an example of a sale not by description: 'It follows that the only sales not by description are sales of specific goods *as such.*'[920]

---

916. (1956) 90 ILTR 40 at 41.
917. [1990] 1 All ER 737.
918. 'The description must have a sufficient influence in the sale to become an essential term of the contract and the correlative of influence is reliance', *per* Nourse LJ, *ibid.*at 744. Although Nourse LJ recognized that in theory a descriptive statement could be made a term of the contract without the buyer relying on it, he held that in practice the description could only have the necessary influence upon the sale if it was 'within the reasonable contemplation of the parties that the buyer was relying on the description', *ibid.* at 744.
919. For the purpose of this analysis, there is no difference between the UK provision and the Irish provision, on sales by description. The buyers also argued, unsuccessfully, breach of s. 14(2) of the 1979 Act, on merchantable quality.
920. Benjamin, *Sale of Goods* para. 11-011 (9th ed., Sweet & Maxwell 2014).

2. What Words Form Part of the Contractual Description?

512. Case law makes clear that not every statement about the description, quality or fitness of the goods can be treated as a part of the contractual description. Some such statements may constitute mere representations, of no binding effect. Even where a statement about the goods forms a part of the contract, it may not form part of the contractual description. It is not easy to predict what words or phrases will be construed as mere representation or terms of the contract; or, ordinary terms of the contract or contractual words of description. The legislation offers some assistance by providing that a reference to goods on a label or other descriptive matter accompanying the goods exposed for sale (such as a sales brochure, or other form of advertisement) may constitute or form part of a description.[921] By way of illustration, the following have been held to form part of the description by which goods are sold: the date of shipment of goods;[922] a statement in a contract for the sale of 3,000 tins of fruit that the tins should be packed in cases of 30 tins;[923] a statement in a contract for sale of wooden staves that the staves should be half an inch thick;[924] a statement as to the situation of goods;[925] and the markings on the goods.[926]

513. Conversely, in *Reardon Smith Line Ltd v. Yngvar Hansen-Tangen,*[927] Japanese shipbuilders contracted to charter a ship to the defendant, to be built to a detailed specification, by the Osaka company, and known as Hull No. 354, until named. The defendant later sub-chartered the ship to the plaintiff, identifying the vessel as 'Yard No. 354 at Osaka Zosen'. The ship was in fact built elsewhere, under a different hull number. By the time the ship was built the market had collapsed due to the oil crisis of 1974 and the charterer sought to reject the ship on the basis that it did not comply with its description. The House of Lords held that the words as to the identification of the vessel and the location of construction were of no legal significance. Lord Wilberforce stated that the implied term as to description was concerned with words that identify 'an essential part of the description of the goods'.[928]

3. What Constitutes Breach of Section 13?

514. Once it is decided that a word or phrase forms part of the description by which the goods are sold, the goods must correspond exactly to that description,

921. 1893 Act, s. 13(3).
922. *Bowes v. Shand* (1877) 2 App. Cas. 455.
923. *Re Moore & Co. Ltd and Landauer & Co ' s Arbitration* [1921] 2 KB 519: there was therefore a breach when the seller delivered the full quantity of tins but some were packed in cases of twenty-four tins. The buyer was entitled to reject the goods for breach of the implied condition as to description.
924. *Arcos Ltd v. E A Ronaasen & Son* [1933] AC 470.
925. *Macphearson Train & Co. v. Howard Ross & Co.* [1955] 1 WKLR 640.
926. *Smith Bros (Hull) Ltd v. Gosta Jacobsson & Co.* [1961] 2 Lloyd's Rep 522.
927. [1976] 3 All ER 570, [1976] 1 WLR 989.
928. [1976] 3 All ER 570 at 577, [1976] 1 WLR 989 at 999.

otherwise there will be a breach of the condition implied by section 13(1) enabling the buyer to reject the goods, terminate the contract and sue for damages. It would seem that the more precise the contractual description of the goods is, the more precisely they must correspond with the description. The issue of breach is a question of fact to be decided in each case. It should also be remembered that liability is strict and accordingly, the seller will be liable regardless of his/her responsibility for the breach.

515. Where the goods delivered are totally different from those contracted for, there is clearly a breach of contract.[929] However, in all other cases, it may be more difficult to decide whether goods correspond to their description or not. Since contractual description depends of the intentions of the parties, the test of compliance may be difficult to apply. Moreover, the parties may intend to describe the goods in broad terms or in minute detail. For instance, in *Ashington Piggeries Ltd. v. Christopher Hill Ltd,*[930] Norwegian suppliers contracted to sell herring meal to buyers to be compounded and used as mink food. The meal supplied was treated with a preservative which reacted with the meal producing a toxin that made it fatal when fed to mink. The buyers argued that the meal supplied did not comply with its description. Four members of the House of Lords held that there was no breach of section 13 because the goods could still properly be described as 'herring meal': contaminated herring meal is still herring meal; 'herring meal' did not implicitly mean 'non-toxic herring meal'. Here the contamination was relevant to the issue of quality or fitness,[931] but it was made clear that not every statement about quality or fitness can be treated as part of the description. This case is notable for the narrow interpretation it gives to section 13 claims.

516. By way of example, courts have found a breach of section 13 where: Western Madras cotton was tendered for Long Staple Salem cotton;[932] a mixture of hemp and rape oil was tendered under a contract for foreign refined rape oil;[933] giant sainfoin was delivered under a contract for common English sainfoin seed;[934] winter wheat seed was supplied under a contract for the sale of spring wheat seed;[935] copra

---

929. For example, in *Fogarty v. Dickson* (1913) 47 ILTR 281 there was a breach of s. 13 where winter wheat was supplied under a contract for 'spring wheat'; and in *O ' Connor v. McCowen & Sons Ltd* (1943) 77 ILTR 64, there was a breach of s. 13 where there was a contract to sell turnip seed and cabbage seed was supplied. *See further*, *Chanter v. Hopkins* (1838) 4 Mee & W 399 at 404 where Lord Abinger CB stated: 'if a man offers to buy peas of another, and he sends him beans, he does not perform his contract, the contract is to sell peas and if he sends him any thing else in their stead, it is a non-performance of it'; approved in *American Can Co. v. Stewart* (1915) 50 ILTR 132.
930. [1972] AC 441.
931. The buyer made a successful claim under s. 14, of the 1893 Act: *see further* paras 499–530.
932. *Azemar v. Casella* (1867) LR 2 CP 677.
933. *Nichol v. Godts* (1854) 10 Exch. 191.
934. *Wallis Son & Wells v. Pratt & Haynes* [1911] AC 394.
935. *Fogarty v. Dickson* (1913) 47 ILTR 281.

cake was contaminated with so large an admixture of caster bean as to render it poisonous;[936] meat and bone meal was contaminated with 5% cocoa husks;[937] and a vaccine was sold under the description H-120 but was of greater potency than usual.[938] Again, it must be stressed that each case was decided on its own special facts.

517. Specifications which form part of the description are usually interpreted strictly. In *Arcos Ltd v. E A Ronaasen & Son,*[939] there was a sale of wooden staves, half an inch thick, for making cement barrels. In fact, only about 5% of the goods conformed to this specification, with the remainder being not more than 9/16 of an inch thick. The goods were perfectly usable for making cement barrels and the court found that they were merchantable and reasonably fit for the purpose they were bought. Nevertheless, the buyer was entitled to reject the goods because the court held that there was a breach of section 13. Lord Atkin stated:

> If the written contract specifies conditions of weight, measurement and the like, those conditions must be complied with. A ton does not mean about a ton, or a yard about a yard. Still less when you descend to minute measurements does 1/2 inch mean about 1/2 inch. If the seller wants a margin he must and in my experience does stipulate for it. No doubt there may be microscopic deviations which business men and therefore lawyers will ignore. But apart from this consideration the right view is that the conditions of the contract must be strictly performed. If a condition is not performed the buyer has a right to reject.[940]

This case has been criticized on the basis that the goods were fit for their purpose and that the buyer's undenied reason for wanting to reject the goods was because the market price for such goods had fallen and they wanted to get out of a bad bargain.[941] Nevertheless, correspondence with description and fitness for purpose are two different concepts and should not be confused. And, the strict application of the correspondence to description requirement can be justified, in the commercial context, on a number of grounds. First, it offers certainty and avoids any delays which would be caused by going to court to determine whether a deviation from the contract was significant or not. Second, in commodity sales, particularly at an international level, the goods are usually bought and resold, numerous times over, using the same description. If there is a dispute over conformity under the first contract,

---

936. *Pinnock Bros v. Lewis & Peat Ltd* [1923] 1 KB 690, where Roche J described the goods as something 'which could not properly be described as copra cake at all', at 697. Cf. *Ashington Piggeries Ltd v. Christopher Hill Ltd* [1972] AC 441.
937. *Robert A Munro & Co. v. Meyer* [1930] 2 KB 312.
938. *O ' Regan v. Micro-Bio (Ireland) & Intervet* (unreported, High Court, 26 Feb. 980).
939. [1933] AC 470.
940. [1933] AC 470 at 479–448.
941. *See*, e.g., Goode, *Commercial Law* 113 (4th ed., Penguin 2010). Similar criticism has been levelled at the decision in *Re Moore & Co. Ltd and Landauer & Co ' s Arbitration* [1921] 2 KB 519: in *Reardon Smith Line Ltd v. Yngvar Hansen- Tangen* [1976] 3 All ER 570, Lord Wilberforce stated that he found the decision in *Re Moore & Co. Ltd and Landauer & Co ' s Arbitration* 'excessively technical and due for fresh consideration by this House', at 576.

a court will not know what purpose the ultimate buyer has in mind for the goods and whether it is such as will entitle him/her to reject; whereas reliance on matters of description offers the advantage of consistency of outcome in string transactions. Third, at an international level, sales contracts are frequently performed not by the parties themselves but by the respective banks whereby the goods are paid for against documents. Banks in these circumstances are not to know whether goods that do not comply with the contract description are fit for their client's, or their client's sub-buyer's, purposes. Hence, it is argued that the only workable rule in relation to correspondence with description is one of strict performance. Finally, the rule can be, and often is, contracted out of by using words of approximation, such as 'about', 'in or about', 'approximately', or 'plus or minus 5%'. Moreover, a price variation clause can be included in the supply contract to take account of any variations in delivery. The Sales Law Review Group recommended that section 13 should be retained in its current form in any future legislation.[942]

B. Merchantable Quality

518. Having stated the basic common law principle *caveat emptor* in subsection (1), section 14 goes on to imply two conditions, which protect the position of the buyer, in relation to the quality of the goods supplied. The goods supplied must be: (i) of merchantable quality; and (ii) reasonably fit for the buyer's particular purpose. These conditions effectively erode the principle caveat emptor, particularly where the buyer deals as a consumer where the conditions can never be excluded. In light of this, the Sales Law Review Group has recommended the repeal of section 14(1).[943] Further to any express terms in the contract,[944] and the statutory implied terms, a term as to quality or fitness may also be implied by usage.[945]

519. Section 14(2) provides:

> Where the seller sells goods in the course of a business there is an implied condition that the goods supplied under the contract are of merchantable quality, except that there is no such condition:
>
> a. as regards defects specifically drawn to the buyer's attention before the contract is made; or
> b. if the buyer examines the goods before the contract is made, as regards defects which that examination ought to have revealed.

942. Sales Law Review Group, *Report on the Legislation Governing the Sale of Goods and Supply of Services* (Dublin, Prn. A11/1576, 2011) para. 4.27.
943. Sales Law Review Group, *Report on the Legislation Governing the Sale of Goods and Supply of Services* (Dublin, Prn. A11/1576, 2011) para. 4.50.
944. Express terms as to description and quality are very common in commercial contracts, which may be standard form in nature, and less common, but not unusual, in consumer contracts: *see further*, e.g., *Cotter v. Brewster* (unreported, High Court, 18 Dec. 1997).
945. 1893 Act, s. 14(5). *See*, e.g., *Peter Darlington Partners Ltd v. Gosho Co. Ltd* [1964] 1 Lloyd's Rep 149, where canary seed was sold and according to the custom of the trade, the buyer was not entitled to reject the goods for impurities in the seed but was entitled to a reduction of the price.

1. Application

520. There are three issues concerning the application of section 14 of the 1893 Act. First, and unlike section 13, section 14 applies to sales 'in the course of a business' only and hence not to sales in a private context. The status of the buyer is irrelevant for these purposes. This phrase is not defined in the legislation.[946] But it was interpreted, for the first time, by the English Court of Appeal, in *Stevenson v. Rogers.*[947] In this case, the defendant, a fisherman, sold his only boat, the *Jelle,* to another fisherman, and replaced it with another boat. The court was asked to rule, as a preliminary issue, whether the sale of the *Jelle* was 'in the course of a business' and so whether the merchantable quality provision applied. Having examined the legislative history of the phrase and the relevant case law, the court opted for a broad interpretation of the phrase and found that the sale was 'in the course of a business'. Accordingly, goods may be sold *in the course of a business* even where the business is not normally involved in dealing in goods of the type, provided that the contract is made for the purpose of the business.

521. Second, the conditions implied in section 14 apply to the goods *supplied* under the contract, not merely the goods sold. Therefore, a defect in the packaging of the goods might render the goods unmerchantable, even if the packaging is returnable. In *Geddling v. Marsh,*[948] mineral water was sold to the plaintiff in a 'returnable' bottle that was bailed to the plaintiff, that is, the bottle was not sold to the plaintiff. The bottle burst and injured the plaintiff. The court held that the bottle was supplied under the sales contract and so the plaintiff could recover damages for breach of the merchantable quality requirement.

522. Finally, as regard the application of the condition of merchantable quality, subsection (2) provides that the condition shall not apply in two circumstances. There is no implied condition as to merchantable quality where defects are disclosed in the sense of being *specifically* drawn to the buyer's attention before the contract is made. It has been suggested elsewhere that a seller would need to do more than include printed words in a written sales contract to satisfy this provision.[949] Personal intervention by the seller, or indeed any other person, drawing the buyer's notice to these printed words, would probably be required. And, if a buyer undertakes to examine the goods before the contract is made, he/she loses the protection afforded by section 14(2) in relation to defects which that examination ought to have revealed. This provision only applies where an actual examination takes

946. 'Business' is defined as including any profession and the activities of any state or local authority: s. 2(1), 1980 Act.

947. [1999] 1 All ER 613.

948. [1920] 1 KB 668; *see further Wilson v. Rickett, Cockerill & Co.* [1954] 1 QB 598 where Coalite sold included an explosive detonator. Even though there was nothing wrong with the Coalite, or even the detonator, the goods were found to be unmerchantable.

949. *See* Adams & MacQueen, ed., *Atiyah ' s Sale of Goods* (12th ed., Harlow, Pearson 2010), 164. Again, a sign nearby the goods being sold and stating that they are 'shop-soiled' arguably would not satisfy this provision. Where a defect becomes known through course of dealings: *see Royal Business Machines v. Lorraine Corporation* 633 F. 2d 34, US Ct. App. 7th Circuit (1980).

place. A buyer is not obliged to make any examination, but, where an examination does occur, the seller will not be liable for any defects which *ought* to have been revealed by *that* examination, and not just for the defects actually revealed by the examination.[950] Where the examination is cursory, the buyer's right to complain about defects which a cursory examination could not reasonably be expected to reveal remains unaffected.[951] It would seem that the burden is on the seller to establish that either of these exemptions applies.

2. The Definition of Merchantable Quality

523. Quality in relation to goods is defined as including their state and condition.[952] Merchantable quality is defined in section 14(3) of the 1893 Act, a definition introduced by the Sale of Goods and Supply of Services Act 1980. Section 14(3) states:

> Goods are of merchantable quality if they are as fit for the purpose or purposes for which goods of that kind are commonly bought and as durable as is reasonable to expect having regard to any description applied to them, the price (if relevant) and all the other relevant circumstances.

524. There is, in fact, relatively little Irish case law on the detailed meaning of merchantable quality, as defined in the legislation. Hence, we have tended to rely on English case law for guidance in this regard. Care needs to be exercised however, because, the English and Irish definitions of merchantable quality, once introduced, never coincided. In particular, the English definition of merchantable quality did not include an express reference to durability, whereas the Irish definition does. Furthermore, the change from a requirement of merchantable quality to a requirement of satisfactory quality (which does refer to durability, amongst a list of other factors), under section 14 of the UK Sale of Goods Act, in 1995, adds to this problem. It remains to be seen to what extent English case law on the meaning of satisfactory quality is of use in Ireland.

525. Section 14(3) specifically mentions some factors to be taken into account in determining merchantability; however, it is clear that other factors may also be relevant. Merchantable quality has proved to be a flexible standard, and this partly explains its longevity. Goods can be of widely varying qualities, from relatively

950. In *Thornett & Fehr v. Beers & Son* [1919] 1 KB 486 glue was being sold and the buyers were encouraged to open and inspect some barrels in which the glue was stored in the seller's warehouse. The buyers merely looked at the outside of the barrels before buying the glue. The buyers later claimed that the glue was unmerchantable but failed on the basis that they had examined the goods and so the implied term as to merchantable quality did not apply. This case was decided on a slightly different worded provision which refers to 'defects which such examination ought to have revealed'.

951. *See Godley v. Perry* [1960] 1 All ER 36 on 1893 Act, s. 15.

952. Unreported, High Court, 26 Feb. 1980.

poor quality to top quality, and still be of merchantable quality, depending on the circumstances of the case and the application of a variety of factors. These factors are considered in more detail below.

a. Fitness for Purpose

526. Fitness for purpose is a core element of merchantable quality. In *O'Regan & Sons Ltd v. Micro-Bio (Ireland) Ltd & Intervet Laboratories Ltd,*[953] the plaintiff company was in the business of rearing broiler chickens and it decided to vaccinate them against certain diseases. It bought a vaccine, Intervet H-120, and administered it according to the instructions. However, rather than immunizing the chickens, an unusually high proportion of chickens died. Expert evidence was produced to the effect that this particular batch of vaccine was more potent than normal. The court found that the purpose of the goods was to vaccinate chickens, and that the evidence showed that the goods were not fit for this purpose. Hence the goods were unmerchantable.[954]

527. The question of fitness for purpose can be more complicated where goods have more than one common purpose. Section 14(3) requires goods to be fit for their *purpose or purposes*. Clearly, where goods have only one common purpose, the goods need only be fit for that one common purpose to be merchantable. But, where goods have more than one purpose, it is unclear from the statutory definition of merchantable quality, whether the goods are merchantable when they are fit for any one common purpose, or whether they must be fit for all the purposes for which they are commonly bought. This question was addressed in the English case of *Aswan Engineering Establishment Co v. Lupdine Ltd,*[955] where it was held, by the Court of Appeal, that where goods have more than one common purpose they will be merchantable provided they are reasonably fit for any one of their common purposes. This decision clearly favoured the seller by placing the onus on the buyer to make known to the seller his/her purpose for buying the goods, thereby allowing the buyer to rely on section 14(4). English law on this point has been changed with the U.K. Sale and Supply of Goods Act 1994. This legislation amended the law in relation to implied terms and the remedy of rejection. In particular, goods must now be of *satisfactory quality,*[956] rather than merchantable quality, and 'fitness for *all* purposes for which goods of the kind in question are commonly supplied' is 'in appropriate cases' an aspect of the quality of the goods.[957] It would seem that the intention behind this amendment was to reverse the decision in *Aswan*, such that a seller could not claim that goods were of satisfactory quality where they were fit for only one of their common purposes.

953. 1893 Act, s. 62. *See further Niblett v. Confectioners ' Materials Ltd* [1921] 3 KB 387.
954. The court also found a breach of ss 13(1) and 14(4).
955. [1987] 1 All ER 135. On this point there is no difference between the English statutory provision then in force and the current Irish legislation. *See further Sumner Permain & Co. Ltd v. Webb & Co. Ltd* [1922] 1 KB 55; and *Henry Kendall & Sons v. William Lillico & Sons Ltd* [1969] 2 AC 31.
956. U.K. Sale of Goods Act 1979, s. 14(2).
957. U.K. Sale of Goods Act 1979, s. 14(2B)(a).

528. The issue of fitness for *purpose or purposes* was considered most recently by the Irish High Court in *James Elliot Construction Ltd v. Irish Asphalt Ltd.*[958] In this case the defendant, Irish Asphalt, supplied hardcore infill ('Clause 804'), a form of crushed rock commonly used under the foundations of buildings and roads, to the plaintiff company which was building the Ballymun Central Youth Facility. The plaintiff claimed that the infill supplied expanded and heaved upwards, due to an excess of pyrite in the infill, causing damage to the building and hence that the goods supplied were unmerchantable. In assessing whether the infill was of merchantable quality or not, Charleton J referred to the characteristics of Clause 804, as indicted by expert evidence, as requiring durability, inertness and strength. In reliance on *Aswan,* it had been argued before the Court, that Clause 804 was capable of a number of uses, and consequently if one of the purposes for which the infill was commonly bought could be proved to be suitable, then the infill would be of merchantable quality. However, Charleton J rejected this reasoning and instead looked to the case of *Rogers v. Parish Ltd,*[959] a case decided four months after *Aswan*, where the Court of Appeal did not accept an argument that a Range Rover motor car which got its purchaser from A to B, but with accompanying extraordinary noises and a rapid decline in its cosmetic appearance was of merchantable quality. In effect, the Court of Appeal dismissed an argument that a car was of merchantable quality if one of its purposes (conveying passengers) was fulfilled. Other purposes of a motor car included being a source of pride to its owner who could not reasonably be expected to put up with weird engine noises and an off-putting exterior. Therefore, noting that the Irish Sale of Goods and Supply of Services Act 1980 completely recast the circumstances of liability as between the purchaser of goods and services and the seller, Charleton J found, on the evidence, that the infill supplied was neither chemically inert, nor durable, nor sufficiently strong. Moreover, it was held that this lack of merchantability was not displaced by any argument that it would be suitable for another purpose such as being put under an external tarmacadamed car park where, it might be argued, the heave of 25–35 mm over a few years variably over the surface tarmacadam laid above it might not make much difference. Accordingly, the goods supplied were found to be unmerchantable.[960]

b. Durability

529. Durability is another core element of merchantable quality. To be merchantable goods must be reasonably durable, that is, in such a condition that they will remain fit for a reasonable time. An illustration of the requirement of durability can be found in the English case, *Mash and Murrell v. Joseph I Emmanuel*[961] where sellers in Cyprus sold potatoes, c & f Liverpool. The potatoes, although sound when loaded, had deteriorated by the time the ship reached Liverpool. It was held that the

958. [2011] IEHC 269; approved by the Supreme Court [2014] IESC 74.
959. [1987] Q.B. 933.
960. Importantly, a claim that the goods were not fit for any particular purpose, under s. 14(4) was not proved as the evidence did not support the communication of a *particular purpose* from the purchaser to the supplier.
961. [1961] 1 All ER 485, reversed by Court of Appeal on other grounds [1962] 1 WLR 16n.

goods were unmerchantable because the goods should have been loaded in 'such a state that they could endure the normal journey and be in a merchantable condition on arrival'.[962]

530. It should be noted, however, that the requirement that goods should be supplied in a reasonably durable condition relates to the time of supply. If goods do break down or deteriorate earlier than would reasonably be expected, this may be evidence of a defect in the goods at the time of supply. If however it is shown that a break down or deterioration is due to some other factor, such as the way the goods are used by the buyer, rather than a defect present at the time of supply, the goods may not be unmerchantable. In order to avoid doubts and disputes a buyer may expressly provide for durability by requiring the seller to give a product guarantee (sometimes called a warranty) covering the goods as regards certain defects, for an agreed period after delivery.

c. Description

531. The description applied to goods will affect the standard that can be reasonably expected of them. For instance, a higher standard would be expected from goods described as 'brand new' or 'deluxe', than those described as 'second-hand', 'seconds' or 'shop-soiled'.[963] In *Rogers v. Parish (Scarborough) Ltd*,[964] a buyer bought a 'new Range Rover' for GBP 14,000. The car suffered from a number of minor defects and was held to be unmerchantable. The Court of Appeal emphasized the importance of the descriptions 'new' and 'Range Rover':

> In the present case the car was sold as new. Deficiencies which might be acceptable in a second-hand vehicle were not to be expected in one purchased as new. Next, the description 'Range Rover' would conjure up a particular set of expectations, not the same as those relating to an ordinary saloon car, as to the balance between performance, handling, comfort and resilience.[965]

It was further held in this case that the fact that the goods are repairable does not mean that the goods are merchantable.[966] Where, under a seller's or manufacturer's

962. *Ibid.* at 488.
963. In *Bartlett v. Sidney Marcus Ltd* [1965] 2 All ER 753, for example, the plaintiff bought a second-hand car for GBP 950. The dealers had informed the plaintiff that the clutch was defective, and they had offered to put it right and sell the car for GBP 975. The defect was more serious than expected and cost GBP 84 to be repaired. Nevertheless, the Court of Appeal held that the car was merchantable because it was sold *as second-hand with a defective clutch.*
964. [1987] QB 933.
965. *Ibid. per* Mustill LJ at 237. *See also Shine v. General Guarantee Corpn Ltd* [1988] 1 All ER 911, at 915.
966. Cf. *Millar of Falkirk v. Turpie* [1976] SLT 66.

product guarantee, defective goods are replaced or repaired, this has no effect on the merchantability of the goods sold, as any rights under any such guarantees are additional to the buyer's statutory rights.[967]

d. Price

532. While the adequacy of consideration is not relevant to the enforceability of a contract, the price may be relevant to the issue of merchantable quality. The same basic goods can be supplied for a wide range of prices: the higher the price, the greater the quality that can reasonably be expected. For example, in *Rogers v. Parish (Scarborough) Ltd,*[968] a car was bought for GBP 14,000, whereas in *Bartlett v. Sidney Marcus Ltd,*[969] a car was bought at a 'reduced price': the standard of quality required in both these cases reflected this difference in price. Resale price of machinery was considered a relevant factor by Moriarty J in *O'Donnell v. Truck Machinery Sales;*[970] however, where the purchase of goods is speculative in nature, price can be less useful as an indication of quality.[971]

e. Other Relevant Factors

533. The factors listed in the definition of merchantable quality – fitness for purpose, durability, description and price – are not exhaustive. Included in the definition is a catch-all phrase, whereby 'all the other relevant circumstances' can be taken into account. The breath of this phrase is illustrated in *O'Donnell v. Truck Machinery Sales,*[972] which involved the sale of mechanical shovels to the defendant company which was in the business of leasing and reselling heavy construction machinery. Moriarty J, in finding no breach of sections 14(2) and 14(4), stated:

> it seems to me, construing the evidence in totality, that given such factors as the relative prices obtained in resale in varying circumstances, the overall hire records, durability and income generated in favour of the [defendant] by those shovels which became part of the hire fleet, the relative incidence of repairs required and the apparent evaluation of the [shovels] in Ireland and other market places by other purchasers and users that neither term has been shown to be infringed.[973]

534. Two particular factors have been identified a number of times by case law as being relevant: safety; and minor or cosmetic defects.

---

967. Cf. *Eurodynamics Ltd v. Automation Ltd* (UK unreported, QBD, 6 Sep. 1988) on computer software.
968. [1987] QB 933.
969. [1965] 2 All ER 753.
970. [1997] 1 ILRM 466.
971. *See*, e.g., *Harlingdon and Leinster Enterprises Ltd v. Christopher Hull Fine Art Ltd* [1990] 1 All ER 737.
972. [1997] 1 ILRM 466.
973. [1997] 1 ILRM 466 at 473.

535. Defects which render goods unsafe may be regarded as making them unmerchantable.[974] This factor has been emphasized in a number of English cases concerning motor cars. In *Bernstein v. Pamson Motors (Golders Green) Ltd*,[975] for example, a new Nissan Laurel car, bought for just under GBP 8,000 seized up after three weeks, and about 140 miles driving, due to a blob of sealant which blocked the oil supply. It was held that the car was unmerchantable. Though the defect was repairable, it had major consequences. The court emphasized the potentially disastrous consequences of the car seizing up while being driven at speed.

536. The safety of motor vehicles is addressed specifically in section 13 of the Sale of Goods and Supply of Services Act 1980. This provision implies a condition, into every contract for the sale of motor vehicles,[976] (except where the buyer is a person whose business it is to deal in motor vehicles) that at the time of delivery, it was free from any defect which would render it a danger to the public, including persons travelling in it.

537. Goods that suffer from minor or cosmetic defects, what are sometimes called non-functional defects, may still be usable for their common purpose. Hence, it can be argued that because the goods are fit for their common purpose they are merchantable. In a commercial case, a court may be reluctant to hold goods unmerchantable, so as to allow the buyer to reject them, where the defect is minor. This was the finding in the English case of *Cehave v. Bremer*[977] where it was held that a cargo of citrus pellets for cattle food that was overheated was 'far from perfect'. Nevertheless, the court found that the goods were merchantable as they could still be used for the buyer's purpose.[978]

538. In contrast, minor or cosmetic defects may be more important in the case of a consumer sale. For instance, in *Rogers v. Parish*,[979] the defects in a new Range Rover included misfiring, oil leaks, paint scratches and engine noise. These were categorized as minor by the Court of Appeal but the car was nevertheless found to be unmerchantable. Mustill LJ said that the purpose for which cars are bought would include:

---

974. Safety is of course a key element under the Liability for Defective Products Act 1991. This legislation however is solely concerned with property damage and personal injury caused by defective products: *see further* paras 956–962.

975. [1987] 2 All ER 220; *see further Lee v. York Coach & Marine* [1977] RTR 35; and *Clegg v. Anderson* [2003] EWCA Civ 320; [2003] 1 All ER (Comm.) 721.

976. For definition of 'motor vehicle' *see* s. 13(1).

977. [1976] QB 44; *see also Arcos Ltd v. E A Ronaasen & Son* [1933] AC 470.

978. Atiyah warns that it might be dangerous to read too much into this case because it was decided on is own peculiar facts and the merits of the case were all on the seller's side. For example, it emerged in court that the buyer having sought to reject the cargo because it was unmerchantable had arranged for an agent to purchase the same cargo, at a reduced price, for himself, and for the same use. *See* Atiyah *Sale of Goods* 184–185 (11th ed., Pearson 2005).

979. [1987] QB 933, [1987] 2 All ER 232.

not merely the driver's purpose of driving the car from one place to another but of doing so with the appropriate degree of comfort, ease of handling and reliability and, one may add, pride in the vehicle's outward and interior appearance.[980]

539. Although there is no reported Irish case on the effect of minor or cosmetic defects in relation to merchantable quality, it is likely that an Irish court would be willing to take account of consumer expectations as to appearance, finish and freedom from minor defects.[981] Indeed, even in a commercial case, minor or cosmetic defects could render goods unmerchantable especially if they were bought for resale, rather than if they were bought as commodities or raw materials which even if defective might still have a commercial value.[982]

540. The Sales Law Review Group stated in its report that the term 'merchantable quality' is archaic and unsuited to modern-day legislation and hence it recommended that the term 'satisfactory quality' should replace 'merchantable quality' as the standard for the purpose of the implied terms as to the quality of goods in any future legislation. Moreover, it is recommended that goods should be defined as being of 'satisfactory quality' if 'they meet the standard that a reasonable person would regard as satisfactory taking account of any description of the goods, the price (if relevant) and all the other relevant circumstances'. Accordingly, an indicative list of the following specific aspects of quality should apply alongside the general definition in appropriate cases: fitness for all the purposes for which goods of the kind in question are commonly supplied; appearance and finish; freedom from minor defects; safety; and durability.[983] This recommendation mirrors the current position in the UK and arguably would have more of an impact on the form rather than the substance of the law.

980. [1987] 2 All ER 232 at 237. In *Shine v. General Guarantee Corpn Ltd* [1988] 1 All ER 911 a car which had been submerged in water for twenty-four to forty-eight hours and hence was an insurance 'write-off' was held by the Court of Appeal to be unmerchantable even though no specific defect or unroadworthiness was alleged. The decisive factor here seemed to be that a dealer gave evidence that if the full facts were revealed, the car would be worth GBP 1,000 less than the price. Further in *Bernstein v. Pamson Motors (Golders Green) Ltd* [1987] 2 All ER 220, although the defect was minor, a blob of sealant in the lubrication system, and easily repairable, the consequences were very serious and hence the car was held to be unmerchantable. Cf. *Millars of Falkirk Ltd v. Turpie* [1976] SLT 66 where a new car was sold with a leak in the power steering system. The defect would have cost GBP 25 to repair and the seller offered to repair the leak, but the buyer refused the offer of repair and immediately sought to reject the car. The court found that the car was merchantable.

981. In *Marah v. Kellehers Ltd* (unreported, High Court, 3 Dec. 1998) *see Cork Examiner,* 4 Dec. 1998, a defect in the paintwork of a car was held to constitute a breach of the implied condition as to merchantable quality.

982. *See*, e.g., *Jackson v. Rotax Motor & Cycle Co.* [1910] 2 KB 937.

983. Sales Law Review Group, *Report on the Legislation Governing the Sale of Goods and Supply of Services* (Dublin, Prn. A11/1576, 2011) paras 4.43 and 4.48.

C. Fitness for Particular Purpose

541. Section 14(4) states:

> Where the seller sells goods in the course of a business and the buyer, expressly or by implication, makes known to the seller any particular purpose for which the goods are being bought, there is an implied condition that the goods supplied under the contract are reasonably fit for that purpose, whether or not that is the purpose for which such goods are commonly supplied, except where the circumstances show that the buyer does not rely, or that it is unreasonable for him to rely, on the seller's skill or judgement.

As with section 14(2), the requirement that goods be fit for the particular purpose of the buyer, under section 14(4), applies only where the seller sells the goods *in the course of a business* and, it applies to goods *supplied* under the contract.

1. Particular Purpose

542. The reference to 'particular' purpose means the purpose indicated by the buyer, rather than any special, or abnormal purpose. Where goods have only one purpose, this has been taken as the particular purpose. This broad interpretation has been pursued to protect the position of consumer buyers. For instance, food has been found to have the particular purpose of being eaten;[984] milk has been found to have the particular purpose of being drunk;[985] and a hot-water bottle has been found to have the particular purpose of being filled with hot-water for the purpose of applying heat to the human body.[986] This broad interpretation of particular purpose is further supported by the words 'whether or not that is the purpose for which such goods are commonly supplied'. However, where goods are bought for their common or normal purpose, and this is found to be the buyer's particular purpose, the application of section 14(4) would appear to add little to the requirement that the goods should be of merchantable quality, under section 14(2). In these circumstances, a buyer would be unlikely to succeed under section 14(4), if he/she could not establish a claim under section 14(2).[987]

543. The buyer's particular purpose can be made known expressly, by word of mouth or in writing, or impliedly. Where there has been a course of dealings between the same parties the buyer may be held to have impliedly made his/her purpose known to the seller.[988]

---

984. *Wallis v. Russell* [1902] 2 IR 585.
985. *Frost v. Aylesbury Dairy Co.* [1905] 1 KB 609.
986. *Priest v. Last* [1903] 2 KB 148.
987. *Aswan Engineering Establishment Co. v. Lupdine Ltd* [1987] 1 All ER 135, *per* Nichols LJ at 157.
988. *Manchester Liners Ltd v. Rea Ltd* [1922] 2 AC 74.

544. The implied condition requires that the goods be *reasonably fit* for the purpose indicated by the buyer. This is therefore not an absolute standard, and in determining reasonable fitness, issues which are also relevant to merchantable quality, such as description, and durability, may be relevant here.

545. Under section 14(4) goods must be reasonably fit for the particular purpose indicated by the buyer. The more precisely the buyer expresses his/her purpose, the more closely the goods must fit that purpose. Accordingly, a buyer should try to be as explicit as possible about the purpose for which the goods are being bought. But, case law suggests that courts may not always require buyers to be as explicit as possible, thereby placing a greater burden on sellers. For instance, in *Ashington Piggeries Ltd v. Christopher Hill Ltd,*[989] feeding compound was mixed by manufacturers to their buyers' formula. The feed contained herring meal sold to the manufacturers by Norwegian suppliers, which was contaminated by a toxic preservative, that proved fatal when fed to the buyer's mink. The manufacturers sued their suppliers for breach of the implied condition that goods must be fit for their particular purpose. Herring meal was commonly used as animal food and fertilizer. The Norwegian suppliers knew that the herring meal was to be used for animal feed but not that it was to be used to feed mink. It was held that the manufacturers had sufficiently made known the particular purpose for which the meal was bought. The making of mink food fell within the broader category of animal feed and was not an unforeseeable use. The toxin affected different species of animals in varying degrees, but was especially harmful to mink.

546. In contrast, in *Aswan Engineering Establishment Co v. Lupdine Ltd,*[990] where pails were sold and used to store waterproofing compound which was lost when the pails were stacked six high in intense heat in Kuwait for several days, the Court of Appeal rejected the buyer's claim that the goods were not fit for their particular purpose.[991] Nicholls LJ found that even if the particular purpose was 'for export' this would not have been enough to find the sellers liable. Where the purpose is stated so broadly, section 14(4) adds little to the requirement of merchantable quality. Goods will be reasonably fit 'for export' under section 14(4) if they are fit for export to most parts of the world. In order for the sellers to be liable under the facts in the *Aswan* case, the buyers would have to have stated their purpose more exactly, such as 'for export to a hot climate', or 'for export to Kuwait'.

547. It would appear that there is no breach of section 14(4) where the failure of the goods to meet the particular purpose arises from an abnormal feature or idiosyncrasy, not made known to the seller, either of the buyer, or in the circumstances of the use of the goods by the buyer. In *Slater v. Finning,*[992] the plaintiff owner of a 'fishing vessel *Aquarius II*' wanted to upgrade the power of the engine, and

989. [1972] AC 441. *See further Henry Kendall & Sons v. William Lillico & Sons Ltd* [1969] 2 AC 31.
990. [1987] 1 All ER 135.
991. The claim for breach of merchantable quality also failed.
992. [1996] 3 WLR 190. *See further Brady v. Cluxton* (1927) 61 ILTR 89 (HC); and *Griffiths v. Peter Conway Ltd* [1939] 1 All ER 685.

accordingly the defendant installed a new camshaft into the engine. This proved unsatisfactory, causing excessive noise and wear and tear to parts of the camshaft. Two further replacement camshafts caused similar difficulties and the plaintiff had to replace the whole engine with a different model. The plaintiff sued for breach of the implied term on fitness for particular purpose. It was accepted by both sides that the damage caused to the camshaft was caused by some unascertained force external to the engine and the camshafts themselves: an idiosyncratic feature of the vessel. Nevertheless, the plaintiff argued that he had made known the particular purpose for the camshafts, that is, to be installed in *Aquarius II*, idiosyncrasies included. The House of Lords rejected this notion that the defendant took the risk that *Aquarius II* might have unknown or unusual features and hence there was no breach of the relevant provision.

2. Reliance

548. Section 14(4) requires that: (a) the buyer rely on the seller's skill and judgment; and (b) such reliance be reasonable. In many cases these requirements will be satisfied easily: for instance, consumer buyers will generally be taken to rely on retailers;[993] a person buying from a manufacturer will generally be taken to rely on the manufacturer.[994] Indeed, the provision, as amended in 1980, raises a presumption of reliance. So now, to avoid the application of section 14(4), the burden of proof is on the seller to show that the buyer did not rely, or that it was unreasonable for him/her to rely, on the seller's skill or judgment.

549. However, where the buyer's purpose is insufficiently communicated, the buyer may not be able reasonably to rely on the seller's skill and judgment. In *Jewson Ltd v. Kelly*,[995] the defendant bought twelve electrical boilers and materials from the claimants for installation in a building to be converted into individual flats. The defendant did not pay for all the goods and the claimant took proceedings to recover the shortfall. The defendant counter-claimed, *inter alia*, that the boilers were not fit for their purpose, in breach of section 14(3) of the UK Sale of Goods Act 1979, because the boilers reduced the 'SAP' ratings (home energy ratings) of the flats. The English Court of Appeal found that whilst the defendant had told the claimant that he wanted the boilers for installation in flats for sale, he had given the claimant no information about the nature of the building being converted. Therefore, it could not be held that the defendant had relied on the skill and judgment of the claimants. The Court found that this was a matter for the defendants and his advisors. This was a case of partial reliance where the defendant relied on the claimants as to the intrinsic quality of the boilers but not as to whether the boilers were suitable for those particular flats having regard to the SAP ratings.

993. Cf. *Brady v. Cluxton* (1927) 61 ILTR 89.
994. *Henry Kendall & Sons v. William Lillico & Sons Ltd* [1969] 2 AC 31.
995. [2003] EWCA Civ 1030; [2003] All ER(D) 470.

550. Difficulties may also arise where goods are manufactured to a specification provided wholly or partly by the buyer. In such a case, the buyer will rely on the seller to follow the specification, provide materials and actually manufacture the goods. In these circumstances, there may be a breach of the implied term if the finished article proves unfit for the buyer's purpose due to any defect within the area of the seller's responsibility. In the *Ashington Piggeries* case,[996] the buyers of the mink food gave the manufacturers/sellers detailed specifications as to how the mink food was to be compounded. But it was held that the buyers were entitled to rely on the manufacturers to ensure that the ingredients used would be fit for animal feed, including feeding to mink, which they were not.

551. In *Cammell Laird & Co Ltd v. Manganese Bronze & Brass Co. Ltd,*[997] the defendant agreed to build two ships' propellers for the plaintiff according to the plaintiffs' specification. However, these specifications were silent on certain points, such as the thickness of the blades, and these matters were left to the defendant. One propeller was unsatisfactory due to defects in matters not covered by the specification. The House of Lords held that there was a breach of the implied condition as to fitness for particular purpose because 'there was a substantial area outside the specification which was not covered by its directions and was therefore necessarily left to the skill and judgment of the seller'.[998] The Sales Law Review Group was of the view that section 14(4) was broadly satisfactory and did not require substantive amendment.[999]

D. Sale by Sample

552. Goods are frequently sold by reference to a sample. For example, in a commercial context, grain is usually bought on the basis that a sample of the grain is provided by the seller, for testing by the buyer. If the buyer is happy with the quality of the sample, he/she can buy the larger quantity by reference to the sample. In a consumer context, carpets are usually bought by reference to a sample. In both these examples, the buyer does not examine the actual goods being bought because it is more convenient to examine a sample. However, a sale is not a sale by sample simply because the buyer is shown a sample. Section 15(1) provides that a sale is by sample where there is an express or implied term to that effect in the contract. Such express terms are more common in commercial sales. In general, it seems that in order for a contract of sale to be regarded as one by sample, the sample must be used to *define* the goods to be supplied.[1000] There is no reason why a sale cannot be

996. [1972] AC 441.
997. [1934] AC 402.
998. [1934] AC 402 at 414, *per* Lord Warrington.
999. Sales Law Review Group, *Report on the Legislation Governing the Sale of Goods and Supply of Services* (Dublin, Prn. A11/1576, 2011) para. 4.49.
1000. A sale will be by sample where the sample 'is to present to the eye the real meaning and intention of the parties with regard to the subject matter of the contract which, owing to the imperfections of language, it may be difficult or impossible to express in words. The sample speaks for itself': *per* Lord MacNaghten in *Drummond v. Van Ingen* (1887) 12 All Cas 284 at 297.

by sample *and* by description, in which case both sections 13 and 15 will apply.[1001] Where a sample is provided to the buyer the contract may therefore include a term making clear whether the sale is or is not a sale by sample within the meaning of the Act: for instance, a provision that any sample provided is merely for the purposes of demonstration might prevent the sale being by sample.

553. Where goods are sold by sample, section 15 implies three conditions:

a. that the bulk will correspond with the sample in quality;[1002]
b. that the buyer will have a reasonable opportunity to compare the bulk with the sample;[1003]
c. that the goods will be free from any defect, rendering them unmerchantable, which would not be apparent on reasonable examination of the sample.[1004]

These requirements largely mirror sections 13, 34 and 14(2) of the 1893 Act respectively and it would seem to add little to them.[1005] However, section 15 is not limited like section 14, in that, the seller does not have to be dealing in the course of a business. Further, where a sale is a sale by sample, the rules on merchantable quality are different from those in ordinary sales. Under section 15(c), the condition implied is that the goods will be free from any defect, which would not be apparent on reasonable examination of the sample, whether or not such examination was made.[1006] Benjamin refers to this latter distinction as support for the proposition that purchases by consumers are less likely to be held as sales by sample, because this rule would be inappropriate for consumers.[1007] Indeed, most if not all of the case law in this area involves business sales. The Sales Law Review Group recommended that section 15 of the 1893 Act should be retained in future legislation, subject to some minor amendments.[1008]

1001. 1893 Act, s. 13(1) provides that if the sale be by sample and by description, it is not sufficient that the bulk of the goods correspond with the sample if the goods do not correspond with the description.
1002. *See*, e.g., *E & S Ruben Ltd v. Faire Bros & Co. Ltd* [1949] 1 All ER 215 where rubber was sold by sample for the manufacture of shoes. The sample was flat and soft while the goods delivered were crinkly and unsuitable for use in the buyer's machines. The court held that there was a breach of s. 15 of the 1893 Act.
1003. Normally this inspection will occur at the place of delivery, although the parties can agree otherwise: *Heilbutt v. Hickson* (1872) R 7 CP 483. *See further Polenghi Bros v. Dried Milk Co. Ltd* (1904) 92 LT 64.
1004. *See*, e.g., *Steel & Busks Ltd v. Bleecker Bik & Co. Ltd* [1956] 1 Lloyd's Rep 228.
1005. On s. 34 *see* para. 550 below.
1006. *See*, e.g., *Godley v. Perry* [1960] 1 All ER 36.
1007. *See further* Benjamin, *Sale of Goods* paras 11–75 and 11–082 (9th ed., Sweet & Maxwell 2014).
1008. Sales Law Review Group, *Report on the Legislation Governing the Sale of Goods and Supply of Services* (Dublin, Prn. A11/1576, 2011) paras 4.57, 4.60 and 4.62.

E. Nature of Liability

554. Liability for breach of the implied terms in sections 13–15 of the 1893 Act is strict. This clearly favours the position of the buyer who does not have to prove fault or negligence on the part of the seller. Equally, it is no defence that the seller was unaware of the defect or that he/she took all reasonable care in relation to the goods. Where goods pass through a chain of supply from a manufacturer, to a distributor, to a retailer and finally to a buyer, it is the retailer/seller who will be liable, on the contract, to the buyer for any defects, even those caused by, say, the manufacturer. The doctrine of privity of contract limits a buyer's rights in such situations.

555. A seller who is liable for breach of any of the implied terms as to quality may, in turn, have a claim for breach of the implied terms against his/her supplier, and so on up the chain of supply. However, the use of exclusion clauses which is permissible between a seller and a buyer, who is not dealing as a consumer, may mean that the full liability to the ultimate consumer cannot be passed back-up the chain of supply. Moreover, this chain of liability may be broken where one of the parties becomes insolvent or cannot be located.

F. Exclusion of Liability

556. The implied terms in sections 13–15 of the 1893 Act cannot be excluded where the buyer deals as a consumer, and in other cases only a fair and reasonable exclusion is allowed.[1009] In the commercial context, any attempt to reasonably exclude liability should use clear wording. For example, in *Robert A Munro & Co Ltd v. Meyer*,[1010] the defendant agreed to buy goods 'with all faults', but it was held by Wright J that this clause did not excuse the seller for failure to supply goods which corresponded with their description, it merely protected the seller from the requirement to supply goods of merchantable quality.[1011]

557. Moreover, a seller may seek to 'exclude' liability under section 13, by preventing the sale from being a sale by description. In *Harlingdon and Leinster Enterprises Ltd v. Christopher Hull Fine Art Ltd*,[1012] for example, the sale was not a sale by description because of the lack of reliance by the buyer on the seller. It is not clear if such 'exclusion of liability' under section 13 is subject to section 55 of the 1893 Act which deals with exclusion of the statutory implied terms. In the *Harlingdon* case, Slade LJ thought that there was no exclusion of section 13, and rather that the sale was simply not a sale by description.[1013] But it has been held that a term in

1009. 1893 Act, s. 55(4), as substituted by the 1980 Act, s. 22. On recommendations for reform, especially as regards consumer sales, *see* Sales Law Review Group, *Report on the Legislation Governing the Sale of Goods and Supply of Services* (Dublin, Prn. A11/1576, 2011) Ch. 5.
1010. [1930] 2 KB 312.
1011. Cf. *Pinnock Bros v. Lewis & Peat Ltd* [1923] 1 KB 690.
1012. [1990] 1 All ER 737.
1013. *Ibid.* at 753.

the contract 'seen as sold' prevented it from being a sale by description and was subject to the rules on exclusion of liability in sales law.[1014]

558. A seller may also seek to 'exclude' liability under section 14(2) on the basis of the two built-in exemptions in that provision. There is no implied condition as to merchantable quality:

- as regards defects specifically drawn to the buyer's attention before the contract is made;
- if the buyer examines the goods before the contract is made, as regards defects which that examination ought to have revealed.

This too, it would seem, would fall outside the rules on exclusion of liability.

G. Implied Warranty Regarding Spare Parts and Servicing

559. The implied terms considered above – as to title; description; merchantable quality; fitness for particular purpose; and, sale by sample – date back to the 1893 Act, although the Sale of Goods and Supply of Services Act 1980 did make some important amendments to the details of these provisions. The 1980 Act introduced two further implied terms in response to changes in the economy and society: an implied warranty as to spare parts and services; and an implied condition regarding defects in motor vehicles.

560. Section 12(1) of the 1980 Act provides that where there is an offer, description or advertisement by the seller representing that spare parts and servicing will be available from himself/herself, or the manufacturer, then in the contract of sale there is implied a warranty that spare parts and adequate services will be made available. If a period is stated in the warranty this must be complied with, if no period is stated then these services must be available for a 'reasonable period'. The Minister may, after consultation, by order, specify what a reasonable period shall be for certain goods.[1015] This power has not been exercised, to date. Further, this warranty can never be excluded.[1016] It is important to note that there is no requirement on a manufacturer or retailer to offer spare parts or after-sales services. But where such an offer is made, this provision ensures that such a promise is elevated to warranty status, the breach of which gives right to a right to claim damages. The Sales Law Review Group recommended that the implied warranty as to the availability of spare parts and an adequate after-sale service at section 12 of the 1980 Act should in principle be retained in future legislation.[1017]

1014. *See Hughes v. Hall* [1981] RTR 430.
1015. 1980 Act, s. 13(2).
1016. 1980 Act, s. 13(3).
1017. Sales Law Review Group, *Report on the Legislation Governing the Sale of Goods and Supply of Services* (Dublin, Prn. A11/1576, 2011) para. 4.68.

H. Implied Condition Regarding Sale of Motor Vehicles

561. Motor vehicles, as goods, when sold must comply with all the implied terms as to description, merchantable quality, fitness for particular purpose and spare parts and after-sales services, as described above. Moreover, the safety of motor vehicles is addressed specifically in section 13 of the Sale of Goods and Supply of Services Act 1980. This provision implies a condition, into every contract for the sale of motor vehicles,[1018] (except where the buyer is a person whose business it is to deal in motor vehicles) that at the time of delivery, it was free from any defect which would render it a danger to the public, including persons travelling in it.[1019]

562. This implied condition can be avoided where: (a) it is agreed that the vehicle is not intended for use in the condition in which it is sold; and (b) a document to this effect is signed by the parties and given to the buyer prior to or at delivery;[1020] and (c) the above agreement is fair and reasonable.[1021]

563. This section provides an exception to the doctrine of privity of contract in that it allows not only the buyer, but also any person using the motor vehicle with the consent of the buyer, who suffers a loss, to sue the seller for breach of section 13(2). However, the generous lifting of the doctrine of privity contract is diminished somewhat by the shorter than usual limitation period for such actions which, under section 13(8), is two years from the date on which the cause of action accrued. The buyer's right to sue for breach of section 13(2) remains unaffected at six years. Finally, in relation to the sale of motor vehicles, any term exempting from all or any of the provisions of section 13 shall be void.[1022] The Sales Law Review Group recommended that the implied condition as to motor vehicles at section 13 of the 1980 Act should in principle be retained in future legislation, subject to minor amendment.[1023]

1018. For definition of 'motor vehicle' *see* s. 13(1).
1019. *See*, e.g., *Glorney v. O ' Brien* (unreported, High Court, 14 Nov. 1988) where a car bought for IEP 250 soon after went out of control on a public road and crashed because of defective suspension. It was held that there was a breach of s. 13 of the 1980 Act and damages were awarded for destruction of the property, physical injury and loss of earnings for several weeks.
1020. 1980 Act, s. 13(5) states that where a document complying with the requirements of this section is not given, and an action is taken for breach of s. 13, it shall be presumed that the defect existed at the time of delivery. Such an evidential presumption is of great benefit to any plaintiff. Furthermore, s. 13(4) and (6) provide that the Minister may make regulations prescribing the form(s) of this document: this power has never been exercised by the Minister.
1021. 1980 Act, s. 13(3). On the meaning of fair and reasonable *see* Schedule to the 1980 Act.
1022. 1980 Act, s. 13(9).
1023. Sales Law Review Group, *Report on the Legislation Governing the Sale of Goods and Supply of Services* (Dublin, Prn. A11/1576, 2011) para. 4.73.

V. Buyer's Remedies

564. A seller's basic duty under a sale of goods contract is to deliver the goods, in accordance with the terms of the sales contract.[1024] Where a seller fails in this basic duty, by making a defective delivery, he/she will be in breach of the contract. In this context, the term 'defective delivery' includes late delivery, non-delivery, defects in quality of the goods delivered and defects in the quantity of the goods delivered.[1025] The Sale of Goods Acts 1893 and 1980 provide remedies for the buyer where the seller makes a defective delivery. These remedies are the subject of this subsection, with one exception. The remedies for delivery of the wrong quantity are dealt with at subsection II above.[1026]

565. Fundamental in determining what remedies are available to an innocent party in relation to a breach of a sale of goods contract is the distinction between conditions and warranties. Section 62 of the 1893 Act provides that a warranty means:

> an agreement with reference to goods which are the subject of a contract of sale, but collateral to the main purpose of such a contract, breach of warrant gives rise to a claim for damages, but not the right to reject the goods and treat the contract as repudiated.

Condition is not defined expressly in the legislation but by implication. Section 11(2) of the 1893 Act states:

> Whether a stipulation in a contract of sale is a condition, the breach of which may give rise to a right to treat the contract as repudiated, or a warranty the breach of which may give rise to a claim for damages but not to a right to reject the goods and treat the contract as repudiated, depends in each case on the construction of the contract.

Further, section 11(3) of the 1893 Act states:

> Where a contract of sale is not severable, and the buyer has accepted the goods, or part thereof, the breach of any condition to be fulfilled by the seller can only be treated as a breach of warranty, and not as a ground for rejecting the goods and treating the contract as repudiated.

Hence, any defective delivery, whether a breach of condition or warranty, amounts to a breach of contract by the seller and entitles the buyer to damages for losses caused by the breach. In addition, where the seller commits a breach of a condition, the buyer may reject the goods and terminate the contract. Section 11(1) of

---

1024. 1893 Act, s. 27.

1025. On the seller's obligations as to title and remedies for breach of implied terms as to title, *see* paras 469–484 above.

1026. *See* paras 466–468 above.

the 1893 Act provides that where a condition is to be fulfilled by the seller, the buyer may waive the condition or elect to treat the breach of a condition as a breach of warranty. Hence, a buyer is not obliged to reject the goods following the breach of a condition: in practice, a buyer often opts to keep the goods and simply claim damages. Other remedies may be available under the general law of contract, including specific performance, interest and rescission of the contract or damages for misrepresentation.

A. The Right to Reject

566. A buyer can reject goods in four circumstances. First, where there is an express right to reject under the contract. Second, the legislation provides a specific right where the seller delivers the wrong quantity.[1027] Third, the legislation provides a general right to reject where the seller has breached a condition. And fourth, it would seem that the common law allows rejection for a serious breach of an innominate term.[1028] A rejection in any other circumstance will not be justified and amounts to a breach of contract by the buyer for which the seller has remedies.

567. Section 11(2) of the 1893 Act makes it clear that where there is a breach of a condition, the innocent party can repudiate or terminate the contract, reject the goods and claim for damages. If any price has been paid under the contract the buyer is also entitled to a refund of the price, on the basis of a claim in restitution, for total failure of consideration.[1029] Where the buyer claims such a refund, or makes an additional claim for damages for any additional losses caused by the breach, the assistance of the court will be needed. But where the price under the contract has not been paid, a buyer rejecting goods is essentially a self-help remedy.

568. Where a buyer wishes to reject goods, he/she must indicate his/her intentions clearly.[1030] If a buyer seeks to reject goods, he/she does not necessarily have to physically return the goods to the seller. Rather he/she must make them available for collection at the delivery point.[1031] Where the goods cannot be made available, for instance, because the goods have been consumed, rejection is not possible.[1032]

569. On rejection, any property in the goods, and any risk associated with it, revests in the seller.[1033] Where the buyer remains in possession following rejection

1027. 1893 Act, s. 30: *see* paras 466–468 above.

1028. *The Hansa Nord* [1976] QB 44. *See also Laird Bros v. Dublin Steampacket* (1990) 34 ILTR 97; *Taylor v. Smyth* [1990] ILRM 377; *Irish Telephone Rentals v. ICS Building Society* [1991] ILRM 880.

1029. 1893 Act, s. 54.

1030. In *Lee v. York Coach and Marine* [1977] RTR 35 the buyer's solicitor wrote to the seller indicating that the buyer had the right to reject and requesting that the seller repair the goods. It was held that the letter was insufficient to amount to a rejection of the goods.

1031. 1893 Act, s. 36.

1032. *See* paras 550–554 below.

1033. *See* paras 590–603 and paras 604–616 below.

he/she would be liable as an involuntary bailee.[1034] However, between delivery and rejection, it would seem that risk rests with the buyer.[1035]

570. The right to reject is a powerful sanction against the seller's breach of condition. In effect, the buyer is legitimately refusing to perform his/her part of the bargain. The buyer does not have to accept the goods and to pay for them. It is then up to the seller to keep or dispose of the goods for his/her own account. Moreover, the effect of lawful rejection is as if the seller had never delivered the goods. Unless the seller is entitled to and makes a replacement delivery, the buyer can sue for non-delivery and further can claim damages for any losses caused by the non-delivery. But the legislation imposes restrictions on a buyer's right to reject.

1. Acceptance

571. A buyer loses his/her right to reject if he/she is deemed to have accepted the goods, under sections 34 and 35 of the 1893 Act.[1036] First, section 34(1) restricts the circumstances in which a buyer will be deemed to have accepted goods. It provides that where goods are delivered to the buyer and he/she has not previously examined them, he/she cannot be deemed to have accepted the goods until he/she has had a reasonable opportunity to examine the goods for the purpose of ascertaining whether they are in conformity with the contract. Reasonable opportunity, in this context, may include a reasonable time to see the goods in operation.[1037] Second, section 34(2) gives the buyer a right of examination in certain circumstances. It provides that, unless otherwise agreed, that when the seller tenders goods for delivery, he/she is bound, on request, to afford the buyer an opportunity to examine the goods for the purpose of ascertaining whether they are in conformity with the contract. This right is made available to a buyer, but only on request by the buyer.

572. Section 35 outlines three ways in which a buyer will be deemed to have accepted goods, and thus lose the right to reject. Section 35 states:

> The buyer is deemed to have accepted the goods when he intimates to the seller that he has accepted them, or, subject to section 34 of this Act, when he does any act in relation to them which is inconsistent with the ownership of the seller or when, without good and sufficient reason, he retains the goods without intimating to the seller that he has rejected them.

Accordingly, a buyer is deemed to have accepted goods when:

- he/she intimates acceptance;
- he/she does any act inconsistent with the seller's ownership of the goods;

1034. *See further* Palmer, *Bailment* (3rd ed., Sweet & Maxwell 2009).
1035. But *see Head v. Tattersall* (1871) LR b7 Exch 7.
1036. 1893 Act, ss 34 and 35, as amended by the 1980 Act, s. 20.
1037. *Bernstein v. Pamsons Motors (Golders Green) Ltd* [1987] 2 All ER 220.

– without good and sufficient reason, he/she retains the goods without intimating rejection.

573. So, for instance, under the first category above, a buyer will lose the right to reject the goods if he/she indicates to the seller that he/she accepts them. Such indication can be in any form: oral, written or by conduct, provided it is clear and unequivocal.[1038]

574. As regards the second category, the law is unclear as to what constitutes an act inconsistent with the seller's ownership. There is authority that administrative acts, such as unloading or sorting goods,[1039] or re-bagging rejected goods is insufficient,[1040] but even the most trivial act when done with knowledge of the seller's breach can constitute acceptance.[1041] For instance, registering ownership of a defective car and advertising it for sale,[1042] and the mere use of such a car,[1043] have been held to constitute acceptance under this category. It has also been held that incorporating goods so that they cannot be detached, constitutes acceptance.[1044]

575. As regards the final category, the key question is how long can a buyer hold goods and not lose the right to reject? This is a question of fact in each case. This time period can be very short as evidenced by *Gill v. Thomas Heiton & Co. Ltd* [1045] where the plaintiff wholesalers sold a barge-load of turf to the defendant retailers. On delivery and shortly after unloading commenced it was noted that the turf was unfit for resale. However, the unloading continued until the whole barge was unloaded. The following day the plaintiff was informed of the defective quality and the defendant sought to reject the goods. The plaintiff argued that the defendant had accepted the goods and demanded the price. The High Court held that the buyer had a right to reject goods for breach of condition, within a reasonable time. However, this right had not been exercised with sufficient promptness or in a manner consistent with the ownership of the seller and so the plaintiff was limited to a claim in damages only. In *Bernstein v. Pamsons Motors (Golders Green) Ltd*,[1046] it was stated that a reasonable time to keep the goods without losing the right to reject was an objectively reasonably time to try out the goods, not necessarily a reasonable time to discover the defect. Here a new car seized up after three weeks driving and 142 miles due to a blob of sealant in the lubrication system. It was held that the car was unmerchantable but the buyer was too late to reject and only had a claim in damages. Rougier J emphasized, from the seller's point of view, 'the commercial desirability of being able to close his ledger reasonably soon after the transaction is

1038. In *Varley v. Whipp* [1900] 1 QB 513 the buyer's 'grumbling' letter arranging a meeting with the seller to discuss a solution was held not to constitute acceptance.
1039. *Libau Wood Company v. H Smith & Sons Ltd* (1930) 37 Ll L Rep 296, at 300.
1040. *Dower & Co. v. Corrie Maccol & Son* (1925) 23 Ll L Rep 100 at 102.
1041. *Gill v. Thomas Heiton & Co. Ltd* [1943] Ir Jur Rep 67.
1042. *Armaghdpwn Motors Ltd v. Gray Motors Ltd* [1963] NZLR 5.
1043. *Lee v. York Coach and Marine* [1977] RTR 35.
1044. *Mechan & Sons Ltd v. Bow, M ' Lachlin & Co. Ltd* 1910 Sess C 758.
1045. [1943] Ir Jur Rep 67.
1046. [1987] 2 All ER 220.

complete'.[1047] But he also stated: '[w]hat is a reasonable time in relation to a bicycle will hardly suffice for a nuclear submarine',[1048] thereby leaving a huge margin of discretion in deciding what constitutes a reasonable time for different goods. For instance, in a Canadian case, *Public Utilities Commission of City of Waterloo v. Burroughs Business Machines*,[1049] based on similar statutory provisions, a computer system which was defective was rejected by the buyers after eight months; however, the buyers continued to use it for a further seven months. It was held that the buyer could reject the goods after fifteen months as the buyers had used their best efforts to make the computer function properly, and the goods were 'complex and novel'.

2. The Rule Against Partial Rejection

576. The rule against partial rejection is based on section 11(3) of the 1893 Act. It provides:

> Where a contract of sale is not severable, and the buyer has accepted the goods, or part thereof, the breach of any condition to be fulfilled by the seller can only be treated as a breach of warranty, and not as a ground for rejecting the goods and treating the contract as repudiated.

Hence, where the contract is not severable, the buyer loses the right to reject if he/she accepts the goods or part of them. Thus, if only some or part of the goods delivered are defective the buyer must accept, or reject, all of them. There are two statutory exceptions to this 'all or nothing' rule:

- where, under section 30(3), the seller delivers goods of the contract description mixed with goods of a different description;
- where, under section 11(3), the contract is severable.

In practice, this rigid 'all or nothing' approach is often not followed. Commercial contracts frequently make provision for partial rejection as this is more in keeping with commercial reality, and, even in the absence of a contractual right to partially reject the goods, a seller will often allow a buyer to reject part of the goods as part of a negotiated settlement.

577. First, under section 30(3), where the seller delivers goods he/she contracted to sell mixed with goods of a different description, the buyer is given two

1047. *Ibid.* 230. However, following statutory amendment in the UK in 1994, in *Clegg v. Anderson* [2003] EWCA Civ 320; [2003] 1 All ER (Comm.) 721, the Court of Appeal held that *Bernstein* no longer represented the law in relation to acceptance.
1048. *Ibid.* 230.
1049. (1974) 52 DLR 481.

options. He/she may either accept the goods which match the contract description and reject the rest – a form of partial rejection – or he/she may reject the whole quantity delivered.

578. Second, section 11(3) is expressed not to apply where the contract is severable, so that where the contract is severable the buyer may reject some goods notwithstanding that he/she has accepted other goods supplied under the contract. An example of a severable contract is given in section 31(2) of the 1893 Act which refers to instalment deliveries. Accordingly, a contract is severable where the goods are to be delivered in separate instalments and are paid for separately. The courts have also interpreted contracts as severable in other circumstances, thereby allowing the application of more flexible rules. For instance, a contract was severable where the contract provided for the goods to be delivered in instalments, to be determined by the seller,[1050] and as required by the buyer,[1051] and where goods were to be paid for by monthly account.[1052] The essence of a severable contract is that it is one contract, with the obligations under the contract, such as the delivery obligations or the payment obligations, being performed in several (two or more) parts.

579. Where the contract is severable and the seller makes one or more defective deliveries it may be necessary to decide whether the buyer can:

(a) reject the defective delivery;
(b) terminate the contract and refuse future deliveries.

a Rejection of the Defective Delivery

580. Where a contract is severable, acceptance of one instalment does not prevent the buyer rejecting another instalment. But, although the position is not clear, the better view is that the buyer may not reject part of an instalment and accept the remainder: in these circumstances an 'all or nothing' approach pertains.

b Termination of the Contract

581. Section 31(2) provides that where the seller makes one or more defective deliveries under a severable contract, whether or not those breaches allow the buyer to terminate the whole contract depends on the terms of the contract and all the circumstances of the case. Hence, where the breach in relation to one or more instalments is sufficiently serious, this may amount to a repudiation of the whole contract and allow the buyer to terminate it.[1053] Factors which may be taken into account in

1050. *Regent OHG v. Francesco of Jermyn St* [1981] 3 All ER 327.
1051. *Jackson v. Rotax* [1910] 2 KB 937.
1052. *Longbottom v. Bass Walker* (1922) WN 245.
1053. *Warinco AG v. Samor SPA* [1977] 2 Lloyd's Rep. 582, *per* Donaldson J at 588.

assessing the seriousness of the breach include: the ratio of the breach to the contract as a whole; and the likelihood of the breach being repeated.[1054] For example, in *Maple Flock Co. Ltd v. Universal Furniture Products (Wembley) Ltd*,[1055] the seller contracted to deliver 100 tons of rag flock in weekly instalments of one-and-a-half tons each. The first fifteen deliveries were satisfactory and were accepted; the sixteenth was contaminated but the next two were acceptable. The buyer purported to terminate the contract for breach in relation to the sixteenth delivery. A further four satisfactory deliveries were tendered and rejected: the seller sued. The court held that, bearing in mind the ratio of the breach to the contract as a whole and the likelihood of the breach being repeated, the breach was not so serious as to justify termination. Therefore the buyer was in breach of contract.[1056]

582. The Sales Law Review Group has made a number of important recommendations for change in relation to a buyer's remedies and the right to reject, in particular. Most notably, in relation to the concept of 'acceptance', the Group has recommended that the rules on acceptance in future legislation should be amended to clarify that, in the case of commercial contracts of sale, the buyer would not be deemed to have accepted goods by means of intimation of acceptance to the seller unless he has had a reasonable opportunity of examining the goods for the purpose of ascertaining their conformity with the contract. And, in the case of consumer contracts of sale, intimation by acceptance should be excluded from the rules governing acceptance in consumer contracts of sale in future legislation.[1057] Further, the Group have recommended that the rules governing acceptance by reason of acts inconsistent with the seller's ownership of the goods should be amended in future legislation to provide that a buyer would not be deemed to have accepted the goods merely because:

a. the goods have been delivered to a third party under a sub-sale, gift or other disposition;
b. the buyer asks for, or agrees to, the repair of the goods.[1058]

Lastly, in relation to acceptance, the Group has recommended the introduction of a default thirty-day period for the exercise of the right to reject goods not in conformity with the contract.[1059] The Group has also recommended that future legislation should give buyers a general right of partial rejection of goods not in conformity with the contract and which do not form part of a commercial unit. This general right of partial rejection should replace the limited right of partial rejection

---

1054. *Maple Flock Co. Ltd v. Universal Furniture Products (Wembley) Ltd* [1934] KB 148.
1055. [1934] KB 148.
1056. *See also Regent OHG v. Francesco of Jermyn St* [1981] 3 All ER 327; *Robt A Munroe & Co. Ltd v. Meyer* [1930] 2 KB 312.
1057. Sales Law Review Group, *Report on the Legislation Governing the Sale of Goods and Supply of Services* (Dublin, Prn. A11/1576, 2011) para. 9.21.
1058. Sales Law Review Group, *Report on the Legislation Governing the Sale of Goods and Supply of Services* (Dublin, Prn. A11/1576, 2011) para. 9.28.
1059. Sales Law Review Group, *Report on the Legislation Governing the Sale of Goods and Supply of Services* (Dublin, Prn. A11/1576, 2011) para. 9.44.

for goods of mixed description at section 30(3) of the 1893 Act. Moreover, future legislation should also state that section 11(3) of the 1893 Act is subject to the provision on partial rejection.[1060]

B. The Right to Damages

583. Any breach of contract by the seller entitles the buyer to claim damages in respect of any losses caused by the breach. Damages are assessed in accordance with the general rules of contract law; the buyer must therefore show that his/her losses were caused by the breach in question, that they are not too remote to be compensatable and that he/she has taken reasonable steps to mitigate his/her loss. Further, any term in the contract fixing the amount of damages payable will be subject to the rule against penalties and will only be enforceable if it is a genuine pre-estimate of the loss. However, these rules are modified by the Sale of Goods Acts 1893 and 1980 and specific rules apply to claims for damages for non-delivery, late delivery and breach of warranty.

1. Damages for Non-delivery

584. Where the seller wrongfully neglects or refuses to deliver, he/she totally fails to perform his/her obligations under the contract and the buyer is released from his/her obligation to accept the goods and to pay for them.[1061] If the buyer has paid the price, or any part thereof, in advance, and no goods are delivered, he/she can also reclaim the price as part of a restitutionary claim because there has been a total failure of consideration on the part of the seller.[1062] Where the buyer has suffered additional losses because of the non-delivery, he/she may sue the seller for damages under section 51(1) of the 1893 Act.

585. The *basic* measure of damages for non-delivery is provided for in section 51(2) of the 1893 Act as 'the estimated loss directly and naturally resulting, in the ordinary course of events, from the seller's breach'. This basic measure of damages is modified where there is an available market for goods of the contract description. It would appear that there is an 'available market' for this purpose if there is an available source of supply from which the buyer could buy replacement goods at a price that fluctuates in line with supply and demand.[1063] In such circumstances, section 51(3) of the 1893 Act applies the 'available market rule'. The available market rule provides that that the buyer's damages for non-delivery are prima facie the difference between the contract price and the market price for similar goods, on the

1060. Sales Law Review Group, *Report on the Legislation Governing the Sale of Goods and Supply of Services* (Dublin, Prn. A11/1576, 2011) para. 8.39.
1061. 1893 Act, s. 27.
1062. 1893 Act, s. 54.
1063. *Charter v. Sullivan* [1957] 2 QB 117.

date(s) when the goods should have been delivered: an objective test.[1064] The rationale for this rule is that the buyer is expected to take reasonable steps to mitigate his/her loss and, where there is an available market, he/she can mitigate by buying replacement goods in the market. Indeed, while the available market rule is only a prima facie rule, in practice, it is applied more commonly than the basic rule.[1065]

586. Where the buyer has contracted to resell the goods but the seller fails to deliver, generally no account is taken of the price at which the buyer contracted to resell:[1066] a replacement purchase in the market will enable him/her to satisfy his/her resale contract. However, the market price rule does not prevent the buyer recovering special damages where they would be recoverable in accordance with general principles.[1067] Thus, where the buyer loses a resale because he/she cannot satisfy his/her resale by buying in the market, special damages may be recoverable to compensate for the lost resale provided they are not too remote.[1068]

2. Damages for Late Delivery

587. Where time is of the essence,[1069] late delivery constitutes a breach of condition and the buyer can reject the goods, terminate the contract and sue for damages for non-delivery, as described above. A buyer can always choose to treat the breach of a condition as a breach of warranty,[1070] and hence pursue a claim in damages only. Where time is not of the essence, the buyer's only remedy is to sue for damages.

588. There are no special legislative rules as to the measure of damages for late delivery. Hence, the general common law rules will apply. Accordingly, where goods were intended for use in the buyer's business, he/she may recover damages for loss of profits caused by their non-availability, provided the loss is not too remote. Where the goods were to be used for some particularly lucrative purpose, the buyer will only be able to claim damages for such lost profits where this particular lucrative purpose was known to the seller at the time of the contract.[1071] Where the goods were intended for resale, the basic measure of damages will be the difference in value of the goods between the contractual date of delivery and the

1064. No account is taken of subjective factors personal to the buyer, such as lack of expertise which might result in him/her paying a higher price: *see Shearson Lehman Hutton Inc v. Maclaine Watson & Co. Ltd (No. 2)* [1990] 3 All ER 723.

1065. The market price rule may be displaced where it would be inappropriate (*see*, e.g., *The Texaco Melbourne* [1994] 1 Lloyd's Rep 473) and it may not apply where the parties have contemplated that it would not provide adequate compensation for the breach (*see WL Thompson Ltd v. Robinson (Gunmakers) Ltd* [1955] Ch. 177 *per* Upjohn J).

1066. *Williams v. Agius* [1914] AC 510.

1067. 1893 Act, s. 54.

1068. *Re R & H Hall & Co. Ltd and W H Pim (Jnr) & Co. Ltd ' s Arbitration* (1927) 30 Ll L Rep 159.

1069. *See* para. 465 above.

1070. 1893 Act s. 11(2).

1071. *Victoria Laundry (Windsor) Ltd v. Newman Industries Ltd* [1949] 2 KB 528.

actual date of delivery:[1072] that is, the amount, if any, by which the value has fallen and the buyer has lost by the delay in reselling. If there is an available market for goods of the contract description, their value will be assessed by reference to the market price at the relevant date. It is not clear whether account can be taken of any actual resale by the buyer in fixing damages.[1073] In practice, commercial buyers rarely seek damages for consequential losses caused by late delivery. Sales contracts often exclude liability for such losses, a force majeure or other clause may extend the time for delivery or a liquidated damages clause may exist to cover the situation.

3. Damages for Breach of Warranty

589. Under section 53(1), where the buyer retains the goods he/she may set-up his/her claim for damages for breach of warranty against the seller's claim for the price and thus withhold some, or all of the price,[1074] or he/she can sue for damages for breach of warranty.[1075] Section 53(4) provides that the basic measure of damages for breach of warranty is 'the estimated loss directly and naturally resulting, in the ordinary course of events, from the breach of warranty'.

590. Section 53(5) is stated to cover the situation where there is a breach of warranty of quality, for example, where the goods delivered are unmerchantable. However, it is assumed that the provision applies to any claim where the goods are defective and for any claim for breach of any of the statutory implied terms. In these circumstances, the measure of damages is prima facie the difference between the value of the goods at the date of delivery and the value they would have had had they satisfied the warranty. In commercial cases, rather than sue for breach of warranty, the parties more usually agree to a variation of the price. Section 53(5) is a prima facie rule only, and can be displaced in certain circumstances.[1076] Special damages may also be recovered provided they are not too remote.[1077]

1072. *Heron II* [1969] 1 AC 350. *See also Croudace Construction v. Cawoods Concrete Products* [1978] 2 Lloyd's Rep. 55 where the goods though delivered late were used as originally intended. In this case, the measure of damages was assessed not by the difference in value but on the basis of the additional costs resulting from the late delivery.

1073. *See Wertheim v. Chicoutimi Pulp Co.* [1911] ACD 301, where it was held that account should be taken of the fact that the buyer had sold the goods at more than the market price current at the date of delivery. Cf. *Slater v. Hoyle and Smith Ltd* [1920] 2 KB 11, where the court refused to follow *Wertheim* and applied the simple 'difference in value' rule.

1074. 1893 Act, s. 53(1)(a).

1075. 1893 Act, s. 53(1)(b).

1076. *Bence Graphics v. Fasson* [1997] 3 WLR 205.

1077. 1893 Act, s. 54.

C. Specific Performance

591. Section 52 of the 1893 Act gives the court discretion to award specific performance in 'any action for breach of contract to deliver specific or ascertained goods'. Specific goods are defined in section 62 of the 1893 Act as goods that are identified and agreed upon at the time the contract is made. However, even if the buyer can establish that the court has a discretion to award a decree of specific performance, he/she must also persuade the court to exercise that discretion in his/her favour. The weight of authority shows that specific performance will rarely, if ever, be ordered where the goods to be supplied are 'ordinary articles of commerce' which the buyer could obtain elsewhere.[1078] In effect, therefore, specific performance will be ordered only where the goods to be supplied are 'unique', and the courts have taken a very narrow view of what is 'unique'. Neither antique furniture[1079] nor ships[1080] are necessarily unique. The basis for this approach is that where the goods are not unique, damages will enable the buyer to buy alternative goods in the market.

D. Other Remedies

592. Where the seller is guilty of misrepresentation, the buyer may claim damages or rescind the contract on the basis of the misrepresentation. There may be advantages in pursuing a claim for misrepresentation rather than a claim for breach of contract. It would appear that delay alone will not bar the right to rescind for misrepresentation, whereas it may amount to acceptance and bar any right to reject the goods under the sales contract. But a court may be reluctant to allow rescission where the right to reject has been lost.[1081] Also, unless the misrepresentation is fraudulent, a court may be inclined to exercise its discretion under Part V of the Sale of Goods and Supply of Services Act 1980 to award damages in lieu of rescission. In practice, both avenues should be pursued where possible.

593. Where the property in the goods has passed to the buyer and he/she is entitled to immediate possession of the goods, he/she may also be able to sue in the tort of conversion for any wrongful interference with the goods.[1082] In such an action the court has a discretion to order specific delivery of the goods, or to award damages based on the value of the goods. Where, for example, a seller refused to

1078. The only reported Irish case, found by the author, where specific performance was ordered is *Clarke v. Reilly* (1962) 96 *ILTR* 96 which involved a contract for the supply of a new car in return for a 'trade-in' plus cash.

1079. *Cohan v. Roche* [1927] 1 KB 169.

1080. *CN Marine Inc v. Stena Line A/B and Reige Voor Maritem Transport (No 2), The Stena Nauticaa* [1982] 2 Lloyd's Rep 336; cf. *Behnke v. Bede Shipping Co. Ltd* [1927] 1 KB 649.

1081. *Leaf v. International Galleries Ltd* [1950] 2 KB 86.

1082. *See generally*, McMahon & Binchy, *Law of Torts* Ch. 30 (3rd ed., Butterworths 2000).

deliver, a claim in conversion may be available, alongside an action for non-delivery. But even where no action for non-delivery lies, for instance, where a third party interferes with the goods, such as a carrier who refused to deliver, a claim in conversion may exist.

VI. Seller's Remedies

594. Section 27 of the 1893 Act provides that the buyer's basic duties are to pay the price and accept the goods, in accordance with the terms of the contract. If the buyer indicates an intention to repudiate the contract, the seller may accept that repudiation and terminate the contract. The seller is then released from his/her obligations under the contract. Furthermore, the legislation provides the seller with a range of personal and real remedies for defective, or non-performance, of the buyer's obligations. Where the buyer defaults on his/her basic duties under the contract, the seller has a personal action on the contract. But a personal remedy, such as a claim for damages, is of limited value where the defendant is insolvent: the claim may, in effect, be worthless. In contrast, a real remedy confers rights against property, and so is unaffected by insolvency.

A. Personal Remedies

595. The 1893 Act provides the seller with three rights of action following the buyer's breach of contract.[1083] First, the seller can sue for the price under section 49 of the 1893 Act. Section 49 provides that where the buyer wrongfully neglects or refuses to pay the price, a seller can sue for the price if the property has passed to the buyer, or even if the property has not passed to the buyer if the price is payable 'on a day certain'. If the seller cannot fit within the above provision, he/she will be limited to a claim for damages for non-acceptance, under section 50 of the 1893 Act. From the seller's point of view a claim for the price has advantages over a claim for damages for non-acceptance: it is a liquidated claim so there is no need to prove causation or loss and there is no duty to mitigate. There are also procedural advantages to such claims.[1084]

596. The seller's second right of action against the buyer comes under section 50 which provides that where the buyer wrongfully neglects or refuses to accept and pay for the goods, the seller can sue the buyer for damages for non-acceptance. The measure of damages is the estimated loss directly and naturally resulting, in the ordinary course of events, from the buyer's breach.[1085] Where there is an available market for the goods of the contract description, the measure of damages is, prima

---

1083. *See* Sales Law Review Group, *Report on the Legislation Governing the Sale of Goods and Supply of Services* (Dublin, Prn. A11/1576, 2011) Ch 11 for more minor recommendations for change in this regard.

1084. *See* Ords 13 and 37 of the Superior Court Rules on the summary summons procedure.

1085. 1893 Act, s. 50(2).

facie, the difference between the contract price and the market price of the goods at the date when they should have been accepted, or if no time was fixed for acceptance, at the time of the refusal to accept.

597. Lastly, a distinction must be made between a buyer failing to accept and pay for the goods, and a buyer failing to take delivery. Where a buyer delays in taking delivery though he/she ultimately accepts and pays for the goods, the seller cannot claim for non-acceptance, or the price. But he/she may have incurred losses due to the delay in taking delivery. Under section 37, where the seller is ready and willing to deliver the goods and he/she requests the buyer to take delivery and the buyer fails to take delivery of the goods within a reasonable time, the buyer is liable to the seller for any loss caused by his/her failure to take delivery and also the buyer must pay the seller a reasonable charge for the care and custody of the goods.

B. Real Remedies

598. Personal claims on the contract, such as the right to sue for the price or damages for non-acceptance, will be of little use where the buyer is insolvent and unable to pay. Sections 38–48 of the 1893 Act therefore give the seller three real remedies which offer some measure of protection against the buyer's failure to pay or inability to pay due to insolvency. They are:

- a lien over the goods
- a right to stop the goods in transit
- a right to resell the goods and terminate the original contract.[1086]

These rights arise automatically, by implication of the law, although they can be augmented by the express terms of the contract. They are available to an unpaid seller only. The real remedies under the legislation protect the seller by giving him/her express rights, in defined circumstances, to withhold delivery, in the form of a lien and a right of stoppage in transit and a right of resale. These real rights apply even where the property in the goods has passed to the buyer. However, the real remedies provided by the 1893 Act are of limited practical value in modern trade and commerce where goods are normally supplied on credit terms and they come into the buyer's possession before the expiry of the credit period. This weakness in the statutory scheme of real remedies, and the superior status of real rights in general, has led to the express inclusion of retention of title clauses in sale of goods contracts since the 1970s, as a means of protecting the seller's interests in sales contracts. The scope and legal effectiveness of such clauses is examined below.

1086. 1893 Act, s. 39(1).

C. Retention of Title Clauses

599. Today, it is common to allow buyers credit. In these circumstances, the buyer will usually have possession of and even property in the goods before payment is effected. In modern commercial circumstances the statutory rights of lien, stoppage in transit and resale offer the seller very limited protection against the buyer's failure to pay the price. Alternatively, the seller's rights to sue for the price and for damages for non-acceptance are personal claims. And, the personal claims of an unpaid seller, who is usually an ordinary unsecured creditor, will rank behind those of the buyer's secured and preferential creditors. In most cases the unpaid seller will only receive a small percentage of the sum due to him/her; in many cases he/she will receive nothing.

600. Thus, a seller may require additional protection against the buyer's inability to pay. The simplest option will often be to retain property in the goods. In appropriate cases the seller may lease the goods to the buyer; alternatively, they may be supplied on hire purchase terms. However, leasing and hire purchase are inappropriate where the goods are supplied to the buyer for resale or for use in manufacturing. A further alternative is for the seller to supply the goods under a conditional sale agreement, retaining title to them until they are paid for. It is now common for commercial sale contracts to contain a 'retention of title clause' whereby the seller retains title to the goods supplied until they are paid for in order to protect himself/herself against the buyer's failure to pay the price. From a commercial perspective, the retention of title clause operates like an extended version of the real rights of lien and stoppage in transit but unlike the real remedies, the retention of title must be expressly provided for. Such clauses are often complex and must be drafted with care.

601. Retention of title by the seller is sanctioned by sections 17 and 19 of the 1893 Act. Section 17 provides that property passes when the parties intend it to pass; section 19 provides that the seller may reserve the right of disposal of the goods until certain conditions are met. At its simplest, a sale subject to a retention of title clause is essentially a conditional sale agreement. However, whereas traditionally goods were only supplied on conditional sale terms where it was expected that they would be retained by the buyer in the form in which they were supplied, retention of title clauses are used in contracts even where it is expected from the outset that the goods may be resold, consumed or used in a manufacturing process before they are paid for.

602. There is now a substantial body of case law and extensive academic literature surrounding retention of title clauses.[1087] Nevertheless, many aspects of the law relating to retention of title clauses remain unclear. The following analysis identifies the different types of claims that have been made in relation to retention of title clauses.

1087. *See*, e.g., McCormack, *Reservation of Titles Clauses* (2nd ed., Sweet & Maxwell 1995); Wheeler, *Reservation of Title Clauses: Impact and Implications* (Clarendon Press 1991).

1. Simple Clauses

603. It is clear that a *simple* clause which retains title to the goods supplied until they are paid for is legally effective.[1088] It had been argued by insolvency practitioners that such a retention of title clause involved the property in goods passing to the buyer and the buyer granting back to the seller a mortgage or charge over the goods to the value of the debt which was unenforceable due to lack of registration under the relevant legislation.[1089] In practice, retention of title clauses are never registered in Ireland not least because the process would be administratively cumbersome requiring a separate registration for each individual clause. This rather complicated charge argument was definitively rejected by the courts, in Ireland and England in the 1980s.

604. EU law also sanctions the use of 'simple clauses'. The EC Directive on combating late payment in commercial transactions[1090] states that Member States shall provide:

> that the seller retains title to goods until they are fully paid for if a retention of title clause has been expressly agreed between the buyer and the seller before the delivery of the goods.[1091]

As noted above, Irish common law was already in compliance with this provision and so no further transposing measure was required in this regard.

605. In *Bernard Somers v. James Allen (Ireland) Ltd,*[1092] the respondent supplied animal feed to a company subject to a simple retention of title clause. On appointment of the receiver the goods were identifiable and had not been used in the manufacturing process. The applicant receiver sought the assistance of the court and argued that a simple retention of title clause was not effective where it was known that the goods would be used in a manufacturing process. It was held by Carroll J, in the High Court, that as long as the goods still existed in the same state in which they were supplied, and as long as they had not been mixed with other goods or transmuted into a manufactured product, then a simple clause would be effective.

1088. *Frigoscandia Ltd v. Continental Irish Meat Ltd* [1982] ILRM 396; *Clough Mill v. Martin* [1984] 3 All ER 982.
1089. Where individuals grant security interests over goods they must be registered under the Bills of Sale (Ireland) Acts 1879 and 1883; where companies grant security interests they must be registered under the Companies Act 2014 (this new Companies Act 2014 replaces the former Companies Acts 1963–2013 on 1 Jun. 2015): *see further* paras 809–821.
1090. Directive 2011/7/EU, [2011] OJ L 48/1.
1091. Article 9.
1092. [1985] IR 340; [1984] ILRM 437; appealed to the Supreme Court, unsuccessfully, on separate point: [1985] IR 340; [1985] ILRM 624. *See also Hendy Lennox v. Grahame Puttick Engines Ltd* [1984] 1 WLR 485.

606. In contrast, where the manufacturing process results in the seller's goods being irreversibly incorporated into a new product, or losing their identity, the seller's title to the original goods will be extinguished as they will cease to exist as an independent item. For instance, in *Peachdart Ltd*,[1093] leather was supplied to manufacture handbags. It was possible to identify which handbags were made from the supplier's leather. However, it was held there that there is a presumption that property passes to the buyer as soon as the goods enter a manufacturing process that will result in the loss of their identity, in this case, once the leather was first cut.

607. Generally, where goods supplied by the seller are incorporated into realty, or the land, they will become part of the realty, and therefore the property of its owner, if the annexation is such as to make them a fixture. In order to determine whether something has become a fixture or not, courts usually consider two things: the degree of annexation and the object of annexation.[1094]

2. Manufactured Goods

608. In order to overcome the above problem of the original goods supplied losing their identity in a manufacturing process, retention of title clauses have been drafted to claim title to the products manufactured using the original goods supplied. However, it will generally be assumed that new products manufactured by the buyer will be the buyer's property, since to recognize them as belonging to the seller would allow him/her to take the benefit of the buyer's labour and of any other goods or materials used in their manufacture. Where the seller's retention of title clause lays claim to such manufactured products it will normally give him/her no more than a charge over the manufactured product to secure the sums owed to him/her, which if not registered is not enforceable.[1095]

3. Claims to Proceeds

609. If the buyer resells the goods before paying for them, the seller's rights over the goods will normally be extinguished because the sub-buyer will take a good title to the goods by virtue of section 25(2) of the 1893 Act.[1096] In order to overcome this problem the seller may seek to claim an interest in the proceeds of the resale. In *Aluminium Industrie Vaasen BV v. Romalpa Aluminium*,[1097] the English Court of Appeal held that, in certain circumstances, the seller was entitled to trace his goods into the proceeds of their resale. A claim to proceeds will only be worthwhile where,

1093. [1984] 1 Ch. 131; *see also Borden v. Scottish Timber Products Ltd* [1981] Ch. 25.
1094. *Holland v. Hodgson* (1872) LR 7 CP 328; *see also In re Galway Concrete Ltd (In Liquidation)* [1983] ILRM 402.
1095. *Kruppstahl AG v. Quitman Products Ltd* [1982] ILRM 551; *see further Clough Mill v. Martin* [1984] 3 All ER 982.
1096. *See* paras 633–634 below.
1097. [1976] 1 WLR 676.

as in the *Romalpa* case itself, the proceeds of resale are received after commencement of the insolvency. A seller's claim to proceeds will only succeed if the seller can show that the relationship between himself/herself and his/her buyer is fiduciary, thereby establishing a right to trace in equity. The establishment of a fiduciary relationship will depend on the wording and construction of the particular retention of title clause and the other provisions of the contract in which it appears. In *Romalpa,* the seller sold aluminium foil to the buyer subject to a retention of title clause which provided that:

(a) the foil should be stored in such a way as to identify it as the seller's property;
(b) products made from the seller's foil were to belong to the seller and be stored so as to make them identifiable as such;
(c) that until resale, the buyer was to hold manufactured products in the capacity of 'fiduciary owner' for the seller;
(d) on demand the buyer should 'hand over' to the seller claims against its customers who bought manufactured products.

The buyer went into receivership without paying for a quantity of foil. However, prior to the receivership, the buyer sold a quantity of foil and it was paid for after the appointment of a receiver. The seller claimed the proceeds of sale from the receiver. The contract contained no express provision to cover such a situation. Counsel for the receiver conceded that the buyer held the foil as bailee for the seller, and the Court of Appeal held, in light of that concession and the provisions of the contract, that: (a) a right for the buyer to sell foil must be implied; and (b) the relationship between the seller and buyer was fiduciary so that on a resale of the foil the seller could trace into the proceeds of sale.

610. However, since the *Romapla* decision in 1976, courts in the UK have been reluctant to recognize a fiduciary relationship between a buyer and a seller when in truth the relationship is really one of debtor and creditor.[1098] In contrast, *Romalpa* type claims have been successful in Ireland,[1099] and a fiduciary relationship may be found to exist between an unpaid seller and a buyer of goods, based on the construction of the retention of title clause and the surrounding circumstances, thereby, enabling a claim to proceeds. For example, a case where the wording of the clause and the surrounding circumstances were found to be lacking was *Carroll Group Distributors v. G & JF Burke.*[1100] In that case, the plaintiff supplied goods to the defendant, subject to a retention of title clause, and four week's credit. The clause provided, *inter alia*, that the goods were to remain the property of the supplier until all sums due were paid; it gave the buyer the express right to resell the goods; where

1098. *Re Andrabell Ltd* [1984] 3 All E.R. 407; *Tatung v. Galex* (1988) 5 B.C.C. 325; *E Pfeiffer v. Arbuthnot* [1988] 1 W.L.R. 150; *Re Weldtech* [1991] B.C.C. 16 and *Compaq Computers v. Abercorn* [1991] B.C.C. 484.

1099. *See*, e.g., *Re Sugar Distributors Ltd* [1982] ILRM 399; *SA Foundaries Du Lion v. International Factors Ltd* [1985] ILRM 66; *Re WJ Hickey Ltd* [1988] IR 126. This line of cases has been referred to as being based on 'the automatic fiduciary relationship proposition': *see* McCormack, *Reservation of Titles Clauses* 88 (2nd ed., Sweet & Maxwell 1995).

1100. [1990] ILRM 285.

goods were resold the clause provided that the buyer did so on their own account and not as agent for the supplier; and the buyer undertook to keep all proceeds of such resale 'in trust' for the supplier and in a separate bank account. The buyer went into liquidation and the supplier sought to trace into the proceeds of sale of the goods. No such separate bank account was ever created and the court found that the supplier was probably aware of this fact. Murphy J, in the High Court, in dismissing the plaintiff's claim, held that had this system operated, the buyer would have sums in a bank account in excess of the supplier's claim, partly because of the mark-up in price. As such, the bank account would be a source of funds to which the supplier could have recourse to discharge monies due though he/she would not be entitled to all the monies in the account. Moreover, the clause expressly provided that where goods were sold to a customer by the buyer, the buyer was acting on its own account and not as agent for the sellers. On the basis of this analysis, the court found that this arrangement possessed all the characteristics of a mortgage or charge which was void for non-registration under section 99 of the Companies Act 1963.

611. More recently, a claim to proceeds initially succeeded in the High Court in *Unitherm Heating Systems Ltd v. Wallace & BHT Group Limited (in liquidation),*[1101] but was subsequently overturned on appeal by the Court of Appeal.[1102] In that case, Unitherm supplied goods to BHT, for resale, subject to a retention of title clause which included a claim to proceeds of sale. On liquidation, over EUR 93,000 was due to the plaintiff in respect of goods supplied which had been sold on to third parties before the appointment of the liquidator. Based on a comprehensively drafted retention of title clause, Unitherm submitted that BHT held the goods as their agent, and hence as a fiduciary, entitling the Unitherm to trace into the proceeds of sale. The liquidator, on the other hand, submitted that the legal effect of the proceeds of sale clause was to create a charge which was registrable under section 99 of the Companies Act, 1963, and in so far as it has not been registered, the charge was void as against the liquidator. Based on the terms and condition of sale, as well as the particular course of trading between the parties, it was found in the High Court that an agency relationship existed between the seller and buyer, despite no express mention of agency in the terms and conditions of sale, and Unitherm was thereby held to be able to trace into the proceeds of sale. On appeal, the Court of Appeal found no such agency relationship, on the facts, instead characterizing the relationship between the parties as a normal buyer/seller relationship. Factors which pointed away from any agency/fiduciary duties included: (i) BHT's right to sell to it's customers in the course of its own business; (ii) credit terms of 60 days; (iii) the standard conditions of sale which sought to impress the entirety of the purchase monies received, including BHT's profit margin, with a trust, the latter being monies to which it had no legal or beneficial entitlement; (iv) the fact that no separate account was ever created for the purchase monies; and (v) the 'all sums due' nature of the retention of title clause.

1101. [2014] IEHC 177.
1102. [2015] IECA 191.

4. All Sums Due Clauses

612. Where a seller relies on a 'simple clause', the seller is only entitled to claim the goods so long as sums remain due under the contract under which the particular goods were supplied. This is not problematic where the seller and buyer transact on a once-off basis. However, where the parties trade more frequently or where there is a continuous trading relationship between the parties, problems of identification can arise for the seller seeking to pursue a claim based on a simple retention of title clause. In order to avoid these identification problems, a seller may use an 'all sums due' clause[1103] which provides that as long as *any* sum is outstanding, whether under the relevant supply contract or otherwise, no property in any goods supplied can pass from the seller to the buyer. In *Armour v. Thyssen*,[1104] the only reported case which addressed this type of clause directly,[1105] the House of Lords held that an all sums due clause was effective to prevent title passing to the buyer until its conditions were fulfilled and it therefore seems that such a clause does not create a charge.

VII. The Passing of Property

613. The legal objective of a contract for the sale of goods is the transfer of property in the goods from seller to buyer. This is recognized by the statutory definition of a contract of sale, and it is one of the features which distinguishes a sale from other, apparently similar, transactions involving the transfer of possession and use of goods.[1106] Because the transfer of property has important practical and legal consequences, the legislation contains detailed rules governing various aspects of it including: the time when property is transferred from seller to buyer, in sections 16–19; the issue of risk, in section 20; and the effect of a purported transfer by someone who is not the owner of the goods, in sections 21–26. The rules on the transfer or passing of property are examined under this heading; the related topics of the passage of risk, and title conflicts are considered later.

614. The statutory rules on the passing of property are based on rules developed at common law prior to the 1893 Act, and they have remained unchanged since 1893. Perhaps surprisingly, the passing of property is not related to the delivery of the goods or the payment of the price. This means that the rules often operate contrary to expectations. Instead, the legislation contains rather technical and complicated rules depending largely on the type of goods sold: specific, unascertained or future.

1103. Also referred to as 'all monies due'; 'all debts due'; 'all liability'; or 'current account' clauses.
1104. [1990] 3 All ER 481.
1105. 'All sums due' clauses were used in a number of Irish cases with success but the 'all sums' aspect of the clauses was not directly in issue: *see*, e.g., *Re Interview Ltd* [1975] IR 382; *Frigoscandia Ltd v. Continental Irish Meat Ltd* [1982] ILRM 396; *Kruppstahl AG v. Quitman Products Ltd* [1982] ILRM 551.
1106. 1893 Act, s. 1.

A. Specific Goods

615. Specific goods are defined as goods which are identified and agreed upon at the time the contract is made.[1107] Under a contract for the sale of specific goods the seller must deliver the specific goods identified and agreed upon and cannot, without the consent of the buyer, tender substitute goods. The first three rules in section 18 contain presumptions of intention as to the passing of property in specific goods. These presumptions can, of course, be rebutted where a contrary intention appears.

616. Rule 1 provides:

> Where there is an unconditional contract for the sale of specific goods, in a deliverable state,[1108] the property in the goods passes to the buyer when the contract is made, and it is immaterial whether the time of payment or the time of delivery, or both, be postponed.

617. Where the goods are not in a deliverable state at the time of the contract, Rule 2 provides:

> Where there is a contract for the sale of specific goods and the seller is bound to do something to the goods, for the purpose of putting them into a deliverable state, property does not pass until the thing is done, and the buyer has notice thereof.

618. Rule 3, which is of limited application, provides:

> Where there is a contract for the sale of specific goods in a deliverable state, but the seller is bound to weigh, measure, test, or do some other act or thing with reference to the goods for the purpose of ascertaining the price, the property does not pass until such act or thing be done and the buyer has notice thereof.

B. Goods on Approval or on Sale or Return

619. Goods may be delivered to a potential buyer in order for him/her to evaluate their suitability for his/her purposes, or to try to resell them, under terms which allow him/her to return them if they prove unsuitable or unsaleable. In such cases the goods are said to be delivered 'on approval' or 'on sale or return' terms, respectively. Strictly, where goods are delivered on approval, or on sale or return terms,

1107. 1893 Act, s. 62.
1108. 1893 Act, s. 62(4) defines deliverable state as 'such a state that the buyer would under the contract be bound to take delivery of them'.

there may, at the time of delivery, be no contract of sale. Instead, there will be an agreement under which the buyer effectively has an option to buy the goods if they are approved or resold.

620. The sale on approval, and the sale or return agreement may contain detailed provisions dealing with the buyer's right to return the goods and the passing of property in them. In the absence of any express or implied agreement as to the passing of property, section 18, Rule 4 provides that property in the goods passes to the buyer in one of the four circumstances:

- when the buyer signifies his/her approval or acceptance of them to the seller;
- when the buyer does any other act adopting the transaction;[1109]
- when the buyer retains the goods, without rejecting them, beyond the time limit fixed for their return;[1110]
- when no time limit for their return is fixed, on the expiry of a reasonable time.

C. Unascertained Goods

621. The category of unascertained goods is not expressly defined in the legislation. But, section 62 of the 1893 Act does define specific goods as goods which are identified and agreed upon at the time the contract is made. The implication is that all other goods are unascertained (also known as 'fungibles'). It is important to note that the relevant time for assessing the nature of goods, whether specific or unascertained, is the time the contract is made. Under the statutory rules, in order for property to pass in unascertained goods, the goods must first become ascertained at some time between the making of the contract and its completion, under section 16, and then property passes when the parties intend it to pass, under section 17, or when the goods are unconditionally appropriated to the contract, under section 18, Rule 5.

622. Section 16 of the 1893 Act provides that:

> where there is a contract for the sale of unascertained goods no property in the goods is transferred to the buyer unless and until the goods are ascertained.

1109. A buyer will be deemed to have adopted the transaction by dealing with the goods, such as reselling or pledging them. However, it has been held that a buyer does not adopt the transaction where he/she is prevented by circumstances outside his/her control from returning the goods – for instance because they are accidentally damaged or destroyed: *Elphick v. Barnes* (1880) 5 CPD 321.

1110. *See Atari Corpn (UK) Ltd v. Electronics Boutique Stores (UK) Ltd* [1998] 2 WLR 66.

This rule cannot be excluded or varied by the terms of the contract or the intention of the parties.

623. It has been said that goods are ascertained when they are 'identified in accordance with the agreement after [the] contract is made'.[1111] An illustration of this rule, and the resulting injustice, can be found in *re Wait*.[1112] Wait bought 1,000 tons of wheat to be loaded on the *mv Challenger*. Wait then resold 500 tons of the cargo to a buyer who paid for that part of the cargo in advance. However, before the ship reached its destination, Wait became bankrupt. It was held that the buyer was unable to claim any part of the cargo. He owned no part of the goods because he had agreed to buy unascertained goods (albeit from an identified source) which had not been separated from the bulk and hence not identified with the buyer's contract. The fact that the goods were unascertained prevented property passing; and it also prevented the buyer obtaining a decree of specific performance.[1113] A claim to an equitable interest in the cargo was also unsuccessful, the court finding that the mere fact of a sale or an agreement to sell part of a specified bulk did not give the buyer an equitable interest in the goods.[1114] The result was that the buyer was left as an unsecured creditor to claim repayment of the price.

624. Once unascertained goods have been ascertained, property passes according to the intention of the parties, under section 17. However, where it is not clear what the parties intended, section 18, Rules 5 provides that property passes to the buyer when goods of the contract description in a deliverable state are unconditionally appropriated to the contract by one party with the consent of the other. The key to the passing of property in unascertained goods under Rule 5(1) is the phrase 'unconditional appropriation'.

1111. *Re Wait* [1927] 1 Ch 606, *per* Atkin LJ at 630.
1112. [1927] 1 Ch 606.
1113. 1893 Act, s. 54.
1114. *Per* Atkin, LJ, 635–636; approved more recently in *Re Goldcorp* [1995] 1 AC 74, at 91; [1994] 2 All ER 806 at 814–815. Hence, it is widely accepted that the legislation contains a complete statement of the proprietary rights conferred by a sale of goods contract: no equitable interest can be created merely by virtue of a sale contract. This is despite the fact that it is well established that equitable rights can arise in relation to the transfer of other types of property such as land or book debts (*Tailby v. Official Recei ver* (1888) 13 App. Cas. 523). Of course, the parties to a sale of goods contract can *expressly agree* to create equitable rights, and indeed include such an agreement as a term of the sales contract, but this is strictly speaking, in Atkin LJ's terminology 'dehors the contract of sale'. *See*, e.g., *Re Kayford Ltd* [1975] 1 All ER 604; [1975] 1 WLR 279; *McCann v. Irish Board Mills Ltd* [1980] ILRM 216. But, it should be noted that *Re Wait* and *Re Goldcorp Exchange* both concerned sales of unascertained goods, and hence the cases could be limited to these circumstances. Lord Mustill's comments in *Re Goldcorp Exchange* related to wholly unascertained goods only, while Atkin LJ's comments in *Re Wait* were strictly speaking *obiter*, and Lord Hamworth MR, who agreed with Atkin LJ in the result in *Re Wait*, seems to have concerned himself with sale of unascertained goods only. Accordingly, it is not conclusively settled that a contract of sale, in itself, can never give rise to an equitable interest before the passing of property. However, the creation of an equitable interest normally depends on the contract being specifically enforceable (*Holroyd v. Marshall* (1862) 10 HL Cas 191). Because courts rarely order specific performance of sales contracts (*see* para. 569), such an equitable interest would only arise in exceptional cases.

625. It is said that goods are unconditionally appropriated to the contract if they have been 'irrevocably attached or earmarked' for use in its performance.[1115] Generally, this requires the seller to do some act which puts the goods out of his/her control, so that he/she cannot use them in the performance of another contract. The simplest way in which this happens is by delivery to the buyer. A statutory example of unconditional appropriation can be found in section 18, Rule 5(2). Accordingly, where the seller delivers goods to the buyer or an independent carrier or bailee for transmission to the buyer, he/she is to be taken as having unconditionally appropriated the goods to the contract unless he/she reserves a right of disposal of the goods. Further examples can be found in case law. In *Aldridge v. Johnson*,[1116] for example, the plaintiff agreed to purchase a quantity of barley from the defendants and sent 200 sacks to the defendants to fill. The defendants filled 155 sacks and then emptied them before becoming insolvent. It was held that the goods had been unconditionally appropriated when the barley was placed in the sacks and property had passed at that stage. Emptying the sacks was of no legal consequence. Pearson J explained this as an example of 'constructive delivery' when the defendant sellers placed the goods in plaintiff buyer's sacks.[1117]

626. In reviewing the rules on the passing of property, the Sales Law Review Group recognized the vulnerable position of pre-paying buyers of goods in bulk who have paid for the goods, and hence the Group focused on section 16 in term of its reform agenda. Having examined the relevant case law, the Group found that the mandatory nature of section 16 was contrary to the principle of freedom of contract and that the provision operated contrary to the reasonable expectations of contracting parties in an anomalous and inconsistent manner. Following the lead of the UK,[1118] the Group recommended that future legislation should provide that where there is a contract for the sale of a specified quantity of unascertained goods forming part of an identified bulk, a buyer who has paid for some or all of the contract goods would obtain an undivided share in the bulk and become a tenant in common of the whole. This tenancy in common would be realizable upon apportionment of the identified quantity to the individual contract of the tenant (i.e., the buyer). Therefore, while ascertainment and appropriation would still be required in order for the goods to be subject to individual proprietary rights, this recommendation would establish new proprietary rights for buyers while the goods remain in bulk – the tenancy in common.[1119]

1115. Atiyah, *Sale of Goods* 334 (11th ed., Pearson 2005).

1116. (1857) 7 E&B 885; *see also Langton v. Higgins* (1859) 4 H&N 402.

1117. *See also Healy v. Howlett & Sons* [1917] 1 KB 337; *Carlos Federspiel & CoSA v. Charles Twigg & Co. Ltd* [1957] 1 Lloyd's Rep 240; *Wardar v. Norwood* [1968] 2 QB 663; [1968] 2 All ER 602; *Spicer-Cowan Ireland Ltd v. Play Print Ltd* (unreported, High Court, 13 Mar. 1980); *Hendy Lennox Ltd v. Graham Puttick Engines Ltd* [1984] 1 WLR 485; and *Cronin v. IMP Midleton Ltd* (unreported, High Court, 31 Jan. 1986).

1118. There the Sale of Goods (Amendment) Act 1995 inserted new ss 20A and 20B in the UK Sale of Goods Act 1979 which reformed the operation of s. 16.

1119. Sales Law Review Group, *Report on the Legislation Governing the Sale of Goods and Supply of Services* (Dublin, Prn. A11/1576, 2011) para. 6.26. The Group recommended no other major changes to the provisions governing the passing of property in ss 16–18 of the 1893 Act: para. 6.33.

D. Future Goods

627. Section 5(1) of the 1893 Act states that goods can be existing, that is, owned or possessed by the seller at the time of the sales contract, or future, that is, goods to be manufactured or acquired by the seller after the making of the sales contract. Such sales of future goods operate as agreements to sell.[1120] Where the contract is for future goods sold by description, in the absence of any indication of the parties' intention, section 18, Rule 5 applies and provides that property passes when goods of that description and in a deliverable state are unconditionally appropriated to the contract with the consent of the other party. For example, in the English case *Carlos Federspiel & CoSA v. Charles Twigg & Co Ltd,* [1121] Twigg agreed to manufacture and sell *fob* a quantity of bicycles to a buyer, Federspiel, in Costa Rica. The buyer paid for the goods in advance. The bicycles were placed in crates marked with the buyer's name. Twigg then became insolvent and the receiver refused to deliver the goods to the buyer. The issue before the court was: who owned the goods; and in particular, had they been unconditionally appropriated to the contract? It was held that the goods had not been unconditionally appropriated to the buyer's contract. Packaging the goods and marking the buyer's name on them was not sufficient, in this case, to constitute unconditional appropriation. Such conduct was considered merely an aspect of the internal administration of the sellers' business. Rather, the act of appropriation will often be the last act a seller will perform, which in this case would have involved placing the goods on board the ship. Hence, the receiver was entitled to remove the bicycles from the crates and sell them to another customer, leaving the buyer an unsecured creditor.

VIII. The Passing of Risk

628. 'Risk' is not defined in the legislation but it is accepted that risk is concerned with events causing damage to or loss of the goods which is not attributable to the act or fault of the seller or buyer. If goods are damaged whilst at the seller's risk, the seller may not be able to require the buyer to accept them in performance of the contract of sale. Therefore, where goods are damaged or lost, the seller may have to repair them or find replacement goods in order to perform his/her contract; such repair or replacement will be at his/her expense. Where the contract is for the sale of specific goods, replacement is not an option without the consent of the buyer. If he/she is unable to repair or replace the goods within the time for performance of the contract he/she may incur liability for late or non-delivery, unless he/she is excused by the contract on the grounds of impossibility. If, on the other hand, the goods are damaged whilst at the buyer's risk, the buyer must accept and pay for them under the contract of sale, unless he/she is excused by the contract on the grounds of impossibility.

1120. 1893 Act, s. 1.
1121. [1957] 1 Lloyd's Rep 240.

629. The party who bears the risk of damage to or loss of goods therefore bears the risk that they may have to be replaced or repaired and may wish to insure against that risk. It has been held that a person who bears the risk of damage to or loss of property has sufficient interest in that property to insure it.[1122] Moreover, the party who bears the risk of damage or loss is still bound by his/her contractual obligations, regardless of any damage or loss, and will be in breach of contract for any failure to perform his/her contractual obligations, unless such performance is excused. Performance of contractual obligations can be excused, on the grounds of impossibility, under the doctrine of frustration. The doctrine of mistake may also provide an excuse for non-performance. Instances of these common law doctrines, excusing performance, are to be found in sections 6 and 7 of the 1893, and the operation of these provisions is linked to the passing of risk. The rules on the passage of risk and sections 6 and 7 excusing performance are considered further below.

A. The Basic Rule on the Passing of Risk

630. The basic common law rule is that the owner of property bears the risk of its damage, deterioration or destruction: *res peruit domino*. Section 20 of the 1893 Act reiterates this rule:

> Unless otherwise agreed, the goods remain at the seller's risk until the property in them is transferred to the buyer, but when the property in them is transferred to the buyer the goods are at the buyer's risk whether delivery has been made or not.

Hence, we say, risk passes with property. In order to determine when risk passes, the different rules on the passing of property, outlined above, must be applied, depending on whether the goods sold are specific, unascertained or future. Where, for example, specific goods are sold but possession is retained by the seller, under section 18 Rule 1, property passes at the time the contract is made and hence, under section 20, risk passes to the buyer at the time of contract, regardless of delivery. Where unascertained goods are sold, no property or risk can pass until the goods are ascertained, under section 16, and then property and risk can pass in accordance with the intention of the parties, under section 17, or, when the goods are unconditionally appropriated to the contract, under section 18, Rule 5. Conversely, where a seller supplies goods subject to a retention of title clause, possession of the goods may pass to the buyer but property and risk will remain with the seller until the goods are paid for.

631. Healy v. Howlett & Sons [1123] is an illustration of this general rule in operation. There, the plaintiff, a fish exporter based in Ireland, agreed to sell twenty cases of mackerel to the defendant, a fishmonger based in London. The plaintiff had two

1122. *Inglis v. Stock* (1885) 10 App. Cas. 263.
1123. [1917] 1 KB 337; *see also Clarke v. Micheal Reilly & Sons* (1962) 96 ILTR 96.

other customers for mackerel and so he dispatched 190 cases of mackerel by train to satisfy all three contracts. The plaintiff gave instructions to the railway company to divide the consignment into three lots for the three customers at Holyhead. However, the train was delayed before the defendant's boxes were earmarked and by the time this was done at Holyhead, the fish had deteriorated. The defendant refused to pay and it was held that no property and hence no risk had passed in the goods to him. Property and risk would not pass until the goods were ascertained and unconditionally appropriated to the contract.

632. The above general rule has been amended recently in relation to consumer sales. The issue of risk in consumer sales is addressed in the EU Consumer Rights Directive[1124] which was transposed in Ireland in Part 6 of the EU (Consumer Information, Cancellation and other Rights) Regulations 2013.[1125] Part 6 makes a number of amendments by way of substituting new provisions into the Sale of Goods Act 1893 in relation to consumer sales. Accordingly, the general rule that risk passes with property in displaced in consumer sales. A new section 20(3) of the Sale of Goods Act 1893, substituted by Regulation 29, provides that this general rule does not apply where:

(a) the buyer deals as consumer;[1126]
(b) the seller dispatches the goods to the buyer.

In such circumstances, Regulation 29(4) states that the goods remain at the seller's risk until the buyer, or a person indicated by the buyer for this purpose, acquires the physical possession of the goods. Hence, the former link between risk and property is broken and, in its place, the passage of risk is linked to possession of the goods, reflecting more closely parties' reasonable expectations. However, this new rule linking risk with possession does not apply where the goods are delivered to a carrier who:

(a) was commissioned by the buyer for the purpose of carrying the goods;
(b) was not proposed by the seller for that purpose.[1127]

In these circumstances, the goods are at the buyer's risk upon delivery to the carrier.

B. Exceptions to the General Rule

633. Because, generally, in commercial sales, risk is linked to property, and not possession, and because the rules on the passing of property are technical and not always in keeping with people's expectations, a person can find himself/herself at

1124. Directive 2011/83, [2011] OJ L304/64.
1125. SI No. 484/2013.
1126. As defined in s. 3 of the Sale of Goods and Supply of Services Act 1980.
1127. Regulation 29(5).

risk without being aware of this fact, without any practical control over the goods and without insurance. However, the general rule that risk passes with property can be modified, and in certain circumstances the issue of possession may be relevant to the passage of risk. For example, section 20 provides that where delivery is delayed through the fault of either buyer or seller, the goods are at the risk of the party at fault as regards any damage or loss that might not have occurred but for such fault.[1128] Section 20 also provides that nothing in this section shall affect the duties or liabilities of either seller or buyer as a bailee or custodier of the goods for the other party. Importantly, the rule in section 20 may be displaced by an express or implied agreement. The contract may contain an express provision as to the passing of risk that contradicts the general rule. This possibility is expressly recognized by section 20 which is a default rule. For example, where goods are sold and the seller retains title to the goods, the agreement often states that risk passes to the buyer with possession of the goods, and requires the buyer to insure the goods. But even where the contract contains no express provision as to the passing of risk, it may be possible to find an implied term governing the subject. For instance, in international sale contracts, it is implied, by custom, that risk usually passes on shipment although property usually does not pass until a later date. The general rule can also be displaced by an implied agreement based on the facts of the case. So, for example, in *Sterns Ltd v. Vickers Ltd*,[1129] the plaintiffs owned 200,000 gallons of white spirit held in a storage tank by a third-party bailee. They agreed to sell 120,000 gallons of the spirit to the defendant buyers and gave the buyers a delivery warrant or order addressed to the bailee to enable them to collect the spirit. The buyers delayed in taking delivery, and when they did collect the spirit it was found that it had deteriorated in quality during the continued storage. It was held that the spirit was at the buyers' risk from the time they were provided with the means to obtain delivery, despite the fact that no property had passed to the buyers during this time because the goods remained unascertained.

C. Goods Damaged in Transit

634. Transit involves further risks for goods. Sections 32 and 33 deal with the allocation of risk when goods are damaged in transit to the buyer and provide a statutory modification to the general rule on the passing of risk. Section 32(1) provides that where, under the sale contract, the seller is authorized or required to send the goods to the buyer, delivery to a carrier, for transmission to the buyer is prima facie deemed to be delivery to the buyer.[1130] It is as if the carrier were the buyer's agent. Such delivery satisfies a seller's section 27 obligation to deliver the goods to the buyer and such delivery may pass property and therefore risk, in the goods, unless property and risk have already passed or unless the seller has reserved his/her right of disposal.[1131] Hence, prima facie the buyer is at risk during transit. This

1128. *See*, e.g., *Demby Hamilton & Co. Ltd v. Barden* [1949] 1 All ER 435.
1129. [1923] 1 KB 78.
1130. Section 32 of the 1893 Act does not apply to consumer sales: SI No. 484/2013. Regulation 31.
1131. 1893 Act, s. 19(1).

presumption can be rebutted. For instance, where the carrier is the seller's agent, the seller will be at risk until the goods reach the delivery point. Or, under international sales contracts, risk passes from seller to buyer when the goods pass the ship's rail, so if goods are damaged while in transit to the port of departure they are at the seller's risk.

635. Where, under section 32(1), the seller makes a contract of carriage on behalf of the buyer, section 32(2) provides that he/she must make a reasonable contract having regard to the nature of the goods and the other circumstances of the case. If he/she fails to do so and the goods are lost or damaged in transit, the buyer may decline to treat delivery of the goods to the carrier as delivery to himself/herself, thus throwing the risk of loss during transit back onto the seller. Alternatively, the buyer may claim damages from the seller in respect of the damage caused by this breach. What is a reasonable contract will depend on all the circumstances of the case. For example, where goods are perishable, a slow or long means of transit may be unreasonable. In one case,[1132] a seller contracted to sell goods 'free on rail' and the seller contracted with the railway company that the goods would be carried at the owner's risk. It transpired that the goods could have been carried at the carrier's risk for the same price, subject to an examination. The court found that the contract was unreasonable.

636. Where the transit involves carriage by sea, section 32(3) provides that the seller must give the buyer such information so as to enable him/her to insure the goods. If the seller fails to do so, the goods are at the seller's risk while in transit.

637. Finally, where the seller agrees to deliver the goods at his/her own risk at a place other than where they were sold, section 33 provides that, unless otherwise agreed, the buyer must take any risk of deterioration in the goods necessarily incidental to the transit. Under this provision a buyer is only at risk for deterioration caused by the ordinary risks of transit. Such risks are greatly reduced today, as opposed to when the provision was drafted, due to improvements in the speed and methods of transportation. Moreover, a seller remains liable for any deterioration caused by his/her own neglect.

D. Impossibility

638. As noted above, if goods to be sold are lost or damaged so as to become unmerchantable, for instance, whilst at the seller's risk, he/she will be unable to insist on the buyer accepting them under the contract and may have to repair or replace them. Where the contract is for specific goods, replacement is not possible without the buyer's consent, so that the seller may be unable to perform the contract, and in any case the delay involved in arranging repair or replacement may put the seller in breach of contract. But, sections 6 and 7 of the 1893 Act contain rules broadly analogous to the general common law rules of mistake and frustration

1132. *Thomas Young & Sons v. Hobson* (1949) 65 TLR 365.

which may excuse the seller from liability if performance becomes impossible. These rules apply in limited circumstances: where specific goods have perished.[1133] Where they apply the general common law rules on mistake and frustration are displaced.

639. Section 6 provides that:

> Where there is a contract for the sale of specific goods and the goods without the knowledge of the seller have perished at the time the contract is made, the contract is void.[1134]

Section 6 is an instance of the doctrine of common mistake as to the existence of the subject matter. It applies where goods have perished before the contract is made. Further, the goods must have perished without the knowledge of the seller. Where a seller seeks to sell goods that he/she knows do not exist, he/she can be sued for non-delivery. The effect of section 6 is that the contract is void. Because the contract is void, no contract ever existed and the parties have no legal obligations to each other: the seller has no obligation to deliver, and the buyer has no obligation to accept and pay.

640. Section 7 provides that:

> Where there is an agreement to sell specific goods and subsequently the goods, without any fault on the part of the seller or buyer, perish before the risk passes to the buyer, the agreement is avoided.

Section 7 is an instance of the doctrine of frustration caused by the destruction of the subject matter of the contract. It applies where goods perish after the contract is made but before risk passes to the buyer. Normally, where specific goods are sold, property and hence risk passes when the contract is made, under section 18, Rule 1 and section 20. Accordingly, this provision has very limited application and will apply only where Rule 1 is displaced by Rules 2 or 3 or a contrary intention, or where section 20 is displaced. Moreover, the perishing must take place without any fault on the part of the seller or the buyer. At common law, frustration cannot be self-induced, and the same rule applies under section 7. Therefore, for example, if goods are totally destroyed due to the negligence of the seller in their storage, the buyer can sue for non-delivery. The effect of section 7 is that the contract is avoided. The initial existence of the contract is not affected, but from the perishing event the contract is avoided, that is, the parties cease to have any contractual obligations to each other: the seller does not have to deliver and the buyer does not have to accept and pay. If the price is paid in advance the buyer can claim a refund, otherwise losses lay where they fall.

1133. *Asfar & Co. v. Blundell* [1896] 1 QB 123; *Barrow, Lane and Ballard Ltd v. Phillip Phillips & Co.* [1929] 1 KB 574; *Horn v. Minister of Food* [1948] 2 All ER 1036.
1134. This provision is said to be based on *Couturier v. Hastie* (1856) 5 HL Cas. 673.

641. In practice, in commercial contracts, the types of events that come within section 7 or otherwise frustrate a contract are often covered by express provision in the contract: force majeure clauses. And rather than rely on the rules in sections 6 and 7, or the relevant common law rules, commercial traders often seek to negotiate their way out of such a situation to maintain a good trading relationship, rather than enforce their strict legal rights.

IX. Title Conflicts

642. It is a fundamental rule of property law that no one can transfer a better title than he/she himself/herself has: *nemo dat quod non habet.* This, or a similar, basic rule applies to sales of goods, land and to other forms of property, to gifts and to bailments, such as contracts of hire and hire purchase. In relation to goods, the basic rule is restated in section 21 of the 1893 Act:

> Subject to the provisions of this Act, where goods are sold by a person who is not the owner thereof, ... the buyer acquires no better title to the goods than the seller had ... .

Over time, a number of common law exceptions to the basic rule were developed, in order to protect bona fide purchasers and thus encourage commercial activity by reinforcing the security of sale transactions. These exceptions are now set out in sections 21–26 of the Sale of Goods Act 1893.[1135] In truth, while the *nemo dat* principle is the starting point in describing Irish law, the exceptions in the Sale of Goods Act effectively render this general rule more commonly honoured in the breach.

A. The Tort of Conversion

643. An owner, or a person with an immediate right to possession of goods, who is wrongfully deprived of possession, may sue, in the tort of conversion,[1136] any person who deprives him/her of possession or who, without his/her authority, deals with the goods intending to assert a right to them inconsistent with his/her right. Provided the defendant has this intention, liability in the tort of conversion is strict. So, a defendant may be liable even though he/she was unaware of the plaintiff's right to the goods or honestly believed that he/she himself/herself was their true owner. In practice, the original owner will generally seek to recover the goods from the buyer, the person in possession. If he/she can do so lawfully, the original owner is entitled to recover the goods without court action; however, if the buyer resists the original owners claim, the original owner will need to bring an action in conversion. In his/her defence, the buyer can rely on any one or more of the exceptions to the *nemo dat* rule. If he/she succeeds, the buyer will acquire a title to the goods

1135. *See also* ss 2, 8 and 9 of the Factors Act 1889 for similar exceptions.
1136. *See* McMahon & Binchy, *Law of Torts* Ch. 30 (4th ed., Bloomsbury Professional 2012).

superior to that of the original owner and therefore be able to resist the original owner's claim. The goods may have changed hands several times via a chain of transactions before coming into the buyer hands. In order to dispute the original owner's entitlement to the goods the buyer must therefore examine each of the transactions in the chain in order to see if any fall within any of the *nemo dat* exceptions.

B. Section 12

644. Following from the above, where the buyer of goods cannot rely on any of the *nemo dat* exceptions he/she will be forced to surrender the goods, or pay their value, to the original. In these circumstances, the buyer has a claim against the seller, his/her vendor, for breach of the implied terms in the contract of sale that the seller has the right to sell the goods and that the buyer should enjoy quiet possession of them, under section 12 of the 1893.[1137] Where such a claim succeeds, according to the leading case of *Rowland v. Divall,*[1138] there will be a total failure of consideration and the buyer will be entitled to a full refund of any price paid, from the seller, irrespective of any beneficial enjoyment the buyer may have had of the goods in question.

C. Exception No. 1: Agency

645. In the Sale of Goods Act 1893, the first two exceptions to the *nemo dat* rule are based on agency principles and are to be found in section 21. There is some overlapping between these first two exceptions. Section 21 provides:

> where goods are sold by a person who is not the owner thereof, and who does not sell them under the authority or with the consent of the owner, the buyer acquires no better title to the goods than the seller had, … .

In addition, section 61 preserves the common law rules of agency. Hence, and unsurprisingly, an owner will be bound by any disposition of his/her goods by an agent acting with his/her authority or consent.

D. Exception No. 2: Estoppel

646. The second agency exception is also found in section 21 of the 1893 Act:

> where goods are sold by a person who is not the owner thereof, and who does not sell them under the authority or with the consent of the owner, the buyer acquires no better title to the goods than the seller had, unless the owner of the goods is by his conduct precluded from denying the seller's authority to sell.

1137. *See* paras 469–484 above.
1138. [1923] 2 KB 500.

The final words of this provision reproduce a common law exception to the general *nemo dat* rule that a person who buys from someone other than the owner may acquire a title to the goods where the owner is precluded or estopped from denying the seller's right to sell the goods. The exception may apply in two different types of case:

- where the owner represents that the seller is the owner's agent, as in cases of apparent authority;
- where the owner represents that the seller is the owner of the goods, sometimes referred to as apparent ownership.

In each case the owner will be prevented from recovering his/her goods, and the buyer will acquire title to them, provided the seller's dealing in the goods is consistent with the appearance created by the owner's conduct.

E. Exception No. 3: Market Overt

647. By a long-established exception to the *nemo dat* rule, section 22 of the 1893 Act provides:

> Where goods are sold in market overt, according to the usage of the market, the buyer acquires a good title to the goods, provided he buys them in good faith and without notice of any defect or want of title on the part of the seller.

Accordingly, the sale must take place in an open, public and legally constituted market, established by Royal Charter, statute or custom. Though Irish case law on the point is scarce, it has been held that the old Prussia Street cattle market in Dublin was a *market overt*.[1139] A list of such *markets overt* does not exist for consultation: the issue of whether a particular market qualifies or not can be addressed only in the context of a dispute in relation to a sale in a particular market. Nevertheless, it seems clear that a private market or a car-boot sale would not qualify as a market overt.[1140] Section 22 expressly provides that the sale must be in accordance with the customs or usages of the market. Finally, and common to many of the *nemo dat* exceptions, the buyer must act in good faith and without notice of any defect in the seller's title to the goods. The Sales Law Review Group has recommended the repeal of this provision on the basis that it is archaic and not appropriate to modern commercial conditions.[1141]

1139. *Ganly v. Ledwidge* (1876) IR 10 CL 33; and *Delaney v. Wallis* (1883) 14 LR Ir 31.
1140. *Lang v. Jones, The Times,* 6 Mar. 1990.
1141. Sales Law Review Group, *Report on the Legislation Governing the Sale of Goods and Supply of Services* (Dublin, Prn. A11/1576, 2011) para. 7.40. Other, mainly minor, amendments to subsequent provisions, ss 23, 25 and 26, are made at para. 7.40.

F. Exception No. 4: Voidable Title

648. Section 23 of the 1893 Act provides:

> When the seller of goods has a voidable title thereto, but his title has not been avoided at the time of the sale, the buyer acquires a good title to the goods, provided he buys them in good faith and without notice of the seller's defect in title.

Accordingly, where a person (B) buys goods from a seller (S) who has only a voidable title to the goods, but his title has not been avoided at the time of the sale to B, B may nevertheless acquire a good title to the goods, provided he buys them in good faith and without notice of S's defect in title.

1. Voidable

649. This section applies only where S's title is voidable. Hence, it can apply in two main situations:

(a) where S acquired the goods under a transaction which was voidable as a result of, most commonly, misrepresentation, or more rarely duress, undue influence, or drunkenness;
(b) where S's title is defective because one of his predecessors in title acquired the goods under a voidable contract.

650. In *Anderson v. Ryan,*[1142] the owner of a Mini car, D, answered an advertisement which offered a Sprite car for sale. D and X met, exchanged cars,[1143] and X left with the Mini. X did not own the Sprite car, which had been stolen, and X ultimately pleaded guilty to a charge of obtaining the Mini by false pretences. X later sold the Mini to the defendant, and the defendant in turn sold it to the plaintiff. It was held, in the High Court, that the contract of exchange was voidable as a result of X's fraudulent misrepresentation of an existing fact, that is, that the Sprite was his property to sell. Hence, X acquired a voidable title to the car. This title had not been avoided by D at the time of the sale to the defendant. Accordingly, the defendant acquired a good title to the car under section 23, which he was able to pass to the plaintiff. As the High Court in *Anderson v. Ryan*[1144] noted, section 23 does not apply where S has no title at all, such as where goods are stolen. Furthermore, it cannot apply where the contract under which S acquired the goods:

(a) purported to transfer only possession of the goods;
(b) was an agreement to sell under which property is to pass at a later date;

1142. [1967] IR 34.
1143. This was a pure contract of exchange, with no money being paid.
1144. [1967] IR 34 at 38.

(c) was wholly void, as opposed to voidable, since a void contract has no legal effect at all.[1145]

2. Avoiding Title

651. B will succeed in a conflict of title with the original owner (O), where S has a voidable title and the title has not been avoided at the time of the sale between S and B. Therefore, O should take immediate steps to rescind the contract with S, in order to recover the goods and prevent their sale to a bona fide purchaser who may be protected by section 23. He may do so without court proceedings merely by notifying S of his intention to avoid the contract between them or by retaking possession of the goods. However, where S is untraceable, O may be able to rescind the contract by taking other steps to recover his property, such as notifying the police or the AA.[1146]

3. Good Faith and without Notice

652. As with the other *nemo dat* exceptions the buyer must act in good faith and without notice of the seller's defect in title. However, the burden of proof under section 23 is different from the other exceptions. It has been held that, under section 23, it is for the original owner to prove that the purchaser did not act in good faith.[1147] Requiring an owner to prove a third party's bad faith is clearly more difficult than requiring a third party to prove his/her good faith: all the relevant evidence is in the hands of the third party.

G. Exception No. 6: Seller in Possession

653. Possession can give the impression of ownership.[1148] However, possession and property are two separate concepts, and we have seen how property in goods can pass before or after physical possession passes.[1149] For this reason, section 25 of the 1893 Act, which mirrors sections 8 and 9 of the Factors Act 1889, is designed to protect persons who deal with sellers or buyers in possession of goods but who no longer, or do not yet, own the goods.

654. Section 25(1) states:

1145. *Cundy v. Lindsay* (1878) 3 App. Cas. 459 an example of a contract rendered void on grounds of mistake of identity. *See further Shogun Finance Ltd v. Hudson* [2003] UKHL 62, [2004] 1 AC 1101, [2004] 1 All ER 641.
1146. *Car and Universal Finance Co. Ltd v. Caldwell* [1965] 1 QB 525.
1147. *Whitehorn Bros v. Davison* [1911] 1 KB 463.
1148. *See also* Factor Act 1889, s. 8.
1149. *See* paras 590–603 above.

> Where a person having sold goods continues or is in possession of the goods, or of the documents of title to the goods, the delivery or transfer by that person, or by a mercantile agent acting for him, of the goods or documents of title under any sale, pledge or other disposition thereof, to any person receiving the same in good faith and without notice of the previous sale, shall have the same effect as if the person making the delivery or transfer were expressly authorised by the owner of the goods to make the same.

This provision covers the situation where a person [S], who has sold goods, retains possession of them after the sale and thus appears to own the goods,[1150] even if property in them has in fact already passed to the buyer [B1]. Other people [B2] may therefore deal with S as if he were still the owner of the goods – for instance, by agreeing to buy the same goods, or to take security over them.[1151] Section 25(1) may protect such a person, B2, who deals with a seller who remains in possession of goods after selling them.

655. It is important to note that this provision deals with the situation where property has passed to B1 under the sale from S, such that B1 becomes the owner [O] and a conflict of title arises between B1/O and B2. Where the property has not passed to B1 under the first contract of sale, S may continue to deal with the goods as owner himself. If S resells the goods to B2, a second buyer, B2 will acquire property in the goods and a title superior to that of B1. S may incur liability to B1 for failure to deliver where the contract with B1 is for specific goods, or where the contract with B1 is for the sale of unascertained goods, if S cannot deliver goods which match the contract description by the delivery date. Hence, section 25(1) only applies where the seller has 'sold' (not 'agreed to sell') goods. Finally, and as with the previous exceptions, B2 will only take priority where he receives the goods in good faith and without notice of S's defect in title. The burden of proof under section 25 is on B2 to prove that he acted in good faith and without notice of S's rights.

656. Where all the above requirements are satisfied, section 25 provides that the transfer to B2 has the same effect as if S were authorized by the owner of the goods, B1/O, to make it. S is thus treated as if he was B1's agent and B1 is therefore bound by S's dealings with the goods.

657. Section 8 of the Factors Act 1889 is similar to section 25(1) of the 1893 Act, but is a little broader because it seeks to validate the transfer of property under any *agreement* to sell, pledge, or otherwise dispose of the goods, as well as under an actual sale, pledge or other disposition. Both provisions are usually pleaded together, if possible.

1150. *See Hanley v. ICC Finance* [1996] ILRM 463; *Pacific Motor Auctions Property Ltd v. Motor Credits (Hire Finance) Ltd* [1965] AC 867; *Worcester Works Finance Ltd v. Cooden Engineering Ltd* [1972] 1 QB 210. *See also Mitchell v. Jones* (1905) 24 NZLR 932.

1151. *Nicholson v. Harper* [1895] 2 Ch. 415; *Worcester Works Finance Ltd v. Cooden* [1972] 1 QB 210.

H. Exception No. 7: Buyer in Possession[1152]

658. Section 25(2) of the 1893 Act states:

> Where a person having bought or agreed to buy goods obtains, with the consent of the seller, possession of the goods or the documents of title to the goods, the delivery or transfer by that person, or by a mercantile agent acting for him, of the goods or documents of title, under any sale pledge or other disposition thereof, to any person receiving the same in good faith and without notice of any lien, or other right of the original seller in respect of the goods, shall have the same effect as if the person making the delivery or transfer were a mercantile agent in possession of the goods or documents of title with the consent of the owner.

This provision covers the situation where a person who has bought or agreed to buy goods (B1)[1153] obtains consensual possession of them before title passes to him and, by being in possession of the goods, may appear to be the owner of the goods; if he resells or otherwise disposes of them before property passes to him, a title or priority dispute may then arise between S, the person who sold the goods to B1, and B2, the person to whom B1 transferred them. Section 25(2) may protect B2 in such a case. Provided that the requirements of the provision are fulfilled, the disposition by B1 has the same effect as if he were a mercantile agent in possession of the goods with the consent of their owner, allowing B2 to take priority over S. It has been held in England that since a disposition by a mercantile agent is only binding on the owner of goods if the agent is in possession of them with the consent of the owner, section 25(2) only applies where B1 is in possession with the consent of *the true owner*.[1154] Thus, if S steals goods from O and sells them to B1, a resale by B1 to B2, and any subsequent resales, are not within the provision, since B1, although in possession with the consent of *his seller*, is not in possession with the consent of *the owner*. As with the previous exceptions, B2 must act in good faith and without notice of any rights of S. As noted above, the burden of proof under section 25 is on B2 to prove that he acted in good faith and without notice of S's rights.

659. Section 9 of the Factors Act 1889 is to the same effect as section 25(2), but is a little broader because it seeks to validate the transfer of property under any *agreement* to sell, pledge, or otherwise dispose of the goods, as well as under an actual sale, pledge or other disposition. Both provisions are usually pleaded together, if possible.

1152. *See also* the Factors Act 1889, s. 9.
1153. Section 25 applies to a sale subject to a reservation of title pending payment *(Lee v. Butler* [1893] 2 QB 318) but not where B1 acquired the goods under a hire purchase contract (*Helby v. Mathews* [1895] AC 471); an agency agreement (*Shaw v. MPC* [1987] 1 WLR 1332); a sale or return agreement (*Weiner v. Harris* [1910] 1 KB 285); or a contract for work and materials (*Dawber Williamason Roofing v. Humberside CC* (1979) 14 BLR 70).
1154. *National Employers Mutual General Insurance Association Ltd v. Jones* [1990] 1 AC 24.

I. Exception No. 8: Sales under Special Powers of Sale or Orders of the Court

660. Section 21(2)(b) of the 1893 Act provides that nothing in the Act shall affect the validity of any contract of sale under any special common law or statutory power of sale or under the order of a court of competent jurisdiction. This provision speaks for itself.

§3. COMMERCIAL SERVICES

661. While contracts for the sale of goods have traditionally been considered to be the backbone of commercial activity, contracts for the supply of services also play a prominent role. Agency contracts,[1155] insurance contracts[1156] and carriage contracts[1157] are all contracts for the supply of services that are often ancillary to commercial sale of goods contracts, for example. Contracts for services cover a wide range of activities from contracts for professional services (such as contracts for the services of engineers, medics and solicitors) to contracts for leisure services (such as contracts for the provision of holidays, hotel accommodation and entertainment). Construction and related contracts are another important type of service contract. A major growth area, in recent years, involves contracts for the supply of financial services,[1158] and e-commerce /digital services.[1159]

662. As with all contracts, the starting point for examining the rights and obligations of the parties are the express terms of the contract. Some services contracts are standard form contracts promoted by the various professional bodies.[1160] In relation to construction contracts, for instance, a significant body of case law exists to define the obligations of the parties under these standard form contracts.[1161] Beyond the express terms of the contract, certain terms may be implied at common law. For example, in agency contracts where it is agreed that an agent should be paid but the amount of remuneration is not expressly agreed between the parties, it is implied that a reasonable sum will be payable.[1162] Moreover, Part IV of the Sale of Goods and Supply of Services Act 1980 implies a set of four terms, related to the quality

1155. *See* paras 644–699 below.
1156. *See* paras 700–719 below.
1157. *See* paras 732–765 below.
1158. Note, e.g., the International Financial Services Center (IFSC), established in 1987, in Dublin: www.ifsc.ie.
1159. *See* Directive 2000/31/EC on certain aspects of information society services, in particular electronic commerce, in the Internal Market [2000] OJ L 178/1. The main objective of the Directive is to ensure the free movement of information society services between Member States. *See further* the Electronic Commerce Act 2000. *See* also the recently adopted Directive (EU) 2019/770 on certain aspects concerning contracts for the supply of digital content and digital services [2019] OJ L136/1.
1160. With regard to building and construction services, a variety of standard form contracts are promoted by the RIAI (Royal Institute of Architects of Ireland); the CIF (Construction Industry Federation); and the Law Society of Ireland, for example.
1161. *See*, e.g., *Chitty on Contracts* vol. 2 Ch. 37 (33rd ed., Sweet & Maxwell 2018).
1162. *Henehan v. Courtney* (1967) 101 ILTR 25: *see* para. 683 below.

of service, into every contract for the supply of services where the supplier is acting in the course of a business. This legislation also deals with the exclusion of liability for breach of these statutory implied terms. Lastly, in particular areas, there may be further regulating legislation and rules such as the Solicitors Acts 1954–2002,[1163] or the Investment Intermediary Act 1995, or the Central Bank's various Codes of Practice.[1164] These more specific forms of regulation are beyond the scope of this work. In this final section on commercial contracts we start by outlining the general provisions of Part IV of the Sale of Goods and Supply of Services Act 1980, before considering, in brief, some other service contracts including contracts with intermediaries such as distribution and franchising agreements, agency contracts, insurance contracts, other financial services and contracts of carriage.

663. Section 39 of the 1980 Act implies four terms into every contract for the supply of services where the supplier is acting in the course of a business.[1165] They are:

a. that the supplier has the necessary skill to render the service;
b. that he/she will supply the service with due skill, care and diligence;[1166]
c. that, where materials are used, they will be sound and reasonably fit for the purpose for which they are required;
d. that, where goods are supplied, they will be of merchantable quality.[1167]

Significantly, section 39 implies 'terms' into the service contract, not conditions or warranties, as is the case with the sales legislation.[1168] Accordingly, these terms are what can be described as 'innominate terms', the effect of the breach of which depends on the seriousness of the breach. Only where the breach of such a term deprives the party not in default of substantially the whole benefit of the contract will the innocent party be able to repudiate the contract; otherwise, his/her remedies are limited to a claim for damages.[1169] Moreover, the four terms arise automatically and unlike the express terms of the contract, have the advantage that they do not need to be proved in evidence.

1163. At the time of writing, the Legal Services Regulation Bill 2011 is before the Houses of the Oireachtas and if passed, it will introduce wide-sweeping changes to the regulation of legal services in Ireland, including the establishment of an independent Legal Services Regulatory Authority. *See* para. 896below.
1164. *See generally* www.centralbank.ie.
1165. A contract for the supply of a service is not defined in the legislation but has been taken to include a simple supply of services contract, such as a consultation with a solicitor (*Lee v. Griffin* (1861) 1 B & S 272); a contract for work and materials, as where a printer prints a book (*Clay v. Yates* (1856) 1 H&N 73); and a contract for the supply of services which involves the supply of a finished item or goods, such as the construction and supply of a ship (*Hyundai v. Papadopoulos*[1980] 2 All ER 29). On 'in the course of a business' *see Stevenson v. Rogers* [1999] 1 All ER 613; *see further* para. 501 above.
1166. *See*, e.g., *Roche v. Peilow* [1986] ILRM 189.
1167. *See*, e.g., *Irish Telephone Rentals v. ICS Building Society* [1991] ILRM 880.
1168. *See* §2 III and §2 IV above on implied terms in sales contracts.
1169. *Irish Telephone Rentals v. ICS Building Society* [1991] ILRM 880.

664. Section 40 states that any term implied by section 39 can be excluded (expressly, or by course of dealings, or by usage) except where the recipient of the service deals as a consumer, in which case the express term limiting or excluding liability must be fair and reasonable and must be specifically brought to the attention of the buyer to be effective. Hence, other than where the recipient of the service deals as a consumer, the common law rules on exclusion clauses prevail.[1170] Moreover, section 41 of the 1980 Act makes it an offence for any person in the course of a business to display, publish or otherwise furnish a statement to the effect that the rights conferred by section 39 are restricted or excluded. A person guilty of an offence under the 1980 Act is liable, on summary conviction, to a fine not exceeding EUR 4,000, and/or imprisonment not exceeding six months; and on indictment, to a fine not exceeding EUR 60,000, and/or imprisonment not exceeding two years.[1171]

665. The Sales Law Review Group reviewed the provisions on contracts for the supply of services in Part IV of the Sale of Goods and Supply of Services Act 1980 and, noting their limited nature, made a number of recommendations to flesh out the provisions and to align more closely the rules on supply of services contracts with those of sale of goods contracts. For example, the Group recommended that a broadly based definition of 'services' should be included in future legislation;[1172] that the existing implied terms as to the quality of services should be classified as conditions of the contract in future legislation;[1173] that future legislation should include an implied term that, where the time of performance of a service is not fixed by the contract, it should be carried out within a reasonable time, and it should also include an implied term that, where the price for a service is not fixed by the contract, the recipient of the service should pay a reasonable price.[1174] Other important recommendations are that future legislation should include a provision along the lines of section 29 of the New Zealand Consumer Guarantees Act 1993 that a service, and any product resulting from it, will be reasonably fit for any particular purpose, and of such a nature and quality that it can reasonably be expected to achieve any particular result that the consumer makes known to the supplier as the particular purpose for which the service is required, or the result that the consumer desires to achieve. This provision should apply to both consumer and commercial contracts.[1175] Lastly, the Group recommended that contract terms which exclude the terms implied by statute into commercial contracts for services should be regulated on the same basis as exemption clauses in contracts of sale, namely that they are

1170. *See* paras 420–426 above.

1171. 1980 Act, s. 6, as amended by s. 81 of the Investment Funds, Companies and Miscellaneous Provisions Act 2005 and the Fines Act 2010.

1172. Sales Law Review Group, *Report on the Legislation Governing the Sale of Goods and Supply of Services* (Dublin, Prn. A11/1576, 2011) para. 14.21.

1173. Sales Law Review Group, *Report on the Legislation Governing the Sale of Goods and Supply of Services* (Dublin, Prn. A11/1576, 2011) para. 14.30.

1174. Sales Law Review Group, *Report on the Legislation Governing the Sale of Goods and Supply of Services* (Dublin, Prn. A11/1576, 2011) para. 14.38.

1175. Sales Law Review Group, *Report on the Legislation Governing the Sale of Goods and Supply of Services* (Dublin, Prn. A11/1576, 2011) para. 14.38.

unenforceable unless shown to be fair and reasonable. Contract terms which exclude the terms implied by statute into consumer contracts for services should be automatically unfair in all circumstances under the European Communities (Unfair Terms in Consumer Contracts) Regulations 1995 and 2000.[1176]

I. Distribution and Franchising

666. Goods and services can be marketed by intermediaries using a variety of networks. Traditionally, agents were utilized for this purpose[1177] but more modern alternatives exist including distribution and franchising networks. Distribution and franchising are services which are virtually unregulated.[1178] The rights, duties and incidents of parties to these contracts turn overwhelmingly on the very terms of the agreements they have made. Many of those agreements are standard form contracts and when a problem arises in relation to a distribution agreement, for instance, normally the answer will be found in the fine print of the contract, against the background of the general principles of the law of contract and of agency.

A. *Distribution Agreements*

667. A manufacturer or supplier of goods may use a network of distributors to market its products. The relationship between the business and an individual distributor will generally be governed by a master agreement which usually imposes restrictions on both parties. For instance, the distributor may agree to purchase all its stock from the business and not to sell products of a rival business: this is commonly referred to as 'exclusive purchasing'. In return, the business may agree not to appoint other distributors in the same area: known as 'a sole distribution arrangement';[1179] and the business may agree not to sell products in competition with the distributor within its area: known as 'an exclusive distribution arrangement'.[1180]

668. Although the relationship between the business and an individual distributor is close, importantly, it does not amount to one of agency. When the business supplies goods to a distributor, they enter into a contract for the sale of goods and the relationship of seller and buyer arises. When the distributor resells the goods, it

1176. Sales Law Review Group, *Report on the Legislation Governing the Sale of Goods and Supply of Services* (Dublin, Prn. A11/1576, 2011), para. 14.44. *See* paras 973–976 below.
1177. *See* paras 644–699 below.
1178. But *see* block exemptions under EU competition law: Regulation No. 330/2010 on the application of Art. 101(3) of the Treaty on the Functioning of the EU to categories of vertical agreements and concerted practices, [2010] OJ L 102/1; and Regulation 461/2010 on the motor vehicle sector [2010] OJ L 129/52. *See also* Irish CCPC, Declaration in respect of Vertical Agreements and Concerted Practices (Decision No. D/10/001, 2010). *See further* Part II, Ch. 4 on competition law.
1179. *See*, e.g., *Bob Bushell Ltd v. Luxel Varese SAS* (unreported, High Court, 20 Feb. 1998).
1180. It has been held that an agreement expressed to give the distributor the 'sole right to sell' the suppliers' products has the same effect: *WT Lamb and Sons v. Goring Brick Company Ltd* [1932] 1 KB 710.

does so on its own behalf, and it, rather than the business, will be liable to customers for performance of the contract of sale. The master agreement between the business and the distributor is not a sale of goods contract, but a contract governing the terms of their relationship, though it can contain terms of sale.

B. Franchising Agreements

669. As with a distribution arrangement, the relationship between a franchisor and a franchisee will be governed by a master agreement. But the relationship between franchisor and franchisee may be even closer than that between a manufacturer and its distributors. The master agreement between the franchisor and each individual franchisee will impose various restrictions on the parties. Basically, the franchisee will be given the right, or a license, to use the franchisor's product or business idea and also its general style, including intellectual property rights such as copyrights and trademarks, in return for payment of a fee.[1181] Indeed, the franchisee will generally be obliged to adopt the franchisor's style. The franchisee will also generally be obliged to purchase some or all of the products to be used in its business from the franchisor. The individual franchisee thus gets the benefit of appearing to be part of a large organization and of the goodwill generated by the franchisor and other franchisees. However, once again, when goods are supplied from franchisor to franchisee the relationship is that of seller and buyer; and when the franchisee resells, it does so as seller on its own behalf and not as agent for the franchisor.

II. Agency Contracts

670. Most businesses use intermediaries in their dealings with the outside world. Many such intermediaries are agents; the need for them is particularly acute where the business wishes to trade on an international basis. Even at a domestic level, once a business develops from a single person enterprise, the need for the use of agents is unavoidable. Where, for instance, a sole trader joins with another to form a partnership, legislation provides that all partners are agents for the other partners and the firm.[1182] Or, where the business is conducted through the medium of a company, which is in law a separate person from its shareholders, the company can only act through human agents. Employees may also act as agents of their employer. Hence, agents and the law of agency are central to the conduct of trade and commerce.

671. In general, no formality is required when appointing an agent. An agent can be appointed by the principal orally, in writing or by deed (usually called a power

1181. This can include an initial fee, and a proportion of annual turnover, usually payable regardless of whether profits are being made.
1182. Partnership Act 1890, s. 5.

of attorney).[1183] Under the Commercial Agents Directive,[1184] as implemented in Ireland,[1185] the agency agreement must be evidenced in writing,[1186] and a commercial agent and his/her principal are each entitled to receive from the other, on request, a signed written statement of the terms of the agency contract.[1187]

672. A number of consequences flow in law from the creation of an agency relationship. First, and arguably most importantly, the agent has the power to affect the principal's legal position with third parties. The most significant aspect of the agent's power in the commercial context is that, as an exception to the doctrine of privity, contracts made by the agent on behalf of the principal are treated in law as the principal's contracts and are directly enforceable by and against him. Therefore, where an agent (A) acting on behalf of a principal (P), negotiates and concludes a contract with a third party (T), the parties to that contract are P and T: P can sue T, and, T can sue P, for breach of contract. The agent may also make binding dispositions of the principal's property or acquire property on the principal's behalf; he may sign documentation on behalf of his/her principal;[1188] his/her statements may bind the principal, both in a contractual context and otherwise. The nature of this power and the effects of its exercise will be outlined below.

673. Second, the law gives the parties to an agency relationship certain rights, and imposes on them certain duties, against each other. Significantly, the agent can occupy a fiduciary position vis-à-vis the principal. In return, the agent is given certain rights at common law and under the EC Commercial Agents Directive 1986,[1189] as implemented in Ireland under the 1994 and 1997 Commercial Agents Regulations.[1190] A brief analysis of these rights and duties is provided below.

674. It is vital to be able to identify whether a person is an agent, or not, in order to advise parties of their legal rights and responsibilities. Not all those referred to as 'agents' in commercial parlance are agents in law; and a person who is an agent in law may not be called an agent. The essential characteristic of an agent is the ability to be able to affect the legal relations of his/her principal with third parties. Where this essential feature is lacking, the simple reference to someone as an agent has no legal consequence. In each case, regardless of the terminology used, a detailed examination of the role of the intermediary is vital to determine his/her legal status. Some of the more common examples of agents, such as partners and company directors, are identified above. But agents, of many different types, have been part of commercial life for hundreds of years. For example, agents may be 'general' or 'special': a general agent has general authority to act for the principal in a particular trade or class of transactions; in contrast, a special agent is authorized only to act in

1183. *See further* Powers of Attorney Act, 1996.
1184. Directive 86/653/EEC, [1986] OJ L 382/17.
1185. SI No. 33 of 1994, and SI No. 31 of 1997.
1186. Article 13(2) of the Directive and Regulation 5, 1994.
1187. Article 13(1) of the Directive.
1188. *Dundalk Football Club v. The Eircom League* [2001] 1 IR 434.
1189. Directive 86/653/EEC, [1986] OJ L 382/17.
1190. SI No. 33 of 1994, and SI No. 31 of 1997.

one particular transaction. This distinction is no longer as significant as it once was. Other agents include factors and brokers. A factor is a commercial agent who handles the goods (or documents of title) of his/her principal in the course of finding a buyer or seller for them;[1191] whereas a broker negotiates contracts for the sale and purchase of goods and other property on behalf of his/her principal without having possession of the goods. But, it should be noted that there are other types of brokers, such as stockbrokers and insurance brokers. A del credere agent negotiates contracts for a principal and guarantees to the principal that the third party will pay any sums due under the contract; this may be important where the third party is not known to the principal. A commission agent buys or sells property on behalf of a principal, but is not authorized to create privity of contract between the principal and the third party with whom he deals. Thus vis-à-vis the third party, the agent contracts as principal and is therefore liable to the third party on the contract but vis-à-vis his/her principal, the agent owes the duties owed by an agent to his/her principal.[1192] Today, this arrangement is more commonly used in civil law systems than in common law systems. In 1994, the concept of 'commercial agent' was introduced into Irish law. The relevant Directive and the implementing Regulations define a 'commercial agent' in the following terms:[1193]

> a self-employed intermediary who has continuing authority to negotiate the sale and the purchase of goods on behalf of another person, hereinafter called the principal, or to negotiate and conclude such transactions on behalf of and in the name of that principal.[1194]

There is also a list of exclusions from this definition, such that the term 'commercial agent' does not include:

- company officers;
- partners of a firm;
- insolvency practitioners;
- unpaid commercial agent;
- commercial agents operating in a commodity exchange or market;
- consumer credit agents and mail order catalogue agents, on the basis that their activities are secondary.[1195]

The legal position of commercial agents vis-à-vis their principals is considered further below.

1191. There are five Factors Acts: 1823; 1825; 1842; 1877; and 1889. *See further* §2 IX above on title conflicts in sale of goods transactions. Factor, in this technical sense, has dropped out of commercial usage. In modern business, the word 'factoring' is used in the unrelated sense of assigning or discounting book-debts.

1192. *Ireland v. Livingstone* (1872) LR 5 HL 395.

1193. Directive 86/653/EEC, [1986] OJ L 382/17, Art. 1(2) and SI No. 33 of 1994, Regulation 2(1).

1194. The leading Irish case on this definition is Kenny v. ROC Ireland [2005] IEHC 241; [2007] 1 IR 448.

1195. Regulation 2(1), 1994.

A. Agent's Authority and Power

675. This heading refers to an agent's ability to legally bind his/her principal in relation to a third party. Sometimes we speak of an agent's *authority* to bind his/her principal but beyond the authority given to an agent by his/her principal, an agent may have *power* to bind his/her principal so that, strictly speaking, the agent's actions are *unauthorized*. In this regard, the word *authority* is used to cover both these situations. An agent's authority can be categorized under the following five sub-headings:

(1) actual authority
(2) apparent authority
(3) usual or customary authority
(4) authority by ratification
(5) agency of necessity.

1. Actual Authority

676. Actual authority exists where the principal consents in advance to the agent's actions, giving the agent actual authority to act in a certain manner and bind the principal. This consensual arrangement can form the basis of a contract, or the relationship between the principal and the agent can be gratuitous.

677. Furthermore:

> actual authority can be express or implied. It is express when it is given by words such as when a board of directors passes a resolution which authorises two of their number to sign cheques. It is implied when it is inferred from the conduct of the parties and the circumstances of the case, such as when a board of directors appoints one of their number to be managing director. They thereby impliedly authorise him to do all such things as fall within the usual scope of that office.[1196]

2. Apparent Authority

678. Apparent authority exists where an agent appears to a third party to have authority, whether he/she actually has it or not, and this appearance is somehow corroborated by the principal. This type of authority can also be identified as a type of *power*, referred to above. The leading case of *Freeman and Lockyer v. Buckhurst Park Properties Ltd*[1197] sets out three requirements which must be fulfilled before a principal can be bound by an agent's apparent authority:

1196. *Hely -Hutchinson v. Brayhead Ltd* [1968] 1 QB 549 at 583.
1197. [1964] 2 QB 480; [1964] 1 All ER 630, approved in Ireland in *Kett v. Shannon & English* [1987] ILRM 364; and *APD v. Walsh & ors* [1991] 2 IR 8.

(a) There must be a representation that a person, the agent, has authority.
(b) The representation must come from someone with authority to make that representation – usually, though not always, the principal.[1198]
(c) The representation must be relied on by the third party.

3. Usual/Customary Authority

679. Usual or customary authority pertains where an agent has authority which a person in his/her position usually, or customarily, has. This type of authority can be seen either to expand the scope of an agent's actual or apparent authority, or to represent an independent head of authority.

680. An agent (A) appointed to a position may either:

(a) implicitly be given[1199] or
(b) appear to have[1200]

the authority which an agent in that position usually has. In each case he may be said to have 'usual authority'. However in scenario: (a) A's usual authority is a species of actual authority, whereas in scenario: (b) it is a species of apparent authority.

681. There is some support for the existence of a separate category of usual authority, distinct from both actual and apparent authority, so that where an agent is appointed to a position, any acts that he/she does, which would be usual for a person in that position to do, are binding on the principal. In *Watteau v. Fenwick,*[1201] A was appointed to manage a public house, which he had previously owned. His name was still over the door as licensee. P expressly limited his actual authority by forbidding him to purchase anything other than bottled ales and mineral waters. In defiance of that prohibition he bought cigars and bovril from T. In a very brief judgment, P was held liable for their price. Clearly, A did not have actual authority: there was an express prohibition. Nor could this be a case of apparent authority as T believed A to be owner of the business and was not aware of P, and so could not rely on any representation made by P. The correct basis of this decision is therefore unclear and various explanations have been offered; one is that an agent appointed to a position has power to bind his/her principal by doing acts which would be usual for an agent in his/her position.

1198. *Armagas Ltd v. Mundogas Ltd* [1985] 1 Lloyd's Rep 1; [1986] 2 All ER 385.
1199. *See*, e.g., *Hely -Hutchinson v. Brayhead Ltd* [1968] 1 QB 549 at 583.
1200. *See*, e.g., *Freeman and Lockyer v. Buckhurst Park Properties Ltd* [1964] 2 QB 480; [1964] 1 All ER 630.
1201. (1893) 1 QB 346.

4. Ratification

682. Authority by ratification occurs where although an agent does not have authority at the time when he/she acts on the principal's behalf, the principal later ratifies or adopts the agent's actions and is thus bound by them. A principal can only ratify an agent's actions if the following conditions are met:

(a) The agent must purport to be acting for a principal.[1202]
(b) The principal must have been in existence at the time when the agent purported to act on his/her behalf.
(c) The principal must have been competent at the time when the agent purported to act on his/her behalf and at the time of ratification.
(d) The principal must have been capable of being ascertained at the time when the agent purported to act on his/her behalf.[1203]
(e) A principal cannot ratify a nullity.
(f) The principal must ratify within a reasonable time.
(g) The principal cannot ratify unless aware of all the material facts.[1204]

683. Moreover, the principal can expressly ratify the relevant transaction, or ratification can be implied from the facts.[1205] The effect of ratification is that the agent is retrospectively deemed to have had authority at all relevant times, so that, the principal can sue, or be sued by, the third party on the contract made by the agent, and any liability the agent may have had to the third party or the principal is extinguished.

5. Agency of Necessity

684. Agency of necessity arises where, due to an emergency situation, the agent is vested, by operation of the law, with authority to act in a way not actually authorized by the principal. There are four preconditions for agency of necessity to arise:

(a) It must be shown that the agent could not get instructions from the principal.[1206]
(b) The agent must have acted in the principal's interests and bona fides.[1207]
(c) The agent's actions must be reasonable.
(d) There must have been some necessity or emergency which caused the agent to act as he/she did.

Developments in modern communications have rendered this type of authority less relevant today.

1202. *Keighley, Maxstead & Co. v. Durant* [1901] AC 240.
1203. *Watson v. Swann* (1862) 11 CBNS 756.
1204. *Brennan v. O ' Connell* [1980] IR 13.
1205. *Barclay ' s Bank v. Breen* (1962) 96 ILTR 179.
1206. *Springer v. Great Western Rly Co.* [1921] 1 KB 257 at 265 *per* Bankes LJ.
1207. *Prager v. Blatspiel, Stamp & Heacock Ltd* [1924] 1 KB 566 at 571–572 *per* McCardie J.

B. The Effects of Agency

685. The typical agency scenario (the paradigm case) is where an agent, A, acting on behalf of a principal, P, and within the scope of the actual authority granted from P to A, concludes a contract with a third party, T, who knows that A is acting for P. The effect is that privity of contract is established between P and T: and A drops out of the picture.[1208] It is said in this situation that the agency is *disclosed*, that is, the third party is aware that the agent is acting on behalf of a principal. The effects of the agency differ depending on whether the agency is *disclosed* or *undisclosed*. In contrast, where the third party believes that the agent is acting on his/her own behalf and not for any other person, at the time of contracting, there is an *undisclosed* agency. If the agency is disclosed, it is of no legal significance that the principal is not *named*.

1. Disclosed Agency

686. There are three particular scenarios which must be outlined to explain the effects of a disclosed agency on the parties. First, where an agent, with the principal's actual authority, concludes a contract on the principal's behalf with a third party and the agency is disclosed, a direct contractual relationship is created between the principal and the third party, and each party can sue the other on the contract (the paradigm case). The agent is not liable on this contract to either the third party or the principal.

687. Second, if an agent concludes a contract outside his/her actual but within his/her apparent authority, the principal will be bound by the contract but cannot enforce it: as apparent authority is based on a form of estoppel it does not give rise to an independent cause of action. Since apparent authority depends on a representation by the principal that the agent has authority, apparent authority can only arise where the (purported) agency is disclosed. The third party may also hold the agent personally liable for breach of warranty of authority,[1209] or in tort.[1210]

688. Third, if an agent acts without the principal's actual authority, the principal can ratify his/her actions, provided that the agent purported to act on his/her behalf; only a disclosed principal can therefore ratify an unauthorized contract. The effect here is that a direct contractual relationship is created between the principal and the third party, and each party can sue the other on the contract. The agent is not liable on this contract to either the third party or the principal.

1208. *Montgomerie v. UK Mutual Steamship Association* [1891] 1 QB 370.
1209. *See* para. 666 below.
1210. *See* para. 666 below.

689. It almost goes without saying that where an agent acts without authority, the principal will incur no liability to a third party.[1211]

2. Undisclosed Agency

690. Where an agent contracts with a third party without disclosing that he/she is acting as an agent, so that the agency is undisclosed, the contract is initially between the agent and the third party and each may enforce the contract against the other. However, if the third party discovers the undisclosed principal's existence, the third party may enforce the contract against either the agent or the principal, but not both.[1212] Moreover, provided that the agent acted with actual authority, the undisclosed principal can intervene and enforce the contract against the third party. The undisclosed principal's right to intervene and enforce the contract made on his/her behalf is limited in several respects. These limitations go some way to rebalance a doctrine which at first sight seems to favour the position of the undisclosed principal over the third party. So, for example, an undisclosed principal can only intervene if he/she was in existence and had the legal capacity to make the contract at the time it was made. Further, an undisclosed principal can only intervene if the agent had *actual* authority to conclude the contract.[1213] And, an undisclosed principal cannot intervene if such intervention is prohibited by the contract, either expressly or impliedly.[1214] There is also authority to support the proposition that an undisclosed principal may be prevented from intervening if it can be shown that the third party contracted with the agent for personal reasons. And, in some cases, it has been said that an undisclosed principal cannot intervene where the third party has personal reasons for not contracting with him/her.[1215] However, it is clear that this rule can only apply where the personal element is 'strikingly present' in the contract;[1216] and it is unlikely to apply in the context of ordinary commercial transactions.[1217]

691. If an undisclosed principal does intervene, he/she does so generally on the same terms on which the agent could have enforced the contract, so that a third party can raise any defences against the undisclosed principal which he/she would have had against the agent. These may include purely personal defences, such as rights of set-off available against the agent.[1218]

1211. *Wiltshire v. Sims* (1808) 1 Camp 258; *Comerford v. Britannic Assurance Co. Ltd* (1908) 24 TLR 593.
1212. *Clarkson, Booker Ltd v. Andjel* [1964] 3 All ER 260.
1213. *Keighley Maxsted & Co. v. Durant* [1901] AC 240.
1214. *See*, e.g., *Humble v. Hunter* (1848) 12 QB 310 where the undisclosed principal was not allowed to intervene where the agent signed a contract to charter a ship as '*owner* of the good ship or vessel called *Ann*'. *See also F Drughorn Ltd v. Rederiaktiebolaget Trans-Atlantic* [1919] AC 203; *Danziger v. Thompson* [1944] KB 654; *Epps v. Rothnie* [1945] KB 562; and *Sui Yin Kwanv. Eastern Insurance* [1994] 2 AC 199; [1994] 1 All ER 213.
1215. *See*, e.g., *Said v. Butt* [1920] 3 KB 497.
1216. *Ibid.* at 503.
1217. *Dyster v. Randall & Sons* [1926] Ch 932.
1218. *Cooke & Sons v. Eshelby* (1887) 12 App. Cas. 271.

3. Agent's Liability

692. Despite the general rule that where an agent concludes a contract on behalf of a principal, the contract is between the principal and the third party, an agent may be liable on or be able to enforce a contract, either together with or to the exclusion of the principal, in the following circumstances. First, an agent will be liable on the contract where, on its proper construction, the agent is a party to the contract. This can occur where an agent contracts on behalf of himself/herself and a principal. Second, in general, if an agent personally executes a deed, he/she is liable on it and able to enforce it to the exclusion of the principal,[1219] except where the deed is executed pursuant to a power of attorney.[1220] Third, an agent who signs a bill of exchange, such as a cheque, may become personally liable on it. A person will be liable on a bill of exchange if his/her name appears on the bill.[1221] A principal will be liable on the bill if his/her signature is written on the bill by someone acting with his/her authority.[1222] Therefore, where an agent signs a bill, he/she should use clear words to indicate that he/she is acting in a representative capacity and not undertaking personal liability. Fourth, as noted above, in cases of undisclosed agency, the third party may elect to enforce the contract against the agent or the undisclosed principal. Equally, the agent may enforce the contract against the third party, if the undisclosed principal does not do so. Fifth, where an agent purports to have authority to act on a principal's behalf but in fact is unauthorized, the agent may be liable to the third party for breach of warranty of authority. An agent will be liable if he/she falsely claims to have authority even though his/her claim is wholly innocent. In contracting on behalf of a principal, an agent is taken impliedly to warrant, or promise, that he/she does have the principal's authority. If he/she has no such authority, he/she can be sued for breach of warranty of authority. An agent's warranty of authority is viewed as being collateral to the main contract; the third party provides consideration for it by entering into the (supposed) main contract with the principal. Since the agent's liability is contractual, it is strict. Lastly, an agent may be liable in tort law. If an agent can be shown to have acted fraudulently, a notoriously difficult concept to prove, when he/she claimed to have authority, knowing that he/she had no authority, he/she may be liable to a third party in the tort of deceit.[1223] Alternatively, an agent may be liable in negligence, under the ruling in *Hedley Byrne & Co Ltd v. Heller & Partners Ltd,*[1224] if it can be shown that he/she was negligent in claiming to have authority. In either case, a third party may claim damages from an agent on a *tortious* basis.

1219. *Re International Contract Co, Pickering ' s Claim* (1871) 6 Ch App 525.
1220. *See further* Power of Attorney Act, 1996.
1221. Bills of Exchange Act 1882, s. 23.
1222. *Ibid.* s. 90(1).
1223. *See generally*, McMahon & Binchy, *Law of Torts* (4th ed., Bloomsbury Professional 2012), Ch. 35.
1224. [1964] AC 465.

C. *Principal/Agent Relations*

693. In general, there are potentially three levels of 'regulation' of the agency relationship in Irish law. The primary source of the parties' rights and duties is their agreement.[1225] The normal rules of construction will apply to give effect to the intentions of the parties, when interpreting this agreement. Further, at common law, an agent is given three basic rights: to remuneration; to an indemnity; and to a lien. The common law traditionally regarded agents as independent businesses and took the view that the agent was in the stronger position than the principal. Hence, the principal was in need of protection. As a result, the law imposed on agents extensive duties, partly because of the fiduciary nature of the agency relationship. In addition, many agency agreements will now be subject to the EC (Commercial Agents) Regulations 1994[1226] and 1997[1227] (hereinafter 'the Regulations'), which partly codify and partly modify the common law. The Regulations were passed to implement the EC Directive on self-employed commercial agents.[1228] The Regulations came into force on 1 January 1994 and apply both to agreements entered into after their commencement and to existing agreements.[1229] Their main impact is to give agents more extensive rights than they enjoy at common law. However, although the Directive and Regulations apply to many commercial agency arrangements, they do not apply to all agencies, and it is therefore necessary to consider their scope.

1. Application of the Regulations

694. The Regulations apply to relations between 'commercial agents' and their principals.[1230] A 'commercial agent' means:

> a self-employed intermediary who has continuing authority[1231] to negotiate the sale and the purchase of goods[1232] on behalf of another person,[1233] hereinafter

1225. An agent's rights and duties may also derive from other sources such as tort law, statute or the law of restitution.
1226. SI No. 33 of 1994.
1227. SI No. 31 of 1997. The 1997 Regulations were introduced to implement properly the Directive, in particular, to enable Ireland to exercise its discretion under Art. 17 of the Directive on the rights of an agent on termination of the agency agreement to 'an indemnity' or 'compensation for damage'.
1228. Directive 86/653/EEC, [1986] OJ L 382/17.
1229. Regulation 3, 1994; Regulation 2, 1997.
1230. Regulation 2(3), 1994.
1231. In *Poseidon Chartering BV v. Marianne Zeeschip VOF and Others*, Case C-3/04, [2006] ECR I-02505, the Court of Justice found that an intermediary with authority to conclude a single contract which is subsequently extended over several years, is not incompatible with the requirement of 'continuing authority'.
1232. In *Tamarind International Ltd v. Eastern Natural Gas (Retail) Ltd* [2000] 26 *Law Society Gazette, Law Reports*, 35, goods was held to include gas and electricity.
1233. In *AMB Imballaggi Plastici SRL v. Pacflex* [1999] 2 All ER Comm 249 it was held that the Directive does not apply to intermediaries other than agents, such as distributors or franchisees.

called the principal, or to negotiate and conclude such transactions[1234] on behalf of and in the name of that principal.[1235]

695. There are a number of exclusions from this definition such that the term 'commercial agent' does not include:

- company officers
- partners of a firm
- insolvency practitioners.[1236]

The Regulations also provide that they shall not apply to commercial agents:

- whose activities are unpaid;
- operating in a commodity exchange or market.[1237]

696. Further, the Directive provides that Member States have the right to specify that the Directive shall not apply to those persons whose activities as commercial agents are considered secondary by the law of the Member State in question.[1238] In implementing this provision, the Irish Regulations provide that there is a presumption that the activities of consumer credit agents and mail order catalogue agents for consumer goods are secondary.[1239] This list is not described as exhaustive and therefore there may be other activities that might be considered secondary, in Irish law.[1240] The Directive provides that Member States may provide that an agency contract shall not be valid unless evidenced in writing.[1241] The Regulations adopt this formal requirement.[1242] Lastly, it has been held that the Directive and hence the Irish Regulations should apply in all cases where the agent undertakes activities within Ireland, unless the contract is subjected to the law of another Member State.[1243]

2. Agent's Duties at Common Law

697. Three duties are imposed at common law: to obey instructions; to exercise reasonable skill and care; and to perform personally. Where the agency is contractual, these duties usually take effect as implied terms of the contract.

1234. *See Parkes v. Esso Petroleum Co. Ltd* [1998] EU LR 550; [1999] TR LR 232; cf. *Kenny v. ROC Ireland* [2005] IEHC 241, [2007] IR 448.
1235. Regulation 2(1), 1994.
1236. Article 1(3) and Regs 2(1)(a)–(c), 1994.
1237. Regulations 2(1)(d) and (e), 1994.
1238. Regulation 2(2), 1994.
1239. Regulations 2(1)(f) and 2(2), 1994.
1240. *See further Parkes v. Esso Petroleum Co. Ltd* [1998] EU LR 550; [1999] TR LR 232; cf. *Kennyv . ROC* [2005] IEHC 241; [2007] IR 448.
1241. Article 13(2).
1242. Regulation 5, 1994. *See further Moore v. Piretta* [1999] 1 All ER 174.
1243. *Ingmar GB Ltd v. Eaton Leonard Technologies Inc* (Case C-381/98) [2000] All ER (D) 1759; [2001] All ER (EC) 57.

698. First, an agent must obey his/her principal's lawful instructions. Where instructions are ambiguous, an agent will not be held liable where he/she acts on a reasonable interpretation of them;[1244] though an agent should seek clarification, where possible.[1245] Where the agency is contractual, the agent is liable for breach of contract if he/she fails to act as instructed.[1246]

699. Second, all agents are required to act with reasonable care. Where the agency is contractual, a term to exercise reasonable care will normally be implied in the contract, at common law.[1247] Where services are provided in the course of a business, a term to exercise reasonable care is implied by statute.[1248]

700. Third, since an agent is often chosen for his/her personal qualities, the general rule is that he/she must perform his/her duties personally and cannot delegate performance unless delegation is authorized by the principal. In practice, delegation is quite common.

3. Agent's Duties in Equity

701. Agents are normally subject to fiduciary duties because agents have the power to affect the legal position of their principals in relation to third parties, and principals normally place trust and confidence in the agent in the exercise of that power. The core duties of a fiduciary are those of loyalty and fidelity.[1249] These core duties have several aspects and an agent's fiduciary duties can be examined under four headings: to avoid conflicts of interest; not to make a secret profit; not to accept a bribe; and to account. Where an agent is in breach of his/her fiduciary duties, a variety of remedies is available: proprietary or personal, at common law or in equity.

702. The agent's primary fiduciary duty is to avoid a conflict of interest:

> It is a rule of universal application, that no one, having [fiduciary] duties to discharge, shall be allowed to enter into engagements in which he has, or can have, a personal interest conflicting, or which possibly may conflict, with the interests of those whom he is bound to protect.[1250]

1244. *Ireland v. Livingstone* (1872) LR 5 HL 395.
1245. *Woodhouse AC Israel Cocoa Ltd SA v. Nigerian Produce Marketing Co. Ltd* [1972] AC 741 at 772 *per* Lord Salmon; *European Asian Bank AG v. Punjab & Sind Bank* [1983] 2 All ER 508 at 517 *per* Goff LJ.
1246. *Turpin v. Bilton* (1843) 5 Man & G 455.
1247. *See*, e.g., *Chariot Inns v. Assicurazioni Geberali SPA* [1981] IR 199 regarding duty of care of insurance brokers.
1248. Sale of Goods and Supply of Services Act 1980, s. 39; *see* para. 638.
1249. *See Bristol and West Building Society v. Mothew* [1998] Ch. 1 *per Millett LJ* at 18.
1250. Lord Cramworth LC in *Aberdeen Rly Co. v. Blaikie Bros* (1854) 1 Macq 461 at 471.

The fact that the agent acted in good faith and produced a benefit for his/her principal is irrelevant to the application of this rule.[1251] Where the duty applies, there is a breach if, for instance, an agent instructed to buy property, sells his/her own property to the principal;[1252] or if an agent instructed to sell property, buys it for himself/herself,[1253] unless all the circumstances are disclosed to the principal and the principal consents to the transaction.[1254]

703. An agent's second fiduciary duty is not to make a secret profit:

> There is no dispute about the law, which is that an agent cannot without the knowledge of his principal make any profit for himself out of services rendered to his principal.[1255]

An agent must account to the principal for all profits made from his/her position. It is irrelevant that the agent acted in good faith, that the principal suffered no loss, that the agent made a profit which the principal could not, or that the principal actually benefited from the agent's actions.[1256]

704. Third, an agent cannot accept a bribe. A bribe is any payment or other inducement made to an agent by a third party which is secret from the principal. It is therefore a particular species of secret profit. In this context, 'bribe' may not necessarily indicate corruption. If an agent receives a bribe, the principal may:

- dismiss the agent without notice;[1257]
- withhold any commission due to the agent on that transaction and recover any commission already paid;[1258]
- rescind the contract with the third party;
- require either the agent or the third party to account for the amount of the bribe as money had and received;[1259]
- claim damages (in the tort of deceit) for any loss he/she suffers as a result of payment of the bribe and entry into the consequent contract; the agent and third party are jointly and severally liable for such damages.[1260]

Additionally, the payment of a bribe may give rise to criminal liability.

1251. *Boardman v. Phipps* [1967] 2 AC 46.
1252. *See*, e.g., *Armstrong v. Jackson* [1917] 2 KB 822.
1253. *See*, e.g., *McPherson v. Watt* (1877) 3 All Cas 254.
1254. *North & South Trust Co. v. Berkeley* [1971] 1 WLR 470 at 484–485. Where an agent buys his/her principal's property or sells his/her own property to the principal, the agent must also show that the price was fair and that he/she did not abuse his/her position: *Gibson v. Jeyes* (1801) 6 Ves 266.
1255. *Sherrard v. Barron* [1923] 1 IR 21, *per* Moore LJ at 24.
1256. *See*, e.g., *Boardman v. Phipps* [1967] 2 AC 46.
1257. *See*, e.g., *Boston Deep Sea Fishing and Ice Co. v. Ansell* (1888) 39 CH D 339; and *Bulfield v. Fournier* (1895) 11 TLR 282.
1258. *Andrews v. Ramsey & Co. Ltd* [1903] 2 KB 635.
1259. *Lister & Co. v. Stubbs* (1890) 45 Ch D 1.
1260. *Arab Monetary Fund v. Hashim* [1993] 1 Lloyd's Rep 543.

705. Lastly, an agent must account to the principal for all property of the principal he/she receives in the course of the agency. He/she must therefore keep his/her own monies and property separate from those of the principal, unless mixing is authorized. If an agent wrongfully mixes his/her property with that of the principal, the principal may claim the whole of the mixed fund, unless the agent can establish any part of it as his/her own property.[1261] Since the relationship between the principal and agent is generally fiduciary, the principal may trace his/her property in equity and thus claim any replacement assets if the agent wrongfully disposes of his/her property.

4. Agent's Duties under the Regulations

706. The Directive appears to restate an agent's common law duties, in broad terms. It provides that a commercial agent has a general duty to look after the interests of his/her principal and act dutifully and in good faith.[1262] In particular, a commercial agent must:

(a) make proper efforts to negotiate and, where appropriate, conclude transactions he/she is instructed to take care of;
(b) communicate to his/her principal all the necessary information available to him/her;
(c) comply with reasonable instructions given by his/her principal.[1263]

Importantly, the parties cannot derogate from these duties.[1264]

5. Principal's Duties

707. No duties, similar to those placed on an agent, are placed on a principal at common law, reflecting the common law position that principals, and not agents, need protection, as noted above. For the first time, under the Directive and Regulations, good faith duties, similar to those placed on an agent, are placed on the principal.[1265] The detail of these duties will have to be developed by case law. In particular, the Directive provides that a principal must:

(a) provide his/her commercial agent with the necessary documentation relating to the goods concerned;
(b) obtain for his/her commercial agent the information necessary for the performance of the agency contract, and in particular notify the commercial agent

1261. *Lupton v. White* (1808) 15 Ves 432.
1262. Article 3(1).
1263. Article 3(2).
1264. Article 5.
1265. Article 4(1).

within a reasonable period once he/she anticipates that the volume of commercial transactions will be significantly lower than that which the commercial agent could normally have expected.[1266]

The parties cannot derogate from these duties and so, the information described above, which a principal might consider confidential, must be provided to the agent.[1267] There is no Irish case law on these provisions although there is a growing body of UK case law, much of which takes a narrow view of principal's good faith duties to their agent. For example, in *Npower Direct Ltd v South of Scotland Power Ltd*[1268] it was held that the duty could not broaden the substance of the obligation contractually agreed (although this is questionable in light of the mandatory nature of these obligations and Article 5). In this case it was argued that the principal had breached Article 4 by asking for a reduction in the volume of sales of 70% for a period and concurrently increasing the price of goods for sale to a level that made it harder to conclude sales. The judge referred to the principle of good faith as requiring 'fair and open dealing'. On the facts, and in light of a price variation right in the contract, it was found that the principle of good faith had not been breached.

6. Agent's Rights at Common Law

708. The agent has three basic rights at common law: a right to remuneration; a right to an indemnity; and a right to a lien.

709. First, an agent is only entitled to remuneration if that has been agreed with the principal and in accordance with the terms of the agreement. The agreement as to remuneration can be express or implied. A right to remuneration will be implied on the same basis that other terms can be implied into contracts. For instance, such a right would probably be implied where the agent is acting in the course of a profession or business, and would more easily be implied where the services have been provided. Where it is agreed that an agent should be paid but the amount of remuneration is not agreed, the agent is entitled to a reasonable sum as a *quantum meruit*.[1269] Where a commission is earned on an agent bringing about a result, he/she will only be entitled to payment if he/she is the effective cause of that result.[1270] Importantly, an agent is only entitled to remuneration where he/she has acted within his/her authority. Moreover, it seems that even where an agent has acted within his/her authority but has committed a serious breach of any of his/her duties to his/her principal, he/she loses his/her right to remuneration.

1266. Article 4(2).
1267. Article 5.
1268. [2005] EWHC 2123.
1269. *Way v. Latilla* [1937] 3 All ER 759; *Henehan v. Courtney* (1967) 101 ILTR 25.
1270. *Millar, Son & Co. v. Radford* (1903) 19 TLR 575; *Judd v. Donegal Tweed Co. Ltd* (1935) 69 ILTR 117; *Stokes & Quirke Ltd v. Clohessy* [1957] IR 84; *Murphy, Buckley & Keogh Ltd v. Pye (Ire) Ltd* [1971] IR 57.

710. Second, an agent is entitled to be indemnified against any expenses and liabilities, contractual or tortious, necessarily incurred on behalf of the principal in performance of his/her duties when acting within the scope of his/her actual authority, or, if his/her actions are later ratified, or if the agency is one of necessity. Where the agency is contractual, the right to indemnity will be an implied term of the contract.

711. Lastly, an agent is entitled to a lien over property – including papers – of the principal, in his/her possession, to secure payment of any remuneration or indemnity due to him/her. Most agents are entitled only to a particular lien – a right to retain property until sums related to that property or any related transaction are paid. However, some agents are entitled to a general lien, a right to retain any property of the principal's to secure payment of any sums due from the principal, whether connected to that property or not. Factors, bankers, solicitors and stockbrokers are entitled to a general lien, for instance.

7. Agent's Rights under the Regulations

712. Where the Directive and Regulations apply, they modify the agent's right to remuneration and give him/her certain additional rights. The common law rights to indemnity and lien remain unchanged.

713. As regards commission, in the absence of any agreement about the level of remuneration payable, a commercial agent is entitled to receive such remuneration as is customarily paid to a commercial agent dealing in the type of goods to which the agreement relates, in the area in which the agent operates. And where there is no custom, a reasonable sum is payable.[1271]

714. A commercial agent is entitled to receive commission on transactions concluded *during* the agency:[1272]

- which result from his/her actions;[1273]
- which result from repeat orders of the same kind from customers introduced by the agent;[1274]
- where the agent has the exclusive right to represent the principal in a specific geographical area or group of customers, on all contracts from customers belonging to that area or group.[1275]

1271. Article 6.
1272. Article 7 and Regulation 4, 1994.
1273. Article 7(1)(a).
1274. Article 7(1)(b).
1275. Article 7(2) and Regulation 4, 1994; *see further Georgios Kontogeorgas v. Kartonpak AE 1* (Case C-104/95) [1996] ECR I-6643.

Broadly speaking, under the Directive, commission becomes due when either the principal or the third party perform their obligations under the contract. Where the principal fails to perform, commission is due when he/she should have performed, or, at the latest, when the third party should have performed had the principal not breached the contract.[1276]

715. There are also various information rights under the Directive. The Directive requires the principal to provide the commercial agent with a detailed statement indicating the amount of commission due to him/her and how it is calculated.[1277] A commercial agent can demand access to information and, in particular, to extracts of the principal's books – but not the full books – to check the amount of commission due.[1278] Moreover, either party may require the other to provide a signed, written statement of the terms of the agency, including any variation.[1279]

8. Termination of Agency

716. Since the formation of an agency relationship depends on consent, the relationship of principal and agent can be terminated, at any time, by either party withdrawing consent. The relationship can also terminate automatically, by operation of law, such as, by effluxion of time, by performance, under the doctrine of frustration or by the bankruptcy or insanity of either party.[1280] Termination of the relationship and of the agent's actual authority may leave the agent with apparent authority and may therefore not deprive him/her of power to bind the principal. In addition, as between the principal and the agent, termination of the agency may give rise to consequent, or secondary, rights, especially where the agency is contractual and termination amounts to a breach of contract. Once again, the general common law rules are modified by the Regulations.

717. Under the Regulations, where an agent is appointed initially for a fixed term but both parties continue to perform the contract after expiry of the term, the agency is treated as continuing as one for an indeterminate period, determinable by notice.[1281] In the case of termination by notice, the notice required by the contract cannot be less than one month in the first year of the relationship, two months in the

1276. Article 10. Commission is payable not later than on the last day of the month following the quarter in which it became due: Art. 10(3). These provisions are mandatory: Art. 10(4).
1277. Article 12(1).
1278. Article 12(2). Derogation from Art. 12(1) and (2) to the detriment of the commercial agent is not permitted: Art. 12(3).
1279. Article 13. Waiver of this right is not permitted: Art. 13(1).
1280. However, an agency may be irrevocable where (i) the agent is given a 'power with an interest', that is, where an agent is given power and a personal interest, as where P owes A money, and appoints A to act as his agent to sell property and thereby rise funds to pay the debt: *see* the Powers of Attorney Act 1996, s. 20; or (ii) where a power of attorney is expressed to be 'enduring' or irrevocable under Part II of the Powers of Attorney Act 1996.
1281. Article 14 and Art. 15(1).

second and three months thereafter.[1282] The parties cannot agree to shorter notice periods but they can agree to longer notice.[1283] In the latter case, the notice to be observed by the principal must not be shorter than that to be observed by the agent.[1284]

718. Moreover, under the Regulations, an agent is entitled to commission on contracts concluded *after* the agency contract has terminated:

(a) if the transaction is mainly attributable to the commercial agent's efforts during the period of the agency contract and if the transaction is entered into within a reasonable time after termination;
(b) if in accordance with the above the order of the third party reached the principal or agent before termination of the agency.[1285]

719. Commercial agents may also have a right to *compensation for damage*, on termination of the agency. Importantly, the right to compensation for damage is different from a claim for damages under the common law. An agent will be entitled to damages at common law if the agency is terminated in breach of contract. But, any losses must not be too remote from the breach and an agent is under a duty to mitigate his/her loss. In contrast, the Regulations introduce a system of 'no-fault' compensation under which, after termination, an agent is entitled to receive compensation for loss of his/her agency regardless of whether the principal is in breach of contract or not. For instance, compensation is payable where the agency is terminated following the agent's death.[1286]

720. Under Article 17(3) of the Directive, a commercial agent is entitled to compensation for damage suffered as a result of the termination of the agency relationship. Such damage is deemed to occur particularly where the termination takes place in circumstances which:

(a) deprive him/her of commission which proper performance of the agency contract would have procured him/her whilst providing the principal with substantial benefits linked to the agent's activities;
(b) prevent him/her from recouping the costs and expenses incurred in performing the agency contract.

These examples are not exhaustive. For example, it has also been held that compensation is payable on insolvency or on closing down of the business.[1287]

1282. Article 15(2); *see further King v. Tunnock* [2000] IRLR 569.
1283. Article 15(2) and (4).
1284. Article 15(4).
1285. Article 8. *See further* e.g., *Tigana v. Decoro* [2003] EWHC 23 (QB).
1286. Article 17(4).
1287. For example, *in King v. Tunnock* [2000] IRLR 569 a long-established agency was terminated when a part of the business was closed and the agent was held to be entitled to a sum equal to two years' commission as compensation.

721. Article 18 of the Directive provides that compensation is not payable where:

a. the principal has terminated the agency contract because of default of the agent which would justify immediate termination under national law;
b. the agent has terminated the agency contract, unless termination is justified by circumstances attributable to the principal or on the grounds of age, infirmity or illness of the agent in consequence of which he/she cannot reasonably be expected to continue his/her activity;
c. with the agreement of the principal, the agent assigns his/her rights under the agency contract to another.[1288]

Moreover, Article 16 provides that nothing in the Directive affects national laws which provide for the immediate termination of the agency contract because of the failure of one party to perform his/her obligations under the contract, or where exceptional circumstances arise. Therefore, if a principal dismisses a commercial agent on grounds of a serious or repudiatory breach of contract by the agent, no compensation is payable. Conversely, if a commercial agent resigns, he/she loses his/her right to compensation unless his/her resignation is justified on one of the grounds listed in Article 18.

722. It would seem that in all other circumstances, other than those listed in Article 18 above, compensation is payable. For instance, and unlike common law damages, compensation may be payable where the principal terminates by giving proper notice, unless the principal would have been justified in terminating without notice because of the agent's serious breach of contract. Compensation may also be payable where an agency terminates by effluxion of time.[1289]

723. In determining the amount payable there is no guidance in legislation. Various options have been put forward including the French model of two years' average commission. In *Tigana v. Decoro*,[1290] a balance sheet approach listing various factors was suggested, including the length of the agency, the period the agency actually lasted for, the terms of the agency, the nature of the agency, any amount of compensation payable under Article 8 and the manner in which the agency terminated. Importantly, the judge in that case found that French precedent in the area was less useful than previously though. More recently, in *Lonsdale v. Howard Hallam*,[1291] both options above were rejected by the House of Lords in favour of valuing compensation with reference to the value of the income stream the agency would have generated. This would require expert valuation, the best evidence being the value of the agency if the agent was to sell his/her agency business on the open market. There is no Irish authority on this point.

1288. Under Art. 19 of the Directive, parties cannot derogate from Art. 18.
1289. *Tigana v. Decoro* [2003] EWHC 23.
1290. *Ibid.*
1291. [2007] UKHL 32.

724. In order to claim compensation under the Directive and Regulations, a commercial agent must deliver a written claim for compensation to the principal within one year of termination of the agency.[1292]

725. Lastly, a restrictive covenant in the agency agreement is enforceable, but the clause must be in writing and shall not apply for more than two years after termination of the agency.[1293]

III. Insurance

726. Insurance contracts involve the allocation of risk to a third party: the insurer. Broadly speaking, in return for a premium, the insurer takes over certain risks from the insured. Should these risks ever materialize, the insurer will compensate or 'indemnify' the insured for any loss or damage caused, under the terms of the insurance contract. There are two main types of insurance business, life assurance and non-life insurance, and the main types of non-life policies are for personal accident, fire, other property damage, pecuniary loss, motor, marine, aviation, and third-party liability. Some forms of insurance are compulsory. For example, where you drive a motor vehicle you are required to have third-party motor liability insurance.[1294] Certain professions, such as solicitors,[1295] may be required by legislation or, by rules of professional conduct, to have minimal professional liability insurance cover. But employer's liability insurance is not compulsory in Ireland.

727. The insurance industry is now highly regulated.[1296] The form of regulation includes requiring that a person cannot carry on business in the State as an insurer or an insurance intermediary without a license from or the authorization of the relevant body. The focus of this section is not on the regulation of the insurance industry but on the aspects of the private law of insurance. The very foundation of insurance law is the law of contract, and the answer to most questions arising between the insurer and insured will be found in the fine print of the insurance policy, which contains the terms of their contract. However, there are a number of particular features of insurance law worthy of mention, in particular as regards the formation of insurance contracts and the principle of indemnity.

1292. Article 17(5); *see Hackett v. Advanced Medical Computer Systems* [1999] CLC 160.
1293. Article 20.
1294. *See* Road Traffic Act 1961, s. 56, as amended.
1295. *See* the Professional Indemnity Insurance Regulations, 1995, SI No. 312/1995, as amended, made under the Solicitors (Amendment) Act 1994, s. 26.
1296. *See further* para. 866.

A. Formation

728. An insurance contract, like any other contract, is subject to the general rules of contract law.[1297] For example, to be properly formed there must be an agreement, supported by consideration and accompanied by an intention to create legal relations. However, specialized rules have developed in relation to insurance contracts and indeed in relation to particular types of insurance contract. In this regard, we will consider the requirement of an insurable interest, the rules as to form and the position as regards misrepresentation and the duty to disclose, in relation to the formation of insurance contracts.

1. Insurable Interest

729. It is a requirement of every insurance contract that the insured has an 'insurable interest' in the event insured against. Where there is no such insurable interest, the insurer may be able to avoid liability at common law, or the contract may be void by statute.[1298] The requirement of an insurable interest is based on the notion that the insured should have an economic interest or a proximate legal relationship with the subject matter insured. Accordingly, an insured would have an insurable interest in his/her own life, or in his/her own property, but not in the property of others. This requirement seeks to prevent 'a mischievous kind of gaming'[1299] which might follow if an insured could obtain insurance cover for an event in which he/she had no such interest. The concept of insurable interest is also closely related to indemnity insurance.[1300] Under indemnity insurance, the insured must have suffered a loss to be indemnified. But where the insured has no interest in the event insured against, he/she cannot have suffered a loss to be compensated. In modern times, Irish courts have adopted a generous interpretation of the requirement of an insurable interest.[1301]

2. Form

730. As noted above, insurance contracts are subject to the general law of contract and hence there must be an agreement, supported by consideration and an

1297. *See* paras 370–399 above.
1298. *See* the Life Assurance Act 1774; the Life Assurance (Ireland) Act 1886; and the Gaming and Lotteries Act 1956.
1299. Life Assurance Act 1774, s. 1.
1300. *See* paras 711–719 below.
1301. *See*, e.g., *Carrigan Ltd & Carrigan v. Norwich Union,* unreported, High Court, Lynch J., 11 Dec. 1987.

intention to create legal relations. Otherwise, there are no other formal requirements and, provided the above requirements are satisfied, an insurance contract may be concluded orally.[1302] In practice, however, standard formation procedures tend to be followed.

731. Marine insurance is the exception to the above general rule that there are no formal requirements in effecting an insurance contract. The Marine Insurance Act 1906 provides that a contract of marine insurance is inadmissible in evidence unless embodied in a marine policy.[1303] Moreover, the policy must specify the name of the insured or his/her agent;[1304] and must be signed by the insured or his/her agent.[1305] The policy may take the form in the First Schedule to the 1906 Act,[1306] but since 1982, Lloyd's of London and the marine insurance companies have used new forms of policies.

3. Misrepresentation and Duty of Disclosure

732. The decision to accept or refuse insurance is based largely on the answers and statements provided by the applicant in an insurance proposal form. Hence, these statements are very important. Commonly, the proposal form will contain a term which provides that these statements form the basis of the contract (a 'basis of the contract' clause) thereby converting such statement into important terms of the contract, known as warranties.[1307] Where such statements take effect as warranties, any false statement will be a serious breach of contract allowing the insurer to repudiate the contract. Even where a statement does not take effect as a term of the contract, any false statement may amount to a misrepresentation. Similar to other contracts, where one party to an insurance contract makes an untrue material statement, a misrepresentation, before the contract is concluded, and this induces the other party to enter the contract, then the contract can be avoided.[1308] So, for example, where an applicant for insurance makes a false statement in the proposal form, the insurer can avoid any subsequent liability. In relation to marine insurance, this position has been put on a statutory basis,[1309] reflecting the common law. Accordingly, a representation is material if it would influence the judgment of a prudent insurer in fixing the premium or determining whether he/she will take the risk

1302. Insurance contracts must be stamped, generally by the insurer (Stamp Duty Consolidation Act 1999, s. 2) but failure to stamp does not invalidate the contract.
1303. 1906 Act, s. 22.
1304. 1906 Act, s. 23.
1305. 1906 Act, s. 24.
1306. 1906 Act, s. 30.
1307. This classification is at odds with the general law of contract where important contractual terms are referred to as 'conditions': *see* paras 411–414 above.
1308. *See* para. 396 above.
1309. Marine Insurance Act 1906, s. 20.

or not.[1310] And, a statement may be a matter of fact, expectation or belief.[1311] A statement as to expectation or belief is true if it is made in good faith, that is, honestly.[1312]

733. In the majority of cases, an insurer's right to rescind the contract for misrepresentation is of little significance because, in one important regard, insurance contracts are different from most other contracts when it comes to pre-formation statements. Unlike the majority of contract types, insurance contracts are contracts of *utmost good faith (uberrimae fides)* and the parties owe each other a duty of utmost good faith. While the law recognizes that this duty of good faith is mutual,[1313] most legal actions involve the insured's duty of good faith to the insurer. For example, the duty of good faith comprises a duty not to make fraudulent claims, and, perhaps more importantly, it comprises a duty of disclosure on the parties. In particular, the insured is under a strict legal duty to actively disclose certain matters to the insurer (usually on the proposal form). Where the insured fails in this duty, the insurer can avoid the contract and liability is repudiated. The rationale for this aspect of the duty of disclosure is that in order to assess the risk the insurer must be informed of all material facts and it is the insured that has the best knowledge of these facts.[1314]

734. The insured's duty of disclosure has been strictly applied.[1315] The duty extends beyond answering the specific questions in the proposal form. In essence, the insured is required to disclose all material facts known to him/her. Under the Marine Insurance Act 1906, the insured must disclose facts which are known to the insured and the insured is deemed to know every fact which, in the ordinary course of business, ought to be known to him/her: constructive knowledge.[1316] It has been held by the Court of Appeal that this rule applies to non-marine insurance.[1317]

735. The insured is required to disclose all *material* facts known to him/her. In assessing what is material, it is neither relevant that the insured did not think the information material, nor is it an excuse that the insured acted with good faith. The

---

1310. 1906 Act, s. 20(2).
1311. 1906 Act, s. 20(3).
1312. 1906 Act, s. 20(5); *Economides v. Commercial Union Assurance plc* [1997] 3 All ER 636.
1313. *Carter v. Boehm* (1766) 3 Burr 1905 at 1909; *Fagan v. General Accident Fire & Life Assurance Corporation plc* (unreported, High Court, 19 Feb. 1993); upheld by the Supreme Court (unreported, Supreme Court, 14 Oct. 1998).
1314. *See Abbott v. Howard* (1832) Hayes 381.
1315. Although exceptions to this strict doctrine may exist as where the contract expressly or impliedly excludes the requirement of full disclosure, *see*, e.g., Aro Road *v. Insurance Corporation* [1986] IR 403 and *Kelleher v. Irish Life Assurance* [1993] 3 IR 393.
1316. 1906 Act, s. 18(1).
1317. *PCW Syndicates v. PCW Reinsurers* [1996] 1 All ER 774. In relation to private individuals, an insured is probably only required to disclose all material facts *actually* known to him/her, provided he/she does not deliberately shut his/her eyes to obvious facts: *Keating v. New Ireland Assurance* [1990] 2 IR 383.

standard for assessing materiality is that of a *prudent insurer*. The common law duty of disclosure was codified in section 18(2) of the Marine Insurance Act 1906 which provides that:

> Every circumstance is material which would influence the judgment of a prudent insurer in fixing the premium or determining whether he will take the risk.[1318]

This test was adopted by Kenny J in the Supreme Court in *Chariot Inns Ltd v. Assicurazioni Spa and Coyle Hamilton.*[1319]

B. The Principle of Indemnity

736. An important distinction in insurance law is between indemnity and contingency insurance. Contingency insurance involves the payment of a *fixed* sum on the happening of an event, such as death or illness. In contrast, indemnity insurance, such as property insurance and liability insurance, involves the insurer undertaking to insure against a risk that may never occur and payment under indemnity insurance seeks to *indemnify* or compensate the insured for the loss sustained. The insurance contract usually sets a ceiling on the amount payable but does not define the exact amount. The basic principle is that an insured is entitled to be indemnified, no more or no less:

> The contract of insurance is a contract of indemnity and of indemnity only and … this contract means that the assured, in case of a loss against which the policy has been made, shall be fully indemnified, but shall never be more than fully indemnified.[1320]

Three sets of rules seek to ensure that the principle of indemnity is applied: the rules involve the measure of loss; the insurer's right of subrogation; and the rules relating to double insurance. The insurer's right of contribution is closely related and is also considered below.

1. The Measure of Loss

737. If a valid claim is made by an insured under an insurance contract, the insurer is obliged to satisfy it. The amount payable is governed by the terms of the contract. Therefore, the amount payable by the insurer is the amount required to indemnify the insured, subject to any ceiling fixed in the contract and any excess

1318. *See also Joel v. Law Union & Crown Insurance Co.* [1908] 2 KB 863.
1319. [1981] IR 199.
1320. *Castellain v. Preston* (1883) 11 QBD 380 *per* Brett LJ at 386; *see also Vance v. Forster* (1841) Ir Cir Rep 47 and *St Albans Investment Co. v. Sun Alliance & London Insurance Ltd & ors* [1983] IR 363.

clause. However, with property insurance, the measure of loss can be more complicated and the rules differ depending on whether the property insured is goods or land, and whether the claim is for total or partial loss.

738. In relation to goods, the measure of loss in the case of total loss is the market value of the goods at the time of the loss. With insurance on land, such as buildings insurance, two basic measures of damage can be used: market value or reinstatement cost.[1321] An insurance contract should clearly indicate which measure is to be used, and where such a clear indication does not exist, the market value measure prevails.[1322]

739. As an alternative to a simple indemnity policy, insurance on property can be affected by means of a *valued* policy, as is common with marine insurance.[1323] Accordingly, the parties agree a value on the property and in the case of total loss, that agreed sum is payable, provided that the sum is not so excessive as to amount to a breach of the duty of good faith. In this way the valuation operates like a liquidated damages clause in a contract,[1324] or the sum assured in a contingency policy.

740. In the case of partial loss, where goods or premises are damaged but not totally destroyed, the measure of loss is essentially the cost of repair, subject to a deduction for betterment if the repair leaves the property better than it was before the loss and subject to any maximum ceiling.[1325] With a valued policy, in the case of partial loss, the insured will be entitled to recover the proportion of the cost of the repair which bears the same relation to the cost of the repair as the policy value bears to the actual value of the property prior to the loss.[1326]

741. Where an insurer refuses or fails to satisfy a valid claim, he/she is in breach of contract and the insured has an action in damages against the insurer. The measure of damages is prima facie the amount of the claim.

2. The Doctrine of Subrogation

742. Essentially, subrogation is the right of the insurer, having indemnified the insured, to pursue any claims the insured might have had against another party in relation to the insurance claim, thereby allowing the insurer to diminish his/her loss, and in turn place legal responsibility on the person at fault. While the right arises at

1321. Other measures are available but should be clearly expressed in any insurance contract. For example, the indemnity can be calculated on the basis of the cost of a similar premises; or on the basis of the cost of erecting a modern premises which would provide the same facilities as the destroyed premises: *see*, e.g., *Reynolds v. Phoenix Assurance Co. Ltd* [1978] 2 Lloyd's Rep 440.
1322. *St Albans Investment Co. v. Sun Alliance & London Insurance Ltd & ors* [1983] IR 363.
1323. Marine Insurance Act 1906, s. 27; cf. *Brodigan v. The Imperial Live Stock and General Insurance Co. Ltd* (1927) 61 ILTR 193.
1324. *See* para. 448 above.
1325. *Vance v. Forster* (1841) Ir Cir Rep 47.
1326. *Elcock v. Thomson* [1949] 2 KB 755, [1949] 2 All ER 381.

common law, most modern insurance contracts will make express provision for this right allowing the insurer to take and defend proceedings in the insured's name and requiring the insured to provide assistance to the insurer. The right of subrogation operates in the same way as an implied assignment of the right of action. The insurance contract may even require the insured to expressly assign his/her right of action allowing the insurer to bring proceedings in his/her own name and entitling him/her to retain all that he/she recovers.

743. In Doyle v. Wicklow County Council[1327] Griffin J stated that:

> it is beyond question that all claims of the insured arising out of any ground of legal responsibility vest in the insurer by subrogation. The value of all benefits received by the insured from claims which have been satisfied before payment under the policy ought to be deducted from the indemnity at the time of payment; equally, after the insurers have paid the insured under the policy, they have an equity in respect of all the insured's claims.[1328]

3. Double Insurance and the Doctrine of Contribution

744. Not infrequently, the insured's loss may be covered by more than one insurance contract. If so, the insured is entitled to claim under either or both insurance contracts until he/she is fully indemnified. But, importantly, the law precludes double recovery as this would be contrary to the principle of indemnity. Where a risk is insured against with more than one insurer and the insured makes a claim and recovers against only one insurer, that insurer can seek a pro-rate contribution from any other insurers under the equitable doctrine of contribution. Again, the insurance contract usually modifies this right to contribution by including a 'rateable proportion clause'. Accordingly, any one insurer is protected from paying more than his/her 'share' of the loss thereby forcing the insured to pursue claims against each insurer for their proportion of the loss. Importantly, double insurance and the doctrine of contribution only operate where the same subject matter is covered by two or more separate insurance contracts, in relation to the same risk.[1329]

1327. [1974] IR 55.
1328. *Ibid.* at 72.
1329. *Hibernian Insurance v. Eagle Star Insurance and Guardian Royal Exchange Assurance* (unreported, High Court, 17 Feb. 1987); *Zurich Insurance Co. v. Shield Insurance Co.* [1988] IR 174; and *In re Kelly ' s Carpetdrome* (unreported, High Court, 14 Apr. 1985).

C. Reform of Consumer Insurance Law

745. Reform of Irish insurance law has recently been proposed by the LRC. Around the same time that authorities in the UK were examining the matter of insurance law reform,[1330] in 2011, the Irish LRC issued a Consultation Paper, *Insurance Contracts*,[1331] which it followed-up with a final report on *Consumer Insurance Contracts* in 2015.[1332] The final report makes 105 recommendations for reform to consumer insurance contracts. The legislative framework proposed in this Report applies in general to contracts of insurance, both life and non-life, made between a consumer and an insurer, and importantly, the definition of consumer is extended to include SMEs with a turnover of less than EUR 3 million.[1333] Matters concerning contracts of reinsurance, or contracts of marine, air or transport (MAT) insurance would be unaffected by the recommendations for reform. Key recommendations relate to pre-contractual duties of utmost good faith, the duty disclosure and proportionate remedies following breach; warranties and terms that describe the risk; insurable interest; privity of contract and third party rights; subrogation and family and other close relationships; post-contractual duties; and unfair and other onerous terms. In particular, and in a bold move, the final report recommends the abolition of the pre-contractual principle of utmost good faith and the pre-contractual duty of disclosure (whether statutory or at common law) as it applies to consumer insurance contracts and instead recommends that there should be specified statutory duties and obligations. For example, the statutory pre-contractual duty of disclosure of a consumer should be confined to providing responses to questions asked by the insurer, and consumers should not be under a duty to volunteer any information over and above that required by such questions. Moreover, it should be the duty of consumers to answer the questions posed by insurers honestly and with reasonable care. In terms of remedies for breach of such duties, the consequences of non-compliance with the reformulated duty of disclosure should be related to the presence or absence of fault by the consumer in making the misrepresentation and be proportionate to the effects of the misrepresentation upon the interests of the insurer and the consumer. This would mean that, where a consumer's non-disclosure, misrepresentation or other breaches of contract are innocent or due to negligence, insurers should not be able to repudiate all liability under the insurance contract but should be required to make proportionate payments to the consumer. The Commission recommended, however, that where a consumer's non-disclosure, misrepresentation or other breaches of contract are fraudulent (i.e., where made intentionally or recklessly), the insurer's right to completely repudiate liability should remain. In relation to warranties in insurance contracts, the Commission recommends the abolition of the concept of warranties in consumer insurance contracts and their

1330. In the UK, *see* now the Consumer Insurance (Disclosure and Representations) Act 2012 and the Insurance Act 2015.

1331. LRC CP 65 – 2011.

1332. LRC 113 – 2015.

1333. This definition of consumer ties in with the statutory jurisdiction of the Financial Services Ombudsman, which provides a mediation service on consumer insurance complaints, and in the Central Bank's *Consumer Protection Code 2012*, which contains important requirements on insurance contracts.

replacement with statutory rules that will enable insurers to continue to include provisions in contracts that (a) precisely identify or define the risk insured and (b) protect consumers from the unfair and unjust effects of the current law. In particular, any provision which purports to convert any statement by a consumer into a contractual warranty, including by means of a declared 'basis of contract' clause or by any comparable clause (including one described as a warranty, a future warranty, a promissory or a continuing warranty), should be invalid. Lastly, it is recommended that the requirement that a consumer must have an 'insurable interest' in the risk being insured should be abolished, and that it should be replaced by a rule that the consumer should simply be asked to prove what actual loss has been sustained when a claim is made. At the time of writing, a private members bill, the Consumer Insurance Contracts Bill 2017 which seeks to implement these recommendations, was making its way through the Houses of the Oireachtas (the Parliament).

IV. Banking and Other Financial Services

746. Banks and other financial institutions play a central role in commercial activity. Banking activity underpins all commercial activity by facilitating the payment for goods and services, and by providing credit facilities. As is explained later in this monograph, banking, and financial services more generally, is perhaps the most highly regulated industry in the State, in terms of the conditions imposed for entry into that business and for remaining in the business.[1334]

747. One of the more traditional services offered by banks is processing cheques and other negotiable instruments. Many features of that service are governed by the Bills of Exchange Act, 1882, and the Cheques Act, 1959, which were considered earlier in this monograph.[1335] The other major banking services are taking deposits and making loans. Indeed, the modern statutory definition of 'a banking business' places the emphasis on these two services. For regulatory purposes, 'a banking business' has been defined as any business that consists of or includes:

(a) receiving money on the person's own account from members of the public either on deposit or as repayable funds;
(b) the granting of credits on own account.[1336]

This statutory definition reflects the common law definition of banking which also focuses on the acceptance of deposits. In *Re Shields Estate*[1337] it was stated by Holmes LJ that: 'The real business of the banker is to obtain deposits of money which he may use for his profit by lending it out again.' Similarly, Diplock LJ in the

1334. *See further* paras 858–871.
1335. *See* Part I, Ch. 7.
1336. Central Bank Act 1971, s. 2, as amended by Regulation 154(1)(a) of the EU (Capital Requirements) Regulations 2014, S.I. No. 158/2014.
1337. [1901] 1 IR 173 at 182.

Court of Appeal, in *United Dominions Trust Ltd v. Kirkwood,*[1338] was of the view that the essential characteristic of banking was the acceptance of deposits. But Lord Denning MR and Harman LJ, relying on expert opinion, agreed that the essential characteristic of banking was the collection and payment of cheques. Diplock LJ was 'inclined to agree' that 'to constitute the business of banker today' the banker must also pay cheques drawn on him/her and collect cheques on behalf of customers. Since these cases were decided, significant changes have occurred in the provision of banking services. In particular, the use of cheques as a means of making payment has declined and is expected to continue to do so, as alternative payment methods, involving the use of credit and debit cards, and electronic funds transfers, have developed.

748. Modern banking is notable both in terms of the range of institutions which offer banking services, and the range of services on offer. There are numerous banks and other credit institutions, such as building societies, as well as credit unions, competing for business and private customer work. More recently, retailers and tech companies have entered the financial services market. Further, at a commercial level, merchant banks offer banking services exclusively to business customers. Merchant banks do not generally have a branch network but operate from a small number of offices, usually centrally located. Discount houses also offer specialist financial services to the commercial community, by buying at a discount, bills of exchange, for example. Other finance houses provide credit facilities, by financing transactions such as hire purchase, equipment leasing and by factoring debts.

749. The range of banking services has also expanded beyond the acceptance of deposits and the making of loans, and the collection and payment of cheques and other payment orders.[1339] Traditionally, banks have provided credit references for customers and facilities for the safe storage of documents and valuables. Today, banks also provide advice on investment and tax, and offer a variety of services, including stockbroking and insurance services. The method of delivering these services has also changed radically with a move away from the branch to electronic, telephone and Internet banking. Moreover, in relation to their business customers, banks provide a further range of services including, factoring of debts, discounting of bills, and letter of credit facilities.

750. In this section, we concentrate on the banker/customer relationship, in particular the establishment of the banker/customer relationship, the duties of bankers and customers and issues around the termination of this relationship. In addition to the many obligations and rights which may arise pursuant to a contract or by law, a number of Codes of Practice exist, including, in a commercial context, the Consumer Protection Code (2012) and the Code of Conduct for Business Lending to

1338. [1966] 2 QB 431, [1966] 1 All ER 968, *see also Re Roes ' Legal Charge* [1982] 2 Lloyd's Rep 370.

1339. *See* more generally Directive 2013/36/EC on access to the activity of credit institutions and the prudential supervision of credit institutions and investment firms, [2013] OJ L 176/338, Annex I for a list of activities carried out by credit institutions, including banks.

Small and Medium Enterprise (2012) which offer customers of banks further protection. Importantly, these Codes have a statutory basis and are binding.[1340] Moreover, the Consumer Protection Code is notable for its wide application. In particular, the Consumer Protection Code defines 'consumer' broadly to include partnerships and other unincorporated bodies, and incorporated bodies with an annual turnover of less than EUR 3 million in the previous financial year. Hence, certain 'smaller' businesses can be afforded protection under the Consumer Code through enforcement by the Central Bank and the Financial Services Ombudsman.[1341] For example, Chapters 2 and 3 of the Code set out general principles and requirements for regulated providers of financial services, including banks, such as requirement to act honestly, fairly and professionally in the best interest of customers and the market, and to act with due skill, care and diligence in the best interests of customers. Chapters 4 and 6 contain various information obligations, while Chapter 5 requires regulated providers of financial services to know their customer and to assess suitability. Further Chapters address rebates and claims; arrears; advertising; errors and complaints; and records and compliance.

A. The Establishment of Banker/Customer Relations

751. The term 'customer' is used in the Bills of Exchange Act 1882 and the Cheques Act 1959, but the Acts offer no definition. It may be important to identify a customer in order to determine whether a bank can rely on the statutory defences available to banks, under these Acts, when paying and collecting cheques.[1342] The classification of a person as a customer is also important because at common law certain incidents attach to the banker/customer relationship, taking effect as implied terms of the contract. At common law, it has been held that a person becomes a customer as soon as he/she opens an account with a bank.[1343] Indeed, it may be that a person becomes a customer earlier in time when the bank agrees to open the account.[1344] However, it should be noted that many banking services, such as loan or credit card services, are offered to persons who do not have a deposit or current account with the bank and hence are not, strictly speaking, customers. More generally, therefore, a customer can be defined as any person who has a contractual relationship with a bank under which the bank provides financial services to the person. Even in these latter circumstances, some of the common law incidents of the banker/customer relationship may apply.

752. The banker/customer relationship is based on contract, although other aspects of the law including agency, equity, property, restitution and tort play an

---

1340. In relation to banks *see* the Central Bank Act 1989, s. 117. *See further* Donnelly, 'The Consumer Protection Code: Regulatory Innovation from the Irish Financial Regulator', [2009] *Yearbook of Consumer Law* 175.
1341. Central Bank and Financial Services Authority of Ireland Act 2004; *see further* www.financialombudsman.ie
1342. *See* 1882 Act, ss 60 and 80, and 1959 Act, ss 1 and 4.
1343. *Ladbroke & Co. v. Todd* (1914) 30 TLR 433.
1344. *Woods v. Martins Bank* [1959] 1 QB 55, [1958] 3 All ER 166.

important role. While many banking services, such as loans, ATM cards and credit card facilities, are provided on the basis of standard form contracts drafted by the bank, the legal incidents of the banker/customer relationship derive from the common law, as implied terms of contract, when a customer opens an account. These legal incidents are based on mercantile expectations and banking practice.[1345] Traditionally, legislative regulation of the banker/customer relationship has been minimal. What legal regulation does exist today derives mainly from the EU. Some of this regulation seeks to protect consumers, such as the EC (Unfair Terms in Consumer Contracts) Regulations 1995, as amended;[1346] while other aspects of EU regulation is broader in scope, such as the EC (Payment Services) Regulations 2009,[1347] and the EC (Electronic Money) Regulations 2011.[1348] These latter two measures are among a package of measures adopted in the context of the Single European Payment Area (SEPA) – a single market for euro payments subject to a common legal framework.

753. As noted above, the opening of an account gives rise to the banker/customer relationship. Essentially, the relationship of banker/customer is that of debtor/creditor.[1349] Accordingly, when a customer opens a deposit or current account, the customer lends the money deposited to the bank, and in return acquires contractual rights to repayment. Repayment may be due at a specified date, as with certain fixed term savings accounts, or on demand as with the more usual deposit and current accounts. Where an account is overdrawn, the relationship is reversed with the bank becoming the creditor and the customer becoming the debtor.

754. Importantly, and as a consequence of the usual debtor/creditor relationship between the bank and the customer, when a customer deposits money with a bank, the customer ceases to own the money and it becomes the property of the bank. Therefore, for example, when the bank makes payment in accordance with the customer's instructions, it does so from its own resources first; subsequently it reimburses itself for the amount paid out by debiting the customer's account and thereby reducing its debt to the customer. Equally, if the bank becomes insolvent, the customer has no real or proprietary rights in relation to the money deposited; rather, the customer becomes an unsecured creditor of the bank.[1350]

1345. *Hare v. Henty* (1861) 10 CBNS 65 at 77.
1346. SI No. 27 of 1995 and SI No. 307 of 2000.
1347. SI No. 383 of 2009 which transposes Directive 2007/64/EC, the Payment Services Directive, [2007] OJ L319/1. *See further* Commission proposals for a revised Payment Services Directive (PSD2), COM (2013) 547 final.
1348. SI No. 183 of 2011 which transposed Directive 2000/46/EC, the e-Money Directive, [2009] O.J. L267/7.
1349. *Foley v. Hill* (1848) 2 HLC 28.
1350. Today, deposit protection legislation seeks to afford some protection to depositors: *see* the Financial Services (Deposit Guarantee Scheme) Act 2009.

B. Banker's Duties

755. As stated above, on the opening of an account, the relationship of banker/customer arises and a number of legal incidents follow. In particular, various duties are implied into the contract between the bank and the customer.[1351] The bank's main duties are:

- to honour the customer's mandate or instruction to make payments to third parties;[1352]
- to obey a customer's countermand, such as by 'stopping' a cheque;[1353]
- to exercise reasonable skill and care in the performance of its functions, including the paying and collecting of cheques;[1354]
- while normally a bank is not in a fiduciary position with its customers because the funds deposited with it are the bank's property and not the customers, a bank may incur extra fiduciary duties as, for example, if it acts as a trustee;[1355]
- to comply with the bank's duty of confidentiality to its customer.[1356]

756. The EU (Payment Services) Regulations 2018[1357] provide further clarification around the payer's and the payee's respective rights and obligations in Part 4. In brief, the Regulations apply to 'payment services' which include credit transfers, debit transfers, standing orders, money remittance and debit and credit card payments but not for example, paper cheques or drafts.[1358] Part 4 of the Regulations applies to consumers, including microenterprises, although for non-consumers, the parties may contract out of certain aspects of the Regulations.[1359] Further, Part 4 applies in respect of payment service providers established in the State or providing a payment service to a user in the State, including through an agent.[1360]

1351. *See Joachimson v. Swiss Bank Corpn* [1921] 3 KB 110.
1352. *See further Kinlan v. Ulster Bank* [1928] IR 171.
1353. Bills of Exchange Act 1882, s. 75. It is not clear whether a customer can countermand a cheque supported by a cheque guarantee card: *see First Sport Ltd v. Barclays Bank plc* [1993] 3 All ER 789.
1354. *See*, e.g., *Tulsk Co-operative Livestock Mart Ltd v. Ulster Bank* (unreported, High Court, 13 May 1983);*Towey v. Ulster Bank* [1987] ILRM 142 where delays in obtaining payment of cheques amounted to negligence; and *Irish Nationwide Building Society v. Malone* (unreported, Supreme Court, 10 Dec. 1998) where it was held that the Building Society had acted as agents for the borrowers when it agreed to arrange insurance in return for an administration fee and hence owed the defendant a duty of care.
1355. *Batnes v. Addy* (1874) 9 Ch. App 244.
1356. *Tournier v. National Provincial and Union Bank of England* [1924] 1 KB 461. In *National Irish Bank v. RTE* the Supreme Court found that, in principle, an injunction could be granted to protect confidentiality, although, in this case, which concerned allegations of bank assisted tax evasion, the public interest demanded disclosure and the injunction was refused.
1357. SI No 6 of 2018.
1358. *See* Schedule to 2018 Regulations for litany of 'payment services' and Regulation 4 for exclusions.
1359. 2018 Regulations, Reg.62(2) and (3) (re Part 3); Reg.85(1) and (2) (re Part 4).
1360. 2018 Regulations, Reg.3(1)(a).

757. Regulation 94 deals with the obligations of the payment service provider, such as a bank or other credit institution. These include:

- Making sure that the personalized security features of the payment instrument are not accessible to anyone other than the user.
- Not sending any unsolicited payment instruments, other than as a replacement for an existing instrument.
- Ensuring that appropriate means are available to enable the user to contact in respect of fulfilling notification requirements.
- To provide, on request, a means for the user to prove for eighteen months after giving a notification that he or she did notify.
- Preventing the use of the instrument once notification is given.

Regulation 95 provides that a payment service user is entitled to rectification from the payment service provider of any unauthorized or incorrectly executed payment transaction. However, this only arises where the user notifies the provider of this no later than thirteen months after the debit date, except in the case where the provider fails to make the necessary information available.

758. Regulations 97 and 98 deal with unauthorized payment transactions. Accordingly, the payment service provider is liable for unauthorized payments, under Regulation 97, provided the payer concerned has given notice. The provider must refund to the payer immediately the value of the transaction, and, if necessary, restore the debited payment account to the state it would have been in had the transaction not taken place. However, Regulation 98 limits the scope of Regulation 97 in a number of ways. For instance, the payer must bear the loss of unauthorized payments up to a total of EUR 50, if the transaction resulted from the use of a lost or stolen payment instrument or from the misappropriation of the instrument, if the payer failed to keep the personalized security features safe. Moreover, the payer bears all losses arising from the use of an unauthorized payment if he incurred these by acting fraudulently or with gross negligence or if he failed to fulfil his obligations under Regulation 93. A payer does not bear any costs after notification unless he was acting fraudulently. And, if a payment service provider does not provide an appropriate mechanism for the payer to give notice of a lost, stolen or misappropriate instrument, the payer is not liable for any of the consequence of the loss unless he acted fraudulently.

C. Customer's Duty of Care

759. At common law, a customer owes a duty of care to its bank, although this duty is not extensive. A customer owes a duty to take reasonable care in drawing cheques so as not to facilitate fraud and the customer is liable to the bank for any loss caused to the bank for breach of that duty.[1361] Subsequently, it was held that a customer owed a duty of care to its bank to inform the bank of any fraud relating

1361. *London Joint Stock Bank Ltd v. Macmillan and Arthur* [1918] AC 77.

to his/her account, of which he/she is aware.[1362] English authority suggests that this duty of care will not be extended further.[1363] Where the EC (Payment Services) Regulations 2009[1364] apply, Regulation 70 addresses the obligations of a payment service user. These include using a payment services instrument in accordance with its terms and conditions and notifying the instrument provider of any loss of the instrument.

D. Termination of the Banker/Customer Relationship

760. The banker/customer relationship may be terminated in a number of ways, by: the customer; the bank; or the operation of the law. The relationship may terminate automatically, under the terms of the banker/customer contract, as where the customer holds a fixed term deposit account and the term expires. In such circumstances, neither the customer nor the bank can unilaterally terminate the relationship before expiry of the fixed time, although in practice banks allow customers to terminate prematurely on payment of a penalty. Otherwise, the relationship can be terminated unilaterally. For example, a customer can always close an account where the sum deposited is payable on demand; however, the customer must also indicate an intention to terminate the relationship. Equally, the bank can terminate the relationship. However, because payments in and out of a customer's account take a number of days to process, a bank can only terminate the relationship by giving reasonable notice to the customer, as a means of avoiding the dishonouring of cheques, for example.[1365] What is reasonable will depend on the facts of the case. The customer may need to be given sufficient time to rearrange his/her banking affairs. In *Prosperity Ltd v. Lloyds Bank Ltd,*[1366] one month's notice was held to be insufficient because the customer was an insurer who had directed clients to make payments directly into his bank account. However, the court did not order that the account be kept open; damages were awarded instead. Where the account is in overdraft without prior approval from the bank or the account is being used for unlawful purposes, the bank can close the account without giving notice.[1367] Because the banker/customer relationship is personal it will automatically terminate where the customer dies,[1368] or becomes insolvent. Clearly, termination of the banker/customer relationship also involves termination of the customer's mandate to the bank. Where the EC (Payment Services) Regulations 2009[1369] apply, Regulation 56

1362. *Greenwood v. Martin ' s Bank Ltd* [1933] AC 51.
1363. *Tai Hing Cotton Mill Ltd v. Liu Chong Hing Bank Ltd* [1986] AC 80, [1985] 2 All ER 947.
1364. SI No. 383 of 2009 which transposes Directive 2007/64/EC, the Payment Services Directive, [2007] OJ L319/1. *See further* Commission proposals for a revised Payment Services Directive (PSD2), COM (2013) 547 final.
1365. *Joachimson v. Swiss Bank Corpn* [1921] 3 KB 110.
1366. (1923) 39 TLR 372.
1367. *Blighty v. Norton* (1862) 3 B & S 305.
1368. *See* Bills of Exchange Act 1882, s. 75(2).
1369. SI No. 383 of 2009 which transposes Directive 2007/64/EC, the Payment Services Directive, [2007] OJ L319/1. *See further* Commission proposals for a revised Payment Services Directive (PSD2), COM (2013) 547 final.

deals with the termination of framework payment services contracts and includes rules concerning notice periods and charges.

V. Carriage of Goods by Road, Sea and Air

761. Traditionally, and unlike continental Europe where goods were frequently carried by road, rail, river or canal, Ireland, being an island, depended largely on goods being imported and exported by sea. More recently, goods that are compact and high value may be carried by air transport. Also, recent years have also seen the advent of multimodal transport, where goods are carried in containers using a combination of the above forms of transport. The legal framework for carriage of goods by road, sea and air is set out below. In broad terms, the rights of duties of the parties are to be found primarily in the contract of carriage; however, various international treaties have been adopted into Irish law which seek to harmonize certain key aspects of the law in relation to the carriage of goods and passengers.

A. Carriage by Road

762. As is the case with carriage by sea and air, carriage of goods by road is regulated primarily by the contract of carriage between the consignor and the carrier. Such contracts are usually standard in form. These contracts are however subject to the Convention for the International Carriage of Goods by Road, 1956 (the CMR Convention), as amended.[1370] The CMR Convention was incorporated into Irish law in the International Carriage of Goods by Road Act 1990 (hereinafter, the 1990 Act).[1371]

1. Application of CMR Convention

763. Section 2 of the 1990 Act provides that CMR Convention shall have the force of law in the State. The Convention applies to every contract for the carriage of goods by road in vehicles for reward, when the place of taking over of the goods and the place designated for delivery, as specified in the contract, are situated in two different countries, of which at least one is a contracting country, irrespective of the place of residence and the nationality of the parties. 'Vehicles' includes motor vehicles, articulated vehicles, trailers and semi-trailers. However, the Convention does not apply to carriage performed under the terms of any international postal convention, funeral consignments or furniture removal.[1372] Importantly, where the vehicle containing the goods is carried over part of the journey by sea, rail, inland waterways or air, and the goods are not unloaded from the vehicle, the Convention

1370. The CMR Convention was amended by a Protocol in 1978 which involved adopting the SDR (Special Drawing Right) as a measure for placing limits on liability.

1371. *See also* SI No. 160/1991.

1372. Article 1.

still applies.[1373] If, however, loss is caused at sea or air the Convention does not apply if the loss is not caused by the road carrier but by the alternative mode of transport. In that event, the relevant international convention applies and if there is no such convention the CMR Convention applies.[1374]

2. The Consignment Note

764. The principal document when goods are carried by road is the consignment note. The CMR Convention contains various rules in relation to such notes. For example, the contract of carriage must be confirmed by the making out of a consignment note. The consignment note must be made out in three original copies signed by the sender and by the carrier. The first copy is handed to the sender, the second accompanies the goods and the third is retained by the carrier. The consignment note must contain certain particulars including: the date of the consignment note and the place at which it is made out; the name and address of the sender; the name and address of the carrier; the place and the date of taking over of the goods and the place designated for delivery; the name and address of the consignee; the description of the nature of the goods; the number of packages and their special marks and numbers; the gross weight of the goods or their quantity otherwise expressed; charges relating to the carriage; instructions for Customs; and a statement that the carriage is subject to the provisions of this Convention. On taking over the goods, the carrier must check the accuracy of these statements. And senders may be responsible for any damage sustained by the carrier by reason of the inaccuracies in the consignment note.

765. The consignment note is prima facie evidence of the making of the contract of carriage, the conditions of the contract and the receipt of the goods by the carrier. And, where the consignment note contains no specific reservations by the carrier, it shall be presumed, unless the contrary is proved, that the goods and their packaging appeared to be in good condition when the carrier took them over and that the number of packages, their marks and numbers corresponded with the statements in the consignment note.[1375]

3. Duties of the Parties

766. The respective rights and obligation of the parties are to be found of the carriage contract which is usually standard in form drafted by the carrier. Under the CMR Convention, the sender's duties include:

1373. Article 2.

1374. *See further Quantum Corp Inc v. Plane Trucking Ltd* [2002] 1 WLR 2678 where it was held that where there is multimodal transport, the CMR Convention applies to the road part of the journey, even where the contract did not provide for carriage by road.

1375. Article 9.

- making out the consignment note;
- liability for inaccuracies in the consignment note;[1376]
- informing the carrier of dangerous goods;[1377]
- providing necessary document for customs;[1378]
- the payment of freight.

Further to the duties set out in the contract, the Convention imposes certain minimum duties on carriers which cannot be contracted out of. The carrier's duties include:

- an implied duty to provide a roadworthy vehicle;
- an implied duty to carefully handle, stow and carry the goods;
- checking the accuracy of statements in the consignment note and the apparent condition of the goods;[1379]
- delivery of the goods and a copy of the consignment note on arrival;[1380]
- liability for total or partial loss of the goods or for damage caused to the goods en route or for delay.[1381]

4. Restrictions on Carrier's Liability

767. The CMR Convention restricts the carrier's liability in several respects. For example, the carrier is not liable if the loss, damage or delay was caused by the wrongful act or neglect of the claimant; by the instructions of the claimant given otherwise than as the result of a wrongful act or neglect on the part of the carrier; by inherent vice of the goods; or through circumstances which the carrier could not avoid and the consequences of which he/she was unable to prevent.[1382] The period of limitation for an action under the Convention is one year, although in the case of wilful misconduct, the period of limitation is three years.[1383] The Convention also sets a ceiling on damages at 8.33 units of account per kilogram of gross weight short.[1384] Lastly, any stipulation which would directly or indirectly derogate from the provisions of this Convention shall be null and void.[1385]

1376. Article 7.
1377. Article 22.
1378. Article 11.
1379. Article 8.
1380. Article 13.
1381. Article 17.
1382. Article 17. These exclusions do not apply where there is 'wilful misconduct' by the carrier, his agents or servants: Art. 29.
1383. Article 32.
1384. Article 23. Section 6 of the 1990 Act provides that the Central Bank issue a certificate as to the value of the unit of account in Irish currency at any particular time.
1385. Article 41.

B. Carriage by Sea

768. International sales contracts often require the goods to be shipped. Depending on the terms of the sales contract, it may be the seller's or the buyer's duty to arrange shipment of the goods. For the purposes of this subsection, the person who arranges the carriage will be referred to as 'the shipper'. In *Heskell v. Continental Express,*[1386] Devlin J outlined the standard practice when shipping goods. First, the shipper or his/her agent needs to determine when a suitable ship is sailing to the particular port and then, book space on the ship for the goods with the carrier and deliver the goods to the port. On delivering the goods to the carrier, the shipper receives a mate's receipt for the goods and, using this, fills in the details on the bill of lading. Next, the bill of lading is presented to the carrier or his/her representative, who checks the details on the bill against the goods and signs the bill, making any necessary amendments, and issues it to the shipper, in return for the mate's receipt. The shipper forwards the bill, by post, to the person responsible for collecting the goods, the consignee. The consignee may be a buyer or someone acting for the shipper. Finally, the consignee presents the bill of lading to the carrier at the destination: the master of the ship usually will not release the goods without presentation of the bill.

769. Important changes have occurred in practice since *Heskell.* For instance, mates' receipts are not used often today; instead goods are usually forwarded to the port with a Standard Shipping Note or, if necessary, a Dangerous Goods Note containing details of the goods which, when signed, is issued to the shipper as a receipt. Also, it is more common now for the carrier to prepare the bill of lading by computer from the details given by the shipper when booking space on the ship. Indeed, the use of bills of lading has declined, for example, when the voyage is short, where they have been replaced by the sea waybill and especially because of the development of containerization and the use of multimodal transport (combining carriage by road, rail and sea, for example), and multimodal or combined transport documents.

770. Another significant development, with the advent of e-commerce, concerns the replacement of hard copy or paper based bills of lading with electronic bills of lading. Electronic bills of lading bring the prospect of many advantages, including speed, cost savings and efficiency. It is not uncommon, for instance, for the goods to reach the port of destination before the bill of lading but the carrier may not be willing to deliver without presentation of the original bill and so the potential to speed-up this process through the use of electronic bills of lading is a welcome development. The Electronic Commerce Act 2000 ensures that electronic bills of lading cannot be denied legal effect, validity or enforceability merely because the bill is in electronic form.[1387] However, other more practical issues arise. In particular, the use of bills of lading as documents of title depends on the transferability of

1386. [1950] 1 All ER 1033.
1387. Electronic Commerce Act 2000, s. 9.

the physical bill from one person to another, via endorsement of the bill and delivery, or sometimes, by mere delivery. An electronic bill cannot be handled in this way and the virtual nature of the bill therefore inhibits its effectiveness. Different solutions have been promoted in this regard. For example, in 1990, the CMI developed Uniform Rules on Electronic Bills of Lading. More recently, and building on the CMI Rules, the concept of a bill of lading registry has been developed further by BOLERO (Bill of Lading Electronic Registry Organization).[1388] A Bolero bill of lading offers the same functionality as a traditional bill using two basic components. First, the Bolero Bill of Lading (BBL) text which, though in electronic form, looks much like a traditional bill of lading and is issued by the carrier to the shipper, and second, the Title Registry, an electronic database which records all transactions in relation to the bill. This central Registry operates as a trusted third party, using secure electronic messaging and digital signatures. The whole system is regulated by the 'Rulebook', which is agreed to by all parties on becoming members. Therefore, where a Bolero bill of lading is created by the carrier, instructions will be sent electronically to the central Title Registry and the shipper will be recorded as holder of the Bolero bill. If the holder wishes to transfer the bill to another party he does so by attornment whereby the holder sends instructions, again electronically, to the Title Registry to record the name of the new holder. Once these instructions are received, the Registry sends an electronic message confirming the new holder. Only the holder can give such instructions to effect a transfer of the bill. Ultimately, the goods are delivered by the carrier to the last holder of the bill and notice of surrender of the bill is given by the Registry to the carrier. Whether in hard copy form or electronic form, and despite their decreasing use, bills of lading still play a vital role in shipping transactions and therefore warrant further examination.

1. Bills of Lading

771. A bill of lading is a transport document with unique characteristics. It has three functions:

- it evidences the contract of carriage;
- it is a receipt for the goods;
- it is a document of title.

Each of these functions is considered further below.

2. The Contract of Carriage

772. The contract of carriage is concluded between the shipper and the carrier, usually before the goods are shipped, such as when the shipper books space on the

1388. *See* www.bolero.net.

ship or on loading.[1389] Hence, the bill of lading cannot be the contract: but it can evidence the contract. On the back of modern standard form bills are detailed the terms and conditions of carriage, so when the bill is issued or signed by the master it evidences a contract that was previously concluded. More recently, a 'short form' bill has been promoted: here the terms and conditions of carriage are not printed on the back of the short form bill, which is issued to the shipper, but are incorporated by reference to the carrier's standard terms which are available for inspection.

773. In order to regulate the shipment of goods, rules were developed by the international shipping community, which set out the duties and liabilities of the parties to the carriage contract. Today, four different sets of rules (each building on its predecessor) are in force:

- the Hague Rules, 1924;[1390]
- the Hague-Visby Rules, 1968/1979;[1391]
- the Hamburg Rules, 1978;[1392]
- the Rotterdam Rules, 2008.[1393]

Currently, the Hague-Visby Rules are incorporated into Irish law by the Merchant Shipping (Liability of Shipowners and Other) Act 1996.[1394]

a. Application of Hague-Visby Rules

774. Article X of the Hague-Visby Rules and sections 31, 33 and 34 of the Merchant Shipping (Liability of Shipowners and Other) Act 1996 provide for the application of the Rules. Section 31 states that the Rules shall have the force of law in the State,[1395] while Article X provides that the Rules apply:[1396]

to every bill of lading relating to the carriage of goods between ports in two different states if:

1389. *Sewell v. Burdick* (1884) 10 App. Cas. 74 at 105 *per* Lord Bramwell; *Heskell v. Continental Express* [1950] 1 All ER 1033.
1390. The Hague Rules were incorporated into Irish law by the Merchant Shipping Act 1947, s. 13 and the Second Schedule. This legislation is now repealed by the Merchant Shipping (Liability of Shipowners and Other) Act 1996, s. 3 and the Fourth Schedule. By 1977, when the Hague-Visby Rules came into effect, there were more than 60 ratifications and accessions to the Hague Rules.
1391. At the time of writing, thirty states and territories, including Ireland and the U.K. (*see* the Carriage of Goods by Sea Act 1971) have adopted the Hague-Visby Rules.
1392. At the time of writing, thirty-four states have ratified the Hamburg Rules, though the total number of parties to the Rules represent a minute proportion of world trade, being developing counties in the main: *see* Wilson, *Carriage of Goods by Sea* (London: Longman, 7th ed., 2010) Ch. 7.
1393. United Nations Convention on Contracts for the International Carriage of Goods Wholly or Partly by Sea (2008). At the time of writing, the Rotterdam Rules are not in force with only four states having ratified the Convention.
1394. 1996 Act, Part IV and the Third Schedule. The 1996 Act came into force on 6 Feb. 1997: SI No. 215 of 1997.
1395. *See Morviken* [1983] 1 Lloyd's Rep 1, where under English law, the Hague-Visby Rules were held to apply despite a choice of law clause in favour of Dutch law.
1396. *See generally*, Wilson, *Carriage of Goods by Sea*) 174–178 (7th ed., Longman 2010).

- the bill of lading is issued in a Contracting State; or
- the carriage is from a port in a Contracting State; or
- the contract contained in or evidenced in the bill of lading provides that the rules of this Convention or legislation in any State giving effect to them are to govern the contract.

whatever may be the nationality of the ship, the carrier, the shipper, the consignee, or any other interested party.

The Rules clearly envisage an international carriage of goods between ports in two different states but section 34 of the 1996 Act extends the operation of the Rules to cover coastal trade. It would also appear that the Rules do not apply to contracts of carriage where a waybill, or other non-transferable document, is issued because these do not constitute documents of title.[1397] However, section 33(1)(b) of the 1996 Act extends the application of the Rules to any receipt which is a non-transferable document which expressly provides that the Rules are to govern the contract as if the receipt was a bill of lading. Further, section 33(2) extends the application of the Rules to a contract of carriage under a bill of lading or receipt of deck cargo and live animals, although deck cargo and live animals are excluded from the definition of goods under Article I(c) of the Rules.

b. Duties of the Parties

775. The Rules set out the duties of the parties. For example, the Rules require the carrier:

- to exercise due diligence, before, and at the beginning of the voyage to, make the ship seaworthy, properly man, equip and supply the ship and generally make the ship fit and safe for the reception, carriage and preservation of the goods;[1398]
- to properly and carefully load, handle, stow, carry, keep, care for and discharge the goods carried;[1399] and
- on demand from the shipper, to issue a bill of lading showing leading marks of identification; either the number of packages or pieces, or the quantity, or weight; and the apparent order and condition of the goods.[1400]

The shipper, on the other hand, is required not to ship dangerous goods without informing the carrier.[1401]

1397. *See also* Art. I(b) which defines a contract of carriage as a contract covered by a bill of lading or any similar document of title, and *see* the 1996 Act, s. 33(3). The Hague Rules were also limited in their application to bills of lading, and in *Burns & Laird Line Ltd v. Hugh Mack & Co. Ltd* (1944) 78 ILTR 56 it was held that the Hague Rules had no application where goods are not sent under a bill of lading but are shipped under a non-transferable receipt.
1398. Article III, Rule 1.
1399. Article III, Rule 2.
1400. Article III, Rule 3.
1401. Article IV, Rule 6.

c. Restrictions on Carrier's Liability

776. The carrier's liability for breach of the carriage contract is excluded in certain circumstances and can be limited in others. Importantly, Article IV, Rule 2 states that the carrier has no liability for loss or damage arising or resulting from, *inter alia*: act, neglect or default of the master, mariner, pilot or the servants of the carrier in the navigation or in the management of the ship; fire, unless caused by the actual fault or privity of the carrier; perils of the sea; act of God; act of war; act of public enemies; seizure under legal process; quarantine restrictions; act or omission of the shipper; strikes; riots; saving or attempting to save life or property at sea; wastage in bulk or weight arising from inherent defect of the goods; insufficient packing; insufficient marks; latent defects; and any other cause arising without the actual fault or privity of the carrier. Moreover, any deviation in saving or attempting to save life or property at sea or any reasonable deviation is not a breach of contract and the carrier is not responsible for any loss or damage resulting therefrom.[1402]

777. In relation to the limitation of liability, unless the nature and value of the goods has been declared before shipment and entered on the bill of lading, the carrier's liability is limited under Article IV, Rule 5. The financial limit is linked to 'the special drawing right' defined by the International Monetary Fund, a variable sum which tracks inflation, and is calculated on the basis of package or weight.[1403] Lastly, and in order to protect the position of shippers, Article III, Rule 8 provides that any clause relieving or lessening the liability of the carrier, as set out in the Rules, shall be null and void. The limitation period for claims is one year from the delivery of the goods or when they should have been delivered.[1404]

d. Actions Against the Carrier

778. Under a contract of carriage, the carrier is contractually responsible for the care of the goods during transit. If the shipper retains ownership of the goods during the transit and, on discharge, it materializes that some or all of the goods have been lost or damaged, the shipper has a contractual right of action against the carrier on the terms of the contract of carriage. Problems arise, however, where the goods are sold while in transit. Under standard international sale contracts, the buyer bears the risk of loss from the time of shipment, but although he/she may have transferred to him/her a document of title representing the goods, and as a result have constructive possession or ownership of the goods, because, he/she is not privy to the contract of carriage he/she would appear to have no contractual recourse

1402. Article IV, Rule 4.
1403. Article IV, Rule 5, and 1996 Act, s. 36.
1404. Article III, Rule 6.

against the carrier. In these circumstances, the buyer can pursue a claim under a number of different heads, including under section 1 of the Bills of Lading Act 1855, and at common law.[1405]

779. The Bills of Lading Act 1855 was passed to remedy the above privity of contract problem by conferring on the buyer a contractual right of action. Section 1 provides:

> Every consignee of goods named in a bill of lading, and every endorsee of a bill of lading to whom the property in the goods therein mentioned shall pass, upon or by reason of such consignment or endorsement, shall have transferred to and vested in him all rights of suit, and be subject to the same liabilities in respect of such goods as if the contract contained in the bill of lading had been made with himself.

However, this provision has a number of limitations. For example, it only operates where 'the property' passes to a consignee or an endorsee and so a pledgee of goods does not acquire 'the property' and hence cannot pursue an action against the carrier based on the contract.[1406] Moreover, section 1 requires that property must pass 'upon or by reason of such consignment or endorsement'. Thus if property passes before, or independently of consignment or endorsement, it has been held that section 1 does not apply.[1407] Therefore, no right of action would arise where goods are shipped in bulk and no property can be passed until the buyer's goods are separated from the bulk, usually at the port of destination,[1408] or where a buyer of goods forming part of a bulk receives no goods at all;[1409] or where the bill is endorsed subject to a retention of title clause, whereby property passes on payment of the price.[1410] Lastly, section 1 of the Bills of Lading Act is limited in its application today because it applies only where bills of lading are consigned or endorsed. Where other shipping documents are used, such as waybills, multimodal transport documents or delivery orders, a buyer must resort to other causes of action, and not always with success.

780. Due to these deficiencies in section 1 of the 1855 Act, alternative causes of action have been recognized. In particular, it is long-established that where a consignee takes delivery of goods from the carrier, by presenting the bill of lading and paying outstanding charges, a contract on the terms of the bill of lading may be

1405. Since goods are normally covered by insurance against loss and damage while in transit, the problems of liability and title to sue are largely faced by insurers and not traders, as a result of the doctrine of subrogation in insurance law: *see generally* paras 717–718.
1406. *Sewell v. Burdick* (1884) 10 App. Cas. 74 involved a bank as pledge. Following this case, doubts also exist about the position of mortgagees.
1407. *The Delfini* [1990] 1 Lloyd's Rep 252. In this case the endorsement happened eleven days after the goods were delivered and the endorsement was not linked to the passing of property.
1408. Sale of Goods Act 1893, s. 16; *see* paras 598–602.
1409. *The Aramis* [1989] 1 Lloyd's Rep 213.
1410. *The Alkiamon* [1986] AC 785; [1986] 2 All ER 145.

implied between consignee and carrier.[1411] Such contracts are often referred to as 'Brandt contracts' after the leading case of *Brandt v. Liverpool, Brazil and River Steam Navigation Co Ltd*.[1412] Alternatively, where contract rights are vested in the shipper, those rights may be assigned to the consignee as choses in action under section 28(6) of the Supreme Court of Judicature (Ireland) Act 1877. However, technicalities as to form, notice and procedure make this an unpopular option. Moreover, an assignment requires the shipper's co-operation. A consignee who bears the risk of loss of or damage to goods may be able to sue the carrier in tort; however, such an action will only succeed if the consignee had property in or an immediate right to possession of the goods at the time when the damage occurred.[1413] Further, under the rule in *Dunlop v. Lambert*,[1414] the shipper may enforce his/her right of action against the carrier for the benefit of the consignee where the latter bears the risk of loss or damage to the goods.[1415]

3. A Receipt

781. It has been stated that a ship must 'deliver what she receives, as she receives it'.[1416] This means that if the goods are lost or damaged while in transit, the carrier may be liable. In order for a shipper or his/her consignee to pursue such a claim, it is necessary to know the quantity and condition of the goods on receipt by the carrier or on shipment. Also, if a shipper is planning to deal with goods while they are at sea, by selling or pledging them, for instance, he/she will require some form of evidence that proves that the goods exist and provides details as to the quantity and condition of the goods. Written records are relied on as evidence for these purposes, the most important being the bill of lading.

782. When the Hague-Visby Rules apply, the shipper is entitled to demand from the carrier a bill of lading showing, *inter alia*:

(a) leading marks of identification;
(b) either the number of packages or pieces, or the quantity, or weight; and
(c) the apparent order and condition of the goods.[1417]

1411. *Cock v. Taylor* (1811) 12 East 399; *Stindt v. Roberts* (1845) 17 LJ QB 166; *Allen v. Coltart* (1883) 11 QBD 782. While this point has not been judicially considered in Ireland, contracts have been implied between parties originally outside the bargain, *see*, e.g., *Fox v. Higgins* (1912) 46 ILTR 222 (HC).

1412. [1924] 1 KB 575; but *see The Aliakmon* [1986] 2 All ER 145 where no contract was implied because the buyer was found to have presented the bill as agent for the seller; and *The Aramis* [1989] 1 Lloyd's Rep 213 where no contract was implied because freight was prepaid.

1413. *See Margarine Union v. Cambay Princes* [1969] 1 QB 219.

1414. (1839) 6 Cl & F 600.

1415. However, the scope of this rule as been restricted by the decision in *The Albezero* [1977] AC 774, where the House of Lords held that where s. 1 of the 1855 Act applied, this rule could no longer be utilized. In this case, the right of action under s. 1 was time barred.

1416. *FC Bradley & Son Ld v. Federal Steam Navigation Co. Ld* (1927) 27 Ll L Rep 395 at 396, *per* Lord Sumner.

1417. Article III, Rule 3.

In return, the shipper is deemed to have guaranteed to the carrier the accuracy of any information supplied by him/her for incorporation in the bill and the shipper is required to indemnify the carrier against any loss, damages or expenses arising from any such inaccuracies.[1418] A shipper should therefore always demand a bill with these details but a carrier can refuse to issue a bill with such information where he/she has reasonable grounds for suspecting that the information supplied is inaccurate or where he/she has no reasonable means of checking.[1419] The evidential status of the bill of lading is addressed in the Hague-Visby Rules, as adopted by the Merchant Shipping (Liability of Shipowners and Others) Act 1996 and at common law, as amended by the Bills of Lading Act 1855.

783. The Hague-Visby Rules provide that a bill of lading is prima facie evidence of the quantity and apparent condition of the goods at the time of loading. As this raises only a presumption, the carrier can produce evidence to dispute any statements in the bill.[1420] However, proof to the contrary is inadmissible when the bill of lading is transferred to a third party acting in good faith. In these circumstances, the bill is *conclusive* evidence as to the quantity and apparent condition of the goods.

784. Where the Hague-Visby rules do not apply, the matter is dealt with at common law, as amended by section 3 of the Bill of Lading Act 1855. Accordingly, in the hands of the original shipper, statements in the bill as to quantity and condition are prima facie evidence. However, once the bill comes into the hands of a third party, statements as to the *condition* of the goods are binding on the carrier. If a bill states that the goods are loaded in ‘good order and condition’, the carrier is estopped from denying the truth of this statement.[1421] This estoppel operates only in favour of a transferee who takes the bill for value in good faith and relies on it. However, if the bill is claused, that is, there is an annotation on the bill to the effect that the goods are in some way defective, the carrier can raise evidence to prove the condition of the goods loaded.

785. The position as regards statements as to *quantity* is different. It was decided in *Grant v. Norway* [1422] that a ship’s master has no authority to sign a bill where goods were not actually loaded. Hence, where the bill overstates the quantity loaded or states that no goods were loaded at all, the carrier may dispute the statement in the bill as to the amount shipped. Today, it is widely recognized that *Grant v. Norway* is inconsistent with general agency principles,[1423] and indeed the courts have

1418. Article III, Rule 5.
1419. Article III, Rule 3.
1420. *Smith v. Bedouin Steam Navigation Co.* [1896] AC 70.
1421. *Compania Naviera Vasconzada v. Churchill and Sim* [1906] 1 KB 237.
1422. (1851) 10 CB 665.
1423. *See*, e.g., *Lloyd v. Grace Smith & Co.* [1912] AC 716 where the House of Lords held that a firm of solicitors was responsible for the fraud of its agent; *see further* Reynolds, ‘Warranty of Authority’, *Law Quarterly Review* (1967): 189.

gone to great lengths to avoid its strict application.[1424] Section 3 of the Bills of Lading Act 1855 was intended to solve the problem of *Grant v. Norway* by providing that the bill should:

> be conclusive evidence of such shipment as against the master or other person signing the same.

However, section 3 is fundamentally flawed. It does not make the bill conclusive evidence against the carrier but only against the master or other signatory, against whom there is usually no cause of action, since such people are rarely contractually liable. Even if the master was personally liable, he/she does not have the same deep pocket as the carrier.

4. A Document of Title

786. A bill of lading performs a third important function. In *Lickbarrow v. Mason,*[1425] a bill of lading was recognized as a document of title, because, in practice, it was treated as such. The bill of lading thus symbolizes the goods, and proper transfer of the bill affects a transfer of property in or ownership of the goods.[1426]

C. Carriage by Air

787. The law regarding air transport is concerned mainly with the position of passengers and their belongings. However, more recently, where goods are compact and high value, air transport has become a more common form for the transport of goods. As noted above, the rights and duties between the parties derive primarily from the contract of carriage. However, there is no equivalent to the Bills of Lading Act 1855,[1427] as regard air carriage and also the courts have not resorted to implying a *Brandt v. Liverpool* type contract, for the benefit of third parties.[1428]

1. The Montreal Convention

788. The main incidents of carriage by air are regulated by international treaty to a greater extent than carriage by sea. The Warsaw Convention (1929) sought to harmonize the law in this regard and strike a balance between the various interested parties.[1429] The Convention has been amended on numerous occasions:[1430] most

1424. The master may be held liable for breach of warranty of authority: *see Rasnoimport v. Guthrie & Co. Ltd* [1966] 1 Lloyd's Rep 1, and 6.4.5; or possibly for negligent misstatement.
1425. (1794) 5 TR 683.
1426. *Bateman v. Green* (1868) IR 2 CL 166.
1427. *See* para. 749 above.
1428. *See* para. 750 above.
1429. Incorporated in Irish law in the Air Navigation and Transport Act 1936.

recently in 1999 a new draft convention on carriage of goods (and passengers and baggage) by air was adopted, in Montreal (known as the Montreal Convention). Ireland has adopted the Montreal Convention in the Air Navigation and Transport (International Conventions) Act 2004.[1431] Under section 4 of the 2004 Act, the applicable provisions of the Carriage by Air Conventions have the force of law in the State in relation to any carriage by air to which they apply, irrespective of the nationality of the aircraft performing that carriage, and if more than one of the Carriage by Air Conventions applies to a carriage by air, the applicable provisions that have the force of law in the State are those of whichever is the most recent applicable Convention in force. The Montreal Convention came into force on 4 November 2003.[1432]

a. Application

789. The Montreal Convention applies to all international carriage of persons, baggage or cargo performed by aircraft for reward. It also applies to gratuitous carriage. Carriage is international where, under the agreement,[1433] the place of departure and the place of destination, whether or not there be a break in the carriage or a transhipment, are situated either within the territories of two contracting States, or within the territory of a single contracting State if there is an agreed stopping place within the territory of another State, even if that State is not a contracting State.[1434] Therefore, carriage by air entirely within one State, and carriage to and from a State which is not a party to the Convention and which does not stop over in another State is excluded by the scope of the Convention.

b. Air Waybills

790. The principal document issued when goods are transported by air is the air waybill.[1435] Where goods are being transported by air, an air waybill must be delivered. Alternatives may be provided and, if requested by the consignor, a cargo receipt may be substituted. The waybill or receipt must include: an indication of the places of departure and destination; if the flight is between two points within one State, an indication of at least one stopping place outside the State; and an indication of the weight of the consignment. The air waybill must be made out by the consignor in three original parts: the first part must be marked 'for the carrier' and is signed by the consignor; the second part is marked 'for the consignee' and must be signed by the consignor and by the carrier; and the third part must be signed by the carrier and it is to be handed to the consignor after the cargo has been accepted. The

---

1430. *See further* the Air Navigation and Transport Act 1959, 1965 and 1988.
1431. *See also* SI No. 390 of 2010.
1432. Sixty days following the deposit by the United States of America of the required thirtieth instrument of ratification.
1433. *Grein v. Imperial Airways Ltd* [1937] 1 KB 50, in determining whether a carriage is international, the courts focus on the contract as agreed as opposed to the actual journey taken.
1434. Article 1.
1435. *See further* Arts 4–16.

consignor is responsible for the correctness of the particulars and statements relating to the cargo in the air waybill and the consignor must indemnify the carrier against all damage suffered, due to the irregularity, incorrectness or incompleteness of the particulars and statements furnished by the consignor.

791. Like bills of lading, the air waybill or the cargo receipt is prima facie evidence of the conclusion of the contract, of the acceptance of the cargo and of the conditions of carriage. Moreover, any statements in the air waybill or the cargo receipt relating to the weight, dimensions and packing of the cargo, as well as those relating to the number of packages, are prima facie evidence of the facts stated. However, statements relating to the quantity, volume and condition of the cargo do not constitute evidence against the carrier except so far as they both have been, and are stated in the air waybill or the cargo receipt to have been, checked by it in the presence of the consignor, or relate to the apparent condition of the cargo. Unlike bills of lading, the air waybill is not recognized, by statute or otherwise, as a document of title to the goods. However, this is not particularly problematic given the speed of air transport.

c. Duties of the Parties

792. The respective rights and obligation of the parties are to be found in the carriage contract which is usually standard in form and drafted by the carrier. Under the Montreal Convention, the consignor's duties include:

- making out the air waybill in three original parts, although the carrier may do this on the consignor's behalf;
- disclosing any dangerous goods;
- supplying any information and documentation necessary in relation to customs;
- indemnifying the carrier as a result of providing wrong information; and the payment of freight.

793. Further to the duties set out in the contract, the Convention imposes certain minimum duties on carriers which cannot be contracted out of. The carrier's duties include:

- an implied duty to provide an airworthy aircraft;
- an implied duty to carefully handle, stow and carry the goods;
- liability for damage sustained because of destruction, loss or damage to cargo, if caused during transit; liability for delay.[1436]

d. Restrictions on Carrier's Liability

794. As regards damage to cargo, the carrier is not liable where the loss resulted from inherent defect, quality or vice of that cargo; defective packing of that cargo performed by a person other than the carrier or its servants or agents; an act of war

1436. Articles 18–19.

or an armed conflict; or an act of public authority carried out in connection with the entry, exit or transit of the cargo.[1437] In relation to delay, the carrier is not be liable for damage occasioned by delay where he/she took all measures that could reasonably be required to avoid the damage or that it was impossible for it or them to take such measures.[1438] Moreover, if the carrier proves that the damage was caused or contributed to by the negligence of the person claiming compensation, the carrier shall be wholly or partly exonerated from its liability to the claimant to the extent that such negligence caused or contributed to the damage.[1439]

795. There are two distinct aspects to the limitation of actions under the Convention. First, there must be timely notice of any complaint. Accordingly, in the case of damage, the person entitled to delivery must complain to the carrier within fourteen days from the date of receipt, in the case of cargo. As regards delay, the complaint must be made at the latest within twenty-one days from the date on which the cargo has been placed at his/her disposal. Moreover, every complaint must be made in writing.[1440] Second, any right to damages is extinguished if an action is not brought within a period of two years, from the date of arrival at the destination, or from the date on which the aircraft ought to have arrived, or from the date on which the carriage stopped.[1441] The Convention provides various financial limits on liability. For example, in relation to the carriage of cargo, the liability of the carrier in the case of destruction, loss, damage or delay is limited to a sum of seventeen Special Drawing Rights per kilogram.[1442] Further, any provision tending to relieve the carrier of liability or to fix a lower limit than that which is laid down in this Convention shall be null and void.[1443]

1437. Article 18.
1438. Article 19.
1439. Article 20.
1440. Article 31.
1441. Article 35.
1442. Article 22.
1443. Article 26.

Chapter 10. Commercial Securities

796. The ingenuity of the commercial community is well illustrated by the variety of arrangements it has developed to fulfil a creditor's need for security. One of the most valuable forms of security is a mortgage or charge over land. The entire question of land charges is very specialized and is ordinarily regarded as falling outside the province of commercial law, even though that form of security can be a vital feature of major commercial transactions.[1444] In this chapter, first, consideration is given to the different types of security, including quasi-security interests, before examining the various forms of real security (pledges, liens, mortgages and charges) and personal security (including guarantees and indemnities).

§1. Types of Security

797. Essentially, security can be *real* or *personal*. Real security gives the creditor real, proprietary rights over some or all of the debtor's assets. Such proprietary rights can be consensual, that is, based on an agreement between the parties, as where a person pledges his/her goods to another as security for a loan; or, they may be non-consensual and arise by operation of the law, as with an unpaid seller's lien. Moreover, real securities can be *possessory*, in the sense that it depends on the creditor having possession of the property over which the security exists (e.g., pledges and liens). Alternatively, real security can be *non-possessory*, that is, it is not dependent on possession by the creditor, as where the creditor has a mortgage or charge over the debtor's property but the debtor remains in possession of the property. The detailed rights of a creditor with real security vary depending on the type of security but essentially all real security allows the creditor to retain or take possession of the property in question, and ultimately to have it sold and the proceeds applied to satisfy his/her debt. In contrast, personal security involves a third party to the contract between the debtor and the creditor entering into a separate contract with the creditor and undertaking responsibility for the debt if the debtor defaults as is the case under a contract of guarantee, or indemnifying the creditor against losses caused by the debtor's failure to perform.

798. Real security protects against the debtor's insolvency by providing the creditor with real rights over the debtor's assets, offering the creditor priority if the debtor becomes insolvent. The effectiveness of personal security will depend on the creditworthiness of the guarantor. For this reason a personal security is often reinforced by requiring the guarantor to grant real security over his/her assets to secure the guarantee.

1444. For mortgages of land *see generally* Lyall, *Land Law in Ireland* (4th ed., Round Hall Sweet & Maxwell 2018); Wylie, *Irish Land Law*, Part V (5th ed., Bloomsbury 2013); and Pearse & Mee, *Land Law*, Ch 18 (3rd ed., Thomson Reuters Round Hall 2011).

I. Quasi-Security

799. A number of other arrangements are available to provide a creditor with 'security' against the debtor's non-payment or insolvency. In particular, a seller who supplies goods on credit terms can protect his/her interests by utilizing the rules on passing of property.[1445] Reservation of ownership under a conditional sale, hire purchase or similar arrangements allow the supplier to retake the goods if the debtor fails to pay and gives him/her priority over the debtor's other creditors if the debtor becomes insolvent. The practical effect of these arrangements is therefore to grant the supplier security; however, the courts have tended not to regard them as security devices so that they avoid the formality and registration requirements which apply to some security interests. For this reason, such devices can be referred to as 'quasi-security'.

A. Retention of Title Devices

800. A supplier of goods on credit terms can secure himself/herself against the buyer's inability to pay by supplying the goods under an arrangement by which he/she reserves ownership of the goods until their price is paid. Such arrangements include hire purchase agreements, conditional sale arrangements and finance leases.

1. Hire Purchase

801. Under a hire purchase agreement the owner/creditor retains property in the goods until all sums due are paid by the hirer/debtor. If the hirer/debtor becomes insolvent before this time, the owner/creditor can reclaim his/her property before it is realized to meet the claims of other creditors.

2. Conditional Sale Arrangements

802. Similarly, under a conditional sale, property in the goods does not pass to the buyer until the condition is met: typically, until the price is paid in full. A sale subject to a reservation of title clause is a conditional sale, expressly sanctioned by section 19(2) of the Sale of Goods Act 1893.[1446] It is now standard practice for sellers to include a clause to the effect that the property in the goods will not pass from the seller to the buyer until the price is paid. If the buyer/debtor becomes insolvent before the price has been paid, the seller/creditor can demand the redelivery of his/her goods. Again, the goods cannot be realized to meet the claims of other creditors. A number of attempts have been made to challenge the effectiveness of reservation of title clauses and argue that they create registrable charges. It is now settled that a simple clause which reserves title in goods until their price is paid does

1445. *See further* paras 590–603.
1446. *See generally* paras 577–589.

not create a charge.[1447] The seller may even reserve property in goods supplied as security for payment of other debts.[1448] Attempts to claim rights over property other than the goods supplied may be construed as creating a charge, however.[1449]

3. Finance Leases[1450]

803. Under a lease the owner of goods (the lessor) transfers possession of the goods to a hirer (the lessee), for use by the lessee, in return for payment, while retaining ownership. Since ownership is retained, the lessor can repossess the goods if the lessee defaults, and is thus effectively granted some security against the lessee's default and insolvency.

804. Leases can be classified as operating leases or finance leases. An operating lease usually involves goods being hired out to a series of different lessees in return for payment of rental; it can be used for a variety of arrangements – anything from the hire of a car for a day, to a five-year lease of an airplane. The owner/lessor is often responsible for such things as maintenance and repair of the goods. A finance lease, on the other hand, is viewed as a financial tool where the retention of ownership is nominal. Here the goods (usually equipment) are acquired by the owner/lessor and hired out for a period equivalent to the working life of the equipment, to one lessee, who is responsible for their maintenance. The rental is calculated so that the owner/lessor will recoup the cost of the goods and a profit. In effect, therefore, the lessor provides financial assistance to the lessee to acquire the goods while the lease provides the lessor with security against the lessee's default. Commercially, such an arrangement achieves much the same effect as a secured credit sale of the goods but it is not recognized at law as creating a security interest.

4. Sale with a Right to Re-purchase

805. This involves a transaction whereby X sells goods to Y, payment to be by instalments. X and Y also agree that if Y defaults on the instalments, X has the right to purchase back the goods, setting off the amount outstanding against the re-purchase price. Although this resembles a mortgage arrangement, if genuine, it will be regarded as a sale. It has been held that there are three points of distinction between a sale and a mortgage or charge:

1447. *Frigoscandia Ltd v. Continental Irish Meat Ltd* [1982] ILRM 396; *Clough Mill v. Martin* [1984] 3 All ER 982, [1985] 1 WLR 111.

1448. *Armour v. Thyssen Edelstahlwerke GmbH* [1990] 3 All ER 481; *see further* para. 589.

1449. *See generally* para. 586.

1450. Further to the International Interests in Mobile Equipment (Cape Town Convention) Act 2005, Ireland was the first Member State of the EU to ratify the Cape Town Convention and the Aircraft Protocol: the International Registry is based in Dublin. *See also* the UNIDROIT Convention on International Finance Leasing (1988) at www.unidroit.org. *See further*, Goode, *Commercial Law*, Ch. 28 (5th ed., Penguin 2016).

(a) under a sale the vendor is not entitled to get back the subject matter of the sale by returning the purchase price; in the case of a mortgage or charge, the mortgagor is entitled, until he/she has been foreclosed, to recover the subject matter of the mortgage or charge on payment of the debt;
(b) if a buyer resells the subject matter of the sale at a profit, that profit is his/her; a mortgagee who realizes the subject matter of the mortgage for a sum greater than is sufficient to repay himself/herself, must account to the mortgagor for the surplus;
(c) a buyer who resells the goods at a loss must bear that loss; but a mortgagee who realizes the subject matter for a sum insufficient to satisfy his/her debt is entitled to look to the mortgagor to make good the balance.[1451]

B. Use of Assets as Quasi-Security

806. There are a number of arrangements which may be used by a business that wishes to raise finance using its assets as security, but without entering into formal legal security arrangements.

1. Sale and Lease-Back

807. Instead of agreeing a mortgage, an owner may sell goods to a finance house, for the purpose of raising funds, and then take them back under a lease, hire purchase or conditional sale agreement. He/she thus has use of the goods and use of their capital value. The effect is very similar to a mortgage of the goods to secure a loan but a genuine sale and lease-back is a valid transaction and is not regarded as a disguised mortgage. Under a variant on this arrangement the goods are leased back not to the original owner but to his/her nominee. Alternatively, the owner may sell the goods to a dealer who then sells them to a finance house which leases them back to the original owner on hire purchase: a refinancing transaction.

2. Discounting of Receivables

808. Just as a business may use its tangible property to obtain financial accommodation in a quasi-security arrangement, it can use its intangible property in the same way. It may sell its receivables (future debts and other obligations owed by third parties) to a creditor in return for an immediate cash payment. Since the creditor is providing a cash advance against future receivables, it will pay less than the full face value of the debts, which are thus said to be 'discounted'; it may also discount to cover the risk of non-payment. The borrower may be required to guarantee

1451. *Re George Inglefield Ltd.* [1933] Ch. 1 at 27, *per* Romer LJ.

payment of the assigned debts. A genuine discounting arrangement does not create a charge, even though its effect is to provide security for a cash advance.[1452]

3. Bills of Exchange

809. Because a bill of exchange creates a contractually binding obligation to pay money which is separate from any underlying contract in connection with which it is given, bills may be used as an alternative to, or to reinforce, other security. For instance, a creditor providing a loan to a debtor may require the debtor to accept bills of exchange for the instalments of the loan; if there is doubt about the debtor's ability to meet the repayments, the creditor could require the debtor to have the bills accepted by some creditworthy third party, such as a bank.[1453]

4. Set-Off Agreements

810. It is common in commercial contracts, where there is a payment obligation on one party, to find a provision which allows that party to set-off against the sum he/she is obliged to pay under the contract, any amount owing to him/her by the other. This contractual right of set-off can operate in a similar fashion to a security but in law it does not create a security interest. It establishes no rights over the creditor's assets but is merely an entitlement to set-off one personal obligation against another: it therefore does not need to be registered.

§2. Real Security

811. The provision of real security involves the creditor obtaining proprietary rights over the property of the debtor. Real security, therefore, gives the debtor an incentive to pay the debt in order to recover his/her property unencumbered. This may be particularly powerful if the property in question is worth more (to the debtor) than the amount of the debt. In this section, we examine the main forms of real security: pledges, liens, mortgages and charges, in relation to personal property and, in particular, goods.[1454] Essentially, pledges and liens are based purely on the common law idea of possession. A mortgage involves the transfer of ownership and can be legal or equitable. A charge, recognized only in equity, is a type of encumbrance on property and may exist in fixed or floating form. We also consider briefly the current system of statutory control regarding the granting of security over personal property.

1452. *Lloyds and Scottish Finance Ltd. v. Cyril Lord Carpets Sales Ltd.* [1979] 129 NLJ 366, [1992] BCLC 609.

1453. *See generally* paras 308–309.

1454. *See further* Breslin, J. & Corcoran, E. *Banking Law* (4th ed., Round Hall 2018); Donnelly, M. *The Law of Credit and Security* (2nd ed., Thomson Round Hall 2015); Bridge et al., *The Law of Personal Property* (2nd ed., Sweet & Maxwell 2017), Ch. 15.

812. As noted above, real security may be classified as possessory or non-possessory. Non-possessory security will be preferable where the debtor needs access to the property to be used as security, for instance, plant and machinery, and is therefore not in a position to transfer possession of it. However, non-possessory securities tend to be subject to a higher degree of statutory control, especially in order to protect third parties. Where a debtor is left in possession of property which is in fact subject to a security interest in favour of a creditor, other potential creditors may believe him/her to be the unencumbered owner of that property and thus be misled as to his/her creditworthiness. In order to avoid the creation of this false impression, non-possessory securities generally have to be registered.[1455]

I. Pledge

813. A pledge is a type of real security which involves a debtor (the pledgor) delivering goods to a creditor (the pledgee) who has the right to retain possession of the goods as security until payment of a debt or until discharge of another obligation upon an express or implied undertaking that the goods shall be restored to the pledgor as soon as the debt or other obligation is met. Pledges are commonly used in commerce; for example, where a buyer of goods under an international sale contract pledges a bill of lading to a bank as security for an advance of money to pay for them.

A. Possession

814. Since a pledge involves the transfer of possession to the pledgee, it gives the pledgee a special property in the goods.[1456] The pledgee is a bailee of the goods for the pledgor and therefore owes the pledgor a duty of care.[1457] The pledgee's possession of the goods can be actual or constructive.[1458] However, if the creditor has only a contractual right to seize the goods to secure a debt, the contract will amount to a security bill of sale or a charge which will be void unless the relevant registration and formality requirements, under the bills of sales or companies legislation, are satisfied.[1459]

815. Actual possession of the goods brings with it the expense of storage and insurance, so the pledgee should make express provision in the pledge agreement that such costs are to be met by the pledgor. As a bailee of the goods, the pledgee is liable for loss of or damage to the goods caused by his/her negligence and the burden of proof is reversed so that the pledgee/bailee must prove that he/she was

1455. Bills of Sale (Ireland) Acts 1879–1883; Companies Act 2014; *see further* paras 809–821.
1456. *Carter v. Wake* (1877) 4 Ch D 605; *Sewell v. Burdick* (1884) 10 App. Cas. 74.
1457. *Coggs v. Bernard* (1703) 2 Ld Raym 909.
1458. *Dublin City Distillery Ltd v. Doherty* [1914] AC 823; Official *Assignee of Madras v. Mercantile Bank of India* [1935] AC 53.
1459. *Dublin City Distillery Ltd v. Doherty* [1914] AC 823.

not negligent. Today, it is far more usual for the pledgee to have constructive possession of the goods, for example, by having possession of a bill of lading which is recognized as a document of title to the goods while the goods are at sea.

816. The main limitation of this type of security is that it is dependent on possession (actual or constructive) and so not applicable to intangible property which cannot be possessed in the physical sense. Other means of security, such as a mortgage or charge, fulfil this function. Moreover, if the pledge agreement allows the pledgor to retain some control over the goods, the pledgee's security may be destroyed.

B. Creation and Formation

817. As a form of consensual security, a pledge is created by the agreement of the parties. Registration is not required: the very fact of possession is sufficient evidence of the pledge and puts third parties on notice of the pledgee's interest. No formality is required for creation of a pledge. However, it is standard banking practice to require the pledgor to sign a document such as a 'letter of pledge'. A letter of pledge may include terms by which:

- the pledgor agrees that the pledgee is to have a pledge over all goods or documents of title delivered by the pledgor or his/her agent into the possession of the pledgee or his/her agent;
- where the credit provided is a revolving facility, the pledgor agrees that the goods and documents are pledged as continuing security for the payment of all sums owed by the pledgor from time to time;
- the pledgor agrees that in the case of his/her default in repayment of any sum or sums on demand, the pledgee has the right to immediate actual possession of the goods and to sell the goods or any part of them, [X] days after the default;
- the pledgor agrees to keep the goods fully insured to their full value, with such persons as the pledgee may approve and provide proof of such insurance, the customer further agrees to notify the insurers of the pledgee's interest in the goods;
- the pledgor agrees to pay all the costs of storage of the goods;
- all risk of loss of or damage to the goods remains, at all times, with the pledgor whether the goods are in his/her possession, the pledgee's possession or the possession of a third party.

C. Power of Sale

818. If the debt is not paid by the date fixed by the pledge agreement, the pledgee can sell the goods.[1460] If no date is stipulated the pledge must be redeemed within a reasonable time. A sale by the pledgee must be reasonable in that the goods

1460. *Ex p Hubbard* (1866) 17 QBD 699; *Re Morritt* (1886) 18 QBD 222.

must be sold at a reasonable price. The pledgee must account to the pledgor for any monies received on the sale in excess of the debt after the costs of selling have been reimbursed.[1461] If the sale fails to meet the debt in full, the pledgee may pursue the pledgor personally for the amount outstanding.[1462]

D. *Termination of the Pledge*

819. In the normal course of events, the pledgee's interest terminates when the underlying debt is paid, thereby releasing the security. A pledgee may also waive his/her rights by, for example, returning the goods to the possession of the pledgor and hence terminate the pledge. Or, a pledge may be terminated where the pledgee breaches an important term of the pledge agreement, for instance, by intentional destruction of the goods. This will rarely occur. Dealing with the goods does not destroy the pledge. Use of the goods by the pledgee may not amount to a breach, at least where use does not adversely affect the goods, although use may be a breach if the goods are adversely affected. In *Cooke v. Hadden,*[1463] the pledge was destroyed when the pledgee of champagne started drinking it! Generally, pledges are not affected by lapse of time. Thus the pledgee's rights under the pledge remain even if the debt secured by the pledge is time barred. Equally, the pledgor can reclaim the goods on payment of the barred debt. However, lapse of time may amount to a waiver.

II. Lien

820. A lien is a relatively primitive form of real security. Essentially, it entitles a person (the lienee) who has provided services for another (the lienor), to retain possession of the lienor's goods or documents until the charges for the services have been paid.[1464] The lienee is said to have a right of retention; hence, it is a 'self-help remedy'.[1465] While the goods are in the lienee's possession, he/she is a bailee of those goods; hence, if the goods are lost or damaged as a result of his/her negligence, he/she will be liable for that loss and the burden of proving that he/she was not negligent rests with him/her.

A. *Types of Lien*

821. Liens derive from many sources including the common law, contract, equity, statute and maritime law. A lien may also be described as general or specific (particular): the former being the rarer case.

1461. *Halliday v. Holgate* (1868) LR 3 Ex 299.
1462. *Jones v. Marshall* (1889) 24 QBD 269.
1463. (1862) 3 F&F 229.
1464. *Re Barrett Apartments Ltd* [1985] IR 350 at 357, [1985] ILRM 679 at 681 *per* Henchy J.
1465. *Tappenden v. Artus* [1964] 2 QB 185.

1. Common Law Lien

822. The common law has recognized that practitioners of certain trades or callings (especially those pursuing 'common callings'[1466]) may have a lien over their customers' property. This is a non-consensual form of security which arises by operation of the law. Examples of common law liens include a ship's master's lien on cargo for freight or on luggage for passage,[1467] an innkeeper's (or hotelier's) lien over a guest's belongings for sums due,[1468] and a repairer's lien over goods repaired for the cost of the repair. It is hard to imagine this common law entitlement being extended to new relationships today.[1469]

823. Possession of the goods by the lienee is essential both for the creation and continued existence of a common law lien.[1470] Generally, the lienee must have an immediate right to possession so that if payment is tendered, at any time, the goods can be immediately returned to the lienor, their owner. Hence, a lien, unlike a pledge, cannot be transferred,[1471] and hence in this respect is weaker than a pledge interest.[1472] Although the common law lien is non-consensual, the terms of a contract may prevent a lien arising if it appears that the parties intended that the goods should not be retained until payment.[1473]

2. Contractual Lien

824. A right of lien may be reserved by contract and any provider of services may find it useful to include such a lien in its contracts of supply as a means of reinforcing its common law rights. Such a term may be implied following a course of dealing or trade custom, but it is preferable that it be expressly provided for. A contractual lien should include an express right to sell.[1474]

1466. In mediaeval times, certain 'service providers' were obliged to render services to the public on demand, such as the common callings of innkeepers, ferrymen, and common carriers, accordingly, they were entitled to a lien for their services.
1467. *The Princess Royal* (1859) 5 IR Jur (ns) 74; *Belfast Harbour Commissioners v. Lawther* (1866) 17 Ir Ch R 54.
1468. *See* now Hotel Proprietor's Act 1963, s. 8. The 1963 Act repeals the Innkeeper's Act 1878: 1963 Act, s. 13 and Second Schedule.
1469. Bridge, *Personal Property Law*, 134 (3rd ed., Oxford U. Press 2002).
1470. *ESSI v. Crown Shipping (Ireland) Ltd* [1991] ILRM 97.
1471. *Legg v. Evans* (1840) 6 M & W 36.
1472. *Donald v. Suckling* (1866) LR 1 QB 585.
1473. In *Wilson v. Lombard Ltd* [1963] 1 WLR 1294 a car mechanic was held to have no lien over a car because the cost of repair was to be charged to the customer's account.
1474. *See*, e.g., *De Lorean Motor Car Ltd v. Northern Ireland Carriers Ltd* [1982] NI 163.

3. Equitable Lien

825. Possession is not necessary for an equitable lien. For instance, the vendor of land has a lien to secure the purchase price,[1475] and the purchaser has a lien to secure repayment of the price if the transaction falls through.[1476] The seller of intangible property, including shares, debts and intellectual property, also has an equitable lien over the property to secure the price, but the unpaid seller of goods has no such lien.[1477] Where a creditor is given a non-possessory equitable lien over *goods* not in his/her possession, this will amount to a security bill of sale which will be void if not formed and registered in accordance with the bills of sale legislation.[1478]

4. Statutory Lien

826. Certain statutes grant creditors liens or similar rights. The most important example of a statutory lien is to be found in sections 41–43 of the Sale of Goods Act, 1893 which provide that a seller of goods who has not been paid has the right to retain the goods even though property in the goods has passed to the buyer.[1479]

5. General or Specific Liens

827. A lien may be general or specific (particular). A general lien allows the creditor to retain possession of any property of the debtor until any debt due from the debtor is paid. Solicitors, bankers, factors, insurance brokers and stockbrokers have all been recognized as having general liens over their client's papers for all sums owing for professional services rendered as a matter of usage. The lien is general in that it is not confined to services provided in relation to the papers in question. A specific or particular lien, on the other hand, only allows the creditor to retain possession of goods or documents as security for payment of debts which relate to the property retained. For instance, a warehouseman has a specific lien over goods for warehouse charges relating to those goods, and a repairer can retain possession of the goods repaired until he/she is paid for the work done on them.

828. Most common law and statutory liens tend to be specific, while general liens are usually the creation of contract. Where parties are in a continuing trading relationship, a general lien will usually be preferred by the parties. A general lien not only offers the lienor greater and more flexible security but also offers advantages to the lienee. If the lienee has only a particular lien he/she may be reluctant to release property until debts relating to that property are paid, thus restricting the

---

1475. *Shaw v. Foster* (1872) LR 5 HL 321.
1476. *Re Barrett Apartments Ltd* [1985] IR 350, [1985] ILRM 679.
1477. *Transport and General Credit v. Morgan* [1939] 2 All ER 17.
1478. *See* paras 810–818.
1479. *See* para. 576.

lienor's trading ability as he/she will have to pay for each transaction as it is completed, in order to regain possession of the goods. If the lienee has a general lien, he/she will be more willing to release goods to the lienor without immediate payment, as long as he/she has possession of some of the lienor's other goods or will have possession of more of the lienor's goods at some future date.

B. Power of Sale

829. At common law, a lien does not confer a right of sale,[1480] and such an act amounts to conversion and also surrenders the lien.[1481] However, a number of statutes give lienees powers of sale, including the Sale of Goods Act 1893.[1482] Moreover, a lienee may reserve a right of sale by contract and in view of the limited rights of sale under the general law this will generally be advisable. Where the lienee has a contractual right of sale, no particular method of sale is prescribed but the sale must be reasonable.

C. Termination of the Lien

830. A lienee's interest in the goods terminates on payment of the debt though a lien may terminate in other circumstances also. For example, a lien will terminate where the lienee loses possession of the goods.[1483] A lien will also terminate where the lienee waives his/her right by returning the goods to the lienor or where, for instance, alternative security is provided. Moreover, where the lienee breaches a term on which he/she holds the goods, the lien will terminate and the immediate right of possession will revest in the lienor. As with pledges, generally, liens are not affected by lapse of time and limitations of actions do not affect a lienee's rights even if the debt is time barred. Equally, the lienor can reclaim the goods on payment when the debt is barred. But again, such a lapse of time may amount to a waiver.

III. Mortgage

831. A mortgage is a non-possessory form of real security, which involves the transfer of ownership of property to a creditor (the mortgagee) by way of security upon condition that the property will be transferred back to the debtor (the mortgagor) when the sum secured is paid.[1484] The mortgagor may retain possession of the mortgaged property – an advantage where the mortgaged property must be used

---

1480. *Thames Iron Works Co. v. Patton Derrick Co.* (1860) 1 J & H 93; *Somes v. British Empire Shipping Co.* (1859) 28 LJQB 220.
1481. *Mulliner v. Florence* (1878) 3 QBD 484.
1482. *See* para. 576.
1483. *Pennington v. Reliance Motor Works Ltd* [1923] 1 KB 127.
1484. *Keith v. Burrows* (1876) CPD 722.

by the mortgagor in its business. The mortgagor has the right to recover ownership of the mortgaged property – known as the 'equity of redemption'– on payment of the debt secured by the mortgage.[1485] Any property can be mortgaged, including real and personal, tangible and intangible, present and future, property. This gives it an advantage over a pledge which cannot be granted over intangible or future property.

A. *Legal or Equitable*

832. A mortgage can be either legal or equitable. A legal mortgage involves the transfer by way of security of legal ownership of the property. An equitable mortgage is created where:

(a) the mortgagor transfers the equitable ownership or confers an equitable interest in the property;
(b) the mortgage is of equitable property – this includes a mortgage of future property to be acquired by the mortgagor, such as a mortgage of future book debts;
(c) the parties enter into a contract to create a mortgage at a future date;
(d) there is a defective execution of a legal mortgage, as for example where the parties fail to comply with any necessary formalities.

In the cases of the binding agreement and the defective execution, (c) and (d) above, equity looks on that as done which ought to be done and decrees that a valid equitable mortgage has been granted, which can, by the equitable remedy of specific performance, be inflated into a legal mortgage.

B. *Formalities*

833. Generally there is no prescribed form for a mortgage of personality.[1486] The manner of transfer will depend on the type of property being transferred. No formality is required for the transfer of goods; property passes when the parties intend it to pass.[1487] However, it will generally be advisable for the mortgage to be in writing. If the mortgagee does not take possession of the mortgaged property, a written transfer by way of mortgage will have to comply with the formal requirements set down by the bills of sale legislation if granted by an individual or other non-corporate association.[1488] In the case of intangible property, transfer is usually by assignment in writing;[1489] in the case of a mortgage of a debt, notice should be given to the debtor to perfect the assignment to make the assignment a legal, as opposed

1485. *Santley v. Wilde* [1899] 2 Ch. 474; *Carter v. Wake* (1877) 4 Ch D 605.
1486. *Flory v. Denny* (1852) 7 Ex 581.
1487. Sale of Goods Act 1893, s. 17: *see further* paras 590–603.
1488. *See* paras 810–818.
1489. *See*, e.g., Patents Act 1992, s. 79 and s. 85; Trade Marks Act 1996, ss 28–29.

to an equitable, assignment and to fix priority as against any other assignee of the debt in accordance with the rule in *Dearle v. Hall*.[1490]

C. Enforcement

834. A mortgagee generally has three rights as a means of enforcing the mortgage:[1491]

- a right to take possession of the mortgaged property; where the mortgage is a security bill of sale, the mortgagee has a special statutory right of seizure;[1492]
- an express or implied power of sale;
- the right to apply to the court for an order for sale or the appointment of a receiver.[1493]

These rights are generally amplified and reinforced by express provisions in the security instrument. The mortgagor's equity of redemption prevents the mortgagee claiming outright ownership and compels him/her to allow the mortgagor to redeem the mortgaged property, by tender of the amount due plus interest. But, the mortgagor's equity of redemption is extinguished by sale. The Land and Conveyancing Law Reform Act 2009 (LCLRA), which despite its title applies to both real and personal property, deals with mortgages over real and personal property in Part 10. The LCLRA makes some important changes to the law in this regard, including the introduction of a general limitation on the exercise of the mortgagee's powers of enforcement, which provides that the mortgagee's powers of enforcement do not become exercisable unless their exercise is for the purpose of protecting the mortgaged property or realizing the mortgagee's security.[1494] Importantly, in a commercial context, the mortgage contract may exclude this provision.[1495]

1490. (1828) 3 Russ 1.
1491. Traditionally, a four right, a right of foreclosure existed. if the debtor failed to redeem the mortgage within a reasonable time after the debt has become due, the mortgagee could apply for a court order for foreclosure. The effect of foreclosure was to end the mortgagor's equity of redemption, leaving the mortgagee outright owner of the property. In practice, foreclosure was not granted: possession and sale were the preferred remedies (e.g., *Bruce v. Brophy* [1906] 1 IR 611). Now the remedy of foreclosure has been abolished by s. 96(2) of the Land and Conveyancing Law Reform Act 2009; moreover, this abolition is not restricted to mortgages created after the commencement of the 2009 Act.
1492. *See* paras 810–818.
1493. *See further* Land and Conveyancing Law Reform Act 2009, ss 100–109.
1494. LCLRA, s. 96(1)(c).
1495. LCLRA, s. 96(3).

IV. Equitable Charge

835. An equitable charge involves the debtor (chargor) granting the creditor (chargee) the right to have designated property of the debtor appropriated to discharge a debt. It involves no transfer of possession or ownership of the property;[1496] the debt is satisfied by the proceeds of sale of the property which can be transacted voluntarily by the chargor or result from an application by the chargee for a court order. As a mere encumbrance without any conveyance or assignment, a charge exists only in equity or under statute. A charge can be created over any class of property, including goods, intangible property and property to be acquired by the debtor. Although charges can be conferred by an individual, they are most often utilized by companies to secure loans.

A. Fixed or Floating

836. Equitable charges can be fixed or floating. A fixed (or specific) charge is one which attaches to the property as soon as the charge is created or the chargor acquires the rights over the property to be charged, whichever is the later. The chargor cannot dispose of the property free of the charge without the chargee's consent, unless the debt secured by the charge is paid. Any person can create a fixed charge. Charges created by an individual are subject to the bills of sale legislation; those created by companies are subject to companies legislation. More flexible is the floating charge which is not dedicated to any particular asset(s) but floats over a designated class of assets, present or future, allowing the chargor to deal with those assets free from the charge as long as it remains floating.[1497] The security fund is therefore constantly changing; but if, for example, a receiver is appointed to the chargor, or the chargor goes into liquidation, the charge *crystallizes*, that is to say it attaches to those assets then owned by the chargor which correspond with the description specified in the charging instrument, limiting the chargor's right to deal with them. Details of the circumstances in which a floating charge will crystallize should be provided for in the charging instrument.[1498] Because of formal requirements imposed by the bills of sale legislation (in particular, the goods which comprise the bill must be listed in a Schedule) it is difficult, if not impossible, for an individual or non-corporate association to create a floating charge over after acquired property. Hence, only a company can create a floating charge.

837. The obvious advantage of the floating charge is that it leaves the chargor free to use and deal with the charged property. The danger for a creditor taking a

1496. *Re Bond Worth Ltd* [1980] Ch. 228.

1497. A floating charge has been described as a 'dormant' security which permits the debtor company to deal with the charged assets until default or other prescribed event which causes the charge to 'crystallize': *Government Stock Investment Co. v. Manila Railway Co.* [1897] AC 81 at 86 *per* Lord Macnaghten.

1498. On the effect of express or 'automatic' crystallization clauses *see In the Matter of J.D. Brian Motors (In Liquidation) & ors* [2011] IEHC 113; *see further* Courtney, T. *The Law of Companies*, 19.102–19.104 (4th ed., Bloomsbury Professional 2016).

floating charge as security is that before crystallization the chargor's freedom to deal with the property, including by selling it or using it as security to raise further loans, may reduce the security fund below the amount due to be repaid. As a result, floating charges tend to be used to supplement fixed charges. For example, a lending institution will usually take a fixed charge over certain assets of a company (e.g., by way of a legal mortgage on its premises, plant and machinery) and then a floating charge over the remainder of its assets.

B. Debentures

838. A charge may be created by contract or trust, but a commercial charge is generally created by contract. A charge created by a contract is often referred to as a 'debenture'. The Companies Act 2014 defines debenture as including debenture stock, bonds and any other securities of a company whether constituting a charge on the assets of the company or not,[1499] but the term can be used more generally to refer to a type of instrument which creates a charge on a company's assets. Lending institutions, such as banks, have their own printed form of debenture which will normally contain:

(1) an undertaking by the company to repay on demand all monies owing, including interest and charges;
(2) an undertaking by the company to create:
   (a) a fixed charge over assets X, Y and Z;
   (b) a floating charge over the company's remaining assets, present and future.
(3) an undertaking by the company to create no mortgage or charge that would rank in priority to or pari passu with the floating charge created herein;
(4) provision that the monies secured by the debenture become payable on the happening of any of the following events:
   (a) a written demand for payment by the bank;
   (b) the commencement of winding up proceedings in respect of the company;
   (c) the cessation of business by the company.
(5) power for the bank to appoint a receiver in certain circumstances, usually at any time after it has demanded payment of the monies secured and whether or not they have become due;
(6) an undertaking by the company to provide the bank quarterly, or on demand, with up-to-date financial records, including a trading account, profit and loss account and balance sheet representing the true position of the company and duly audited, to enable the bank to review the financial situation and health of the company;
(7) an undertaking by the company to insure all its assets to their full value with such persons as the bank may approve, and provide proof of such insurance.

1499. 2014 Act, s. 2.

V. Statutory Control

839. Non-possessory securities – mortgages and equitable charges – are subject to a high degree of statutory control, which requires the registration of security interests as a means of providing third parties with notice of them. The basic rationale is to protect creditors from advancing credit facilities to debtors who look sound because they have possession of property even though that property is subject to a security interest in favour of an earlier creditor. Where the debtor is an individual, the bills of sale legislation lays down various requirements as to form and registration. Where the debtor is a company, security interests in the form of a charge (including mortgages) must be registered under the Companies Act 2014. Moreover, there are various statutes which establish separate registers and which set out different rules for specific types of property, including the:

- Mercantile Marine Act, 1955
- Agricultural Credits Act, 1978
- Patents Act, 1992
- Trade Marks Act, 1996
- Industrial Designs Act, 2001.

For the purpose of this chapter, the two most important systems of regulation are those in the bills of sale legislation and the Companies Act 2014, both of which are examined further below.

A. Bills of Sale

840. Broadly speaking, a bill of sale is an instrument in writing whereby one party transfers property in goods to another party but remains in possession. There are two types of bills of sale:

(1) an absolute bill;
(2) a conditional bill, more usually called a 'security bill'.

A bill is absolute if given otherwise than as security for payment of money; a bill is conditional or a security bill if it is given to secure a money payment.

1. Application of the Legislation

841. The bills of sale legislation provides for a public registration system for bills of sale to protect third parties who are contemplating taking security in return for credit. The potential creditor has the opportunity to examine the register to see if other prior security interests exist, before advancing the credit. The legislation also seeks to protect the debtor from poor deals and oppressive enforcement measures by requiring bills to be in a prescribed form and restricting enforcement procedures. The courts have been astute to prevent creditors evading the statutory controls; therefore where an individual or other non-corporate entity, such as a trading partnership, gives security over goods, the bills of sale legislation comes into play and the transaction must be considered in order to decide if the legislation applies.

842. The governing legislation in this jurisdiction is:

- the Bills of Sale (Ireland) Act 1879 (which applies to absolute bills of sale);
- the Bills of Sale (Ireland) Act 1879 Amendment Act 1883 (which applies specifically to security bills of sale).

The 1879 and 1883 Acts must be read together regarding bills of sale given by way of security for a money payment. A transaction comes within the scope of the Acts if five conditions are met:

(a) there must be a document, hence oral transactions are not affected by the legislation;[1500]
(b) the document must be a bill of sale as defined by the legislation;[1501]
(c) the document must relate to personal chattels as defined in the legislation, so that security over intangible property is excluded;[1502]
(d) the document must confer on the transferee a right to seize or take possession of the goods;
(e) this right to possession must derive from the document.

843. The legislation does not apply when security is given by a company.[1503] Further exclusions are found in section 4 of the 1879 Act including: assignments for the benefit of creditors and marriage settlements which involve security, and transfers of goods in the ordinary course of business of any trade or calling.

2. Formalities

844. Section 9 of the 1883 Act makes a security bill of sale void unless made in a deed in the form prescribed in the Schedule to the Act, though minor departures from the prescribed form have been tolerated.[1504] The bill must include:

- the names, addresses and description of the parties;
- the consideration given by the creditor;
- the details of the repayment – amount, interest, time and manner;
- the details of insurance;
- the enforcement terms;

1500. 1879 Act, s. 4; *Charlesworth v. Mills* [1892] AC 231; *Newlove v. Shrewsbury* (1888) 21 QBD 41.
1501. 1879 Act, s. 4.
1502. 1879 Act, s. 4.
1503. 1883 Act, s. 17.
1504. *Re Morritt* (1886) 18 QBD 222; *Thomas v. Kelly* (1888) 13 App. Cas. 506.

– a reasonably detailed inventory of the chattels affected.[1505]

Non-compliance not only means that the security interest cannot be enforced, but also that the underlying loan is void.

3. Registration and Attestation

845. The 1883 Act requires that all security transactions covered by the Acts must be attested and registered within seven days,[1506] and for an absolute bill, if necessary, the registration must be renewed every five years.[1507] Attestation must be made by at least one credible witness.[1508] The bill, together with its due execution and attestation and certain personal details of the maker of the bill and the witness, has to be filed in the Central Office of the High Court. If the bill of sale is not duly attested and registered, in compliance with the legislation, it is void and not enforceable.[1509] Registration is also important because if two or more bills of sale have been given they will take priority in the order in which they were registered.[1510] However, this position is modified where an absolute bill is followed by a security bill. If a grantor first gives an absolute bill followed by a security bill over the same goods, the absolute bill will take priority notwithstanding that the security bill was first registered.[1511]

4. Enforcement

846. The 1883 Act gives the creditor limited powers to seize and sell personal chattels secured by the bill of sale. The secured chattels may be seized by the creditor on five grounds:[1512]

(a) if the debtor is in default, or fails to comply with any obligations necessary to maintain the security;
(b) if the debtor becomes bankrupt, or suffers the goods to be distrained for rent, rates or taxes;
(c) if the debtor fraudulently removes or allows the goods to be removed from an agreed premises;
(d) if the debtor fails to comply with a written request for his/her last receipts of rent, rates and taxes;
(e) if execution has been levied against the debtor's goods.

1505. 1883 Act, s. 4.
1506. 1879 Act, s. 8, and 1883 Act, s. 8.
1507. 1879 Act, s. 11.
1508. 1879 Act, s. 8, and 1883 Act, s. 10.
1509. 1883 Act, s. 8.
1510. 1879 Act, s. 10.
1511. 1883 Act, s. 5.
1512. 1883 Act, s. 7.

If seized the goods cannot be removed from the debtor's premises for five days and in that time the debtor can apply to the court for relief.[1513]

847. The extensive formality and registration requirements means that, in practice, in spite of the draconian effect of failure to comply, the vast majority of bills of sale are not registered. Coupled with the statutory restrictions on enforcement procedures, the formal requirements of the legislation mean that mortgages and charges of goods by individuals are little used.

B. Companies Act

848. From 1 June 2015, section 409 of the Companies Act 2014 requires that every charge created by a company must be registered with the Registrar of Companies.[1514] Unlike the bills of sale legislation, the Companies Act seeks to protect only third parties, not the debtor company itself.

1. Registration

849. Section 408 of the Companies Act 2014 defines a 'charge' as being a mortgage or a charge (written or oral) created over any interest in any property of a company. However, the Act specifically excludes the following from the definition of a charge:

- a mortgage or charge created over cash;
- money credited to an account of a financial institution, or any other deposits;
- shares, bonds or debt instruments;
- units in collective investment undertakings or money market instruments;
- claims and rights, such as dividends or interest, in respect of any of the foregoing, except for cash.

850. Particulars of a registrable charge must be registered at the CRO within a specified time period. The 2014 Act provides that registration of the particulars of a charge can be processed by way of either the 'one-stage procedure' or the 'two-stage procedure'. Whichever procedure is chosen by a company may have an effect on determining priority of a charge and importantly, the date of creation of the charge no longer determines priority. However, there are exceptions to this such as: where priority is governed by some other regime, or where lenders agree among themselves to priorities that differ from those set out in the Act. The 'one-stage procedure' is similar to the pre-existing system for registration. Accordingly, particulars must be delivered, in the prescribed form, called a form C1, not later than twenty-one days after the date of the charge's creation. In contrast, the 'two-stage procedure' is a new procedure and involves the submission of prescribed particulars

1513. 1883 Act, ss 7 and 13.
1514. Pre- 1 Jun. 2015, *see* ss 99–106, 108–110 and 112 of the Act of the Companies Act 1963.

on two separate forms. The first of these forms must be submitted to the CRO is the form C1A which is a notice of intention by a company to create a charge. This form must be delivered to the CRO in advance of the charge being created. The second form, a form C1B, must be delivered to the CRO within twenty-one days of the submission of the form C1A. The details to be completed on a form C1B essentially confirm that the charge as detailed in the form C1A has been created.

851. Moreover, from 1 June 2015, CRO has introduced mandatory e-filing for the above forms, incorporating electronic signatures,[1515] thereby providing certainty as to the date and time of registration for the purposes of priority, and visibility of charge submissions on the Register.

852. Failure to register a charge as required renders the charge void against a liquidator and any creditor of the company. The duty to register the charge is imposed on the company, in the first instance, but in practice, to ensure registration, the secured creditor usually registers the charge.[1516] When registration is completed the Companies Registrar issues to the applicant a certificate of registration which is conclusive evidence that the statutory requirements as to registration have been complied with but only to the extent of the particular assets detailed on the form.[1517] The register of charges is a public register, available for consultation by the public.[1518] Any person contemplating advancing loan or credit facilities on the basis of security offered by a limited company should inspect the register for prior registered charges. Non-compliance with this registration requirement mean that the security is void *against the liquidator and any creditor* of the company so that against them the creditor is unsecured, but it remains valid against all other persons: so it continues to bind the company and any purchaser of the charged assets.

2. Priority

853. Registration of a charge is required to perfect the chargee's security. The Companies Act 2014 has introduced a new priority regime for charges, from 1 June 2015, which seeks to minimize the potential for abuse, by giving priority to the creditor who files the first in time. Accordingly, section 412(3) provides that the priority is determined by the date and time of receipt by the Registrar of a fully filed charge submission. The date of creation of the deed of charge will no longer determine priority.

854. In particular, under the 'one-stage procedure', an e-filed and e-signed C1, filed within twenty-one days of creation, receives priority from the e-filing date. The new 'two-stage procedure' allows creditors to secure the earliest possible priority

1515. Companies Act 2014, s. 897.
1516. Companies Act 2014, s. 410.
1517. Companies Act, s. 415.
1518. *See* www.cro.ie.

date by e-filing and e-signing the C1A-notice of intention to create a charge, followed within twenty-one days by e-filing and e-signing the C1B-confirmation of creation of the charge. The date of priority will be that of the e-filed C1A. Moreover, pursuant to the 2014 Act, particulars contained in a form C1, C1A or C1B which attempt to fix notice on a subsequent lender of the existence of a negative pledge will be deemed to be 'extraneous material' and will not be recorded on the register.

§3. Personal Security

855. Personal security is provided by means of contracts of suretyship, whereby one person, the surety, agrees to be answerable for the debt of another, the principal debtor. It therefore involves a tripartite relationship between creditor, principal debtor and surety. Importantly, the debtor is not a party to the contract of surety. A contract of surety gives the creditor a personal right of action against the surety but no real rights over any property. Its value thus depends entirely on the creditworthiness of the surety. However, the surety may be required to reinforce his/her personal undertaking by providing real security to secure his/her performance.

856. Contracts of suretyship take two forms: guarantees and indemnities.[1519] A guarantee is an undertaking, given by a third party, to answer for another's default. The guarantee is based on the debtor's default so, it is referred to as a secondary obligation; the primary obligation to pay lies with the principal debtor. The secondary liability of a surety under a guarantee can be compared with the surety's primary liability under an indemnity. Like a guarantee, an indemnity is a personal security undertaking given by a third party, but under an indemnity the surety's obligation is independent of the debtor/creditor relationship. It is therefore a primary liability, not dependent on the debtor's default.[1520] In practice, guarantees and indemnities are often used to reinforce each other. In this section, we concentrate on the use of guarantees as a form of personal security, making brief reference to indemnities where relevant, before looking at some alternatives to guarantees, including letters of comfort.

I. Guarantees

857. A guarantee can be used to secure both fixed debts and revolving debts. For example, before agreeing to sell goods on credit terms, a seller may require that a creditworthy third-party guarantee payment of the price. Similarly, a bank contemplating providing overdraft facilities may require a creditworthy third party to guarantee repayment. Guarantees are used not only to secure the repayment of a loan or overdraft but also can be given to guarantee tender or performance of a contract.

1519. *Birkmyr v. Darnell* (1704) 1 Salk 27.
1520. *See*, e.g., *Gulf Bank KSC v. Mitsubishi Heavy Industries Ltd (No. 2)* [1994] 2 Lloyd's Rep 145.

Such transactions are known as performance guarantees or bonds but they do not comply with the strict legal meaning of guarantees.[1521]

A. *Formation of a Guarantee*

858. Guarantees must conform to the general requirements for the formation of a contract: there must be an agreement, supported by consideration (unless made by deed) and an intention to create legal relations. Moreover, the guarantee, to be enforceable, must be evidenced by a note or memorandum in writing and signed by the guarantor or other authorized person.[1522] In *Bank of Ireland v. McCabe,*[1523] the defendant had signed an earlier guarantee but, in relation to a new loan, no separate or new guarantee was signed. The court held that the earlier guarantee applied only to a previous loan and hence there was no enforceable guarantee to support the new loan.

1. Revocability of the Guarantor's Undertaking

859. A guarantee may be a unilateral or a bilateral contract. If the creditor agrees that, in consideration of the surety's guarantee, it will provide credit to the debtor, the contract is bilateral. More often the creditor will not actually promise to advance credit. In that case the contract is unilateral: the surety's undertaking is that *if* the creditor advances credit, the surety will guarantee the debt. The creditor accepts that offer, and provides consideration for the surety's promise, by advancing the credit. Where the contract is unilateral the surety can revoke its offer at any time before it is accepted. Once credit is advanced the surety is bound. In some cases, however, such as where the surety guarantees a revolving credit facility, the correct analysis may be that the surety's undertaking is a standing offer which the creditor accepts each time it makes a new advance to the debtor. In that case, the surety can at any time revoke its offer and thus terminate its liability in respect of future advances; it remains liable in respect of advances made before revocation. The terms of the guarantee will normally require the surety to give notice before revoking the offer in this way. Whether a continuing guarantee is revocable in this way depends on the construction of the contract.

1521. *See further* para. 843.
1522. Statute of Frauds (Ireland) 1695, s. 2. Importantly, the Statute of Frauds does not apply to contracts of indemnity.
1523. Unreported, Supreme Court, 19 Dec. 1994.

2. Duress and Undue Influence

860. If the surety's undertaking is obtained by duress, undue influence or misrepresentation *by the creditor*, the guarantee will be voidable.[1524] Unlike contracts of insurance, contracts of suretyship are not contracts of *utmost good faith*, that is, the creditor is not under a legal duty to disclose all materials facts to the guarantor.[1525] However, it has been recognized that a creditor owes a limited duty to disclose unusual features of the principal contract unknown to the surety.[1526]

861. The guarantee may also be invalidated by duress, undue influence or misrepresentation by the *debtor*, a third party to the guarantee, if:

(a) the debtor was acting as the creditor's agent – for instance, in obtaining the surety's agreement to the transaction;
(b) the creditor has actual or constructive notice of the debtor's improper conduct.

In *Barclays Bank v. O'Brien,*[1527] the House of Lords held that where a wife gave a guarantee to secure her husband's debt, and the guarantee was not to the wife's advantage (as, for instance, where the secured debt was the sole liability of the husband[1528]), there was a substantial risk of the husband committing a wrong which would allow the wife to set the transaction aside and the creditor would have constructive notice of the debtor's conduct unless the creditor took reasonable steps to ensure that the guarantee had been properly obtained. In this case, the husband had mis-represented the amount and duration of the loan to his wife. The same rule applies where surety and debtor are cohabitees, and the creditor is aware of the personal relationship between them, or in any other relationship where the creditor is aware that the guarantor reposes trust and confidence in the principal debtor.[1529] To avoid being fixed with such notice, the creditor should inform the surety of the nature of the transaction and of the risks involved and of the advisability of obtaining independent advice. In *Royal Bank of Scotland plc v. Etridge and ors,*[1530] the House of Lords sought to indicate clear, simple and practically operable, minimum requirements for the procedures to be followed when a bank is obtaining security. In particular, a bank would satisfy the minimum requirements by taking steps to bring to a wife's attention the risks of standing as surety for her husband if it insisted that the wife attend a private meeting with a representative of the bank where:

1524. *See*, e.g., *Lloyds Bank Ltd v. Bundy* [1975] QB 326; *National Westminster Bank plc v. Morgan* [1985] AC 686; *Bank of Nova Scotia v. Hogan* (unreported, High Court, 21 Dec. 1992), [1997] 1 ILRM 407; *Carroll v. Carroll* [1998] 2 ILRM 218.
1525. On the distinction between insurance contracts and contracts of guarantee *see Seaton v. Heath* [1899] 1 QB 782; *International Commercial Bank v. ICI* [1991] ILRM 726; *Hong Kong and Shanghai Banking Corpn v. Icarom plc* (unreported, Supreme Court, 31 Jul. 1992). On contracts of insurance *see generally* paras 700–719.
1526. *Levett & ors v. Barclays Bank* [1995] 2 All ER 615.
1527. [1993] WLR 786.
1528. Cf. *Ulster Bank Ireland Ltd v. Fitzgerald* (unreported, High Court, 9 Nov. 2001).
1529. *See*, e.g., *Credit Lyonaisse v. Burch* [1997] 1 All ER 144 where the relationship of surety and principal debtor was that of employee and employer.
1530. [2001] 4 All ER 449, [2001] 2 All ER Comm 1061.

(a) she was told of the extent of her liability as surety;
(b) she was warned of the risk she was running;
(c) she was urged to take separate legal advice.

To be safe, a bank could insist that she take separate legal advice. The House of Lords also set out the minimum content of the legal advice that a solicitor advising the wife should give. Where the guarantee is not for the *sole* benefit of the debtor – as, for instance, where a wife guarantees a loan made to her and her husband jointly and secures the guarantee by giving a mortgage over her property – the creditor is not fixed with constructive notice of improper conduct by the debtor.[1531]

862. The Irish position is less clear-cut. In *Bank of Ireland v. Smyth,*[1532] the defendant's wife gave her consent to a deed of charge in favour of the plaintiff bank over lands owned by her husband (as required by section 3(1) of the Family Home Protection Act 1976). When the bank sought possession of the lands following the husband's default, the defendant's wife argued that her consent was invalid because she had not understood that in the event of default the family home could be sold. The Supreme Court held that because the defendant's wife was not 'fully informed,' her consent was invalid and hence the relevant conveyance was incapable of creating a valid mortgage over the family home. The matter of the enforceability of guarantees and improper conduct by the debtor was considered by the Supreme Court in *Bank of Nova Scotia v. Hogan.*[1533] The case actually involved an allegation that the bank itself had exercised undue influence over the surety, but the case was dismissed for lack of evidence supporting the claim. However, Murphy J., speaking *obiter* for the Supreme Court, appears to have approved the reasoning of the *O'Brien* decision.

863. The matter of third-party duress in relation to a guarantee came before the Irish courts in *Ulster Bank v. Fitzgerald,*[1534] a case decided a few weeks after the House of Lords decision in *Royal Bank of Scotland v. Etridge* but which did not refer to the *Etridge* decision. The second defendant, Ms Williams, had signed two guarantees in respect of the liabilities of a company controlled by her husband, Mr Fitzgerald. When the plaintiff bank sought to enforce the guarantees, Williams argued that she had entered into the guarantees as a result of the undue influence of her husband, and as a result of this undue influence the bank should be precluded from enforcing the guarantees. In deciding against the second defendant, O'Donovan J focussed on the concept of notice. He stated that while it 'may well' have been the case that Williams had signed the guarantees as a result of undue influence from Fitzgerald, it was not necessary for him to reach a conclusion on this point because the bank would not have been affected by any undue influence which took place. He was satisfied that none of the representatives of the plaintiff bank had either actual or constructive notice of any undue influence which might have taken

1531. *CIBC Mortgages plc v. Pitt* [1993] WLR 802.
1532. [1993] 2 I.R. 102.
1533. [1997] 1 I.L.R.M. 407.
1534. Unreported, High Court, O'Donovan, J., 9 Nov. 2001.

place (although it is not clear on what basis this finding is grounded). The learned judge distinguished two earlier authorities: *Bank of Ireland v. Smyth* and *Barclays Bank v. O'Brien* on the basis that both cases concerned a direct threat to a family home. *O'Brien* had involved a transaction in which the wife had had no financial stake, while *Smyth* concerned an attempt to recover possession of a family home. According to O'Donovan J, neither of these cases assisted Williams' case, since there was no threat to her family home and 'in any event, she had a financial stake in both of those guarantees'. Moreover, O'Donovan J rejected the proposition that the bank was obliged to take any special steps to ensure that Williams obtained independent advice before signing the guarantees, stressing that 'the courts are not required to intervene to protect a contracting party from ill-advised action'. O'Donovan J's ultimate conclusion was that the two guarantees were enforceable against Williams and accordingly he gave judgment against her for approximately GBP 130,000.

864. However, more recently, Clark J in *Ulster Bank v. Roche & Anor*[1535] took a more sympathetic view of the second defendant guarantor's position, finding that the bank in question was unable to rely on a guarantee procured by the undue influence of the first defendant. In doing so, the Court while not fully endorsing the decision in *Etridge,* went a considerable way in that direction. Clarke J stated:

> It seems to me that the academic critici*sm of Fitz*gerald is well founded. A regime which places no obligation on a bank to take any steps to ascertain whether, in the presence of circumstances suggesting a non-commercial aspect to a guarantee, the party offering the guarantee may not be fully and freely entering into same, gives insufficient protection to potentially vulnerable sureties. While not necessarily accepting that the precise parameters, identifi*ed in E*tridge, are those which give rise to an obligation on the bank to inquire, and thus represent the law in this jurisdiction, I am satisfied that the general principle, which under*lies E*tridge, is to the effect that a bank is placed on inquiry where it is aware of facts which suggest, or ought to suggest, that there may be a non-commercial element to a guarantee.[1536]

Clark J went on to consider what a bank must do when placed on inquiry. Again, while not fully endorsing the approach in *Etridge,* he found that a bank which is placed on inquiry is obliged to take at least some measures to seek to ensure that the proposed surety is openly and freely agreeing to provide the requested security.

B. Relations Between the Guarantor and the Creditor

865. Unless agreed otherwise, the guarantor's liability is coterminous with that of the principal debtor, so that the guarantor is not liable unless the debtor defaults,

---

1535. [2012] IEHC 166.
1536. [2012] IEHC 166 at para. 5.14. *See* further *ACC Loan Management Ltd v Connelly* [2017] IECA 119.

and, where the debtor pays the secured debt in full, the guarantee terminates. If the debtor defaults, it is not necessary for the creditor to sue or even to make a claim against the principal debtor before calling on the guarantor unless the contract of guarantee expressly so provides;[1537] it is unlikely that a bank would agree to such a provision.

1. Nature of the Guarantor's Liability

866. The extent of the guarantor's liability depends on the construction of the contract but usually the guarantor's responsibility is not merely to pay a sum of money to the creditor if the principal debtor fails to do so, but to procure the debtor's performance. In *Moschi v. Lep Air Services Ltd,*[1538] freight forwarders agreed to relinquish their lien over the debtor's goods in return for the debtor's agreement to pay GBP 40,000 in instalments. The appellants guaranteed performance of the debtor's obligation. The debtor defaulted and the creditors, treating this as a repudiation of the agreement, terminated the contract and claimed against the appellants. The appellants argued that termination of the contract with the principal debtors released them from liability. The House of Lords held that the undertaking to guarantee was not to pay the instalments on the debtor's default but to procure performance by the debtor of his/her obligations under the contract, so that the guarantors were liable for damages equal to the amount the debtor would have paid, plus interest.

2. Invalidity of the Principal Contract

867. The effect on the surety's liability of invalidity or unenforceability of the main contract depends on the construction of the surety contract and whether it is classified as a guarantee or an indemnity. Since a guarantee is ancillary to the main contract, if the principal contract is void and unenforceable, so too is the contract of guarantee. This point is illustrated by the case of *Coutts & Co v. Browne-Lecky*[1539] where a guarantee of a minor's overdraft at a bank could not be enforced due to the Infants Relief Act 1874 which provided that the infant was not liable to repay the loan. In contrast, if the surety is properly construed as an indemnity, the surety incurs primary liability so that he remains liable even though the principal contract is unenforceable against the principal debtor. To avoid any uncertainty over classification of the surety, an express provision should be included that the surety shall be liable even in circumstances where the principal debtor is not.[1540]

1537. *AG v. Sun Alliance and London Insurances Ltd* [1985] ILRM 522. In *Holl v. Hadley* (1828) 5 Bing 54 the contract required the creditor to use 'the utmost efforts and legal proceedings' against the debtor, and thus, it was held that the creditor was obliged to sue the principal debtor.

1538. [1973] AC 331.

1539. [1947] KB 104.

1540. *See Heald v. O ' Connor* [1971] 1 WLR 497.

868. If the surety contract itself is void or voidable it is irrelevant that it is an indemnity rather than a guarantee. In *Associated Japanese Bank (International) v. Credit de Nord,*[1541] the defendant guaranteed payment of rentals due to the plaintiff under a sale and lease-back arrangement of machinery and undertook that they would be liable as 'sole or principal debtor'. In fact the machinery which was the subject of the sale and lease-back contract did not exist. It was held that the guarantee contract itself was void *ab initio* for mistake so that the plaintiff could recover nothing under the guarantee. In addition, the court found that on the construction of the contract there was an express (or at least implied) condition precedent to the guarantee agreement that the machinery existed.

C. *Relations Between the Guarantor and the Debtor*

869. The guarantor has two basic rights against the principal debtor: a right to indemnity, and a right of subrogation. Where there is a contract between surety and debtor these may be supplemented by express, or implied, provisions of the contract.

1. A Right to Indemnity

870. If the guarantee is given at the request of the debtor, the guarantor has an implied contractual right to be indemnified by the debtor against all liabilities he/she incurs: including the sum paid and any interest which has accrued from the date of payment.[1542] This is an example of the general rule that if one party incurs expenditure or liabilities at another party's request or with his/her authority, then that party is entitled to be compensated or indemnified, since the request or authority implies a promise to compensate or indemnify the creditor.[1543] However, the guarantor's right of indemnity is often restricted by the contract of guarantee, whereby the guarantor agrees not to pursue his/her right of indemnity, and hence reduce the pool of assets available to satisfy the creditor's claim, until the creditor's claim has been satisfied.

2. A Right of Subrogation

871. Where the guarantor discharges the debt which he/she has guaranteed, he/she is entitled to step into the shoes of the creditor and, under the doctrine of subrogation, pursue any claims against the debtor which the creditor had, including enforcing securities held by the creditor for the debt, whether made before or after the guarantee. The doctrine of subrogation arises by operation of the law to prevent

1541. [1989] 1 WLR 255.
1542. *Re Fox Walker & Co,* ex parte *Bishop* (1880) 15 Ch. 400.
1543. *Re a Debtor* [1937] 1 All ER 1 at 7–8, *per* Greene LJ; *see further Owen v. Tate* [1976] QB 402.

the debtor being unjustly enriched.[1544] It is available whether the guarantee was given at the request of the debtor or the creditor. For the purposes of subrogation, although the payment of the debt extinguishes the debt, any other securities are kept alive for the benefit of the guarantor who is entitled to have them transferred to him/her together with any judgment obtained by the creditor. The guarantor ranks in the same priority as the creditor. The guarantor can only claim a right to subrogation to securities or other rights of the creditor where he/she has paid the debt in full: a proportionate right of subrogation does not exist.[1545]

872. As noted above, under the doctrine of subrogation, the guarantor is entitled to step into the shoes of the creditor. Therefore, a guarantor's rights cannot be more extensive than the rights which the creditor would have had. This point is illustrated in *Re Chipboard Ltd (in liquidation),*[1546] where the Minister for Finance gave two guarantees as security for bank loans to Chipboard Ltd which subsequently became insolvent. The bank loans were in fact secured in two ways: first, by a charge in favour of the bank over the assets of the company, including book debts; and second, by the Minister's guarantees. The Minister's guarantees were, in turn, secured by a charge on the company's assets, excluding the book debts. The charge in favour of the bank entitled the bank to interest at the current rate of simple interest. The charge in favour of the Minister entitled him to interest set at 5% above the bank's lending rate. The guarantees supplied by the Minister were called upon by the bank and the Minister paid. The Minister then sought to exercise his right to be subrogated to the securities held by the bank: the charge over the company's assets, including the book debts. It was held first that the fact that the Minister had other securities himself did not preclude him from exercising his right of subrogation.[1547] But, because he had opted to exercise his right of subrogation, he was limited to the rate of interest specified in the bank's charge – a lesser rate than his own charge.

D. Rights Against Co-guarantors

873. Where two or more guarantors are liable for the same obligation to the same amount, the extent of the liability is shared equally between them, unless otherwise agreed. So, where one guarantor has paid the full guaranteed amount, he/she is entitled to claim reimbursement from his/her co-guarantor in an equitable action for contribution (the debtor and any other co-guarantors should be joined as co-defendants in the action to avoid multiplicity of actions).[1548] The guarantees need not be created by the same instrument and indeed the fact that each guarantor is unaware of the other's existence does not affect the right to contribution. Where the

1544. *Highland Finance v. Sacred Heart College* [1992] 1 IR 472.
1545. *Re Sass* [1896] 2 QB 12.
1546. [1994] 3 IR 164.
1547. Cf. *Bank of Ireland v. Daly* [1978] IR 79; and *Highland Finance v. Sacred Heart College* [1992] 1 IR 472.
1548. *In re PMPA (Longmile) Ltd* [1993] 1 IR 190. *See further Bank of Ireland v. O ' Shea* (unreported, High Court, 31 Jul. 1992).

guarantees cover the same obligation but in different amounts, each guarantor must contribute in proportion to their respective liabilities.

E. Discharge of the Guarantor

874. A guarantee is usually discharged where the creditor does any act which alters the guarantor's rights, or the debtor is discharged from liability.[1549]

1. Where the Guarantor's Rights Are Altered

875. Unless otherwise agreed, any acts or omissions by the creditor which alter or extinguish the guarantor's rights (e.g., by releasing a co-guarantor,[1550] or giving the debtor more time[1551]) operates to discharge the guarantee.[1552] In *Holme v. Brunskill,*[1553] it was held that if the alteration was not obviously insubstantial or non-prejudicial to the guarantor, the guarantor should be discharged from liability, unless he/she consents otherwise. This test clearly favours the guarantor who does not have to prove actual loss or damage. In *MacEnroe v. AIB,*[1554] the plaintiff agreed to guarantee loans advanced to a company whether 'on foot of current account or otherwise', subject to a limit of IEP 75,000. At the time of the guarantee the company had two bank accounts, both overdrawn. After the guarantee was executed a third account was opened and this fact was known to the guarantor. It was agreed between the bank and the company that this third account could not be set-off against the debts in the other two accounts. The plaintiff argued that the opening of the third account altered the guarantee contract and therefore he should be discharged from liability. The Supreme Court held that the opening of the account was not a 'material variation' of the guarantee and hence the guarantor was not discharged. It has been argued that this difference in terminology between 'not obviously insubstantial or non-prejudicial to the guarantor' and 'material alteration' means that an Irish court will be less sympathetic to guarantors seeking release from their obligation following an alteration of the guarantee contract.[1555] To avoid discharge following a 'material alternation', the guarantee should include a provision such as:

> The guarantor agrees and consents to any alteration, variation, amendment or extinction of his rights to indemnity and subrogation made by the creditor.[1556]

1549. *See further Bank of India v. Trans Continental Commodity Merchants Ltd* [1982] 1 Lloyd's Rep 506 at 514–515, *per* Bingham J; [1983] 2 Lloyd's Rep 298.
1550. *Ward v. National Bank of New Zealand* (1883) 8 App. Cas. 755.
1551. *Prendergast v. Devey* (1821) 6 Madd.124; *Munster & Leinster Bank v. France* (1889) 24 LR Ir 82.
1552. *Holme v. Brunskill* (1878) 3 QBD 495; *MacEnroe v. AIB* [1980] ILRM 171; *ADM Ltd v. Kavanagh* (unreported, Supreme Court 10 May 2002).
1553. (1878) 3 QBD 495.
1554. [1980] ILRM 171.
1555. Donnelly, *The Law of Banks and Credit Institutions* (Round Hall Sweet & Maxwell 2000), at 443.
1556. *See*, e.g., *Allied Irish Bank PLC v. Sean Keane & Ors* [2012] IEHC 516.

2. Discharge of the Debtor

876. Under a contract of guarantee, because a guarantor's liability is coterminous with that of the debtor's, the guarantor's liability is discharged if the debt is paid, or the debtor is discharged from liability, or the liability to pay is extinguished by operation of the law. If, on proper construction of the guarantee, the guarantor is responsible for the procurement of the debtor's performance, the guarantor is not released if the creditor terminates the principal contract in response to a serious breach of contract by the debtor.[1557] The debtor's primary liability in debt is converted into a liability in damages and this secondary obligation is also guaranteed. Under a contract of indemnity, since the surety's liability is independent of the debtor's, discharge of the debtor does not necessarily release the surety.

II. Letters of Credit

877. Letters of credit or documentary credits are utilized as a means of securing payment in international sales contracts. They are used to give a seller of goods an assurance of payment: the buyer arranges for a bank to give the seller an undertaking to pay the price if certain conditions are fulfilled. They thus resemble a guarantee. However, the bank's undertaking under a letter of credit is generally a primary obligation, independent of the underlying contract and the seller looks to the bank rather than to the buyer for payment.

III. Performance Guarantees

878. Performance guarantees (sometimes referred to as bank guarantees or performance bonds) are not guarantees in the strict common law sense, in that they are not secondary obligations which come into operation on the debtor's default, but are primary autonomous obligations. They are undertakings by a bank or similar institution to pay money, used in a similar way to letters of credit to provide an assurance of payment or performance of another obligation.

IV. Letters of Comfort

879. A letter of comfort may be used as an alternative to a guarantee. The use of letters of comfort has become more common in recent years, as a means of reassuring potential creditors that their loan or credit facilities will be repaid, without actually guaranteeing repayment. It is usually given by a parent company to support an advance of credit facilities to its subsidiary by a lending institution.

1557. *Moschi v. Lep Air Services Ltd* [1973] AC 331.

880. A typical comfort letter provides:

- a statement of the awareness of a parent company of the advances made to the subsidiary;
- a promise that the parent company will not, without the lender's consent, relinquish or reduce control of the subsidiary before repayment;
- words of comfort, stating how far the parent company is prepared to go on supporting its subsidiary, often beginning 'it is our intention', or 'it is our policy'.

Whether the words of comfort in (iii) above have contractual effect depends on the construction of the letter. Despite the presumption, in commercial dealings, that parties intend their agreements to have legal effect, it seems that generally letters of comfort will be regarded as not intended to be binding. In *Kleinwort Benson Ltd v. Malaysia Mining Corporation Ltd,*[1558] a creditor agreed a loan with a subsidiary company based on two letters of comfort provided by the parent company (who had been unwilling to guarantee the loan) along the following lines:

> It is our policy to ensure that the business of [the subsidiary] is at all times in a position to meet its liabilities to you.

The subsidiary company went into liquidation and the creditors sought repayment from the parent company. The Court of Appeal held that the letters of comfort were not intended to create a contractual promise as to future conduct. The court did not consider the possibility that the letters contained an *implied* future promise but took the view that letters of comfort are generally commercially regarded as intended to create a moral but not a legally binding obligation. As a result, a letter of comfort represents a poor substitute for a binding personal security undertaking and creditors may be reluctant to advance credit on the basis of letters of comfort alone. However, where a parent company is unwilling to provide a guarantee, a letter of comfort may be the only 'security' available to the creditor.

1558. [1989] 1 WLR 379; approved in *Re Atlantic Computers plc* [1995] BCC 696.

Part II. Economic Law

Chapter 1. State Intervention in Economic Affairs

881. The State intervenes in economic affairs in numerous ways, apart from enacting legislation that is aimed exclusively at commercial operations. A clear example is the law regarding land ownership and the law of trusts. Other examples include the law of employment and of industrial relations; and environmental law, including planning law; although these are usually treated as separate subjects in their own right.

882. One mode of state intervention is through legislation providing for extensive regulation of a particular industry. Examples include the Central Bank Acts, 1942–2018, the Insurance Acts, 1909–2000 and the Road Transport Acts, 1935–1999. The regulation of economic activity, in terms of establishment and supervision of certain activities, is considered further in the next chapter.

883. Another mode of state intervention is either assisting or imposing burdens on particular industries or types of industry or locations through the tax code. Thus since 2003, the standard rate of corporation tax is 12.5%; whereas an additional tax (excise duty) maybe payable on certain products and services, including tobacco and alcohol.

884. Moreover, through the IDA,[1559] the State plays a very prominent role in offering financial incentives in the form of grants, such as capital grants and R&D grants, to foreign firms which need financial support before undertaking major investments. So far as the law is concerned, the award of these grants is entirely discretionary.

§1. Planning

885. There is no detailed prescriptive State planning of economic development; however, starting in 1987, Ireland utilized 'social partnership agreements', of which there were seven, and which many identified as being key to Ireland's former economic prosperity. However, the last agreement, *Towards 2016: Ten Year Framework Social Partnership Agreement 2006–2015*, which represented a negotiated

1559. *See* www.idaireland.ie.

agreement covering a range of issues, including pay, the workplace and employment rights and compliance, as well as issues concerning the macro-economy, infrastructure, the environment and social policy, effectively collapsed at the end of 2009 when the Government imposed income cuts of between 5% and 8% for about 315,000 public servants in its Budget. The Government also publishes on a periodic basis a 'national development plan' (NDP) which provides a strategic framework and financial investment plan for the country. The current NDP runs from 2018 to 2027, and is linked to Project Ireland 2040 which presents a longer-term strategic vision for development.[1560]

§2. State Shareholding

886. Several major economic undertakings were established by the State, which still owns them, most notably public utilities like the ESB;[1561] Bord Gáis;[1562] CIE;[1563] RTE;[1564] and Bord na Móna plc.[1565] Ireland never pursued a nationalization programme along the lines of what happened in Britain in the late 1940s and in France in the early 1980s. Indeed, more recently the State has pursued a policy of denationalization or, as it is more popularly known, privatization to a more limited extent. For example, in the early 1990s the former Irish Sugar Company[1566] and the Irish Life Insurance Company[1567] were floated on the Stock Exchange, and subsequently Telecom Éireann[1568] and Aer Lingus[1569] were privatized.

887. Several of the State-owned utilities and commercial undertakings are statutory corporations, having been constituted by their own statute and not subject to all the rules and requirements of Company Law, for instance, the ESB, Bord Gáis, RTE, CIE and the VHI. The relevant legislation provides for the establishment of these bodies and for how they should be run. To have any of these bodies dissolved, it would appear that special legislation to that effect would have to be passed; they cannot be wound up by the High Court under the Companies Act 2014.[1570]

888. Many other State businesses are companies registered under the Companies Act but whose internal regulations contain various provisions specified in the legislation that authorized registration of the company in question. For instance,

1560. *See generally*, https://www.gov.ie/en/publication/83fec4-national-development-plan/
1561. Established in 1927 as a statutory corporation: Electricity Supply Act 1927.
1562. Established in 1976 as a statutory corporation: Gas Act 1976.
1563. Established in 1944, and reconstituted in 1950, as a statutory corporation: Transport Acts 1944 and 1950.
1564. *See* Broadcasting Authority Acts 1960–2001.
1565. Established as a statutory corporation under the Turf Development Act 1946, it became a plc in 1999: Turf Development Act 1998.
1566. Sugar Act 1991.
1567. Insurance Act 1990.
1568. Telecommunications (Miscellaneous Provisions) Act 1996.
1569. Aer Lingus was the former state airline: *see* Aer Lingus Act 2004.
1570. For example, the Electricity Supply (Amendment) Act 2001, paved the way for the privatization of the ESB.

under the Postal and Telecommunications Services Act, 1983, the Minister was required to arrange for two limited companies, named An Post (or the Post Office) and Board Telecom Éireann (or The Irish Telecommunications Board) to be formed and registered under the then Companies Acts. The 1983 Act then went on to set out in considerable detail the principal features of these two companies, like their authorized share capital, their principal objects, the contents of their articles of association, the issue of and subscription for shares in them. Other State-owned bodies which have been constituted in this manner include An Post National Lottery Company; Dublin Airport Authority plc, the Irish Aviation Authority and Irish Rail.

§3. Principles of Economic Law

889. Regulation of business activities must be in accordance with the provisions of the Constitution (1937), the European Convention on Human Rights (1950)[1571] and more generally EU law[1572] and administrative law.[1573]

890. For example, the fundamental rights provisions of the Constitution have been used on a number of occasions to challenge the constitutionality of legislation aimed at regulating particular commercial activities, such as the since-repealed Pigs and Bacon Acts, 1935–1937, and the Industrial and Provident Societies (Amendment) Act, 1978. On both occasions the contention that these measures constituted unjust attacks on property rights was rejected. The courts have exhibited a disinclination to strike down economic laws merely because they interfered with persons' freedom to conduct their own businesses.[1574] However, more recently, *In the matter of Article 26 and the Employment Equality Bill 1996*,[1575] the Supreme Court struck down provisions of the Employment Equality Bill because they represented an unjust attack on the property rights of employers: employers, and not society in general, would have to carry the cost of integrating disabled workers into the workforce, and this the court deemed was unfair.

891. Regulatory measures must also provide for fair procedures; exactly what procedure is fair for these purposes depends entirely on the nature of the statute or statutory instrument in question. Where the measure does not expressly set out the

1571. European Convention on Human Rights Act, 2003.

1572. Principally, the Treaty on the Functioning of the European Union (TFEU) and related treaties and rules.

1573. Hogan et al, *Kelly: The Irish Constitution* (5th ed., Bloomsbury 2018); Hogan & Morgan, *Administrative Law in Ireland* (4th ed., Sweet & Maxwell 2010).

1574. *See further*, e.g., *AG and Minister for Posts and Telegraphs v. Paperlink Ltd* [1984] ILRM 373 where a challenge by a private courier company against a state monopoly was dismissed; and *Hand v. Dublin Corporation* [1991] 1 IR 409 where legislation regulating casual trading was upheld.

1575. [1997] 2 IR 321.

procedures for its implementation, the courts will imply into it a requirement that fair procedures must be observed; in particular, that persons who stand to be directly prejudiced by an administrative decision are given a reasonable opportunity to have their case against that decision heard before the matter is decided on.

Chapter 2. Law of Establishment and Supervision of Economic Activities

892. Most industries and occupations are unregulated in the sense that you do not need special authorization to establish yourself as a producer or supplier of goods or services, nor are your economic activities supervised. Nevertheless, there is a growing cohort of businesses which are the subject of detailed regulation, much of which derives from EU Regulations and Directives. Moreover, almost the entire farming and fishing industry is carried on within the framework of the EU's Common Agricultural Policy and Fishery Policy, respectively. In this chapter, the law of establishment and supervision in relation to various commercial activities, namely financial services, transport, communications, utility services, leisure services, property services, auditing and legal services, is described.[1576]

§1. Financial Services

893. Probably the most highly regulated commercial sector is the financial services sector which involves the provision of banking, insurance and investment services, amongst others. Much of the regulation derives from EU measures. Irish institutional regulation in this area has recently been reformed and centralized under the Irish Central Bank. The Central Bank Reform Act 2010, created a new single unitary body – the Central Bank of Ireland – responsible for both central banking and financial regulation. This new structure replaces the previous related entities, the Central Bank and the Financial Services Authority of Ireland, and, the Financial Regulator. The Act commenced on 1 October 2010.

894. The Central Bank Commission, established by the Central Bank Reform Act 2010, is responsible for ensuring that the statutory functions of the Bank are properly discharged. It consists of the Governor and two Deputy Governors of the Central Bank, the Secretary General of the Department of Finance, and six to eight members appointed by the Minister. The Central Bank is organized into directorates which report to the Deputy Governor (Central Banking), the Deputy Governor (Prudential Regulation) or the Chief Operations Officer. The remit of the Central Bank covers monetary and economic policy, financial stability as well as financial services regulation.[1577]

1576. There are many other regulatory schemes. *See*, e.g., Private Security Services Act, 2004 in relation to security services; Casual Trading Act, 1995 as regards casual trading; Irish Medicines Board Act, 1995, Health (Nursing Homes) Act, 1990, and Control of Clinical Trials Act, 1987 in relation to various health services; Employment Agencies Act, 1971 as regards employment agencies, etc.

1577. Financial service providers which require a licence, approval or authorization from the Central Bank to carry business in Ireland include: Approved Professional Bodies; Brokers / Retail Intermediaries; Bureaux de Change; Credit Institutions; Credit Unions; Debt Management Firms; Electronic Money Institutions; Funds; Fund Service Providers; Insurance/Reinsurance Undertakings; Investment Firms; Moneylenders; Money Transmission Businesses; Payment Institutions; Regulated Markets; and Retail Credit Firms/Home Reversion Firms.

895. The Central Bank also has a consumer protection function. A statutory Consumer Protection Code was introduced in 2006 and revised in 2012. Moreover, since 2004, a Financial Services Ombudsman has been established with an extensive remit to resolve complaints against financial service providers.[1578]

I. Banking

896. The recent financial and economic crisis resulted in unprecedented and dramatic changes to the regulatory structure of banking in Ireland. The regulatory response ranged from short-term changes, to more long-term changes, with some interim measures in between. For example, in the shorter term, on 30 September 2008 the Government announced that it was guaranteeing the debt obligations of Irish banks pursuant to the Credit Institutions (Financial Support) Act 2008.[1579] A more interim measure involved the establishment of NAMA, the National Assets Management Agency, pursuant to the National Asset Management Agency Act 2009 whose function was to acquire property-related loans from participating banks, at a discount, so as to remove those loans from their balance sheets and restore liquidity to the covered banks. In the longer term, structural reforms introduced by the Central Bank of Ireland and Financial Services Regulatory Authority Acts of 2003 and 2004 were reversed, pursuant to the Central Bank Reform Act 2010. Accordingly, the Irish Financial Services Regulatory Authority ('IFSRA') and the Central Bank and Financial Services Regulatory Authority ('CBFSRA') were merged back into a unitary Central Bank, with enhanced regulatory and enforcement powers.[1580]

897. Historically, the Irish Central Bank had overall responsibility for the authorization and supervision of credit institutions, including banks, operating in Ireland. However, from 4 November 2014 this position has changed with a number of supervisory responsibilities and decision-making powers moving to the ECB)through the establishment of the Single Supervisory Mechanism (SSM). The SSM has been established pursuant to Council Regulation 1024/2013 conferring specific tasks on the ECB concerning policies relating to the prudential supervision of credit institutions (the 'SSM Regulation') whereby the ECB is responsible for all core supervisory responsibilities, as defined in the Regulation.[1581] The Regulation was a direct

---

1578. Central Bank and Financial Services Authority of Ireland Act, 2004, s. 16.
1579. This guarantee lasted two years and was replaced by The Eligible Liability Guarantee Scheme (*see*, e.g., The Credit Institutions (Eligible Liabilities Guarantee) Scheme 2009 (S.I. No. 490 of 2009), as amended, which lasted up to 2013. In addition, for depositors, *see further* limited protection offered under the Financial Services (Deposit Guarantee Scheme) Act 2009 and the European Communities (Deposit Guarantee Schemes) Regulations 1995, SI No. S.I. No. 168 of 1995, as amended. *See also* recast Deposit Guarantee Schemes, Directive 2014/49, [2014] OJ L 173/149.
1580. *See also* Central Bank (Supervision and Enforcement) Act 2013.
1581. [2013] OJ L 287/63; *see further* the EU (Single Supervisory Mechanism) Regulations SI No. 495/2014.

response to the recent financial and economic crisis and it seeks to intensify the integration of banking supervision in the EU in order to restore financial stability and lay the basis for economic recovery.[1582] The SSM's three main objectives are to:

- ensure the safety and soundness of the European banking system;
- increase financial integration and stability;
- ensure consistent supervision.

For 'Significant Institutions',[1583] consisting of the larger institutions operating within Ireland, a Joint Supervisory Team, led by the ECB and consisting of both ECB and Central Bank supervisors will directly supervise these firms. Accordingly, the ECB is responsible for the granting of banking licences, with the exception of credit institutions seeking authorization under section 9A of the Central Bank Act 1971 (as amended). The Central Bank remains responsible for the supervision of activities defined in the SSM Regulation as non-core.

898. Those institutions defined as 'Less Significant' will continue to be directly supervised by Central Bank supervision teams. Importantly, today, virtually all of Ireland's banking regulation derives from EU measures. In this regard, and since 1942, a current banker's license (or 'authorization' in EU terminology) has been a prerequisite to carrying on the business of a bank.[1584] For regulatory purposes, 'a banking business' is been defined as any business that consists of or includes:

(a) receiving money on the person's own account from members of the public either on deposit or as repayable funds;
(b) the granting of credits on own account.[1585]

Section 7(1) of the Central Bank Act 1971 provides:

> a person, … , shall not, in or outside the State, carry on banking business or hold himself out or represent himself as a banker or as carrying on banking business or accept deposits or other repayable funds from the public, unless he is the holder of a licence or authorisation under section 9A.

Moreover, the legislation prohibits persons other than licensed banks from advertising for or otherwise soliciting deposits or other repayable funds from the public.[1586] And building societies, any industrial and provident societies, friendly

1582. Recital 2.
1583. *See* www.ecb.europa.eu/pub/pdf/other/ssm-listofsupervisedentities1409en.pdf?59d76de0c5663687f594250ebf228c6b for list of Significant Institutions.
1584. Central Bank Act, 1942, Part VI, now repealed and replaced by Central Bank Act 1971, Part II, as amended.
1585. Central Bank Act 1971, s. 2, as amended by Regulation 154(1)(a) of the EU (Capital Requirements) Regulations 2014, S.I. No. 158/2014. There are numerous statutory exclusions from this definition.
1586. Central Bank Act 1971, s. 27.

societies, credit unions, investment trust companies and unit trusts cannot use in their names the words 'bank', 'banker' or 'banking'.[1587]

899. Thus, only companies or 'credit institutions' envisaged in the relevant EU Banking Directive and Regulation (known as the 'CRD IV' regime) may hold a banking license.[1588] The effect of CRD IV is to exempt a credit institution authorized in another Member State from the need to obtain a banking licence in Ireland. The legislation also gives the Central Bank the power to impose conditions on a banking licence[1589] and it sets out the grounds on which a banking license may be revoked.[1590]

900. In addition to the licensing function, the Central Bank exercises other regulatory functions. For example, the Central Bank has the following powers: the power to obtain an injunction to restrain the carrying on of banking business by an unauthorized person;[1591] the power to direct a bank to cease operations;[1592] the power to conduct inquiries under Part IIIC of the Central Bank Act 1942; and the power to issue directions in relation to advertisements.[1593]

901. To maintain solvency, the Central Bank may prescribe bank capital and liquidity requirements. The EU legislative basis for this financial regulation is the 'CRD IV' regime which comprises Directive 2013/36/EU on access to the activity of credit institutions and the prudential supervision of credit institutions and investment firms,[1594] and Regulation 575/2013 on prudential requirements for credit institutions and investment firms.[1595] This regime introduces a new system for the prudential regulation of banks and credit institutions following the banking crisis which began in 2008. The regulatory framework was devised by the Committee on Banking Supervision based at the Bank for International Settlements (the 'BIS') in Basel, Switzerland: referred to as the 'Basel Committee'. Moreover, rules in the Bank Recovery and Resolution Directive ('BRRD') aim to provide for the resolution of failing banks without the use of taxpayers' money.[1596] The rules introduce a 'bail-in mechanism' whereby shareholders and creditors of the bank will contribute towards the stabilization of failing banks with any additional funds required being

1587. *Ibid.* s. 14.
1588. Directive 2013/36/EU on access to the activity of credit institutions and the prudential supervision of credit institutions and investment firms (CRD IV) [2013] OJ L 176/423, and Regulation (EU) No. 575/2013 on prudential requirements for credit institutions and investment firms (CRR) [2013] OJ L 176/1. *See further* EU (Capital Requirement) Regulations, SI No. 158/2014.
1589. Central Bank Act 1971, s.10.
1590. Central Bank Act 1971, s. 11.
1591. Central Bank Act 1997, s. 74.
1592. Central Bank Act 1971, s. 21.
1593. Central Bank Act 1971, s. 22.
1594. CRD IV; [2013] OJ L 176/423, transposed by the EU (Capital Requirement) Regulations, SI No. 158/2014.
1595. CRR; [2013] OJ L 176/1.
1596. Directive 2014/59 establishing a framework for the recovery and resolution of credit institutions and investment firms, [2014] OJ L L173/190.

provided by national resolution funds set-up under the Directive. The BRRD provides the legal mechanics for bank resolutions within the EU, while the Single Resolution Mechanism (the 'SRM') will provide the funding of such resolutions by way of the establishment of a single resolution fund.[1597]

II. Insurance

902. Since 1936 one has had to hold an insurer's license or authorization to engage in most types of insurance business, except for trade unions and friendly societies. Part II of the Insurance Act 1989, along with various statutory instruments giving effect to EC Directives, establishes an extensive regulatory regime. In 2003, the Financial Regulator (now the Central Bank) became the regulatory authority, except in relation to private health insurance where a Health Insurance Authority has jurisdiction.[1598]

III. Other Financial Services

903. The establishment and operation of building societies are subject to the Building Societies Act 1989, and in 2003, building societies came within the remit of the Financial Regulator (now the Central Bank).[1599] A building society cannot raise funds, or advertise for or otherwise solicit deposits or subscriptions for shares unless duly licensed.[1600]

904. The establishment and operation of credit unions is regulated by the Credit Union Act 1997, Part VI of which deals with their regulation by the Registrar of Credit Unions, an appointee of the Central Bank.

905. Conducting 'investment business' and insurance intermediaries are regulated by the Investment Intermediaries Act 1995, as amended, Part III of which deals with regulation by the Central Bank. In addition, the Investor Compensation Act 1998 establishes a mechanism for payment of compensation to investors who have lost money through authorized investment businesses.

906. Unit trusts are governed by the Unit Trust Act 1990, as amended,[1601] and a register of unit trusts is maintained by the Central Bank.

1597. Regulation 806/2014 establishing uniform rules and a uniform procedure for the resolution of credit institutions and certain investment firms in the framework of a single resolution mechanism and a single resolution fund [2014] OJ L225/1.
1598. *See* Health Insurance Acts, 1994–2007.
1599. *See* Building Society Act, 1989, ss 37–47.
1600. Building Society Act, 1989, s. 17.
1601. There are a number of Undertakings for Collective Investment in Transferable Securities (UCITS) Regulations which amend this legislation: *see*, e.g., SI No. 211 of 2003 and SI No. 497 of 2003.

907. Stock exchanges are governed by the EU (Markets in Financial Instruments) Regulations, 2017[1602] as a 'regulated market', and come within the remit of the Central Bank.[1603] Financial future and options exchanges are governed by Chapter VIII of the Central Bank Act 1989. *Bureaux de change* and money transmission businesses are regulated by Part V of the Central Bank Act 1997, as amended in 2004. And, carrying on business in Dublin's IFSC is subject to sections 41–45 of the Finance Act 1986, as amended.

§2. TRANSPORT

908. The carriage of passengers and of freight is another industry that has traditionally been the subject of extensive regulation.[1604] The common law placed various obligations on common carriers regarding charges and other conditions of carriage. Railways and canals tended to be natural monopolies which, in the nineteenth century, it was feared would abuse their dominant position unless regulated.

909. State-ownership in the transport sector is common in many jurisdictions although the modern trend is towards privatization. In Ireland, the national railway network is owned and operated by Irish Rail, a subsidiary of CIE, a statutory corporation established in 1944 and reconstituted in 1950. Two other CIE subsidiaries, Dublin Bus and Bus Éireann operate the principal road passenger services.[1605] The main international air carrier, Aer Lingus, was privatized in 2006,[1606] but the major airports remain in public ownership under the control of the Dublin, Shannon and Cork Airport Authorities plc.[1607] The major harbours are also owned and operated by State-owned harbour companies, which operate under the Harbours Acts 1996–2000.

I. Road

910. The carriage of passengers and freight by road is a highly regulated activity. Under the Road Transport Acts, 1933–2011, subject to certain exceptions, in order to carry goods for hire, the haulier must possess a road freight carrier's license. Possession of a haulier's license entitles the person to carry on a merchandise road transport business in any part of the State with the vehicle specified in the license. If it is an international road haulage license, it entitles the person to carry goods outside the State as well.

911. Access to the market for carrying passengers by road is governed by the Public Transport Regulation Act 2009. Much of the market remains dominated by

1602. SI No. 375 of 2017.
1603. *See* paras 362–367.
1604. *See further* Arts 90–100 (TFEU) for European transport policy.
1605. *See* Transport (Reorganization of CIE) Act, 1986.
1606. Aer Lingus Act, 2004.
1607. State Airports Act, 2004.

the State-owned companies, Dublin Bus and Bus Éireann, which are the subsidiaries of CIE. A public bus passenger services can only operate under license.[1608] To obtain a license, application must be made to the National Transport Authority.[1609] In making a decision about the granting of a license, the Authority must consider various criteria, laid down in the legislation, including demand for the service; various policy documents; demographic, economic and socials trends; tourism strategies and plans; and local authority development plans.[1610]

912. The Commission for Taxi Regulation, a statutory corporation, was established under the Taxi Regulation Act 2003, to regulate the licensing of taxis and to control their ownership and operation, including setting maximum fares that might be charged.[1611]

913. Schemes for toll-roads are governed by the Roads Acts 1993–2015 and regulated by the National Roads Authority whose primary function is to secure the provision of a safe and efficient network of national roads. For this purpose, it has overall responsibility for the planning, supervision of construction, road network management and maintenance on national roads.

II. Rail

914. In Ireland, the national railway network is owned and operated by Irish Rail, a subsidiary of CIE, established in 1986.[1612] The Transport Acts of 1944 and 1950, as amended, regulate rail transport in Ireland. The 1944 Act also addressed conditions of rail carriage and charges.

915. More recently, the Railway Procurement Agency, established in 2001, is a statutory corporation whose remit is to secure the provision of light railway and metro railway infrastructure as may be determined from time to time by the Minister, and to supervise safety on those services.[1613]

III. Air

916. The Irish Aviation Authority (IAA) is a State-owned private company, established in 1994, which regulates aviation in Ireland,[1614] in particular in relation

1608. Public Transport Regulation Act, 2009, s. 6.
1609. Public Transport Regulation Act, 2009, s. 30.
1610. Public Transport Regulation Act, 2009, s. 10.
1611. Part 4 of the Public Transport Regulation Act, 2009, makes provision for the dissolution of the Commission for Taxi Regulation and the transfer of its powers to the National Transport Authority. This transfer is expected to happen in 2010.
1612. *See* Transport (Reorganization of CIE) Act, 1986.
1613. The Transport (Railway Infrastructure) Act, 2001; *see further* www.rpa.ie.
1614. IAA Act, 1993: *see further* www.iaa.ie.

to air navigation services in Irish-controlled airspace, and safety standards. Its functions include: certifying and registering aircraft airworthiness; licensing personnel and organizations involved in aircraft maintenance; licensing pilots, air traffic controllers and aerodromes; and approving and monitoring air carrier operating standards. Many of the rules in this area derive from internationally set safety standards emanating from the International Civil Aviation Organization; European Joint Aviation Authorities; EUROCONTROL; amongst others. Moreover, the IAA must comply with directions from the Minister.[1615] However, the IAA has no role in relation to charges imposed by air carriers or their terms and condition of carriage. Terms of carriage are subject to the Montreal Convention, 1999.[1616]

917. The Commission for Aviation Regulation, a statutory corporation established in 2001,[1617] regulates airport charges and aviation terminal charges, imposed largely by the State-owned proprietors of airports.[1618] In discharging its role the Commission must ensure that all decisions are 'objectively justified and shall be non-discriminatory, proportionate and transparent'.[1619] On a periodic basis, it must fix maximum charges in accordance with stated criteria, having considered representations made to it by interested parties.[1620] Objections to the charges may be made before an appeal panel and provision is also made for the judicial review of Commission decisions.[1621]

§3. Communications

918. Traditionally, the communications industry, including broadcasting, telephony and postal services, were owned by the State and private enterprise was excluded from this sector.[1622] Today, the principal radio and television stations are owned and operated by RTÉ, a statutory corporation established in 1960. And, the main postal services are provided by An Post, another statutory corporation. This area is also subject to significant European regulation.

1615. IAA Act, 1993, s. 7.
1616. *See* paras 757–765.
1617. Aviation Regulation Act, 2001, as amended by the State Airports Act, 2004 and the Aviation Act 2006.
1618. Aviation Regulation Act, 2001, s. 7: *see* www.aviationreg.ie. The Commission is also responsible for licensing the travel trade in Ireland, and grants licenses to both tour operators and travel age nts. As part of this function, the Commission administers a bonding scheme to reimburse consu mers in the event of a travel agent collapse. The Commission also licenses airlines and approves ground handling services providers under regulations implementing EU legislation.
1619. Aviation Regulation Act, 2001, s. 5.
1620. Aviation Regulation Act, 2001, ss 32–33 and 35–36, as amended by the State Airports Act, 2004.
1621. Aviation Regulation Act, 2001, s. 40 and s. 38 respectively.
1622. *See*, e.g., *AG and Minister for Posts and Telegraphs v. Paperlink Ltd* [1984] ILRM 373 where the statutory monopoly of the Post Office was upheld following a constitutional challenge.

I. Broadcasting

919. Broadcasting is regulated by the Broadcasting Authority of Ireland (BAI), a statutory corporation, established in 2009.[1623] Under the Broadcasting Act 2009, the functions of the Authority include: to develop a strategy for the regulation of broadcasting; to develop codes and rules for broadcasting; to develop a right of reply scheme; to license broadcasting and multiplex services; and to consult with the relevant Minister and the Commission for Communications Regulation (ComReg) on a range of issues. Particular functions under the Act relate to the BAI's oversight of public service broadcasters and the allocation of public funding.

920. The Broadcasting Act 2009 sets out a range of general objectives for the BAI and specifies that it shall endeavour to ensure:

a. that the number and categories of broadcasting services made available in the State best serves the needs of the people of the island of Ireland, bearing in mind their languages and traditions and their religious, ethical and cultural diversity;
b. that the democratic values enshrined in the Constitution, especially those relating to rightful liberty of expression, are upheld;
c. the provision of open and pluralistic broadcasting services.[1624]

The Act also sets out a range of other specific objectives which include to:

a. stimulate the provision of high quality, diverse and innovative programming by commercial, community and public service broadcasters and independent producers;
b. facilitate public service broadcasters in the fulfilment of their public service objects as set out in this Act;
c. promote diversity in control of the more influential commercial and community broadcasting services;
d. provide a regulatory environment that will sustain independent and impartial journalism;
e. provide a regulatory environment that will sustain compliance with applicable employment law;
f. protect the interests of children taking into account the vulnerability of children and childhood to undue commercial exploitation;
g. provide a regulatory environment that will facilitate the development of a broadcasting sector in Ireland that is responsive to audience needs and in particular is accessible to people with disabilities;
h. promote and stimulate the development of Irish language programming and broadcasting services.

1623. The Broadcasting Act 2009: www.bai.ie. The BAI replaced the Broadcasting Commission of Ire land which in turn replaced the Independent Radio and Television Commission established under the Radio and Television Act, 1988: *see also* Broadcasting Act, 2001 and Broadcasting (Funding) Act, 2003.

1624. 2009 Act, s. 25.

II. Telecommunications

921. In 1999, the State-owned telephone system was privatized and the regulatory regime restructured in 2002, with the establishment of the ComReg, a statutory corporation.[1625] ComReg is responsible for the regulation of the electronic communications sector (telecommunications, radio communications and broadcasting transmission) and the postal sector. ComReg's functions include issuing telecommunications licenses and where there is no competition or one supplier is in a dominant position, it may specify a price cap in respect of certain telecommunication services. Public service requirements in relation to permanence and availability of the service can be imposed on licensed operators by the Minister.[1626] The Minister may give directions to ComReg provided they do not relate to individual undertakings[1627] and ComReg though stated to be 'independent in the exercise of its function'[1628] is required to have regard to Government policy statements.[1629]

§4. Other Utilities

922. The electricity market is now regulated by the Commission for Regulation of Utilities (CRU), a statutory corporation first established in 1999 and renamed most recently in 2017.[1630] Its principal function is to assist in the liberalization of the electricity market in line with national and EU energy policy which seeks to create a single European electricity market.[1631] At a more practical level, this involves a break-up of the monopoly position previously enjoyed by the ESB. The CER's functions include granting licenses for electricity generating, authorizing the construction of new electricity plants, approving a grid code and a distribution code prepared by the ESB which allows others access to the grid and distribution systems owned by the ESB and approving connection charges paid to the ESB. The Minister can give directions to the Commission as regards the performance of its functions under the legislation, including directions in relation to the terms and conditions of licenses, but the Minister cannot give directions in respect of the persons to whom licenses may be granted, or the performance of its functions in relation to individual holders of licenses.[1632] Moreover, the legislation states that the Minister and the CRU must exercise their statutory function in a manner which does

1625. Telecommunications (Miscellaneous Provisions) Act, 1996 and Communications Regulation Act, 2002: *see* www.comreg.ie. The Commission's full remit covers the electronic communications sec tor (telecommunications, radio communications and broadcasting transmission) and the postal ser vice.
1626. Communications Regulation Act, 2002, s. 36.
1627. Communications Regulation Act, 2002, s. 13.
1628. Communications Regulation Act, 2002, s. 11.
1629. Communications Regulation Act, 2002, s. 12.
1630. Electricity Regulation Act, 1999; Gas (Interim) Regulation, Act 2002; and the Energy Act 2016: *see* www.cru.ie
1631. *See*, e.g. the Energy (Miscellaneous Provisions) Act 2006; Electricity Regulation (Amendment) (Single Electricity Market) Act 2007; and the Petroleum (Exploration and Extraction) Safety Act 2010.
1632. Electricity Regulation Act, 1999, s. 10.

not discriminate unfairly between applicants or holders of licenses and the ESB, and which protects the interests of final customers.[1633] The Minister may direct the CRU to impose various public service obligations on the ESB and other licensees in relation to a range of issues including security of supply, regularity, quality and price of supplies, environmental protection, and use of indigenous energy sources.[1634] Objections to or representations about certain decisions of the CRU may be the subject of public hearings.[1635] Moreover, the legislation provides for Appeals Panels, which are independent of the CRU, to determine appeals against certain decisions made by the CER.[1636] The Appeals Panels are given the same powers vested in the High Court to enforce the attendance of witnesses and their examination on oath or otherwise, and to compel the production of documents.

923. The natural gas market also comes within the remit of the CRU where again the CRU's function is to assist in the liberalization of the market for gas and to break-up the previous monopoly position of Bord Gáis in line with the national and European energy policy.[1637] As with the electricity market, similar public service obligations can be imposed on natural gas undertakings.[1638]

924. More recently, the CRU's functions have been expanded into the water sector pursuant to the Water Services Acts 2007-17. The water regulatory functions assigned to CRU include:

(a) the fixing of charges in respect of the provision of such water services;
(b) the specification of minimum standards of service with respect to the provision of such water services;
(c) the protection of the interests of persons to whom water services are provided.[1639]

§5. Leisure Services

I. Tour Operators and Travel Agents

925. Under the Transport (Travel Trade) Acts 1982–1995, as amended, a person or body cannot engage in the business of tour operator or travel agent without possessing a current license from the Commission for Aviation Regulation, a statutory corporation established in 2001.[1640] Before such a license can be obtained, the applicant must satisfy the Commission that his/her financial and other resources are adequate for discharging his/her actual and potential obligations in respect of his/

1633. Electricity Regulation Act, 1999, s. 9(3).
1634. Electricity Regulation Act, 1999, s. 39.
1635. Electricity Regulation Act, 1999, s. 21.
1636. Electricity Regulation Act, 1999, ss 29–32.
1637. Gas (Interim) Regulation Act, 2002.
1638. Gas (Interim) Regulation Act, 2002, s. 21.
1639. Water Services Act 2013, s. 27.
1640. Aviation Regulation Act, 2001, s. 9: *see* www.aviationreg.ie.

her activities and that he/she is 'a fit and proper person' to carry on that business. Moreover, before a license is granted, the tour operator or travel agents must enter into a bond, to the satisfaction of the Commission, for the protection of persons who, during the period of validity of the license, enter into contracts with him/her relating to overseas travel. A license can be revoked by the Commission if it is satisfied that any of those conditions are no longer being met. Additionally, every licensed undertaking in this business must make a specified contribution to a Traveller's Protection Fund; payments are made from this fund to customers of the licensed undertaking which collapsed or otherwise failed to discharge its obligations.

926. Further consumer protection measures were introduced under the Package Holidays and Travel Trade Act 1995, as amended, which transposes EU Directive 2015/2301 on package travel and linked travel arrangements.[1641] Part II of the 1995 Act imposes obligations on travel service providers and others in relation to package holidays and linked travel arrangements for travellers. For example, certain minimum information must be provided pre-contract and in a particular form. Most significantly perhaps, the organizer is responsible for the performance of the travel services included in the package travel contract, irrespective of whether those services are to be performed by the organizer, the retailer or other suppliers of services.[1642]

II. Hotels

927. The National Tourism Development Authority, known as Fáilte Ireland, a statutory corporation established in 2003, has responsibility to promote tourist traffic within the State and more particularly to establish and maintain a register of hotels and other forms of tourist accommodation.[1643] Hotels and other places of accommodation must comply with the Tourist Traffic Acts 1939–2016 before they can register with the Authority and it is prohibited to describe a premises as a hotel, guesthouse, hostel or holiday camp unless duly registered. The Authority also has responsibility for grading of hotels and other accommodation and periodic inspection of such premises. Rights and obligations vis-à-vis guests, arising under common law, are replaced by those in the Hotel Proprietors Act, 1963. The 1963 Act addresses the duty to receive 'all comers' and their property and to take reasonable care of them and imposes liability for loss or damage to property, subject to a monetary ceiling.

1641. *See* S.I. No. 80/2019.
1642. 1995 Act, s. 19, as amended: *see further Scaife v. Falcon Leisure Group* [2007] IESC 57.
1643. National Tourism Development Authority Act, 2003: *see* www.failteireland.ie.

III. Sport

928. The majority of sporting activities are not regulated by legislation, although disputes within sporting organizations may find their way to the courts. However, a number of sports, namely horseracing and greyhound racing and coursing, are regulated, in part, by legislation.

929. Horse Racing Ireland, a statutory corporation, established in 2001,[1644] in conjunction with the Irish Turf Club (for flat racing) and the Irish National Hunt Steeplechase Committee (for national hunt racing), regulates horseracing in Ireland, within the framework of the Irish Horseracing Industry Act, 1994. The Greyhound Industry Act 1958–1993 established Bord na gCon, which is charged with supervising the greyhound racing industry.

IV. Gambling

930. Gambling is regulated by a number of pieces of legislation. Bookmaking and betting is governed by the Betting Act, 1931, the Greyhound Industry Act, 1958 and the Irish Horseracing Industry Act, 1994.[1645] Further, the Gaming and Lotteries Acts, 1956–2013, regulate gaming, amusement halls, funfairs and lotteries. There is also a National Lottery and a National Lottery Regulator, pursuant to the National Lotteries Act 2013. But beyond the National Lottery, there is no centralized regulatory authority in this broad area, instead the legislation is administered by the Gardaí (Irish police force) and the courts. The legislation establishes similar regimes for licensing the person carrying on the relevant business and for licensing each business premises. Several types of gambling and lotteries are prohibited. At the time of writing, a Gambling Control Bill 2018 is before the Houses of the Oireachtas (the Parliament), though progress with this legislation has been very slow. As drafted, the Bill would repeal existing legislation in this regard and replace it with a comprehensive new unified licensing and regulatory framework for gambling in Ireland.

§6. Property Services: Including Auctioneers and Estate Agents

931. A new regulatory regime was introduced in Ireland for auctioneers, estate agents and others offering property services, pursuant to the Property Services (Regulation) Act 2011.[1646] The legislation, and implementing Regulations, provide for the establishment of the Property Services Regulatory Authority, since 2012, whose main function is to control and regulate Property Services Providers (i.e., Auctioneers/Estate Agents, Letting Agents and Management Agents). This involves

---

1644. Horse and Greyhound Racing Act, 2001.
1645. *See also* Horse and Greyhound Racing (Betting Charges and Levies) Act, 1999.
1646. *See also* www. pav.ie.

the licensing of all such services providers; the establishment of a complaints investigation and redress system for consumers; the setting and enforcement of standards in the provision of property services; rules around the administration of client accounts; the establishment of a compensation fund; and the creation of three Public Registers. The Authority has three such registers namely, the 'Register of Licensed Property Services Providers', the 'Residential Property Price Register' and the 'Commercial Leases Register': all of which can be accessed online.[1647]

§7. AUDITING

932. The auditing of books and accounts of registered companies, including who is entitled to be appointed as a statutory auditor, is regulated by the EC (Statutory Audits) (Directive 2006/43/EC) Regulations 2010,[1648] as amended, and Part 6 of the Companies Act 2014. In broad terms, the Regulations provide for the approval of statutory auditors and audit firms, by recognized competent authorities, and the officers of the company must ensure that their auditor is registered on the Public Register of Auditors which may be viewed on the CRO website.[1649] The Regulations include provisions requiring continuing education and professional ethics as well as standards of objectivity and independence. In particular, a statutory auditor must be independent of, and not involved in the decision-taking of, the audited entity.[1650]

§8. LEGAL SERVICES

933. Professional legal services are provided by either solicitors or barristers, in Ireland. Most solicitors operate in private practice, as sole traders or within a partnership,[1651] providing a wide range of legal services directly to the public. Solicitors are both represented and regulated by the Law Society of Ireland. The Law Society, established in 1773, exercises statutory functions under the Solicitors Acts 1954–2015 in relation to the education, admission, enrolment and discipline of the solicitors' profession.[1652] Barristers, in contrast, do not offer legal services directly to the public but are usually engaged by solicitors on behalf of their clients. Barristers must operate as independent sole traders. They specialize in advocacy and the provision of legal opinions. The Bar Council is the representative and regulatory body for practicing barristers, while the Honourable Society of King's Inns is the sole provider of training and hence regulates entry into the profession.[1653]

1647. www.psr.ie.
1648. SI No. 220/2010.
1649. www.cro.ie
1650. *See further* Part 7 of I No. 220/2010.
1651. Solicitors are prohibited from establishing as corporate entities: Solicitors Act, 1954, s. 64.
1652. *See* www.lawsociety.ie.
1653. *See* www.lawlibrary.ie and www.kingsinns.ie.

934. As a condition of Ireland's EU-IMF bailout programme, the Legal Services Regulation Act 2015 was enacted establishing an independent Legal Services Regulatory Authority with the remit to regulate the provision of legal services by legal practitioners in Ireland and to ensure the maintenance and improvement of standards in the provision of legal services in the State. From 7 October 2019, the Authority started to accept complaints from the public about legal practitioners.

Chapter 3. State Incentives for Economic Activities

935. The principal methods by which the State encourages economic activities are by way of subsidies and by tax incentives. In the past, the State has also encouraged particular kinds of activities by undertaking them itself, either by constituting a statutory corporation or by forming a company to engage in an activity or else by acquiring all or some of the shares in a company already engaged in that activity. More recently, the trend has been in the direction of privatizing such enterprises.

§1. Subsidies

936. A considerable variety of subsidies, grants and other incentives for industry and commerce are made available by the State. Perhaps the most important source of these is the IDA, which was founded in 1949 as a part of a government department and became an autonomous statutory corporation under the Industrial Development Act, 1969.[1654] Among the main grants it provides to foreign companies are employment grants, training grants, grants towards research and development and capital grants. While the IDA focuses on foreign investment, Enterprise Ireland is the government agency responsible for the development and promotion of the indigenous business sector through the provision of financial and other services.[1655] Grants to attract industry to Gaeltacht areas are administered by Údarás na Gaeltachta;[1656] grants to attract industry to the Shannon area (Limerick and Clare) are administered by Shannon Development.[1657] Other public bodies providing advice and financial incentives include the Local Enterprise Offices,[1658] and the Education and Training Boards Ireland.[1659]

§2. Tax Incentives

937. Practically all economic activity of significance is carried on by companies within the definition of the Taxes Consolidation Act, 1997, meaning 'any body corporate', with the exception of enumerated public bodies.[1660] Companies resident in the State, with some exceptions, and non-resident companies who trade through a branch or agency are subject to Irish corporation tax. However, a variety of incentives exists to encourage investment by foreign and indigenous enterprises including low corporation tax rates, research and development tax credits, a favourable holding company regime and a patent royalty income exemption. Moreover, Ireland

1654. www.idaireland.ie.
1655. www.enterprise-ireland.com.
1656. www.udaras.ie.
1657. www.shannondevelopment.ie.
1658. www.localenterprise.ie/.
1659. www.etbi.ie.
1660. 1997 Act, s. 4.

has double taxation agreements with seventy-four countries, of which seventy-three are in effect[1661] and continues to negotiate agreements with many other jurisdictions.

938. Since 2003, the standard rate of corporation tax is 12.5% on chargeable profits.[1662] 'Profits' for corporation tax purposes consist of income (business or trading income comprising active income, and investment income comprising passive income) and capital gains, which arise on the disposal of capital assets.[1663]

939. In 2004, Ireland introduced a new Research & Development (R&D) Tax Credit which was designed to encourage both foreign and indigenous companies to undertake new and/or additional R&D activity in Ireland. For example, both revenue and capital expenditure on scientific research is allowable as a trading expense in the year in which the expenditure is incurred. Moreover, a patent royalty exemption (limited to EUR 5 million per annum) applies in respect of royalty income for qualifying patents, i.e., a patent on which the main research and development was conducted in the EEA. The recipient of the royalty income must be Irish tax resident.

940. Also, recent legislation has put Ireland in a position to compete with existing holding company locations within Europe. Until recently, investment in Ireland was likely to be routed through a holding company in another European location. With these new changes, an Irish company can now act as a European/Regional holding or intermediate holding company.

1661. *See* www.revenue.ie.
1662. This rate compares favourable with many jurisdictions including China at 25%; the UK at 28%; Japan and Germany at 30%; France at 34.43% and the USA at 39.5%: *Deloitte & Touche, 2008.*
1663. A higher rate of 25% applies to non-trading income such as interest gains, foreign sourced income and profits and rental income.

Chapter 4. Competition Law

§1. Antitrust Law

941. Both Irish law and EU law contain rules designed to promote competition. Articles 101 and 102 of the Treaty on the Functioning of the European Union (TFEU) form the basis of EU competition law, dealing with cartels and anti-competitive agreements, and abuse of market power respectively. Regulation 139/2004 (the Merger Regulation) deals with mergers which have a Community dimension. Moreover, from 1 May 2004, Articles 101 and 102 have been directly applicable in Member States and hence the application and enforcement of Articles 101 and 102 is shared between the European Commission[1664] and national competition authorities (NCAs), including the Irish CCPC,[1665] and the courts. The main source of Irish competition law is the Competition Acts 2002–2017 which regulate cartels and anti-competitive agreements, abuse of market power and mergers. The legislation is closely modelled on the provisions of EU law.

942. Some conduct is prohibited by domestic law, some by EU law, some by both. In general, EU law applies wherever conduct has an effect on trade within the community between Member States. Where conduct has effect only within Ireland, domestic law applies. In the past the European authorities have adopted a fairly broad interpretation of 'conduct which has effects on trade between Member States' effectively widening the area of application of EU law. Where conduct with such effect is permitted by domestic law but prohibited by EU law, EU law takes priority and the conduct is prohibited. The situation where conduct with effects on inter-state trade is prohibited by national law but permitted by EU law is covered by Article 3 of Regulation 1/2003 (the Modernization Regulation). Article 3(1) provides that NCAs and national courts must always apply Article 101 to agreements which 'may affect trade between Member States within the meaning of that provision'. Moreover, Article 3(2) provides that the application of national competition law may not lead to the prohibition of agreements which may affect trade between Member States that do not restrict competition within the meaning of Article 101(1) or that fulfil the conditions of Article 101(3). The position is different with regard to conduct which may amount to abuse of a dominant position within the scope of Article 102, where national law is permitted to have stricter effects than EU law.

943. The legal position under both European and Irish law will be outlined below.

1664. *See* http://ec.europa.eu/comm/competition/index_en.html.
1665. *See* www.ccpc.ie.

I. Restrictive Practices

A. *European Law*

944. Article 101(1) prohibits certain anti-competitive agreements and activities. An agreement or activity which contravenes this prohibition is automatically void under Article 101(2) unless exempted under Article 101(3).

1. The Article 101(1) Prohibition

945. Article 101 (TFEU) prohibits as incompatible with the common market:

> all agreements between undertakings, decisions by associations of undertakings and concerted practices which may affect trade between Member States and which have as their object or effect the prevention, restriction or distortion of competition within the common market, and in particular those which:
>
> a. directly or indirectly fix purchase or selling prices or any other trading conditions;
> b. limit or control production, markets, technical development, or investment;
> c. share markets or sources of supply;
> d. apply dissimilar conditions to equivalent trading transactions with other trading parties, thereby placing them at a competitive disadvantage;
> e. make the conclusion of contracts subject to the acceptance by other parties of supplementary obligations which, by their nature or according to commercial usage, have no connection with the subject of such contracts.

Accordingly, the prohibition in Article 101(1) only applies if four conditions are fulfilled. First, Article 101 applies to agreements between and decisions and concerted practices of 'undertakings'. The Commission has defined an undertaking as 'any entity carrying on a commercial activity'.[1666] Companies, partnerships, individuals and nationalized industries are therefore all 'undertakings'.

946. Second, Article 101 does not apply only to legally enforceable contracts but also to 'concerted practices' so that it can cover informal 'gentlemen's agreements'. In the *Sugar Cartel case,*[1667] the Court of Justice explained that Article 101 prohibits:

1666. *Re Polypropylene Cartel* [1988] 4 CMLR 347.
1667. [1975] ECR 1916.

> a form of co-ordination between undertakings which, without having reached the stage where an agreement properly so-called has been concluded, knowingly substitutes for the risks of competition practical cooperation between them which leads to conditions of competition which do not correspond to the market.

947. Third, if the object of an agreement is the restriction of competition, it contravenes Article 101.[1668] Thus any agreement to fix prices, limit production or divide markets will contravene Article 101, even if the agreement would not in fact have achieved its object. If the object of the agreement is not the restriction of competition, one must consider its effect. The Commission must consider not only the agreement itself, but any surrounding agreements and the generally prevailing market conditions.[1669] Article 101(1) lists five types of distortion or restriction of competition; however, it has also been applied to conduct far less obviously restrictive of competition. For instance, it has been held that Article 101 is contravened if certain types of information are exchanged;[1670] and if there is any kind of restriction on the right of a party to the agreement to export or import goods to or from other Member States.[1671]

948. Lastly, Article 101 applies only where the agreement in question has an effect on inter-state trade. The Court of Justice and Commission have, unsurprisingly, taken a wide view of what is meant by an effect on inter-state trade: the Commission need only prove that there is a possibility of an impact on trade, which can be direct or indirect.[1672] Thus, an agreement will affect inter-state trade whenever it causes a change in the volume of trade that is not *de minimis*, or has the potential to cause such a change. There will also be an effect on inter-state trade if there will be a significant change in the structure of the market, for example, if there is a possibility that new firms will enter the market or an existing supplier will leave it.[1673] Agreements with only a minimal impact on inter-state trade are not caught by Article 101, but this *de minimis* doctrine is narrowly construed. Whether an agreement is too trivial to come within the terms of Article 101 is a matter of fact in each case,[1674] but the Commission has issued Notices of Guidance which, while not binding on it, indicate the approach which it will take.[1675]

2. Article 101(2)

949. An agreement which contravenes Article 101(1) is automatically void unless exempted under Article 101(3). It cannot be enforced by any of the parties,

1668. *Société Technique Minière v. Maschinenbau Ulm* [1966] ECR 235.
1669. *Brasserie de Haecht SA v. WilkinJanssen* [1967] ECR 407.
1670. *Soda Ash Cartel* case [1991] 4 CMLR 502.
1671. *Consten SA and Grundig-Verkaufs GmbH v. Commission* [1966] ECR 299.
1672. *Consten and Grundig v. Commission* [1966] ECR 299.
1673. *Commercial Solvents* [1974] ECR 223.
1674. *Volk v. Vervaecke* [1969] CMLR 273.
1675. *See* latest Notice on agreements of minor importance at [2014] OJ C 291/01.

and, in addition, third parties who are adversely affected can bring civil proceedings.[1676] The parties may also be liable to substantial fines.[1677]

3. Exemption under Article 101(3)

950. Under Article 101(3), Article 101(1) may be declared inapplicable to:

> any agreement or category of agreements between undertakings; any decision or category of decisions by associations of undertakings; any concerted practice or category of concerted practices; which contributes to improving the production or distribution of goods or to promoting technical or economic progress, while allowing consumers a fair share of the resulting benefit, and which does not:
>
> a. impose on the undertakings concerned restrictions which are not indispensable to the attainment of these objectives;
> b. afford such undertakings the possibility of eliminating competition in respect of a substantial part of the products in question.

This power may be exercised to grant exemption to an individual agreement; it has also been used to grant 'block' exemptions to certain categories of agreement.

951. The Commission has issued several 'block' exemptions which set out the conditions under which particular types of agreement will qualify for exemption from Article 101(1), including block exemptions relating to:

a. vertical restraints;[1678]
b. motor vehicle distribution;[1679]
c. specialization;[1680]
d. research and development;[1681]
e. technology transfer agreements.[1682]

1676. *Garden Cottage Foods Ltd v. Milk Marketing Board* [1984] AC 130; *Inntrepreneur v. Crehan* [2004] UKHL 38; *see further* Directive 2014/104/EU on antitrust damages actions under national law [2014] OJ L 349/1. For example, the Directive clarifies that victims are entitled to full compensation for the harm suffered, covering compensation for actual loss, loss of profit, plus interest. The Directive establishes a rebuttable presumption that cartels cause harm. And any participant in an infringement will be responsible towards the victims for the whole harm caused by the infringement (joint and several liability), with the possibility of obtaining a contribution from other infringers for their share of responsibility. Member States need to implement the Directive in their legal systems by 27 Dec. 2016.
1677. *See Guidelines on the method of setting fines* [2006] OJ C 210/2.
1678. Regulation 330/2010 [2010] OJ L 102/1.
1679. Regulation 461/2010 [2010] OJ L 129/52.
1680. Regulation 1218/2010 [2010] OJ L 335/4
1681. Regulation 1217/2010 [2010] OJ L 335/36.
1682. Regulation 316/2014 [2014] OJ L93/17.

952. From 1 May 2004, the Commission's former monopoly over the granting of individual exemptions under Article 101(3) has been eliminated pursuant to Regulation 1/2003.[1683] Accordingly, Article 101(3) is now directly applicable by national courts and NCAs. In particular, subject to the final control of the Court of Justice of the European Union (CJEU), national courts and NCAs have the power and obligation to rule on the application of Article 101(3). Importantly, however, national courts and NCAs are not empowered to grant individual exemptions to applicants under Regulation 1/2003. Instead, as with the Commission, individual NCAs will apply Article 101(3) in the context of other proceedings, such as infringement proceedings. Similarly, national courts will apply Article 101(3) in the context of ordinary civil proceedings, such as where damages for breach of Article 101 and/or the enforceability of an agreement are at issue. To assist undertakings in this task, the Commission has issued a series of Notices setting out principles developed by the CJEU and the Commission's interpretation of these principles.[1684]

B. *Irish Law*

953. Section 4 of the Competition Act 2002 deals with anti-competitive agreements and practices. Its terminology mirrors closely that of Article 101. Certain anti-competitive agreements and practices are prohibited and void under section 4(1) unless exempted under section 4(2).

1. Section 4(1) Prohibition

954. As with Article 101, there are four conditions to the section 4(1) prohibition. First, and like Article 101, section 4(1) applies to agreements between and decisions and concerted practices of 'undertakings'. Section 3(1) of the 2002 Act defines undertaking as:

> a person being an individual, a body corporate or an unincorporated body of persons engaged for gain in the production, supply or distribution of goods or the provision of a service.

1683. [2003] OJ L 1/1.

1684. *See*, e.g., *Guidelines on the effect on trade concept contained in Arts 81 and 82*, [2004] OJ C 101/81; and *Guidelines on the application of Art. 81(3)*, [2004] OJ C 101/97. Moreover, the Commission has issued a *Notice on informal guidance relating to novel questions concerning Arts 81 and 82 that arise in individual cases*, whereby undertakings can seek informal guidance on a novel question in a written statement, known as 'guidance letters', from the Commission (*see further* [2004] OJ C 101/78).

It has been held that the term 'for gain' does not equate to 'for profit' and in *Deane v. VHI*[1685] the Supreme Court held that the term 'for gain' covers activity carried on or a service supplied in return for a charge or payment, and hence the VHI, a non-profit organization was held to be an undertaking for the purpose of section 4.

955. Second, section 4(1) applies to agreements, decisions and concerted practices. For example, in *The Booksellers Association (Currency Conversion Agreement),*[1686] the Booksellers Association circulated a currency conversion chart for the conversion of printed sterling on books, called a 'ready reckoner', to its members. The Competition Authority identified this as a decision of an association, finding that compliance with the chart would have an appreciable effect on the market.

956. Third, the object or effect of the agreement, decision or concerted practice must be to prevent, restrict or distort competition. It was noted in *Masterfoods v. HB Ice-cream Ltd*[1687] the term 'object or effect' can be read disjunctively. Accordingly, even if the undertakings did not intend to prevent, restrict or distort competition, but the effect of their agreements or conduct does so, then section 4 will be breached. Moreover, in assessing the object of an agreement it has been held that it is important to consider the objective circumstances of the case and not the subjective intentions of the parties.[1688]

957. Lastly, the arrangement under scrutiny must prevent, restrict or distort competition in trade-in any goods or services in the State or any part of the State. However, unlike Article 101, there is no *de minimis* doctrine and therefore, in theory, even arrangements with a minimal impact can be prohibited by section 4(1). In *Nallan/O'Toole,*[1689] the Competition Authority decided not to adopt a strict literal interpretation of section 4(1) because:

> virtually every form of business agreement effectively prohibits others from concluding the very same contract with the original parties. Such an interpretation would render it virtually impossible for business to operate.

Like Article 101, section 4(1) provides a non-exhaustive list of types of prohibited behaviour including price-fixing, quote-fixing and market division.

2. Section 4(2) Exemption

958. Section 4(2) states:

1685. [1992] 2 IR 319.
1686. Decision No. 348 (1994).
1687. [1993] ILMR 145.
1688. *Chanelle Veterinary Ltd v. Pfizer (Ireland) Ltd* [1998] ILRM 161.
1689. Decision No. 1 (1992).

> An agreement, decision or concerted practice shall not be prohibited under subsection (1) if it complies with the conditions referred to in subsection (5) or falls within a category of agreements, decisions, or concerted practices the subject of a declaration for the time being in force under subsection (3).

Subsection (3) allows the CCPC to issue written declarations that in its opinion a specified category of agreement, decision or concerted practice complies with the conditions laid down in subsection (5).[1690] These conditions mirror those in Article 101(3). This automatic exemption scheme replaces a previous notification and individual exemption scheme, and is in line with changes introduced by the EU's Modernization Regulation discussed above.

3. Effect of Breach of Section 4(1)

959. Under section 4(1), prohibited arrangements are void and unenforceable. Further, any person aggrieved by such arrangements has a civil right of action against the undertaking involved.[1691] Action can be taken in the Circuit Court or the High Court and remedies available include an injunction or declaration and/or damages, including exemplary damages. Moreover, section 6(1) of the 2002 Act makes it a criminal offence to breach section 4(1) or Article 101. An undertaking guilty of an offence is liable on summary conviction, in the case of an undertaking that is not an individual, to a fine not exceeding EUR 5,000, or in the case of an individual, to such a fine or to imprisonment for a term not exceeding six months or to both such fine and such imprisonment. On conviction on indictment, the sanctions increase. In the case of an undertaking that is not an individual, the undertaking is liable to a fine not exceeding whichever of the following amounts is the greater, namely, EUR 5,000,000 or 10% of the turnover of the undertaking in the financial year ending in the twelve months prior to the conviction, or in the case of an individual, the undertaking is liable to a fine not exceeding whichever of the following amounts is the greater, namely, EUR 5,000,000 or 10% of the turnover of the individual in the financial year ending in the twelve months prior to the conviction or to imprisonment for a term not exceeding ten years or to both.[1692]

II. Monopolies and Abuse of Dominant Position

A. *European Law*

960. Article 102 (TFEU) is designed to prevent the exploitation of market power. It reads as follows:

1690. Category Licences issued under the Competition Act 1991 remain in effect as declaration under Sch. 2 of the 2002 Act.
1691. 2002 Act, s. 14.
1692. 2002 Act, s. 8, as amended.

Any abuse by one or more undertakings of a dominant position within the common market or in a substantial part of it shall be prohibited as incompatible with the common market in so far as it may affect trade between Member States. Such abuse may, in particular, consist in:

a. directly or indirectly imposing unfair purchase prices or unfair trading conditions;
b. limiting production, markets or technical development to the prejudice of consumers;
c. applying dissimilar conditions to equivalent transactions with other trading parties, thereby placing them at a competitive disadvantage;
d. making the conclusion of contracts subject to acceptance by the other parties of supplementary obligations which, by their nature or according to commercial usage, have no connection with the subject of such contracts.

There are thus four questions to be addressed: what is the relevant market; what constitutes 'dominance'; what is a 'substantial' part of the common market; and what constitutes 'abuse' of a dominant position?[1693]

1. The Relevant Market

961. An undertaking cannot simply be 'dominant'; it must be dominant in relation to a particular product and geographical market.[1694] The definition of the product market therefore becomes of crucial importance: if the market is defined narrowly, the undertaking in question will have a larger share than it would if the market were to be given a wide definition. For example, in one of the first major Article 102 decisions, *Europemballage Corp and Continental Can Co Inc v. Commission,*[1695] the Commission found that the undertaking in question was dominant because of its large share in the markets for cans for meat, cans for fish and metal tops. The appellant successfully contended that the market should have been defined more widely, as the market for packaging for food generally. As its market share for packaging generally was not as high, it was not in a dominant position.

962. A number of factors are relevant to defining the relevant market. The first is the interchangeability of demand and supply (or, to use economic language, 'cross-elasticity'). If consumers will buy product A instead of product B when the price of product B goes up, then A and B are part of the same market. Similarly, if manufacturer C puts up its prices and manufacturer D starts supplying similar products, there is interchangeability of supply, and any consideration of C's market power has to take into account the threat to it from D. Other factors are relevant in

1693. *See further* Guidance on the Commission's enforcement priorities in applying Art. 82 (now 102) [2009] OJ C 45/7 which sets out an economic and effects-based approach to exclusionary conduct under European law, in line with more recent case law.
1694. *Notice on the definition of the relevant market for the purposes of Arts 85 and 86* (now Arts 101 and 102), [1997] OJ C 372/5; [1998] 4 CMLR 117.
1695. [1973] ECR 215 (the *Continental Can* case).

identifying the relevant market. For example, in *United Brands v. Commission,*[1696] the Court of Justice held that price, physical characteristics and intended use must be taken into account so that, applying these criteria, the market for bananas was separate from that for fruit generally.

2. Dominance

963. Having defined the relevant market, the next question is whether the undertaking is 'dominant'. A company is dominant where it is able to act independently of its suppliers and customers (e.g., by dictating the prices at which it will buy and sell things), and where it is able to prevent effective competition.[1697] In later cases, undertakings have been found to be dominant where competition is seriously restricted, but is not altogether eliminated.[1698]

964. The most important factor in determining dominance is the market share of the undertaking, together with the market shares of other members of the market. In *Hoffman La Roche,* the Court of justice said that a high market share (probably in excess of 65%–70%) will almost certainly be enough to prove dominance, unless the undertaking can show that special factors exist (e.g., that there is a major producer ready to enter the market if customers no longer believe that they are getting a good deal). However, dominance can exist where the market share is as low as 40%–45%, provided that the other members of the market are too small and fragmented to present a serious threat. The Commission can also take into account the power resulting from: intellectual property rights;[1699] superior distribution systems;[1700] and overall size and strength.[1701]

3. A Substantial Part of the Common Market

965. There is no simple definition of what amounts to a substantial part of the common market based on geographical or other criteria. An entire Member State will be regarded as a substantial part of the EU,[1702] as will a large part of a large Member State.[1703] In *RTE v. Commission,*[1704] it was held by the Court of First Instance that where dominance exists over the whole of one Member State and part

1696. [1978] 1 CMLR 429.
1697. *Hoffman La Roche v. Commission* [1979] ECR 461.
1698. *See*, e.g., *AKZO Chemie BV v. EC Commission* [1991] 1 ECR 3359.
1699. *Tetra Pak v. Commission* [1997] 4 CMLR 662.
1700. *United Brands v. Commission.*
1701. *Hoffman La Roche.*
1702. *BRT v. SABAM* [1974] ECR 313.
1703. For example, southern Germany: *Suiker Unie v. Commission* [1975] ECR 1663.
1704. [1991] 4 CMLR 586.

of another, there is definitely dominance in a substantial part of the common market. Where the dominance covers only part of a Member State, it will be necessary to consider the share of the total EU market represented by the area in question, along with geographical considerations.

4. Abuse

966. Article 102 includes a non-exhaustive list of types of conduct which may be regarded as an 'abuse' for its purposes. Other conduct which may attract sanctions includes:

(a) predatory pricing, where the monopolist prices below-cost to drive out competitors (with the intention of raising prices once it is alone in the market again);[1705]
(b) the practice of giving 'loyalty' discounts when a purchaser obtains all or most of its requirements from the dominant firm;[1706]
(c) the use of intellectual property rights to restrict access to the market by competitors;[1707]
(d) any attempt to impose export bans on trade between Member States in order to keep prices high;[1708]
(e) refusing to supply a customer with raw materials which will be used to make products to compete with the manufacturer in another market, or to discriminate between customers when allocating scarce goods.[1709]

967. The Court of Justice has developed the concept of 'objective justification' to determine whether particular conduct is abusive. For example, in deciding whether a system of rebates and discounts contravenes Article 102, the Commission should look at whether they reflect matters such as economies of scale or reductions in cost arising from the reduced risk of not being able to sell all one's products, or whether they are unrelated to such factors but are designed to deter customers from finding new suppliers. Similarly, a refusal to supply may be objectively justified on the grounds that the purchaser does not know how to use the products properly, and so may cause accidents or otherwise damage the reputation of the manufacturer.

B. Irish Law

968. Abuses of dominant power are prohibited under section 5 of the 2002 Act which mirrors closely the wording of Article 102. Therefore, the relevant market

---

1705. *AKZO Chemie BV v. EC Commission* [1991] 1 ECR 3359.
1706. *Hoffman La Roche v. Commission* [1979] ECR 461; *Michelin v. Commission* [1983] ECR 3461.
1707. *Tetra Pak Rausing v. Commission* [1991] 4 CMLR 344.
1708. *United Brands v. Commission* [1978] ECR 207.
1709. *Commercial Solvents* [1974] ECR 223; *BPB Industries plc v. Commission* [1993] 5 CMLR 32.

must be identified;[1710] the undertaking must be dominant, in that market, in trade for goods or services in the State or any part of the State;[1711] and there must be abuse. Abuse is not defined but, like Article 102, section 5 provides a non-exhaustive list of abusive behaviour including price-fixing, market-sharing; limiting output; discriminatory treatment and tying arrangements. Any person aggrieved by such abuse has a civil right of action against the undertaking involved.[1712] Actions can be taken in the Circuit Court or the High Court and remedies available include an injunction or declaration and/or damages, including exemplary damages. Further, section 7 renders it a criminal offence to abuse a dominant position under section 5(1) and Article 102. The same penalties apply as with section 6.[1713]

III. Mergers and Acquisitions

A. *European Law*

969. Regulation 139/2004 (the Merger Regulation) governs all mergers or 'concentrations' with a 'Community dimension'.[1714] The Merger Regulation requires all concentrations of a particular size to be notified to the Commission before they are put into effect.[1715]

970. A 'concentration' occurs when two or more undertakings merge,[1716] or when one person who already controls one undertaking acquires direct or indirect control over another.[1717] A person has 'control' if, for example, he/she has sufficient voting rights to exercise 'decisive influence' over the undertaking in question.[1718]

1710. *See*, e.g., *Competition Authority v. O ' Regan & Ors* [2007] IESC 22; *Masterfoods v. HB Ice-cream Ltd* [1993] ILMR 145.
1711. In *Deane v. VHI* [1992] 2 IR 319 the VHI were found to be dominant in the health insurance market with a market share of 92%; in *Masterfoods v. HB Ice-cream Ltd* [1993] ILMR 145, HB were found dominant with a market share of 70% in the impulse ice-cream market. *See further Meridian Communication Ltd and Cellular Three Ltd v. Eircell Ltd* [2002] 1 IR 17 where the market share of rivals was considered in determining dominance. In this case Eircell held a 60% share and Esat Digifone a 40% share. The fact that Esat had acquired its share in a three-year period meant that Eircell was not in a dominant position.
1712. 2002 Act, s. 14.
1713. 2002 Act, s. 8, as amended.
1714. The Merger Regulation, [2004] OJ L 24/1; *see also* Regulation 802/2004 implementing Regulation 139/2004, [2004] OJ L 133/1, as amended. The Merger Regulation was reviewed: *see* White Paper, *Towards more effective EU merger control,* COM(2014) 449 final.
1715. For procedures *see* Implementing Regulation 802/2004, [2004] OJ L 133/1, as amended.
1716. *See* Consolidated Jurisdictional Notice under Council Regulation (EC) No. 139/2004 on the control of concentrations between undertakings (2008/C 95/01).
1717. Article 3.
1718. Article 3(2).

Acquisition of a substantial minority shareholding can thus amount to a concentration.[1719] And the creation of a joint venture performing on a lasting basis all the functions of an autonomous economic entity constitutes a concentration.[1720]

971. A concentration has a Community dimension if:

(a) the combined aggregate worldwide turnover of all the undertakings concerned exceeds EUR 5,000 million;
(b) the aggregate EU turnover of each of at least two of the undertakings concerned exceeds EUR 250 million.[1721]

If, however, each of the undertakings concerned achieves more than two-thirds of its EU turnover in one Member State, the concentration will not have a Community dimension but will be left to the Member State, where the bulk of the turnover occurs, to deal with it. Furthermore, a concentration which does not meet the above thresholds has a Community dimension where:

(a) the combined aggregate worldwide turnover of all the undertakings concerned is more than EUR 2,500 million;
(b) in each of at least three Member States, the combined aggregate turnover of all the undertakings is more than EUR 100 million;
(c) in each of at least three Member States included for the purpose of (b), the aggregate turnover of each of at least two of the undertakings concerned is more than EUR 25 million;
(d) the aggregate Community-wide turnover of each of at least two of the undertakings concerned is more than EUR 100 million;

unless each of the undertakings concerned achieves more than two-thirds of its aggregate Community-wide turnover within one and the same Member State.[1722]

972. Once a concentration has been notified, the Commission considers whether it would be compatible with the common market. A concentration will be incompatible with the common market when it would significantly impede effective competition, in the common market or in a substantial part of it, in particular as a result of the creation or strengthening of a dominant position.[1723] In deciding whether a concentration is compatible with the common market, the Commission is to have regard to:

1719. *See further* Consolidated Jurisdictional Notice under Council Regulation (EC) No. 139/2004 on the control of concentrations between undertakings (2008/C 95/01).
1720. Article 3(4); *see further* Consolidated Jurisdictional Notice under Council Regulation (EC) No. 139/2004 on the control of concentrations between undertakings (2008/C 95/01).
1721. Article 1.
1722. Article 1(3), and Art. 5: *see also* Commission Consolidated Jurisdictional Notice under Council Regulation (EC) No. 139/2004 on the control of concentrations between undertakings (2008/C 95/01).
1723. Article 2(3).

(a) the need to maintain and develop effective competition;
(b) the market position of the undertakings concerned and their economic and financial power;
(c) alternatives available to suppliers and users;
(d) their access to supplies or markets;
(e) legal and other barriers to entry;
(f) trends of supply and demand;
(g) the interests of consumers;
(h) the development of technical and economic progress where this is not achieved at the expense of the consumer.[1724]

The criteria on which decisions are to be made are exclusively economic. Other factors, such as employment, are not relevant.

B. Irish Law

973. The Competition Act 2002 introduced a new merger control regime in Ireland.[1725] It also introduced a new substantive test for determining the compatibility of mergers with competition law. Similar to the test applied in the US, it asks: does the merger result or is it likely to result in a substantial lessening of competition in the market.[1726]

974. In line with the EU's Merger Regulation, section 16, as amended, provides that a merger or acquisition takes place if:

a. two or more undertakings, previously independent of one another, merge;
b. one or more individuals who already control one or more undertakings, or one or more undertakings, acquire direct or indirect control of the whole or part of one or more other undertakings;
c. the acquisition of part of an undertaking, although not involving the acquisition of a corporate legal entity, involves the acquisition of assets that constitute a business to which a turnover can be attributed, and for the purposes of this paragraph 'assets' includes goodwill.

Moreover, the creation of a joint venture to perform all the functions of an autonomous economic entity constitutes a merger under section 16(4). In contrast, there is no merger where, for example:

a. the person acquiring control is a receiver or liquidator acting as such or is an underwriter or jobber acting as such;

1724. Article 2(1).
1725. The Competition and Consumer Protection Act 2014 contains particular rules in relation to media mergers in Part 4.
1726. Sections 4 and 5 of the 2002 Act have no application as regards notifiable mergers: s. 4(8) and s. 5(3), 2002 Act.

b. all of the undertakings involved in the merger or acquisition are, directly or indirectly, under the control of the same undertaking;
c. control is acquired by an undertaking the normal activities of which include the carrying out of transactions and dealings in securities for its own account or for the account of others.[1727]

975. Section 18 requires certain undertakings to notify the CCPC of mergers for clearance or approval. The main trigger for notification is where, in the most recent financial year:

- the aggregate turnover in the State of the undertakings involved is not less than EUR 50,000,000;
- the turnover in the State of each of two or more of the undertakings involved is not less than EUR 3,000,000.[1728]

Section 18, as amended, also allows mergers and acquisitions below these thresholds to notify voluntarily. Section 19(1), as amended, provides that a notifiable merger or acquisition cannot be put into effect until it is notified to the CCPC and the Commission has done one of four things:

- issued a clearance decision;
- issued a conditional decision;
- failed to inform the parties within one month of the appropriate date that it has determined that the merger does not substantially lessen competition under section 21(2)(a) or that a full investigation will not be launched under section 21(2)(b);
- failed to make a decision within 120 working days after the appropriate date has elapsed.[1729]

Section 20 provides for the process of examination of a merger by the CCPC and determinations can be made without a full investigation, under section 21, or following a full investigation, under section 22. Accordingly, the CCPC can decide that the merger can be put into effect; can be put into effect subject to conditions, or, cannot be put into effect. An appeal to the High Court against a prohibition on mergers or the approval of conditional mergers exists under section 24.

1727. 2002, Act, s. 16(6)(7) (8) and (8A).
1728. Failure to notify is a criminal offence: 2002 Act, s. 18(9). Mergers that do not meet this threshold are subject to ss 4–5 of the 2002 Act: *see* CCPC *Notice in respect of the review of non-notifiable mergers and acquisitions* (31 Oct. 2014).
1729. The appropriate date is usually the date of receipt of notification by the CCPC: 2002 Act, s. 19(6).

§2. Law of Unfair Competition and Trade Practices

976. As well as the civil and criminal rights of action outlined above, there are other grounds under which a person aggravated by anti-competitive conduct may seek redress.

I. Inducing Breach of Contract

977. It is a tort to persuade or to induce a party to a contract with another to break that contract. Thus, where the competitor persuades a person's supplier or his/her customer to break the contract under which they do that business, that person is entitled to damages from the inducer for the loss resulting from the breach. Similarly, inducing a person's employee to quit his/her job without giving 'due notice' or inducing an employee to disclose confidential information about his/her employer's business is an actionable wrong. Many of the authorities which define the scope of this tort involve industrial relations disputes. A defence of justification exists where, in all the circumstances, the court regards the inducer's actions as justifiable. But mere economic self-interest is not a justification for this tort, such as extending the scope of one's business, earning larger profits or putting a competitor at a disadvantage. It is a good defence if the terms of the contract which was broken were inconsistent with an earlier contract between the inducer and the party who broke the contract, or if the defendant was asserting some other 'equal or superior right'.

II. Interference with Contract by Unlawful Means

978. It is also an actionable wrong to interfere with a person's performance of a contract by unlawful means, even if no actual breach of the contract takes place. The principal form of interference contemplated here is preventing performance which does not amount to an actual breach, such as rendering performance more difficult but not impossible, or disrupting performance where the contract contains a force majeure clause. Most of the authorities on this tort are also industrial relations cases. The interference in question must have been caused by the defendant's actions, which must have been deliberately taken in order to disrupt the contractual relationship. 'Unlawful means' in the context includes the commission of crimes and of torts, and even breaking or threatening to break a contract. For instance, where a tyre company had agreed with a car manufacturer that all cars it exhibited would be fitted with the company's tyres, but a competitor secretly removed them and substituted his own tyres, he was held liable for unlawful interference with contractual relations. It is not essential that the person against whom that unlawful act was committed actually suffered loss; the commission or even the threat of an independently unlawful act suffices. Where appropriate, the courts will enjoin activity that constitutes unlawful interference with contractual relations. Interference with contractual relations by threatening to do something illegal is sometimes described as the tort of intimidation; where the interference or the threat emanates from more than one person, it is often called the tort of conspiracy.

979. It must be proved that the defendant took the unlawful action in order to interfere with the performance of the contract. Malice need not be proved, in the sense of a predominant purpose to cause injury to the plaintiff; but it is not enough that disrupting performance of a contract was an accidental (though foreseeable) consequence of what was done. Provided the defendant knew that a contract existed between the parties (although not of its precise terms) and he/she then deliberately sought to disrupt performance of it, regardless of whether a breach would ensue, he/she is liable for losses thereby incurred by the parties.

III. Injurious Falsehood

980. The tort of injurious falsehood is an offshoot of the tort of defamation. A defamatory statement is words which tend to lower a person in the estimation of his/her fellow men and women by making them think less of him/her. Commercial rivalry not infrequently erupts into one party making libellous or slanderous statements about another. Injurious falsehood concerns statements not made regarding what another is alleged to have done or not done but is more directed against his/her property, goods or business. Often it will be difficult to draw the line between these two types of actionable statements. The typical injurious falsehood is making false claims to legal rights and making disparaging criticisms of a competitor's goods or business. This does not mean that business rivals must be exceptionally careful in what they say about each others' enterprises and products, for the courts have confined this tort to situations where the words are incontrovertibly unjustifiable. The classic formulation of the tort is that an action will lie for written or oral falsehoods, not actionable per se nor even defamatory, where they are maliciously published, where they are calculated in the ordinary course of things to produce and where they do produce, actual damage.

981. It is principally the requirement of malice that perhaps has prevented the courts from being flooded with actions under this heading. Malice has different connotations in law, thereby giving rise to a degree of confusion. In this particular context, the term connotes that the defendant knew his statement was false or that he acted for some sinister purpose or dishonest motive. If the defendant knew that his statement was false, there is malice even though he intended only to benefit himself and not to injure the person with reference to whom the statement was made. If, however, the defendant simply did not believe what was said but he went ahead and said it in order to injure the plaintiff, that would ground a claim. The other way in which this tort was kept in check was the requirement that the plaintiff must prove that he suffered special damage, such as that his business lost trade as a direct result of the false statement. Business plaintiffs were not always required to prove actual transactions or contracts which were lost in consequence of the defendant's remarks. For instance, when the defendant said in a press report that the plaintiff had ceased trading, it might be enough to prove that his sales had immediately fallen, if his customers were normally unknown and changing. But this would not be so where those customers were regular and known to the plaintiff. The requirement to prove special damages has since been removed by section 20 of the Defamation Act, 1961, in two cases. One is where the words are 'calculated to cause pecuniary damage to the plaintiff in respect of any office, profession, calling, trade or business' he/she held or carried on at the time the statement was published. That is to say, special damages need not be proved where the words used are such as are likely to damage or very probably would damage the plaintiff in his/her occupation. The other case is where the false statement is made in writing or in some other permanent form and very likely would cause the plaintiff financial loss.

IV. Passing-Off

982. Another form of unlawful action to which commercial competition can give rise is where one trader represents or passes off his/her goods or services as being those of a rival trader so as to mislead the public and thereby cause an appreciable risk of detriment to the other trader.[1730] In *Reckitt & Colman Products v. Borden Inc,*[1731] Lord Oliver outlined three essential features of passing-off which the plaintiff must establish:

(1) a goodwill or reputation attaching to the goods or services which in the minds of the public is associated with an identifying 'get-up' (e.g., brand name, trade description, individual features, labelling or packaging) and which is distinctive specifically of the plaintiff's goods or services;
(2) that the defendant made a misrepresentation (intentional or otherwise) which leads or is likely to lead the public to believe that the goods or services offered by the defendant are in fact offered by the plaintiff;
(3) proof that the plaintiff has suffered or is likely to suffer as a result of the erroneous belief engendered by the defendant's misrepresentation.

Damages, to compensate for the resulting loss, such as the diversion of sales or injurious association, and an injunction to prevent any further confusion, may be available in an action for passing-off.

1730. *See* paras 243–254.
1731. [1990] 1 WLR 491 at 499, approved by Laffoy J in *DSG Retail Ltd v. World Ltd* (unreported, High Court, 13 Jan. 1998); *see also Erven Warnick Besloten Vennootschap v. J Townend & Sons (Hull) Ltd* (the 'Advocaat' case) [1979] AC 731 at 741, applied in numerous Irish cases including *Falcon Travel Ltd v. Owners Abroad Group plc* [1991] 1 IR 175 (HC); *An Post v. Irish Permanent plc* [1995] 1 IR 140; *Smithkline Beecham plc v. Antigen Pharmaceuticals Ltd* [1999] 2 ILRM 190.

V. Infringement of Trademarks

983. The protection of registered trademarks overlaps to an extent with the law of passing-off and is intended to remedy deficiencies in the common law protection. Section 13 of the Trade Mark Act 1996 states that the owner of a registered trademark has exclusive rights in the trademark and such rights are infringed by the use of the trademark in the State without the owner's consent. Importantly, there is no need to prove a reputation or to show actual or likely damage as is the case with the tort of passing-off. Section 14 specifies various infringing acts. Accordingly, a person infringes a registered trademark if that person uses in the course of trade[1732] a sign which:

- is identical with the trademark, in relation to goods or services which are identical with those for which it is registered;
- because the sign is identical with the trademark and is used in relation to goods or services similar to those for which the trademark is registered, there exists a likelihood of confusion on the part of the public, which includes the likelihood of association of the sign with the trademark;
- because the sign is similar to the trademark and is used in relation to goods or services identical with or similar to those for which the trademark is registered, there exists a likelihood of confusion on the part of the public, which includes the likelihood of association of the sign with the trademark;
- is identical with or similar to the trademark where the trademark has a reputation in the State and the use of the sign, being without due cause, takes unfair advantage of, or is detrimental to, the distinctive character or the reputation of the trademark.[1733]

984. Both civil and criminal law are used to protect the position of trademark owners and licensees. As regards civil remedies, the legislation provides that where a registered trademark is infringed, the owner and/or a licensee can sue for damages or an account of profits, an injunction, or otherwise.[1734]

1732. In *British Sugar plc v. James Robertson & Sons Ltd* [1996] RPC 281, it was held that infringement included non-trade mark use.

1733. 1996 Act, s. 14(3), as substituted by s. 39 of the Patents (Amendment) Act 2006; Directive, Art. 5(2). This provision was optional under the Directive.

1734. 1996 Act, s. 18 and s. 34.

Chapter 5. State Regulation of the Conditions of Commercial Transactions

985. As regards the conditions of commercial transactions the general principle is one of laissez-faire. The most common form of regulation exists to protect persons perceived to be in a weaker bargaining position, namely consumers. Protectionist legislation has also been enacted to protect commercial agents.[1735] Therefore, apart from measures designed to protect consumers, as described below, there is comparatively little detailed prescription regarding the terms and conditions of commercial transactions.

§1. Price and Supply Regulation

986. Until 2007, legislation existed in the form of the Prices Acts, 1958–1972, which enabled the Minister for Business, Enterprise and Innovation to intervene and fix maximum prices and charges in respect of most types of goods and services, in certain circumstances.[1736] However, the Consumer Protection Act 2007 repealed the Prices Acts following the recommendation of an expert group which found that price controls were ineffective and that freely functioning competitive markets were more effective at setting 'fair prices' than any form of price control.[1737]

987. Moreover, for eighteen years, legislation existed in the form of the Groceries Order, 1987 which banned below-cost selling, or more accurately selling below net-invoice price, of grocery goods, as defined.[1738] The Order was enacted to protect smaller retail interests from the larger multiples but a view was taken that instead of encouraging a competitive grocery market the Order had the effect of keeping prices of groceries in Ireland at an artificially high level by allowing suppliers to specify minimum prices below which products could not be sold. Therefore, following a review and public consultation process,[1739] the Groceries Order was abolished pursuant to the Competition (Amendment) Act 2006.[1740]

1735. *See further* paras 667–699 above.
1736. These powers were used most recently in 2000 to set the maximum price in relation to certain drinks sold in pubs, hotels and restaurants.
1737. *See* Report of Consumer Strategy Group, *Making Consumers Count* (2005), Ch. 14. The only aspect of the Prices Acts which remains comprise a series of ministerial orders requiring the display of prices in relation to certain goods and services, including hairdressing services, diesel and petrol, and, beverages in licensed premises: Consumer Protection Act 2007, s. 92.
1738. Restrictive Practices (Grocery Order) 1987, SI No. 142 of 1987. The original Groceries Order was introduced in 1956 with the objective of prohibiting resale price maintenance.
1739. *See* www.entemp.ie/commerce/consumer/groceriesorderreport.htm The abolition of the Groceries Order was also recommended in the Consumer Strategy Group, *Make Consumers Count* (2005), Ch. 13 and a variety of earlier reports and reviews.
1740. 2006 Act, s. 4.

988. The above reforms indicate a general trend away from price controls; nevertheless, price controls remain in relation to certain services, including utilities services, such as electricity and gas, and transport services. For example, any increase in gas and electricity retail prices must first be reviewed and approved by the CRU.[1741] And, in the transport sector, for instance, the Commission for Taxi Regulation is empowered to set maximum fares for taxis.[1742] There are also Government plans to introduce minimum pricing for alcohol, on health grounds.

§2. Consumer Law

I. General Principles, Institutional Aspects and Representation of Consumer Interests

989. The general assumption is that consumers of goods and services are in a weaker bargaining position than suppliers and manufacturers and hence, the law tends to give consumers more extensive protection than that enjoyed by businesspersons carrying out ordinary commercial transactions. The movement to protect the consumer interest through the legal system commenced, in earnest, in Ireland, with the enactment of the Consumer Information Act 1978 (now repealed) which amongst other things established the Office of Director of Consumer Affairs, and which sought to prevent the dissemination of false or misleading information to consumers.[1743] Shortly thereafter the Sale of Goods and Supply of Services Act, 1980 was enacted. The 1980 Act amended the original 1893 Sale of Goods Act, with particular reference to the consumer interest. Subsequently, the vast majority of consumer legislation has emanated from the EU, in the form of Directives. The main consumer Directives, as transposed into Irish law, are considered further below.[1744]

990. In relation to the institutional aspects of consumer law, in 2014, the CCPC was established. The Commission merged the former National Consumer Agency[1745] and the former Competition Authority into one public body.[1746] Although this institutional merger was first proposed in a time of economic crisis, the merger is not simply a cost-cutting exercise. The intention was to create an 'effective and integrated organization'[1747] with stronger powers and more resources to deal with competition and consumer issues. The functions of the Commission, as outlined in section 10(1) of the CCPC Act 2014, are:

1741. Electricity Regulation Act 1999 and the Gas (Interim Regulation) Act 2002; *see generally* www.cer.ie.
1742. Taxi Regulation Act 2003, s. 42, and Taxi Regulation Act 2003 (Maximum Fares) Order 2006, SI No. 438 of 2006. *See generally* www.taxiregulator.ie.
1743. *See* now the CCPC at www.ccpc.ie.
1744. *See* paras 972–985.
1745. In 2007, the National Consumer Agency (NCA) was established as the statutory body to represent the consumer interest in Ireland under the Consumer Protection Act 2007; the NCA replaced the Office of the Director of Consumer Affairs, itself established in 1978 under the Consumer Information Act 1978.
1746. Competition and Consumer Protection Act 2014, s. 9 and s. 38. *See further* www.ccpc.ie.
1747. Dáil Debates, 16 Apr. 2014.

1. To promote competition.
2. To promote and protect the interests and welfare of consumers.
3. To carry out an investigation, either or its own initiative, or in response to a complaint made to it by any person, into any suspected breach of:
   - the relevant statutory provisions, that may be occurring or has occurred, Articles 101 and 102 of the TFEU.
   - the Competition Acts 1991–1996 (notwithstanding their repeal).
4. To enforce the relevant statutory provisions.
5. To encourage compliance with the relevant statutory provisions, which may include the publication of notices containing practical guidance as to how these provisions may be complied with.
6. To set the strategic objectives for the Commission.
7. To ensure that appropriate systems and procedures are in place to achieve the Commission's strategic objectives and to take all reasonable steps available to it to achieve these objectives.

991. Other bodies, public and private, exist to represent the consumer interest, although it has been noted in the past that there is not a strong consumer lobby established in Ireland.[1748] Regulators such as the CRU[1749] and the ComReg,[1750] have a specific consumer interest remit. At a private level, the Consumer Association of Ireland (CAI) has existed since 1966, as a non-profit non-governmental organization, to protect and educate consumers.[1751]

II. Consumer Information

992. In the past, when goods were being sold or hired, or services were being provided, there was no legal obligation to provide information to the purchaser, hirer or user about the subject matter of the contract. The underlying principle was that of *caveat emptor* – let the buyer beware.[1752] Generally, the seller did not impliedly warrant (promise) the quality of the goods he/she sold, nor was he/she under a duty to disclose defects known to him/her. However, the Sale of Goods Act, 1893, implied terms regarding title, description, quality and fitness into sale of goods contracts, the exclusion of which is regulated by statute.[1753] Similar terms are now also applied into consumer hire purchase contracts and contracts for the supply of services.[1754]

1748. *See further* OECD, *Regulatory Reform in Ireland* (2001) available at www.oecd.org/dataoecd/48/35/2475450.pdf; 48/35/2475450.pdf; *see also* Consumer Strategy Group, *Make Consumers Count* (2005).
1749. *See* www.cru.ie.
1750. *See* www.comreg.ie.
1751. *See* www.consumerassociation.ie.
1752. *See*, e.g., s. 14(1) of the Sale of Goods Act 1893, still in force which gives statutory effect to this principle.
1753. *See* paras 469–541.
1754. *See* Part IV of the Consumer Credit Act 1995 and Part IV of the Sale of Goods and Supply of Services Act 1980.

993. More recently, as regards contracts with consumers, the trend has been to impose various information obligations on suppliers of goods and services in order to better inform the consumer of his/her rights and obligations. For instance, a number of EU Directives require suppliers to provide certain pre- and post-contractual information to enable the consumer to make an informed choice about entering into contractual relations and whether to maintain such relations or, whether to withdraw from or cancel the contract within a defined period.[1755] Moreover, legislation in the form of Part 3 of the Consumer Protection Act 2007, which transposes the Unfair Commercial Practices Directive,[1756] exists to protect consumer from misleading and deceptive information.[1757]

III. The Safety of Goods and Services

994. Consumers may have a claim against suppliers, producers and others where they suffer loss or injury caused by dangerous products or services. The supplier of goods and services may be contractually liable for their lack of safety under the statutory implied terms.[1758] In particular, case law has identified that safety is a factor to be taken into account in assessing whether goods are of merchantable quality or not, under section 14(2) of the Sale of Goods Act 1893.[1759] Moreover, the safety of motor vehicles is addressed specifically in section 13 of the Sale of Goods and Supply of Services Act 1980, which implies a condition, into every contract for the sale of motor vehicles (except where the buyer is a person whose business it is to deal in motor vehicles) that at the time of delivery, it was free from any defect which would render it a danger to the public, including persons travelling in it.[1760]

995. Producers may be directly liable to consumers, in negligence, based on the *Donoghue v. Stevenson* principle,[1761] for damage or injury caused by a defective product.[1762] Traditionally, liability was restricted to 'dangerous defects', that is, defects which involve physical damage to the person or other property, as opposed to the product itself. It was felt that contract law and not tort law was the proper avenue for redress for defects in the produce itself, that is, 'non-dangerous defects'. However, in Britain in 1983, liability in negligence for non-dangerous defects was recognized, in *Junior Books Ltd v. Veitchi,*[1763] which was followed in Ireland in *Ward v. McMaster.*[1764] This more radical position was soon resiled from Britain

1755. *See*, e.g., paras 977–979 below.
1756. Directive 2005/29/EC.
1757. *See further* para. 982.
1758. *See* paras 485–541.
1759. *See*, e.g., *Bernstein v. Pamson Motors (Golders Green) Ltd* [1987] 2 All ER 220 and *Clegg and another v. Olle Andersson* [2003] EWCA Civ 320; [2003] 1 All ER (Comm) 721.
1760. *See*, e.g., *Glorney v. O ' Brien* (unreported, High Court, 14 Nov. 1988).
1761. [1932] AC 562.
1762. *Power v. Bedford Motor Co.* [1959] IR 391.
1763. [1983] 1 AC 520, a case concerning the defective laying of a factory floor which was not in itself dangerous but had to be removed and re-laid, at significant cost.
1764. [1985] IR 29, a case where the defendant seller built a house with both dangerous and non-dangerous defects.

where there has been a return to the general principle that liability under the *Donoghue v. Stevenson* principle should not arise in respect of qualitative defects in products.[1765] Irish courts have been slower to return to this tradition position although there are indications that such a process may be underway.[1766]

996. Further, since the enactment of the Liability for Defective Products Act 1991,[1767] which seeks to transpose Directive 85/374/EEC concerning liability for defective products,[1768] producers and others may be strictly liable for defective products which cause damage or injury. Under the Act an 'injured party' can sue the 'producer' for damages in tort, for 'damage' caused by a defect in his/her 'product'.[1769] As is usual, the onus is on the injured party to prove the damage, the defect and a causal link between the two.[1770] 'Injured party' is defined as:

> a person who has suffered damage … caused by a defect in a product or, or if he has died, his personal representative … or dependants.[1771]

This includes any buyer of the product, recipient of the product as a gift, consumer or user of the product or even an innocent bystander injured by the product. The defendant in all these claims is the 'producer'. Producer is defined in the legislation as including:

- the manufacturer or producer of a finished product, or any raw material, or of a component part of a product;
- any person who, by putting his/her name, trade mark or other distinguishing feature on the product, has held himself/herself out to be the producer of the product;
- any person who has imported the product into a Member State from a place outside the European Communities in order, in the course of any business of his/her, to supply it to another.[1772]

Where there is more than one defendant, for the same damage, liability is joint and several.[1773]

1765. *See*, e.g., *Murphy v. Brentwood DC* [1991] 1 AC 398.
1766. In particular, in *Glencar Exploration plc v. Mayo County Council* [2002] 1 IR 84, the Supreme Court refused to allow an action for pure economic loss, on the facts, and Keane CJ expressly 'reserved for another occasion' the question of whether *Junior Books* should be followed in Ireland. More recently, in *Beatty v. The Rent Tribunal* [2006] 1 ILRM 164 Geoghegan J stated that the law in this question 'has not been finally determined in Ireland'.
1767. *See further* the EC (Liability for Defective Products) Regulations 2000, SI No. 401 of 2000.
1768. *See* [1985] OJ L 210/29.
1769. 1991 Act, s. 2(1).
1770. 1991 Act, s. 4.
1771. 1991 Act, s. 1.
1772. 1991 Act, s. 2(2).
1773. 1991 Act, s. 8.

997. Importantly, the types of damage which can be compensated for under this legislation are more limited than in contract law. ‘Damage’ under the legislation means:

> death or personal injury, or loss of, damage to, or destruction of, any item of property, other than the defective product itself.[1774]

Therefore, any damage to, or loss in value of, the product itself cannot be compensated for under this legislation. In contrast, in a claim in contract law, an award of damages for breach of the statutory implied terms, or indeed any contractual terms, may include damages for death, personal injury, damage to other property and any other economic loss, including the reduced value of the defective goods themselves.

998. ‘Product’ is defined as meaning all moveables, including primary agricultural products that have not undergone initial processing, and includes electricity.[1775] And a product is defective, for the purposes of the Act, if it fails to provide *the safety* which a person is entitled to expect, taking all circumstances into account, including:

(a) the presentation of the product;
(b) the use to which it could reasonably be expected that the product would be put; and
(c) the time when the product was put into circulation.[1776]

The circumstances listed above are not exhaustive and other relevant circumstances might include any instructions or warning issued with the product.

999. A major advantage of this legislation in contrast to product liability at common law is that, under the Act, liability is strict. Nevertheless, the legislation provides a series of defences for the producer. So, for example, a producer is not liable under the Act if he/she proves that:

(a) he/she did not put the product into circulation;
(b) having regard to the circumstances, it is probable that the defect which caused the damage did not exist at the time when the product was put into circulation by him/her or that the defect came into being afterwards;
(c) the product was neither manufactured by him/her for sale or for any form of distribution for an economic purpose nor manufactured or distributed by him/her in the course of his/her business;

1774. 1991 Act, s. 1.
1775. 1991 Act, s. 1, as amended.
1776. 1991 Act, s. 5. This last circumstance allows a court to consider the ‘state of the art’ at the time the product was put on the market. *See further* s. 5(2) which provides: A product shall not be considered defective for the sole reason that a better product is subsequently put into circulation.

(d) the defect concerned is due to compliance by the product with any requirement imposed by or under any enactment or any requirement of the law of the European Communities;
(e) the state of scientific and technical knowledge at the time when he/she put the product into circulation was not such as to enable the existence of the defect to be discovered;[1777]
(f) in the case of the manufacturer of a component or the producer of a raw material, the defect is attributable entirely to the design of the product in which the component has been fitted or the raw material has been incorporated or to the instructions given by the manufacturer of the product.[1778]

Additionally, any defences available in a tort action, such a contributory negligence or *volenti non fit in juria*, are available in a claim under this legislation.[1779] But, liability under this legislation cannot be limited or excluded by any contract terms or notice or other provision.[1780]

1000. Finally, the limitation period for actions under the Act is three years from the date of the damage or injury.[1781] Where such damage or injury is not immediately apparent the limitation period starts to run from the date on which the injured party became aware or should reasonably have become aware of the damage, the defect and the identity of the producer. However, a final cut-off point for producers is provided for in the legislation and no claim can be brought more than ten years after the product was put into circulation.[1782] Fears that the introduction of strict liability would lead to a flood of claims, as in the United States, have so far proved unfounded.

IV. The Quality of Goods and Services

A. *Sale of Goods Acts 1893–1980*

1001. Sections 13–15 of the Sale of Goods Acts 1893[1783] imply various terms as to quality in contracts for the sale of goods between sellers and buyers, including consumer buyers.[1784] In general, the terms require that:

- where goods are sold by description, that the goods correspond with the description (section 13);

1777. Known as the 'development risk defence': an optional provision in the Directive. This defence is particularly important regarding high-tech products including new drugs.
1778. 1991 Act, s. 6.
1779. 1991 Act, s. 9.
1780. 1991 Act, s. 10.
1781. 1991 Act, s. 7.
1782. 1991 Act, s. 7(2).
1783. As substituted by s. 10 of the 1980 Act.
1784. Similar terms are implied in consumer hire and hire purchase agreements: Consumer Credit Act 1995, Parts VI and VII.

- where goods are sold in the course of a business, they are of merchantable quality (sections 14(2) and 14(3));
- where goods are sold in the course of a business, and, the buyer makes known to the seller a particular purpose for the goods, the goods will be fit for that particular purpose (section 14(4));
- where goods are sold by sample, the goods will correspond to the sample (section 15).[1785]

Moreover, the Sale of Goods and Supply of Services Act 1980 implies two further terms in relation to the availability of spare parts and after sales services;[1786] and the safety of motor vehicles.[1787] The 1980 Act also provides for the enforceability of any guarantee offered by a manufacturer or retailer to a consumer, despite the lack of privity of contract between the manufacturer and the consumer.[1788]

1002. These statutory implied terms have a number of distinctive features, which can aid a consumer/buyer in pursuing a claim against a seller for their breach. First, and unlike other terms which may have to be proved in evidence, the statutory terms arise automatically, by implication. Second, it should be noted that liability for breach of the statutory implied terms is strict: the usual contractual standard. Therefore, even though the seller is not at fault, he/she will be liable for breach of the statutory implied terms. Third, the statutory implied terms are all, bar one, classified as conditions, breach of which by the seller allows the buyer to reject the goods and claim a full refund of any price paid. Finally, the exemption or exclusion of liability for breach of the statutory implied terms is regulated by statute, further increasing their protective force.[1789] In particular, where the buyer 'deals as a consumer', the effect of the statutory implied terms can never be excluded or restricted.

1003. A party to a contract is said to deal as consumer in relation to another party if:

(a) he neither makes the contract in the course of a business nor holds himself out as doing so;
(b) the other party does make the contract in the course of a business;
(c) the goods supplied under or in pursuance of the contract are of a type ordinarily supplied for private use or consumption.[1790]

This definition has been considered in two Irish cases, of the same year, by the same judge.[1791] In *In re Henry O'Callaghan v. Hamilton Leasing (Ireland) Ltd and Access Refrigeration and Shop Fitting Ltd*,[1792] a case not involving exclusion

1785. For a more detailed analysis of these provisions *see* paras 485–541.
1786. 1980 Act, s. 12.
1787. 1980 Act, s. 13.
1788. 1980 Act, ss 15–19.
1789. 1893 Act, s. 55 and 1980 Act, s. 22.
1790. 1980 Act, s. 3.
1791. Cf. *R&B Customs Brokers v. United Dominion Trust* [1988] 1 WLR 321.
1792. [1984] ILRM 146.

clauses, the plaintiff owned a take-away restaurant. He bought a drink vending machine from the second named defendant to be used in the restaurant. The purchase was financed by a leasing agreement between the plaintiff and the first named defendant. The machine proved to be defective. The legal issue before the High Court was whether the plaintiff could maintain an action against the first named defendant under section 14 or 38 of the 1980 Act.[1793] To do so, the plaintiff had to show that he was dealing as a consumer. In the High Court, McWilliam J., in a short judgment, held that the contract was made *in the course of the plaintiff's business* (contrary to paragraph (a) above) and hence the plaintiff did not deal as a consumer and his action was dismissed. McWilliam J. found that the purchase was made *for the purpose of* the business although he recognized that the business was not involved in the resale or further dealing with the goods. Accordingly, it would seem that *in the course of a business* does not require that the business is normally involved in dealing in goods of the type in question. It is sufficient that the contract is made for the purpose of the business.

1004. In *Cunningham v. Woodchester Investments and Inter-call Ltd*,[1794] the plaintiff was the bursar of a large agricultural college that sold a lot of its produce. Although the college was a non-profit making educational organization, its annual turnover from the sale of its produce was about IR 1 million. It leased a telephone system from the defendant that proved faulty. In order to maintain the action, again under section 14 of the 1980 Act, the plaintiff had to be dealing as a consumer. Again, McWilliam J. in the High Court held that the plaintiff was acting in the course of a business contrary to paragraph (a) of section 3(1) of the 1980 Act. The equipment was mainly used as part of the farming activity and regardless of what was done with the profits from this activity McWilliam J. felt constrained to hold that this activity constituted carrying on a business. It would seem that an organization with mixed activities, such as in this case, where the college was involved in educational and business activities, can be treated as acting in the course of a business with regard to some activities and not others. Further, the lack of a profit motive is not a bar to acting in the course of a business.

1005. Lastly, it is a criminal offence to make a statement which purports to restrict the buyer's rights under these statutory implied terms.[1795]

1793. Section 14 of the 1980 Act deals with the joint liability of finance houses for the supply of defective goods; and s. 38 (*see* now s. 80, Consumer Credit Act 1995) dealt with letting agreements other than hire purchase agreements and liability for defective goods thereunder.

1794. Unreported, High Court, 16 Nov. 1984.

1795. 1980 Act, s. 11.

B. Part IV of the Sale of Goods and Supply of Services Act, 1980

1006. As regards the quality of the supply of services, section 39 of the Sale of Goods and Supply of Services Act 1980 implies four terms into every contract for the supply of services where the supplier is acting in the course of a business. They are:

- that the supplier has the necessary skill to render the service;
- that he/she will supply the service with due skill, care and diligence;[1796]
- that where materials are used, they will be sound and reasonably fit for the purpose for which they are required;
- that where goods are supplied they will be of merchantable quality.[1797]

1007. Significantly, section 39 implies 'terms' into the service contract, not conditions or warranties, as is the case with the sale of goods legislation. Accordingly, these terms are what can be described as 'innominate terms', the effect of the breach of which depends on the seriousness of the breach. Only where the breach of such a term deprives the party not in default of substantially the whole benefit of the contract will the innocent party be able to repudiate the contract, otherwise his/her remedies are limited to a claim for damages.[1798]

1008. Section 40 states that any term implied by section 39 can be excluded (expressly, or by course of dealings, or by usage) except where the recipient of the service deals as a consumer, in which case the express term limiting or excluding liability must be fair and reasonable and must be specifically brought to the attention of the buyer to be effective.[1799] Moreover, section 41 of the 1980 Act makes it an offence for any person in the course of a business to display, publish or otherwise furnish a statement to the effect that the rights conferred by section 39 are restricted or excluded.[1800]

C. EC (Certain Aspects of the Sale of Consumer Goods and Associated Guarantees) Regulations, 2003

1009. In addition to the rights and remedies provided under the Sale of Goods Act 1893 and the Sale of Goods and Supply of Services Act 1980, a further layer of protection is offered to consumer buyers of goods by the EC (Certain Aspects of the Sale of Consumer Goods and Associated Guarantees) Regulations, 2003.[1801] These Regulations mirror many aspects of the pre-existing legislation. In broad terms,

---

1796. *See*, e.g., *Roche v. Peilow* [1986] ILRM 189.
1797. *See*, e.g., *Irish Telephone Rentals v. ICS Building Society* [1991] ILRM 880.
1798. *Irish Telephone Rentals v. ICS Building Society* [1991] ILRM 880.
1799. *See* Schedule to 1980 Act on factors relevant to assessing whether a term is fair and reasonable.
1800. 1980 Act, s. 6, as amended by s. 81 of the Investment Funds, Companies and Miscellaneous Provisions Act 2005.
1801. SI No. 11 of 2003 which transposes Directive 99/44, [1999] OJ L 171/12.

under the Regulations, consumer goods delivered under a contract of sale to the consumer must be in conformity with that contract.[1802] Conformity is presumed and is judged with reference to a list of factors including, compliance with description; fitness for any particular purpose; fitness for normal purpose; and quality and performance. Where there is a breach of the conformity requirement the consumer is offered a hierarchy of remedies, namely, repair or replacement, or reduction in the price or rescission of the contract. Importantly, any lack of conformity which becomes apparent within six months from the date of delivery of the goods is presumed to have existed at the time of delivery of the goods.[1803] The Regulations also address the enforceability of product guarantees.

V. Other Consumer Contracts

1010. As well as the legislation which exists to protect consumers in the context of contracts for the sale, hire, and hire purchase of goods and the supply of services as described above, there is a plethora of other legislation, derived from EU Directives, which seeks to protect consumers in particular circumstances. Chief among this legislation are the EC (Unfair Terms in Consumer Contract) Regulations, 1995 and 2000.[1804] Other such legislation includes the Package Holidays and Travel Trade Act 1995, as amended;[1805] the EU (Protection of Consumers in respect of Timeshare, Long-term Holiday Product, Resale and Exchange Contracts) Regulations 2011;[1806] and the EU (Consumer Information, Cancellation and other Rights) Regulations, 2013.[1807] The main provisions of this legislation are outlined below.

A. EC (Unfair Terms in Consumer Contract) Regulations, 1995 and 2000

1011. These Regulations seek to protect consumers from unfair contract terms in standard form contracts. They apply to any term in a contract concluded between a seller of goods or suppliers of services and a consumer which has not been individually negotiated.[1808] The Regulations basically provide that an unfair term in a contract concluded with a consumer by a seller or supplier shall not be binding on

---

1802. Regulation 5.
1803. Regulation 8.
1804. SI No. 27 of 1995, as amended by SI No. 307 of 2000: which transpose Council Directive 93/13 on unfair terms in consumer contracts; [1993] OJ L 95/29.
1805. Which transposes Directive 2015/2302 on package travel and linked travel arrangements, [2015] OJ L 326/1.
1806. SI No. 73/2011, which transposed Council Directive 2008/122/EC on the protection of consumers in respect of certain aspects of timeshare, long-term holiday product, resale and exchange contracts, [2008] OJ L 33/10.
1807. SI No. 484/2013: which transposes Directive 2011/83 on consumer rights, [2011] OJ L 3304/64.
1808. Regulation 3.

the consumer.[1809] But core terms of the contract (terms which relate to the definition of the subject matter of the contract or the adequacy of the price and remuneration) are not subject to this fairness test, so long as they are in plain and intelligible language.[1810]

1012. A term is unfair if, contrary to the requirement of good faith, it causes significant imbalance of the parties' rights and obligations to the detriment of the consumer.[1811] To determine whether a term satisfies the good faith requirement Schedule 2 sets out relevant considerations:

- the strength of the bargaining position of the parties;
- whether the consumer was induced to agree to the term;
- whether the goods, etc. were sold to the special order of the consumer;
- the extent to which the consumer was treated fairly and equitably.

1013. Schedule 3 then sets out an indicative, though not an exhaustive, list of unfair terms including terms which have the object or effect of:

- excluding/limiting liability for death or personal injury;
- inappropriately excluding/limiting legal rights of consumer re non-performance or defective performance by seller of obligation under contract;
- requiring consumer who fails to fulfil an obligation to pay disproportionate compensation;
- authorizing seller to terminate where customer has not the same right;
- excluding or hindering the consumer's right to take legal action or exercise any other legal remedy.

Moreover, where the contract is in writing it must be drafted in plain and intelligible language and where there is ambiguity an interpretation in favour of the consumer will prevail.[1812]

1014. Individual consumers can utilize these Regulations, arguing that a particular term is unfair, in a dispute with a business. Indeed, following the CJEU decision of *Aziz v. Caixa d'Estalvis de Catalunya*[1813] national courts are now charged to assess, *of their own motion,* whether terms falling within the scope of Directive 93/13 on unfair terms in consumer contracts are unfair or not.[1814] More broadly, the CCPC or a consumer organization can obtain a court order prohibiting the continued use of an unfair term. To assist in its enforcement function, the CCPC or the Minister can appoint an authorized officer to enter premises, to inspect and copy books, etc. and demand the provision of information in general, for these purposes.

1809. Regulation 6.
1810. Regulation 4.
1811. Regulation 3.
1812. Regulation 5.
1813. Case C-415/11.
1814. *Allied Irish Bank v. Counihan & Anor* [2016] IEHC 752.

B. Package Holidays and Travel Trade Act 1995, as amended

1015. Part II of the 1995 Act,[1815] as amended, imposes obligations on traders whether acting as an organizer, retailer, or trader facilitating a linked travel arrangement or as a travel service provider, in their dealings with travellers. For example, specified information must be provided pre-contract and in a particular form.[1816] Certain aspects of this pre-contract information are legally binding and can only be altered following express agreement of the parties.[1817] Post-contract, the organizer must ensure that the contract or confirmation contains the full content of the agreement[1818] and a copy of the contract or confirmation must be provided to the traveller in a durable medium.[1819] Alteration of the price[1820] and other terms[1821] post-contract is strictly regulated and the traveller is given various rights to transfer the package travel contract[1822] or to terminate it (although fees may be payable).[1823] Most significantly perhaps, the organizer is responsible for the performance of the travel services included in the package travel contract, irrespective of whether those services are to be performed by the organizer, the retailer or other suppliers of services.[1824]

C. EU (Protection of Consumers in Respect of Timeshare, Long-Term Holiday Product, Resale and Exchange Contracts) Regulations 2011

1016. These Regulations apply to timeshares, long-term holiday products, resale or exchange contracts (known as 'regulated contracts') between a trader and a consumer. Accordingly, traders have various information obligations to consumers, in relation to advertising; pre-contract information; the contract and the right of withdrawal.[1825] Moreover, the consumer has the right to withdraw from the contract, without reason, within fourteen days of the conclusion of the contract or the consumer receiving a copy of the contract, whichever is later.[1826] Where the contract does not contain the relevant information this period can be extended up to three months and ten days.

1815. *See* in particular S.I. No. 80/2019 EU (Package Travel and Linked Travel Arrangements) Regulations 2019.
1816. 1995 Act, s. 10, as amended5.
1817. 1995 Act, s. 10A.
1818. 1995 Act, s. 13, as amended.
1819. 1995 Act, s. 15, as amended.
1820. 1995 Act, s. 17, as amended.
1821. 1995 Act, s.18, as amended.
1822. 1995 Act, s.16, as amended.
1823. 1995 Act, s. 18A.
1824. 1995 Act, s. 19, as amended: *see further Scaife v. Falcon Leisure Group* [2007] IESC 57.
1825. Regs 5–12.
1826. Regulation 13.

D. EU (Consumer Information, Cancellation and Other Rights) Regulations, 2013[1827]

1017. These Regulations apply to contracts between traders and consumer of goods, services, digital content and utilities, which are concluded on-premises, off-premises and online, subject to various exemptions.[1828] In such circumstances, suppliers are required to provide certain pre- and post-contractual information about the contract.[1829] Failure to do so has both civil and criminal law implications for the trader.[1830] Moreover, the consumer is provided with a right to cancel the contract fourteen days from the date of conclusion of the contract or the delivery of the goods, without reason and without penalty.[1831]

VI. Unfair Commercial Practices

1018. Part 3 of the Consumer Protection Act 2007 transposes into Irish law Directive 2005/28/EC on unfair commercial practices.[1832] Accordingly, a range of unfair,[1833] misleading[1834] and aggressive[1835] trading practices are prohibited. Moreover, the Act lists thirty-two activities that are always prohibited, including false claims:

- that the trader or product has an approval, authorization or endorsement that it does not have;
- that the trader is about to cease trading;
- about cures for illnesses;
- indicating that the product is free when it costs the consumer more than the reasonable costs responding to the representation or collecting the product or having it delivered;
- that there is limited available to encourage quick sales.[1836]

VII. Consumer Redress

1019. There is a variety of avenues of redress for consumers depending on the particular circumstances: civil and criminal; individual and collective; using litigation and alternative dispute resolution methods. Where a civil wrong is committed,

1827. SI No. 484 of 2013.
1828. Regs 3, 4, 6 and 13.
1829. Regs 5, and 7–12.
1830. *See*, e.g., Regulations 7(7) and (8).
1831. *See* Part 4.
1832. [2005] OJ L 149/22. The Act also repealed earlier legislation including the Consumer Information Act 1978.
1833. 2007 Act, s. 41.
1834. 2007 Act, ss 42–51.
1835. 2007 Act, ss 52–54.
1836. 2007 Act, s. 55.

either a breach of contract or a tort, the usual remedy is an action for damages to compensate the innocent party. In relation to the sale of goods and supply of services where a condition of the contract is breached, or, an innominate term is breached with serious consequences, the consumer may also have a right to reject any goods supplied and seek a refund of the price. Moreover, recourse to the criminal law may be possible where a trader engages in certain activities. For example, as noted above, it is a criminal offence to make a statement which purports to restrict a buyer of goods' rights under the statutory implied terms of the Sale of Goods Acts 1893–1980.[1837] Equally, where suppliers fail to comply with various information requirements, criminal sanction may apply.[1838] Usually, under the relevant legislation, it is the CCPC which initiates such prosecutions.

1020. The CCPC also has a role in the protection of the collective interest of consumers. Under the EC (Protection of Consumers' Collective Interests) Regulations, 2001,[1839] the NCA may apply for an injunction to protect the 'collective interest' of consumers. No such application has been made to date, in Ireland.

1021. As well as using civil and criminal court procedures, alternative dispute resolution mechanisms exist. In particular, the Small Claims Court operates to provide consumers (and businesses in relation to small claims) with a cheap and quick resolution to disputes where the claim does not exceed EUR 2000.[1840] The Small Claims service is provided through the District Court offices wherein the Registrar seeks to settle disputes which fall within jurisdiction. The Small Claims service is also provided online. If no settlement can be reached, the matter is then set down for court hearing. Consumer complaints are also frequently referred to the CCPC, and, if cross-border in nature, the European Consumer Centre, for settlement.[1841]

1022. More recently, a number of European measures which seek to improve consumer redress in a cross-border and online context have been transposed into Irish law. In particular, Directive 2013/11 on alternative dispute resolution for consumer disputes (ADR Directive)[1842] sets out the required infrastructure for ADR schemes as well as provisions on accessibility and availability and has been transposed by the EU (Alternative Dispute Resolution for Consumer Disputes) Regulations 2015.[1843] Further, Regulation 524/2013 on online dispute resolution for consumer disputes (ODR Regulation)[1844] establishes an ODR online platform which serves as a bridge between consumers and ADR entities, thus facilitating consumers

1837. 1980 Act, s. 1.
1838. *See*, e.g., Regulation 5(3) of the EU (Consumer Information, Cancellation and other Rights) Regulations, 2013, SI No. 484 of 2013.
1839. SI No. 449 of 2001.
1840. *See* District Court (Small Claims) Rules 2009, SI 2009/519; *see further* www.courts.ie.
1841. *See* www.eccdublin.ie.
1842. [2013] OJ L 165/63.
1843. S.I. No. 343 of 2015.
1844. [2013] O.J. L165/1.

in accessing ADR schemes which comply with the ADR Directive. The ODR Regulation has been transposed in Ireland by the EU (Online Dispute Resolution for Consumer Disputes) Regulations 2015.[1845] These Regulations appoint a single competent authority in respect of the legislation: the CCPC.[1846] ADR is not made mandatory for traders (beyond those circumstances in which it is already mandatory, such as in respect of financial services) and to date, only 2 ADR entities in Ireland are accessible through the ODR platform: Netneutrals.eu and the CRU.

1845. S.I. No. 500 of 2015.
1846. Reg 5(1).

Selected Bibliography

The State and Public Administration

Byrne, R. & McCutcheon, J.P. *The Irish Legal System,* 6th edn (Haywards Heath: Bloomsbury Professional, 2014).

Donson, F. & O'Donovan, D. *Law and Public Administration in Ireland* (Dublin: Clarus Press, forthcoming 2015).

Forde, M. & Leonard, D. *Constitutional Law of Ireland,* 3rd edn (Haywards Heath: Bloomsbury Professional, 2013).

Hogan, G. et al *The Irish Constitution,* 5th edn (London: Bloomsbury, 2018).

Kenneally, A. & Tully, J. *The Irish Legal System* (Dublin: Clarus Press, 2013).

Morgan, D.G. & G. Hogan. *Administrative Law in Ireland,* 4th edn (Dublin: Round Hall Sweet & Maxwell, 2010).

Ryan, F. *Constitutional Law,* 3rd edn (Dublin: Round Hall Sweet & Maxwell, 2018).

Thornton, L., Ní Mhuirthile, T. & O'Sullivan, C. *Fundamental of the Irish Legal System* (Dublin: Round Hall, 2016).

Commercial Law

Breslin, J. & Corcoran, E. *Banking Law,* 4th edn. Dublin: Round Hall, 2018.

Buckley, A. *Insurance Law,* 4th edn. Dublin: Thomson Round Hall, 2016.

Burke, J. & A. Comyn. *Personal Insolvency Law,* Haywards Heath: Bloomsbury Professional, 2014.

Clark, R., Smyth, S, & Hall, N, *Intellectual Property Law in Ireland*, 4th edn. Haywards Heath: Tottel, 2016.

Courtney, T. et al, *The Law of Companies,* 4th 3rd edn. Haywards Heath: Bloomsbury Professional, 2016.

Donnelly, M. *The Law of Credit and Security,* 2nd edn. Dublin: Thomson Round Hall, 2015.

Dowling, S. *The Commercial Court,* 2nd edn. Dublin: Round Hall, 2012.

Dowling-Hussey, A. & D. Dunne. *Arbitration Law,* 3rd edn. Dublin: Round Hall, 2018.

Forde, M. *Commercial Law,* 3rd edn. Haywards Heath: Tottel, 2005.

Forde, M. & H. Kennedy. *Company Law,* 5th edn. Dublin: Round Hall 2017.

Forde, M. & Simms. *Bankruptcy Law,* 2nd edn. Dublin: Round Hall, 2009.

Forde, M., H. Kennedy & D. Simms. *Law of Company Insolvency,* 3rd edn. Dublin: Round Hall, 2015.

Hickey, M. *Merger Control in Ireland,* Dublin: Round Hall, 2013.

Selected Bibliography

Hutchinson, B. *Arbitration and ADR in Construction Disputes,* Dublin: Round Hall, 2010.

Johnson, W. et al. *Arthur Cox Banking Law Handbook,* Haywards Heath, Bloomsbury Professional, 2007.

Keane, H. *Company Law,* 5th edn. Haywards Heath: Bloomsbury Professional, 2016.

Lynch-Fannon, I. & G. Murphy. *Corporate Insolvency and Rescue,* 2nd edn. Haywards Heath: Bloomsbury Professional, 2012.

Mansfield, B. *Arbitration Act 2010 and Model Law: A Commentary.* 2nd edn. Dublin: Clarus Press, 2018.

Murphy, F. *Financial Services Law in Ireland,* Dublin: Round Hall, 2018.

McCarthy, A. & V. Power. *Irish Competition Law: The Competition Act 2002,* Dublin: Tottel, 2006.

Nagle, E. *Intellectual Property Law,* Dublin: Round Hall, 2012.

Power, V. *Competition Law and Practice,* Dublin: Butterworths, 2001.

Sanfey, M. & B. Holohan. *Bankruptcy Law and Practice in Ireland,* 2nd edn. Dublin: Round Hall Press, 2010.

Twomey, M. *Partnership Law,* Dublin: Butterworths, 2000.

White, F. *Commercial Law,* 2nd edn. Dublin: Thomson Round Hall, 2012.

Index

The numbers here refer to paragraph numbers.

Index

Index

www.ingramcontent.com/pod-product-compliance
Ingram Content Group UK Ltd.
Pitfield, Milton Keynes, MK11 3LW, UK
UKHW020132290926
15471UKWH00003B/426

9 789403 52092